D0022960

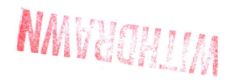

Joyce Wieland

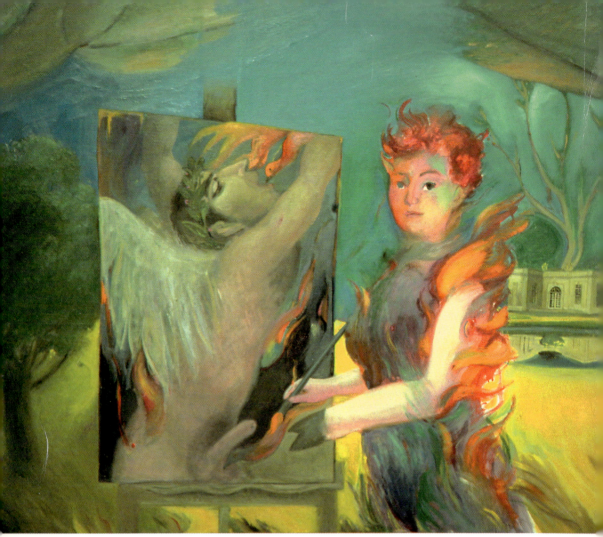

Artist on Fire, 1983.

THE PROBLEM is to go into oneself and find out what one is and to suffer what it is to be oneself. Go to the darkest parts and the brightest parts and find out what you like and want, and to validate that... It's not just a question of art and finding out who you are and to make this wonderful thing happen out of yourself, but it's the responsibility to the society and to care about other people... A lot of people think art is to be separate, but art is to embrace others—whether to convey something difficult or talk about light—work that comes from the spirit, journeys into the spirit are what we need now. Spirit has always been in art.   —*Joyce Wieland*

Joyce Wieland
Artist on Fire

Jane Lind

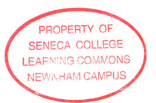
James Lorimer & Company Ltd., Publishers
Toronto, 2001

James Lorimer & Company Ltd. acknowledges the support of the Ontario Arts Council for our publishing program. We acknowledge the support of the Government of Canada through the Book Publishing Industry Development Program (BPIDP) for our publishing activities. We acknowledge the support of the Canada Council for the Arts for our publishing program.

Lorimer also wishes to thank an anonymous donor for her generous contribution to the publication of this book and the Guelph Arts Council for acting as charitable trustee.

Designed by Nick Shinn
Typefaces: Brown, Cartier Book, Shinn Sans

CANADIAN CATALOGUING IN PUBLICATION DATA

Lind, Jane
    Joyce Wieland: Artist on Fire

Includes index.
ISBN 1-55028-695-1

1. Wieland, Joyce, 1931- . 2. Artists – Canada – Biography. 3. Motion picture producers and directors – Canada – Biography. I. Title.

N6549.W53L56 2000   709'.2   C00-931885-2

James Lorimer & Company Ltd., Publishers
35 Britain Street
Toronto, Ontario
M5A 1R7

Printed and bound in Canada.

Contents

The artworks

Acknowledgements

As part of my research for this book, I interviewed many of Joyce Wieland's family members, friends and colleagues, whose contributions are acknowledged in notes throughout the text. I was impressed with their generosity and eagerness to talk about Joyce.

Joan Stewart Prowd, Joyce's sister, cared for Joyce after the death of their parents. I had the privilege and good fortune of taping three conversations with Joan before her death in 1993. An intelligent woman with a sharp wit and a clear memory, she contributed immeasurably to this book, particularly to the story of Joyce's family during their first years in Canada. Joan's daughters and son, Allison McComb, Nadine Schwartz, Lois Taylor and Keith Stewart, also deserve thanks for their help.

Joyce's brother Sidney died in 1967. Two of his sons, Glenn Wieland and David Wieland, spent time answering my questions and sharing their memories of Joyce and the family. Thank you. Joyce's long-time friends each spent many hours in conversations about Joyce and answered myriad questions: Sara Bowser, Betty Ferguson, the late Donna Montague and Colette Perron Sharp. Without their generosity, Joyce's story would not have been complete. My thanks to Judy Steed, Joyce's friend and colleague in *The Far Shore*, who shared her perceptions of Joyce in a number of interviews.

Michael Snow was generous with his time and shared his memories, for which I am grateful. His sister, Denise Rynard, and her daughter Su Rynard, a filmmaker, also contributed their memories of Joyce when she was a part of their family. Antoinette Lévesque Snow Roig, at age ninety-two, told me of her experience of Joyce. Thank you, all.

Barbara King Graham, Joyce's bosom friend at Central Technical School in the 1940s, impressed me with her clear memory of Joyce. She was articulate, direct and honest and answered many questions in interviews and in telephone calls.

I am grateful for the many others who also told me of their experiences with Joyce, and who all together gave hundreds of hours of their time.

I also want to thank the following people who helped me as I gradually put together Joyce's story: Kent Haworth and his staff at the Archives and Special Collections at the Scott Library of York University; Larry Pfaff and Randall Speller at the Art Gallery of Ontario archives; at the Cinémathèque Québécois, Gisele Côté in Montreal and at the archives in Boucherville, Serge Desauliniers, who spent most of a week threading films and audio tapes for me; and the Canadian Filmmakers Distribution Centre for screening Wieland films for me many times over a period of nearly ten years.

My thanks to Douglas McPherson, the executor of the Joyce Wieland Estate, for his help and cooperation.

Joyce's journals and jottings on scraps of paper provided insights into her life and work. I have quoted these verbatim without correcting errors.

My family deserves my appreciation for accepting another person who filled my head and my heart, especially during the last two years. Though for many years I've had the prerequisite room of my own, the necessary guineas Virginia Woolf suggested were another matter during the time required for writing the book. Woolf acknowledged — how slowly things change — that "Women are poorer than men because — this and that."[1] I thank my husband, Loren Lind, for his understanding and for paying the bills because of the many "thises" and "thats."

Thanks to both James Lorimer and Diane Young for their enthusiasm for the book. Special thanks to Diane for her astute insights and editorial comments, and to Ward McBurney and the Lorimer staff for their hard work.

Finally, I appreciate the generosity of an anonymous donor and the charitable trusteeship of the Guelph Arts Council in supporting publication of the book, and the Ontario Arts Council Writers' Reserve program.

For Salome, Mary, Lydia and Elizabeth, and for my other foremothers whose names are lost to me, and who will never be mentioned in history books.

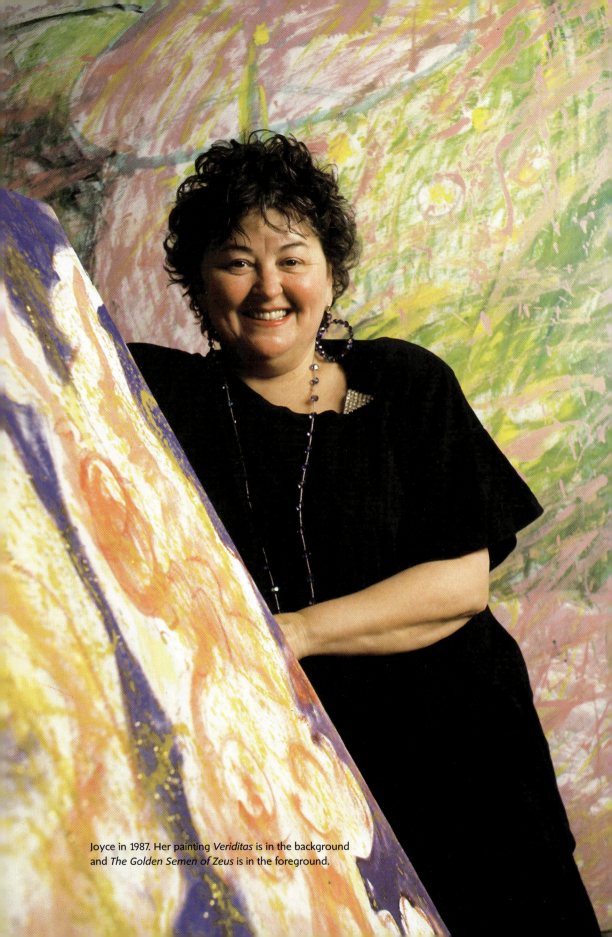

Joyce in 1987. Her painting *Veriditas* is in the background
and *The Golden Semen of Zeus* is in the foreground.

Introduction

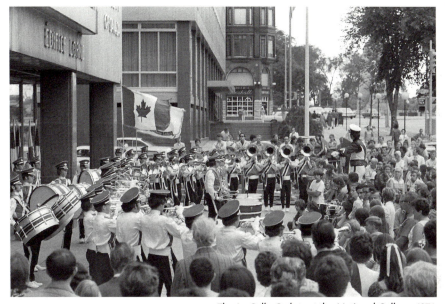

The La Salle Cadets at the National Gallery, 1971.

CANADA DAY, July 1, 1971. A large banner hanging across the front of the National Gallery of Canada in Ottawa announced a new exhibition, "True Patriot Love — Joyce Wieland — Véritable amour patriotique." At six o'clock that evening the National Gallery's first major show by a living female artist opened. The hundred-strong La Salle Cadets' drum and bugle corps marched up the steps and played on the gallery terrace while several hundred guests listened and watched.

Years later, Joyce Wieland recalled those moments when the band members, from ten years old up, dressed in gold shirts printed with a red lightning pattern, some carrying big banners, played trumpets and trombones — "like Dizzy Gillespie," she said. "They [the cadets] played and kneeled and stood up and did all that stuff and they crossed their banners, and these cherubs in the front row, really blasting it out ... playing 'Born Free'

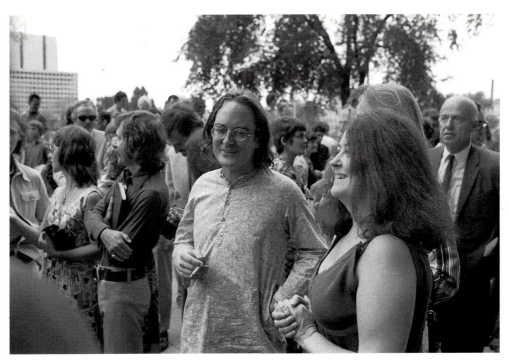
Joyce in the crowd listening to the band at the opening of her show in Ottawa in 1971.

to the universe. That was one of the best things I've ever heard in my life."[1]

Inside the gallery, more gentle sounds filled the air — the taped calls of loons and songbirds. Potted pine trees here and there scented the rooms. Drawings, sculptures, quilted cloth hangings that included knitting and embroidery, and screenings of the artist's films, along with an installation of two dozen ducks cordoned off by knee-high plexiglass walls, filled the ground floor of the gallery.

What remained in the memory of many guests was the giant six-foot-round *Arctic Passion Cake*. Jan Van Dierendonck, executive chef to the parliamentary restaurant, had built the cake of styrofoam covered with icing sugar according to Joyce's sketch. Around the bottom were three thousand stone-shaped petits fours for guests to eat. A sugar-paste polar bear lying dead and bleeding on the top of the cake revealed that the work was not just something sweet. In fact, the cake provided a clue to reading the entire exhibition, revealing that this artist's work warned of the slow erosion of Canada's resources. The title of the show stated clearly that it was also about the artist's love for her country and its people.

To some visitors, the exhibition was a surprise, a paean to the work that women do: piecing together quilts, stitching and sewing to create warmth

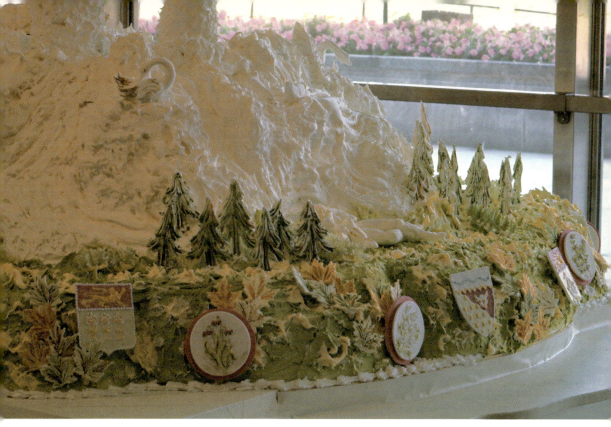

Arctic Passion Cake, (detail) 1971.

for Canada's cold winter nights. Joyce broke down the hard walls of Canada's auspicious institution of high art with the soft work traditionally assigned to women and their domesticity and gave it a place of honour. Ensuring she had cohorts in her "subversive" activity, Joyce had hired other women for some of the textiles in her exhibition.

Pierre Théberge, who was then Curator of Contemporary Canadian Art and now the Director of the National Gallery, was the man responsible for the show. Théberge and Joyce also had the support and enthusiasm of Jean Sutherland Boggs, who was then the gallery's director.

The audacity to mount this type of exhibition in a national institution, which was expected to uphold more than a modicum of propriety, evoked the ire of some traditionalists. For these people, art was not a site for an irreverent sense of humour, and they did not want their concept of art shattered, especially not by live ducks being cared for by gallery staff in rubber boots. Nevertheless, the show created a strong presence in the gallery for more than a month with the artist's keen wit evident in many of the multi-media objects and installations, even though her themes and the statement she made about her country were serious.

Letters to editors in Ottawa newspapers expressed consternation, anger

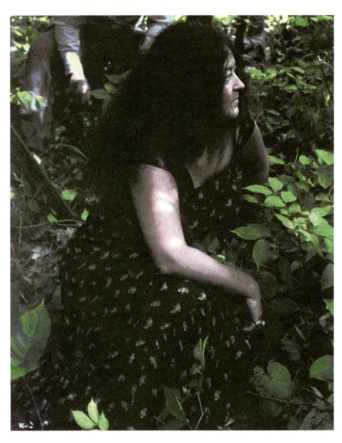

Joyce during filming
The Far Shore,
1975.

and disgust, but some defended and commended the gallery for putting on this festival of colour and texture. And all the while the artist herself delighted in the whole business and felt proud of what she had accomplished.

For those who took time to find out, "True Patriot Love/Véritable Amour Patriotique" revealed what kind of artist Joyce Wieland was. She was a myth-maker, or as Théberge called her, a visionary. She dredged the bottom of the ocean of the imagination and brought back visions, gifts of colours so fine that some people rejected them outright as too ethereal, and too much out of sync with the art world to be taken seriously. The images she brought back told us things we did not know we needed to find out.

She was also a myth-maker in a personal sense. As a young woman, she set out to create a mythology for herself and to write the script for her own life. However, she found out very quickly that if she dared "to be a woman unto herself ... a woman whose identity and life are shaped through her ideas, her actions and her own projects," she was on a difficult path in a patriarchal society.[2] She cast about for role models, looking for other women who had written their own scripts, and was not satisfied with what she found in art history's stories of mostly male painters. Yet when she discovered Colette, George Sand and Katherine Mansfield, their writing confirmed that women did have options other than those prescribed by a patriarchy, giving her the courage to follow her passion.

From the beginning of her career, Joyce did not try to paint like a man, even at a time when mainly men's work was considered authentic art. Working from the wellspring of who she was, a woman and a feminist — before the term was used — meant accepting an inescapable identity that modified her position in art; as a woman she was marginal even though she was the country's leading (woman) artist by the late sixties.[3] Despite this conundrum, she persisted, and her 1971 show in Ottawa was a milestone in Canadian art.

Joyce Wieland's art was her life and her life was her art. She discovered early in her career that "... time in plenty and an abundance of ideas are the necessary basics of creativity."[4] She dreamed and used her ideas to create works from her own experiences and the layers of who she was. The early loss of her parents and the dissolution of her family formed the raw material of her life and work. In her paintings of an intense blue sky, a plane crashed or a sailboat went down in the ocean's waves. She did not try to hide the two extremes in her life and work: her passionate joy and exuberance, as well as her tragedies and wounds. In later years, as new personal difficulties and traumas pervaded her life, she moved away from the themes of Canada and the environment to more personal subjects, as revealed in *Paint Phantom* (1983-84) and *Artist on Fire* (1983), and to her exploration of spirituality.

Joyce had an earthy sense of humour, creating fun with her friends; she loved celebrations and dramatic parties, which seemed at times a declaration of triumph over her personal pain. Joyce's journey to become her own person and create a strong artistic practice has influenced many women, as well as men. She called herself a pioneer because she cleared a space in the landscape of art where women could live and work, and opened up new horizons for herself and the women who came after her.

This artist was an extremely complicated person of tangled emotions, and it's impossible to say definitively who she was, even for a biographer who has spent years researching and thinking about her. She lived in a way that was anything but linear, so to trace her life story on paper inside the covers of a book that moves from beginning to end can seem a confinement. But her story demands telling. This particular account is one person's perceptions — the result of the fluid process of research and writing — which are altered and transformed with the new understandings the writer gleans and the changes she herself experiences as she explores and weaves her way through the story, back and forth in time.

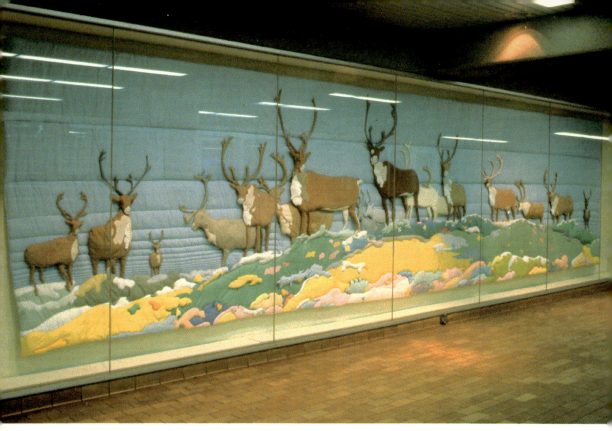

Barren Ground Caribou, 1978.

My introduction to Joyce Wieland's work was in the Kendal Avenue exit of the Spadina subway station near my home in Toronto in the late seventies. There on a brick wall I saw a large hanging, quilted and appliquéd — seventeen caribou against the sky in the Canadian tundra. I noticed the soft, delicate colours and wondered about an artist who would tackle such an enormous ... what was it? A quilt? Or would one call it a hanging? And why was this beautiful, softly coloured depiction of caribou placed underground in a little-used subway station exit in downtown Toronto?

Preoccupied with looking after a family and working as a freelance book editor and artist, I nevertheless kept the name of Joyce Wieland in the back of my mind and began looking for her work in galleries.

In the mid-eighties, while writing the books in The Canadian Artists Series for young people, I taped a series of conversations with Joyce Wieland and was captivated by her life story. She was a woman with dark hair and a round, moon face, with eyes that sparkled when she revealed her mischievous sense of humour and sharp wit, a wit that sometimes slid into dagger-tongued comments about such "fools" as art critics or theorists she disliked.

Joyce was not many inches over five feet tall, but there was something about her spirit and her physical stature that made her seem large and small at the same time. She bounced around as she spoke, gesturing with her small hands, and hummed and sang when she left the room to get a book or to refill a coffee cup — she thought nothing of stirring her coffee with a pencil. She spoke openly of her traumatic early life and its effect on her as an adult. Joyce praised Doris McCarthy for pointing out her gifts when she was a teenager. She spoke of her experience as a woman in a pack of male artists at the beginning of her career. She spoke of her life in New York City, making experimental films and beginning the quilts, and how she found her domestic subject matter and her vision of Canada and returned to live here. She spoke of the heavy price she paid in making *The Far Shore*, the trauma and loss in the breakup of her marriage, the pain of her inability to bear children and the struggle to put her life back together in a new way.

I discovered that her vision evoked in other people an enthusiasm not only for art, but for life itself, and I felt compelled to tell her story. In 1989 I met with Joyce to discuss the possibility of my writing this biography, and she agreed.

As I did my research and talked to Joyce's family, friends and colleagues, I discovered she was a person who elicited strong feelings. Her friends have their own personal Joyce — sometimes to the point of seeming possessive — and often these "Joyces" are different. I found one commonality, however: they all loved her.

As is true for all of us, Joyce Wieland's life was not a neat and tidy progression from point A to point B, but a rather messy business moving back and forth and winding in circles, even though her overall direction was fixed on a certain path. I debated with myself about the various ways of weaving together the strands of this artist's life. In the end, to avoid confusion, I chose a chronological framework. I hope this portrait of Joyce Wieland will illuminate how, like her, we are all absorbed in our own predicament of finding our particular ways of being human — and Canadian.

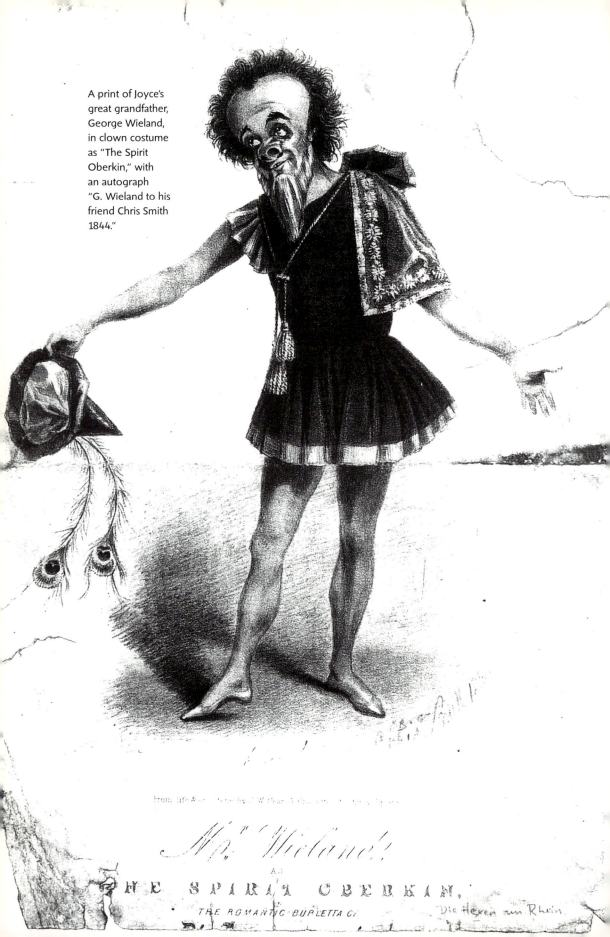

A print of Joyce's great grandfather, George Wieland, in clown costume as "The Spirit Oberkin," with an autograph "G. Wieland to his friend Chris Smith 1844."

1

The family trajectory

Of our fathers we know always some fact, some distinction.
They were soldiers or they were sailors; they filled that
office or they made that law. But of our mothers, our
grandmothers, our great-grandmothers, what remains?
Nothing but a tradition. One was beautiful; one was redhaired; one was kissed by a Queen. We know nothing
of them except their names and the dates of their marriages
and the number of children they bore. —Virginia Woolf[1]

AT THE PARISH CHURCH in Lancashire's market town of Wigan stood an
ancient monument, a man in a coat of mail sitting cross-legged and a woman
in a praying posture wearing a robe. The monument was in memory of Sir
William and Lady Mabel Bradshaigh.

As was fairly common for men during the 1300s, Sir William went on a
quest to the Holy Land. Of course, he left his fair Mabel at home to pray for
his good fortune. However, after a number of years she became tired of
playing the widow and married her suitor, a Welsh knight, Sir Osmund Nevil.

After a ten-year absence, Sir William showed up in Wigan one day dressed
as a pilgrim. Mabel recognized him even in his disguise, and dutiful woman
that she was, "… acknowledged her lawful lord and returned to her
allegiance."[2] Sir Osmond fled but Sir William pursued him and killed him
with his sword. Nor was Mabel totally off the hook. She had to do penance

for giving up on her "lawful lord" by walking barefoot two miles every week, north-west from Haigh-hall to a cross that stood at the top of Standishgate, thereafter called Mab's Cross.[3]

This story of the monument would have appealed to Wigan descendant Joyce Wieland. All her life she had an unquenchable thirst for learning about her ancestors. Whenever she was in England in the 1980s, she researched the family tree of both her parents, even calling every Wieland in London's phone book. Because of the fame of her paternal ancestors in London's music halls in the 1800s, finding information about the Wielands was relatively easy. However, her mother's family was not so well known. Through a Toronto friend's parents, who had done a great deal of research on the Nottingham area, Joyce found records of her mother's line of Coopers and Watsons.[4] She even brought back to Toronto with her a copy of the birth certificate of her mother — Rosetta Amelia Watson — dated May 5, 1890, as well as a small scrap of wallpaper from the room in which her mother was born at 19 Marshall Street in Sherwood, Nottinghamshire.

Wigan, a market town about twenty miles from the coastal city of Liverpool and two hundred miles north-west of London, was where Joyce's maternal grandparents, Mary Jane and Charles Watson, raised their family — more accurately, where Charles started raising his family, and left Mary Jane to finish what the two had started.

Mary Jane Cooper's family came from Cotton Mill, a small hamlet made up of cottages for mill workers, situated in the rolling countryside north of Nottingham, England's centre for lacemaking. Rosetta, one of the Watsons' middle children in a family of five girls and three boys, was the most spirited of the daughters. She inherited her father's black hair and stature — she was taller than her sisters, prompting her brothers to call her "the Titanic." Early in life she was also nicknamed Billy, most likely because she was a tomboy, and that was the name she used the rest of her life instead of the beautiful name she was given at birth.

Charles McKiller Watson was a tall, handsome Scotsman from Dundee, with black hair and a beard, who spoke Gaelic and read Robbie Burns in the evenings. A draper who worked in heavy tapestries, in taffetas and brocades, he travelled all over Scotland and northern England. Joyce claimed, with delight, that he not only hung and draped, but also sculpted fabrics to create forms.[5]

Like Sir William Bradshaigh, Charles Watson had a roaming nature. He left home for South Africa in 1904 to do the drapery work for Boer leader Paul Kruger's funeral and never returned. His parting "gift" to Mary Jane was a load of coal, but the bill for her to pay came later by post. However, he sent home bolts of black and purple velvet left over from his Kruger job, and for

THEATRE ROYAL, DRURY LANE.

☞ POSITIVELY
THE LAST NIGHTS
OF THE
Present Arrangements,
OWING TO THE IMMEDIATE PRODUCTION OF
IMPORTANT NOVELTIES!

This present MONDAY, January 25th, 1841.
The Performances will commence with, (33rd time) the New Grand Opera of

THE BONDMAN.

Marquis de Vernon,	-	Mr. WEISS,
Count Floreville,	- (his Son) -	Mr. RAFTER,
Viscount Morliere	-	Mr. H. HORNCASTLE,
Ardenford,	(the Bondman)	Mr. W. HARRISON,
Mal-a-propos,	(Ardenford's Valet & Book-keeper)	Mr. HARLEY,
madame Corinne,		Mr. S. JONES,
Grisette,		Miss ROMER,
Frivole,	(Corinne's Waiting Maid)	Miss REBECCA ISAACS, Mrs. HUGHES.

After which, (20th time) the Grand Christmas Pantomime, being a mixture of the Historical and Legendary, entitled

HARLEQUIN,
AND
St. GEORGE AND THE DRAGON

Scene 1. ABODE OF KALYBA, THE ENCHANTRESS.

Kalyba,	the Enchantress, (not by BALFE) Mistress of all the Elements, except those of "Arithmetic," having quite misunderstood her power,	Mr. N. HORNCASTLE,
Fiends and Furies,	illustrating a common expression of speech, with anything but a common expression of countenance,	Mess. W. MORGAN, BURT, CONNELL & N. PAYNE,
Earth, Air, Fire, and Water,	the Four Elements, with a strong love of mischief	BY DEALERS IN EACH!
The March of Intellect,	Travelling "incog" as "Young England," a true bit of British blood, by Intellect, out of Industry, Dam by Reason, out of Perseverance, has never been beaten & can be matched against anything	Mr. PAYNE.

Scene II. Interior of INFANT SCHOOL.

Schoolmaster,	Mr. BIGWIG,

(Who, at the request of his "Illustrious Visitor," gives the boys a half-holiday on the occasion)

Scene III. EXTERIOR AND BARBACAN OF COVENTRY CASTLE.

The Earl of Coventry,	Lord High Steward of England, and his own into the bargain	Mr. MAZZONI.
The Countess of Coventry,	(a good Housewife, and supposed to have been the inventor of the celebrated "Coventry Cake,")	Miss MAINS.
Head Nurse,	(with a good character from her last place)	Mr. CHEEL.
Master George,	afterwards celebrated for a Battle he fought with a Dragon, but at present, without any knowledge of "arms," except his nurse's,	Miss MARKS.
Masters Andrew, David, Patrick, Denis, James, Anthony,	very youthful Knights, but destined, with their "cousin George" to astonish the natives by and bye, as "The Seven Champions of Christendom,"	Master COYLE, Master SAVELL, Master DIX, Master WELSH, Master DESBOROUGH Master FRANCIS.

How the youthful St. George is feted on his birth-day,—how he makes his FIRST and nearly his LAST appearance in public on the occasion,—how his "Cousins" Andrew, David, Patrick, Denis, James, and Anthony, come to wish him many happy returns of the day—and how, Kalyba shows her "love of children," by taking the "whole brood under her wing."

Scene IV. Kalyba's House of Correction!

St. George of England,	(a rum'un to look at, but a rum'un to go)	Mr. W. H. PAYNE,
St. Andrew, of Scotland. St. David, of Wales. St. Patrick, of Ireland. St. Denis, of France. St. James, of Spain. St. Anthony, of Italy.	all, pretty much of the same kidney!	Mr. HEATH. Mr. SANGER. Mr. MARKS. Mr. CHAPINO. Mr. MARTIN. Mr. J. PAYNE.

How St. George and his brother Champions (considerably grown since their last appearance in public) are kept in durance vile and on "very short commons" by Kalyba,—how Kalyba pens her affections on St. George, who "can't abide her"—in short, how—but we won't anticipate,—merely observing, that the upshot is

Downfall of Kalyba, and the Emancipation of the Seven Champions.

Scene V.—Dover Roads. Scene VI.—Banks of the Nile.

Almanzor, King of Morocco.	his own Lord High Admiral, Commander-in-Chief, &c. &c., on his way to King Ptolemy's Court, to court King Ptolemy's Daughter,	Mr. T. MATTHEWS.
Ptolemy, King of Egypt.	rather a remote ancestor of Ibrahim Pasha, better known, as "Abraham Parker"	Mr. PRIORSON.

Scene VII. GRAND HALL in the PALACE
OF PTOLEMY THE FIRST, KING OF EGYPT.

The Princess Sabra,	about to be married to the King of Morocco, but patriotically devoting herself to the dignified orgasms of	Mr. HANCE,
The Dragon,	a gentleman, whose prodigious allowance of JAW, enables him to speak for himself	Mr. WIELAND,

Arming of St. George for the approaching Fight!

Latest odds at "the Corner"—1000 to 0 on the Dragon. [TAKEN]

Program for Theatre Royal, Drury Lane, listing George Wieland near the bottom.

years afterward the family wore velvet, so the story goes. Mary Jane never heard from him again. Unlike Mabel Bradshaigh, who submitted to penance for taking charge of her life, Mary Jane succeeded in her independence and opened a sweet shop to support her large family without her husband.

Billy was fourteen when her father disappeared, and two or three years later she, too, left home and headed for London. Joyce recounted that her mother stuffed her corsets up the chimney, cut off her hair and ran away at age sixteen, taking the train to London and then making paper flowers to support herself. However, Joan, Joyce's sister, claimed that their mother apprenticed as a cook and went to London in 1907 to work at a hotel. Joan's is the more probable story.[6]

Billy and the other girls who worked at the hotel were strictly supervised, but they all sneaked out from time to time, presumably to meet their boyfriends, and had to climb up a drain pipe to get back to their room without being found out. It is likely that Billy met Sidney Arthur Wieland at the hotel where she worked.

From the Wielands, Joyce absorbed the spirit of two women she admired: great-aunt Clara, a dancer who performed in the Palace Theatre in London and was reviewed by George Bernard Shaw; and great Aunt Zaeo whose "wonderfully graceful aerial feats" were among the main attractions in the London Aquarium in the early 1890s.[7] A monotype of Zaeo hung on Joyce's dining-room wall, and late in her life, she made big photocopied blow-ups of it and taped them all around the room. That Zaeo's contemporaries saw her as risqué made her even more appealing to Joyce, beyond the skill she had with her ropes.

Joyce's branch of Wielands arrived in London from Holland in the late 1600s, around the time that William of Orange, later King William III, married the English Princess Mary. George Wieland, Joyce's great-great-grandfather, was a famous theatrical agent who handled his daughter Clara's engagements. At one time he specialized in representing gymnastic acts for theatres and took circuses to Europe.[8] Joyce's great-grandfather, also named George, got his first job imitating monkeys when he was only nine years old in the early 1800s during the craze for stage monkeys among theatre goers. Later he became famous as "The Great Wieland" (his son, Joyce's grandfather, was called "Little Wieland") because of his act as a clown-juggler, and was reviewed by Charles Dickens as having a "... grotesque humour of no ordinary kind."[9] Among Joyce's memorabilia was a copy of a 1838 bill for Theatre Royal on Drury lane, listing her great-grandfather as Asmodeus in a popular ballet, *The Devil on Two Sticks*. Another, for Monday, January 25, 1847, advertises Wieland as the dragon in *St. George and the Dragon*. Joyce also had an 1844 signed lithograph of George Wieland, a clown with a bulbous nose, doleful eyes and wide forehead with scraggly hair on a partly bald head. Joyce's pride in these ancestors was unbounded.

Sidney Arthur, Joyce's father, was born three months premature in 1877, and survived by being kept warm in a box on the oven door.[10] Like other children in this family, when Sidney was just an infant he was massaged and exercised to make his muscles strong. With the birth of each child, the number of performers increased. Sidney and his brothers became known as The Five Wieland Brothers and put on singing and dancing acts as late as the 1890s, but Joyce never found out why and when they disbanded. However, we do know that Sidney was among the last of at least four generations who performed in London's music halls.

After Sidney left the stage, he had a varied career. According to a copy of his résumé among family memorabilia, at age eighteen he began working for Simpsons, a large restaurant in London, and after fourteen years there he became manager of a café, and then manager of the Argosy Hotel. However, it seems he lied about his age when he moved from one job to the other, which makes tracking dates difficult. At one time he had an exterminating business. Joyce's sister Joan, had a copy of his recipe for killing rats, in her father's handwriting.[11]

When Sidney met Billy, he was already married and had three children. Billy, a beautiful young woman with blue eyes and two moles on her cheeks she claimed were given to her by fate, was engaged to another man, but her fiancé had gone to Australia to find his fortune, and she fell in love with Sidney. The two began living together. He loved gardening and they had a plot of land in London where Sidney successfully crossbred roses.

A son, also named Sidney, was born in 1920 and a daughter, Joan Amelia, in 1921. For a time Sidney had a job as steward on ocean liners, which meant he could juggle two families without either of the women knowing about the other because he was out of the country much of the time. Later, Sidney and his brother Jack decided to start a hotel in Brighton. However, Sidney's duplicity became impossible to maintain, so in 1925 he sailed for New York, cutting off all contact with his first family and leaving Billy, Sidney and Joan behind.

Sidney claimed that in New York he found a job only when he was down to his last quarter.[12] The next year he sent for Billy to come to New York — without the children. She tried to get her mother, still living in Wigan, to look after Sidney and Joan, but one of her sisters convinced Mary Jane she was too old to be looking after lively, young children. As a result, Billy left her children with the family of a former nursemaid, the Peppers. Close to a year later, the Peppers' apparent neglect of the children alarmed Billy's friends, Jim and Martha Hart. Joan and Sidney were so undernourished that the Harts

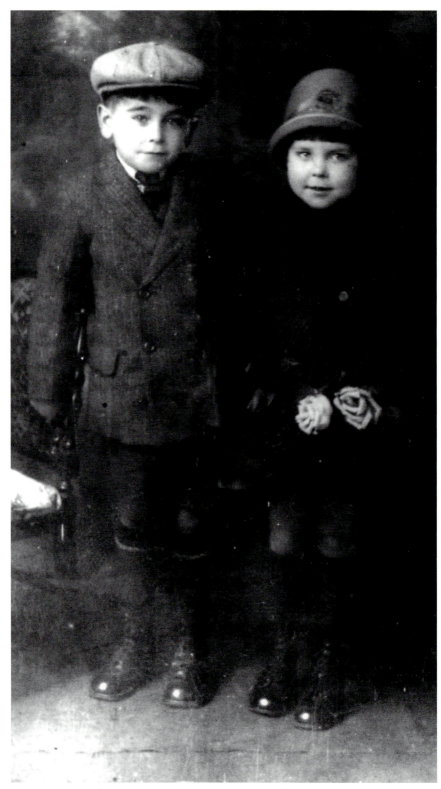

Joyce's brother and sister, Sidney Wieland and Joan Wieland,
dressed for their voyage to Canada in 1927.

took them home and wrote to Sidney and Billy, saying they must have the children sent to them immediately. By then, Sidney and Billy had gone to Ontario, presumably because Sidney's wife would have more difficulty finding him there.

According to a receipt dated April 22, 1927, Billy (R.A. Wieland) paid $102.40 for the passage of the two children to Canada. A notice from the office of Canadian Pacific Steamships posted on May 21, 1927 to Mrs. R.A. Wieland at Oakridges, Ontario, stated that Master Sidney and Miss Joan Wieland would arrive in Quebec on May 25th, 1927.

The Harts' generosity and warmth is evident in a letter dated two days later in which they told Sidney and Billy how they had worried whether the children had arrived safely. Martha Hart said that to prepare them for their voyage, she and Jim had bought new clothes for Joan and Sidney and washed and ironed and aired the few old ones that were still wearable. Before they put the children on the ship, the Harts bought them a good lunch, and they were happy until Jim and Martha said goodbye and left them with the nurse on the ship. They both cried, and the big rocking horse and toys in the ship's nursery "had no charm."[13]

Joan remembered considerable abuse from the Peppers, which seemed confirmed by Martha Hart's letter to Billy and Sidney: "I don't know how they [the children] would have got on if they had been left to the mercy altogether of those people but I shall never tell you — you would be too upset."[14]

When the Harts put Joan and Sidney on the *Montroyal*, the ship nurse had promised that the children would never be left alone. However, Joan remembered the two of them being locked into their small, dark room below deck and feeling that the walls were pushing in on her.

As the *Montroyal* neared its destination, the nurse pointed out icebergs in the distance. At the end of her life Joan still remembered sitting on a big rocking horse looking at the icebergs and sighting land. The nurse told her that was Canada. She did not know exactly what that meant, except that it was a place where she would see her mother again. It seemed a long time until the ship finally docked in Quebec City on May 25, 1927. The day was bright, the first sunshine Joan had seen since they had left Southampton.[15]

In Quebec City a woman took the children to the train bound for Toronto. Joan collapsed and slept for most of the train trip. As they sat in Union Station waiting for Sidney and Billy, Joan began to cry and the woman tried to comfort her, but Joan could not stop sobbing. Finally, through her tears she saw a black-haired woman hurrying toward them; her brother began running. It was not until the woman picked Joan up that she realized it was her mother, and she clung to her and cried uncontrollably. Sixty-six years later, with tears in her eyes, Joan still remembered the feeling of her mother's wet face against her own.

Outside the station, a man stood on the sidewalk watching the three of them, then Joan saw her brother running to meet him. The man lifted Sid and spun him around. This man — Joan did not recognize him as her father — seemed a complete stranger and somewhat frightening. Nothing about him was familiar. As they walked toward the man, Joan clung to her mother's hand.

The first summer that the family was together again, they lived in a small house on a farm near Maple, Ontario, where Sidney worked as a hired hand for a farmer who boarded a herd of horses to be trained for the army. But for Sidney this job was only an interim arrangement, and by the end of the summer, he had found work as caretaker at a movie theatre in Toronto. He moved his family to an apartment above the theatre.

Apparently he still felt he had to hide his identity for years afterwards, even in a city the size of Toronto — he always tried to avoid being photographed. Joan also noticed that her father's mail was frequently addressed to Sidney Spinks, and when she asked him about it, he refused to answer.[16] Since the mail obviously belonged to him, she wondered what he was hiding. His secrecy increased the distrust she had felt for him ever since he had suddenly abandoned the family in England.

Sometime after Sidney's death, Billy told Joan the story behind their coming to Canada, and what her father had been hiding — his other family in England.[17] His duplicitous life distressed Joan. She could only conclude that his real wife had been searching for him. Then, during World War II when the young Sidney was in Europe, he found the Harts, gave them Joan's address, and they sent her a letter saying that her parents had not been married. This also upset her.

The questions about her family were compounded with Joyce's discovery that in the registry of St. Catherine's House in Somerset, England, were birth certificates for a Joan Wieland and Joyce Wieland who would have been the exact age of her father's other family. That their father might have given the same names to daughters in both families disturbed Joan and Joyce, and the issue remained unresolved because they weren't absolutely sure. Yet this scenario fit with what they discovered was a pattern of deceit in their father, so they surmised these other girls were probably their half sisters.

This unsettling aspect of her father's past spread a cloud over what Joyce wanted her family history to be — a romantic, carefree, flamboyant ancestry. But her romantic notions also embraced the troubling traditions embedded in the Wigan story of Mab's Cross, traditions Joyce tried to reconcile with her passion for her art.

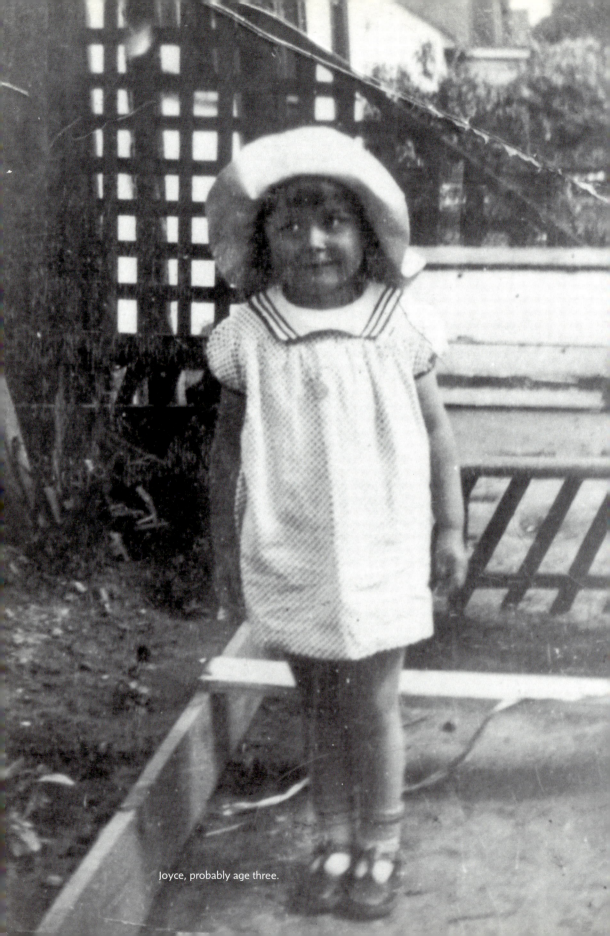

Joyce, probably age three.

2

A daughter
of Canada

I always drew, but we couldn't afford much paper and stuff
and I drew in my sister's books, whatever she had, where
ever there was paper ... My sister taught me about books.
She'd get books from the library ... Those were the things
I liked, and dressing my dolls and I finally got a doll
carriage. That was it. I never looked back after I got the
doll carriage. —Joyce Wieland[1]

TWO HOURS into June 30, 1930, Joyce June Wieland was born in an upstairs
bedroom at 99 1/2 Claremont Street, three years after her family had moved
to the city of Toronto.[2] Throughout her life, Joyce kept alive several dramatic
stories about her birth.

To begin with, her mother led her to believe she delivered herself
because the family doctor was away, and when Billy went into labour
Sidney ran down the street to the police station to call a doctor. When the
doctor arrived, he sat with a newspaper in front of his face waiting for the
baby. Billy noticed that he was "reading" the newspaper upside down,
leading her to believe that he was more nervous than she about the birth.
But the facts about whether the doctor helped with the delivery were
missing from Billy's story.

Joyce claimed that she was born during a thunderstorm so severe that it

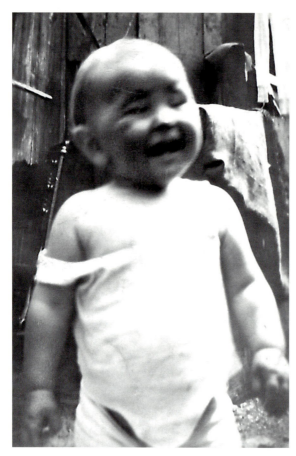

Joyce as a
crying baby.

shook the bed. Not so, said Joan, who was afraid of storms and insisted that she would not have slept through the birth if there had been a storm. Joan was sure Joyce's story was the result of her huge, dramatic imagination. Regardless of who was right about the particulars, according to Toronto newspapers, thunderstorms characterized the weather at the end of June and the beginning of July of that year.

However, for the Wielands and others on Claremont Street, the storms were nothing compared to the devastating consequences of the Great Depression. Canada was among the nations suffering the most severe effects of the events of 1929, partly because of the country's dependence on exports at the time world trading collapsed. In the Prairies, the price of wheat was so low that farmers lost money on every stalk. As if that were not enough, drought and dust storms intensified the effects of economic hardship to such an extent that at one point in Saskatchewan two-thirds of people in the rural areas were on relief.[3] In British Columbia, by 1935 the federal government had set up work camps for single unemployed men, who lived on two meals a day. By the middle of the decade, in Toronto close to 120,000 in a population of 650,000 to 700,000 were out of work and on relief.[4] Many families nearly froze and starved in tar-paper shacks. Slogans and exhortations such as "Be of Good Hope" and "Faith and Work are Antidotes to Fever of Depression," which appeared in Toronto's *Globe* at the beginning of the New Year six months after Joyce's birth, did little to cheer parents who could not find work to feed hungry children.

The situation in Toronto was typical of many of the metropolitan areas of Canada, but the inequity that characterized the disparities between the regions of the country became apparent in the 1930s. For example, in Calgary a family of five drew $60 a month for relief, whereas in Halifax they could count on only $19.[5] The desperate economic plight of such a large number of Canadians — since surely it couldn't be the fault of all these people individually — provided impetus for a close scrutiny of the country's institutions and the whole of society.[6] Many people believed a change of government was the way to repair what was going wrong in what everyone had once thought was a flourishing industrial society. But the Great Depression turned out to be more than just a glitch in the normal state of affairs, and Canadians looked for political leaders who could figure out the roots of the problem.

The same summer that Joyce was born, R.B. Bennett, by promising to conquer the Depression, brought in a four-year interruption of William Lyon Mackenzie King's years in power. At the end of the next year, the *Statute of Westminster* was passed, recognizing that Canada and the other dominions of Great Britain were sovereign states. Although in reality the country was still largely a British colony, particularly in the way Canadians thought of themselves, this new formal autonomy did give rise to questions and discussions during the following decade about who Canadians really were and what set them apart.

Several attempts were made in the 1930s to bring women into the political system. King, before he was ousted from power, appointed the first woman to the senate, Cairine Reay Wilson (1885-1962). The new Cooperative Commonwealth Federation (CCF), which held its first national convention in Regina in 1933, "endorsed the full participation of women and provided many women with a forum for involvement in the political process."[7] However, for the most part, the traditional parties did not open up their policies to include women, which meant that the number of women in office did not increase. In the election in the middle of the decade, Canadians weren't willing to risk a government more adventurous than King and the Liberals, who were a known quantity. Fifty years later, though more women had entered politics by then, Joyce Wieland and some others would work on

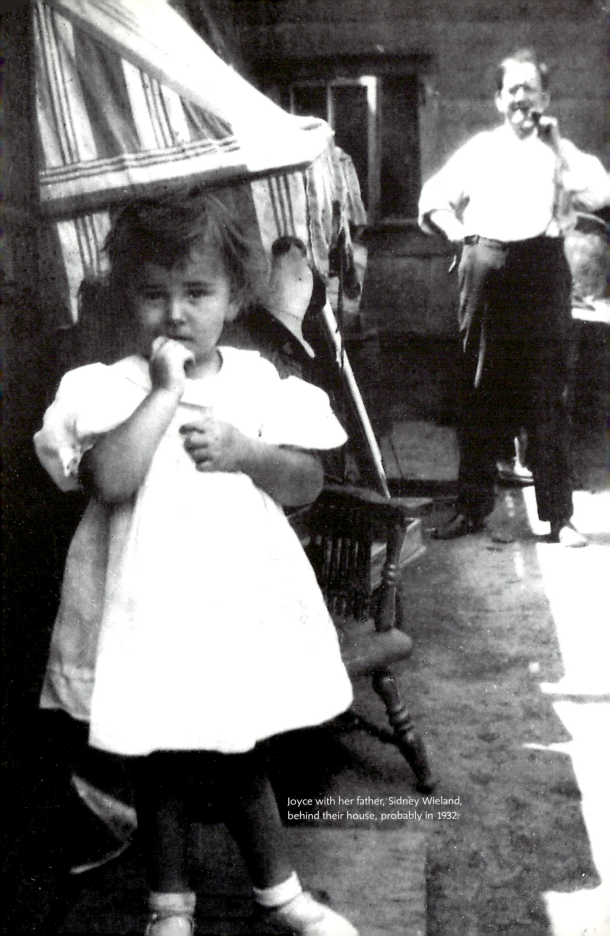

Joyce with her father, Sidney Wieland, behind their house, probably in 1932.

strategies to get enough women elected to create a fifty-fifty balance of men and women in Parliament, as well as elect a female prime minister. The fifty per cent goal still has not been achieved.

At the provincial level, in the 1930s new parties emerged with "colourful leaders ... Duff Patullo and the Liberals in British Columbia, 'Bible Bill' Aberhart and the Social Credit in Alberta, Mitchell Hepburn and the Liberals in Ontario, and Maurice Duplessis and the Union Nationale in Quebec all rode to power on a wave of protest against incumbents long ensconced in their respective legislatures."[8]

The Canadian Broadcasting Corporation, patterned after the British Broadcasting Corporation, came into being in the middle of the decade, as did the Governor General Awards for Literature, and in 1939 the National Film Board was established. By the end of the decade, the threat of another great war injected a different kind of drama into the day-to-day lives of Canadians, a turbulence few people wanted.

No one could have predicted that the new English-Scottish Wieland baby — a female child in a working-class, immigrant family, born the same year that Emily Carr showed her work in Toronto for the first time with Group of Seven painters — would grow up to delineate the uniqueness of this country, a country described by Margaret Atwood as "too big for anyone to inhabit completely ..."[9] Joyce would nonetheless try to inhabit all of Canada by creating a mythology that embraced not only the country's history, but also its people, its landscape and its animals. The mythology she would create would reach into the Canadian political and social fabric, warning that American imperialism would result in the loss of Canada's sovereignty. Sixty-eight years after her birth, at the close of Joyce Wieland's life, Canadians were still preoccupied with their identity; and the fight to protect Canada's sovereignty in every sector of society appeared at times to be a losing enterprise, a fight that, looking back, seemed barely to have begun in 1930.

Three years after R. B. Bennett came to power, people were already disillusioned by his government and were driving "Bennett buggies," cars towed by horses because there was no money to buy gasoline. Sidney Wieland, a short man, not handsome, with "strange hypnotic eyes ... and dimples,"[10] had neither horse nor car, but he did have a job. He had spent three years working as a caretaker at movie theatres, including the Orpheum on Toronto's Queen Street West, now a building used for a tool rental business.

By the time Joyce was born, Sidney was a waiter at the biggest hotel in the British Empire, the new, glamorous one-thousand-room Royal York Hotel, which had opened the same year the stock markets fell. He worked there for most of the thirties, and supplemented his meagre pay by pilfering fine foods. Into huge, specially sewn pockets on the inside of his coats, he stuffed meats, pastries and other delicacies to bring home for his family, foods they could not possibly afford.

As an adult, Joyce spoke with fondness of her memory of sitting on her father's knee in the middle of the night eating pastries. When he came home from work he would lift her out of bed and hold her as she ate as much as she pleased while he and his mother quietly chatted. However, Joyce was at the same time troubled by her father's deceit. As she saw it, his imagination was most active when he was figuring out how to steal food from the hotel — hiding a chicken in a cloth bag behind the door till he went home and filling his secret pockets. She wished he had used his imagination to get better jobs rather than using it to figure out "ten imaginative ways of stealing."[11] Yet Joyce felt that the interweaving of dishonesty with imagination was an integral part of his character.

Although Joyce's point that her father could have used his imagination honestly to feed his family is valid, likely he experienced a great deal of stress trying to earn enough in the extreme circumstances of the 1930s. He probably felt his stealing was justified, if he thought about it at all. With his Royal York Hotel loot and the fresh vegetables he grew in the backyard, for a while at least his family ate better than many in the neighbourhood, some of whom had larger houses.

The Wielands' four-room house at 99 1/2 Claremont, north of Queen Street, was a poorly built home of white stucco and green trim, with floors sloping so much that the back legs of the kitchen stove were set on blocks. This monstrous stove was intended to heat the entire house, an impossible task. However, it did provide warmth for the Saturday night baths if the tin tub was set right in front of it.

The small, dingy kitchen was the back room of the house, and behind it, a shed that included the outhouse extended into the yard. In the front room, the table and chairs and the stairway to the second floor took up most of the space.[12]

Claremont Street was — and is still — a working-class neighbourhood two blocks east of Trinity-Bellwoods Park. When the Wielands lived there, British immigrants like themselves shared the street with others from Poland, Romania and Czechoslovakia — a mixture of Jews and Gentiles. People who spoke the same language stuck together, which meant that there was little interchange between immigrants from different countries. As a result, misunderstandings between neighbours were common, with people shouting in their own languages and shaking their fists at each other.

Wooden-wheeled carts pulled by horses clattered up and down the street delivering bread and milk. Peddlers also brought tea, cheese and produce,

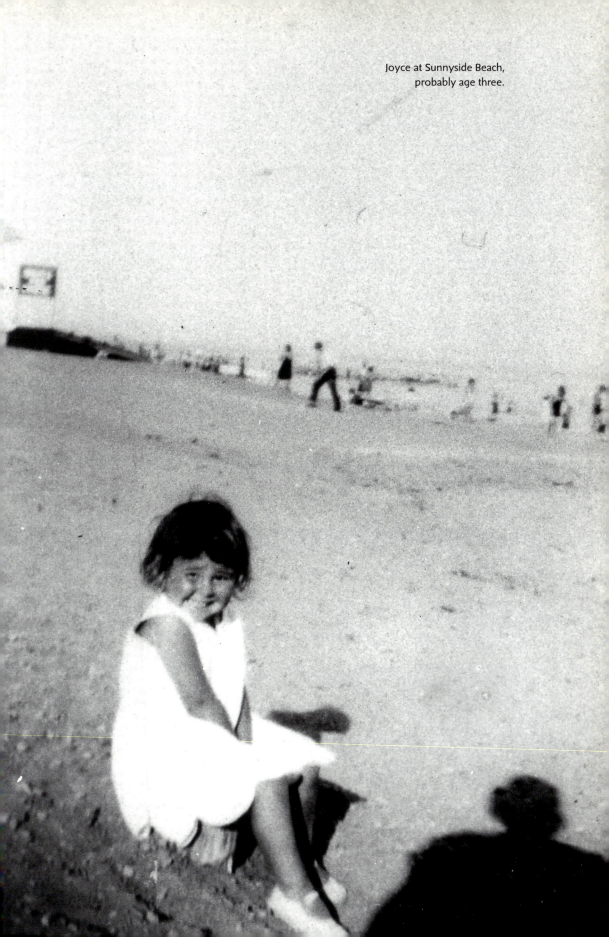

Joyce at Sunnyside Beach,
probably age three.

and on Fridays the fish man came. Because coal was burned for cooking and heating, the coal man also made deliveries every week. The frequency of horses on the street meant that the droppings were free for the scooping to fertilize vegetable gardens, and Sidney assigned this task to Joan, a job she detested and considered humiliating.

One block almost directly west of 99 1/2 Claremont stood a beautiful little Anglican brick church, St. Matthias, with its high, peaked ceiling and glowing stained glass windows. In this church, still standing, Joyce was baptized when she was six months old, and years later in the 1980s, at a ceremony for the blessing of the animals, Joyce would return there with her cat Thomas, who needed all the blessings he could get.

Around the time Joyce was three years old, Sidney moved his family next door to 101 Claremont, a similar four-room cottage, but slightly larger. Joyce's best childhood memories seem to be located in this house, a cosy and secure place, with Billy — dressed in a colourful house dress and a large apron made of sugar sacks with coloured piping — singing in the kitchen, hovering over the large, round kitchen table and stove, and going in and out to the back shed to get wood for the fire. In the mornings when Joyce woke up, her mother kissed her, took her out of bed and for breakfast gave her a boiled egg in a yellow dish. As an adult, Joyce would return to this house through a dream in which she — a little girl — floated high above everything, looking at the top of cupboards and other places she never had seen before.[13]

In such a small house, the kitchen table was the only place Joan had to do her homework, and in winter it was the warmest room. Joyce hung around Joan in the evenings and on the sly drew pictures in her school books.

For all of Joyce's romanticized memories of her life during this period, Joan remembered feelings of desolation and need in their cramped quarters. She and Joyce shared a bedroom, and her brother slept on a couch in the sitting room. In winter she often shivered in bed in both of those poorly built lathe-and-plaster cottages on Claremont Street.

For Joan, the cold house also symbolized an emotional coldness from her father. She felt he had always rejected her; at Joyce's birth she felt he turned his back on his older daughter even more. Sidney was extremely proud of Joyce when she was a baby; he entered her into beauty contests and boasted to his buddies about how beautiful she was with her dimpled cheeks. He also openly showed he preferred Joyce over Joan. However, there was one thing he could not tolerate: Joyce cried for hours at a time, it seemed. Sidney would often send Joan out with the crying baby in the pram to push her up and down the streets, something that Joan resented and never forgot.

Sidney's rejection of Joan cut so deeply that the hurt remained with her all her life. In fact, Joyce also admitted to experiencing the cold side of her father. She recalled that when she was about six years old, she found a Christmas light on the street, an object she thought was incredibly beautiful. In a moment of deep love she offered it to her father as a gift. He brushed her aside, and she was crushed.[14]

According to his daughters' accounts, Sidney paid attention to his children at his own whim. He indulged Joyce and was harsh with Joan. He would not allow his two older children to talk at meal time — a practice that Joan changed dramatically when she had a family. However, Joyce was allowed to eat wherever she pleased. She sometimes sat on the doorstep and food was brought to her there. It seems Sidney could see his daughters only in relation to himself, favouring one and rejecting the other. Meanwhile, he let his son fade into the background, although Joan thought of him as their mother's favourite, which left her without a place.

Although Sidney did not know how to relate to his children, he did care about their living conditions and their health. Whenever they moved to a different house, he stripped down the wallpaper and applied the special concoction he had used in his exterminating business in England to get rid of bedbugs and cockroaches, then painted the walls. In fact, both Joyce and Joan remembered the sitting-room walls Sidney refinished at 101 Claremont. After he had taken off the old wallpaper, he rubbed white, gold and deep blue paints into the plaster to achieve a beautiful embossed effect.

To keep the family healthy, Sidney made a tonic from malt, beef marrow and cod liver oil, which the children had to take every day, despite its vile taste. On Saturdays at bath time, they also submitted to a dose of epsom salts, supposedly to keep their bowels functioning. If someone had a sore throat, Sidney painted it with iodine. The taste was so horrible he used a nickel to bribe whoever needed the treatment.[15] Despite the heavy-handedness of these strategies, they may have been the best options available at the time.

Sidney insisted that Billy use only granite cooking pots — aluminum was not allowed in the house because he thought it was dangerous to one's health. Nor would he allow the family to eat tinned foods. He grew vegetables in the backyard in summer, and often sent the children after school to the Italian or Jewish markets if there was nothing in the garden. At 101 Claremont, he began keeping chickens for fresh eggs. By then, Kensington Market offered anything from live fowl to yard goods, and that is likely where Billy got her cloth for sewing on her treadle sewing machine.

From the time Joyce was a baby, her father spent hours massaging her legs and arms to make her strong so that she could follow his family's traditions and become a dancer. When she was three or four years old, he began taking her to Saturday-morning dance classes at Queen Street and Dovercourt Road. Joyce hated these classes; dancing with little boys in shirts and bow-ties was

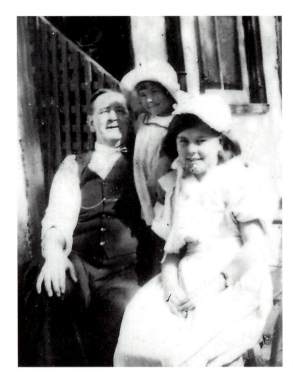

Joyce's father, Sidney,
with Joyce and Joan in
the 1930s.

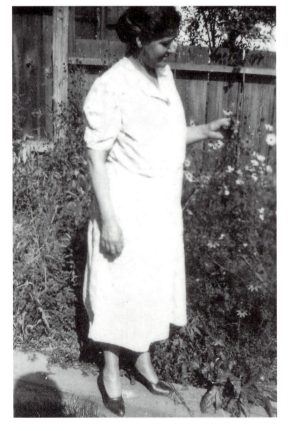

Joyce's mother, Billy
(Rosetta Amelia) Wieland.

not how she wanted to spend Saturday mornings.[16] When her father overruled her objections, she kicked and screamed until he finally gave up. But it seems he continued dreaming of her as a dancer, for on one of his frequent walks with Joyce, he pointed to a revolving dancing figurine in a store window and told her someday she would dance like that. As an adult, Joyce felt her father should not have forced dancing on her, but Joan could see nothing wrong with it. "I would have given my eye teeth to have [dancing lessons]," she said.[17]

When Joyce was five, Billy took her to kindergarten at the Charles G. Fraser School, a red-brick building on Robinson Street, a short walk east from their house. Just as Joyce had objected to Saturday-morning dance classes, she protested against being sent to school, but she handled it differently. She simply left and walked home, and to her mother's exasperation, sometimes arrived home before Billy. It made no difference to her that the Toronto school system had established kindergarten more than a half century earlier and was recognized as a leader in this area of education in Canada, the United States and Britain. The first five years of Joyce's life had not prepared her for a precisely scheduled day broken into blocks of time varying from fifteen minutes to half an hour, beginning with "Morning Circle," the time for emphasis on the spiritual and the duties of citizenship and health and safety rules.[18]

Kindergarten certainly offered her a larger variety of activities than she had at home. The children had access to sand tables, plasticine, crayons, paints, pencils, scissors, paste, needles, wool. They dramatized the story of "Goldilocks and the Three Bears" and listened to such fairy tales as "The Shoemaker and His Elves," "Red, Red Rose," and "Hansel and Gretel." For "Picture Appreciation" the curriculum listed French artist J.-B. Camille Corot's *Spring Landscape* and *Dancing Children*, along with *The Angelus* by Jean François Millet. Rhythm bands and singing were also part of the curriculum, with the guidelines that children's voices should be "unconsciously guided from a loud strident tone to a happy, light, sweet tone."[19] However, for a child who was previously allowed to do as she pleased, kindergarten, with its emphasis on sweetness and conformity, would have sent shock waves through her small world. She tried to be "sick" as often as possible, so she could play with her dolls underneath the kitchen table with a long cloth draped to the floor. At her request her mother would sew doll dresses and coats and hats. And in summer she could forget about school. On hot days she loved to sit in a tin tub filled with water in her mother's watercress patch under the lilac tree, eating cress sandwiches while her mother sat beside her drinking tea.[20]

When Joyce was six years old, Sidney again moved his family, this time to a

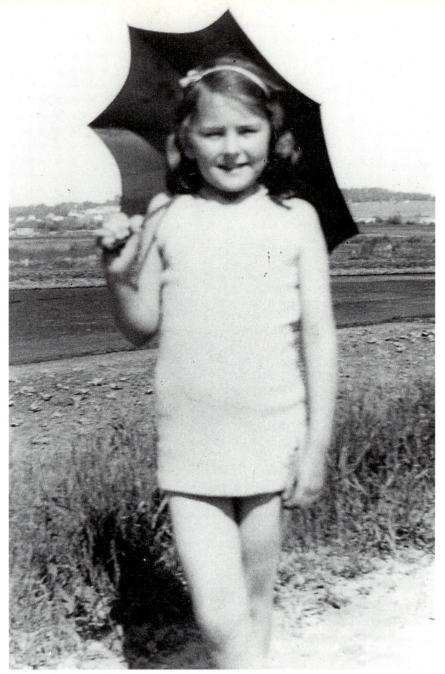
Joyce, eight years old.

better house at 145 Dovercourt Road, a semi-detached brick house with a lot nearly twice the size of the one on Claremont. Joan was delighted to have more space, with six rooms instead of four, and for the first time, a bathroom with an indoor toilet and a tub, though the water for baths still had to be heated on the stove. But her pleasure was short-lived; soon after they moved, Sidney's hours were cut back at the hotel. To make up for his loss of wages, he and Billy took in a boarder whom Joan hated. For Joyce, the move to

Dovercourt destroyed the feeling of security she had experienced in the little house on Claremont, and she also had to change schools — she began attending Givins Street Public School.

The following year, Sidney became ill with heart disease and the doctors told him he would never be able to work again. Survival was precarious without Sidney's earnings, and the household became fractious when Sidney and Billy insisted that Joan find a job. Joan desperately wanted to stay in school so she could become a writer. Furthermore, she felt that her brother should be the one to get a job because he had no interest in his classes anyway, and she loved going to school and earned good grades. No doubt Joan, at age fifteen and a half, was pushed to become the breadwinner because the family was desperate, but she felt it was because her mother favoured Sid, just as her father did Joyce. Joan was furious, but she eventually realized she had no choice. She knew how to type and take dictation and do basic bookkeeping, but she looked suspiciously young and had no diploma. Over and over Joan went to factories and offices and stood in long lines of people in equally dire circumstances looking for work, but in every case someone else was better qualified and wore better clothes.

Joan continued to come home and report that there were no jobs, but when her mother threatened her with going into "service," Joan was horrified at the thought of cleaning up after other people and she doubled her efforts. She found out that a girl who was a neighbour had landed a job at Neilson's chocolate plant, so Joan applied, lied about her age and appealed to the woman giving her the interview, saying her father was sick and the family was desperate. Joan was hired as a "temporary" at 25¢ an hour, which meant she brought home about $10 a week. For a family of five to survive on that amount would have been almost impossible, even though one could buy a loaf of bread for ten cents, hamburger for five cents a pound and shoes for seventy-nine cents. At least half of Joan's monthly earnings would have been used for rent alone.

Eventually the young Sidney was also offered a job at a country club in Islington if he agreed to live there, which he did, and he sent home a bit of money. But by October he had lost his job and returned home. Joan became enraged when she discovered her mother giving Sid spending money out of her pay envelope, which she dutifully turned over to her mother every week.

At the same time the situation must have caused considerable stress and anxiety for Billy. Besides persuading Joan and Sidney to get jobs, she had to keep the house quiet because complete bedrest and a calm house were the only known treatments for cardiac patients. For ten months, Joyce was allowed only at certain times to go into the bedroom where her father lay. Between these visits, wanting to make her father feel better, she drew

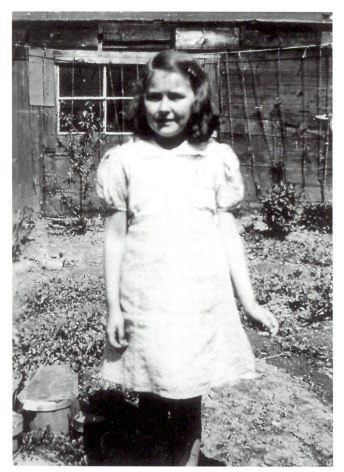

Joyce, eight years old, about a year after her father's death.

pictures to take to him. She poured her love for him into these drawings, and in return, he gave her his attention and affection.[21] This was the beginning of her profound belief that art is love and through art she could establish connections with other people.

In November 1937, Sidney died. It was devastating for Joyce that her drawings had not helped her father recover, and the connection between them was severed. For a seven-year-old girl the emotions accompanying her father's death would have been overwhelming — anger, despair and guilt for not having been able to save him. Young children who experience the death of parents can become wounded to such an extent that they often do not heal. The writer Margaret Laurence, whose parents also died when she was young, still mourned the loss of her mother at the end of her life.[22] Joyce was similarly traumatized.

Billy's grief and anxiety over how they would all survive must have hung like a dark cloud over the family. She had to borrow money to pay for her

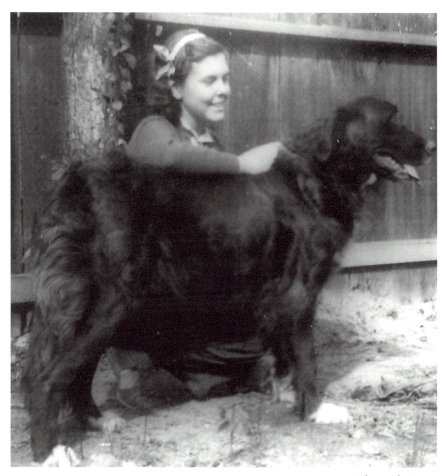

Joan in her early teens.

husband's funeral. Her church friends comforted her — they were the only friends she had — but the comfort did not buy food for the four of them or pay the rent and heat. One winter day, Billy gave Joyce a few pennies and a sack and told her to go to the coal yard on Queen Street to get coal. She pulled her sleigh home with the sack only a quarter full because that was all her few coins could buy.[23]

After Christmas, Neilson had no more work for Joan. She spent January and February of 1938 looking for another job, and out of desperation Billy applied for welfare, even though she had so far refused to do so because she felt it was like begging. However, in March, with the prospect of the Easter candy market, Joan had work at Neilson again. She learned to hand-wrap boxes of chocolates, sitting at the end of the line and taking the boxes off the belt and wrapping them in sheets of cellophane. She was fast and was pleased to have earned a small raise. She became so saturated with the smell of chocolate during those years that she hated it for the rest of her life, but she brought chocolate home for Joyce — the beginning of her chocolate obsession.

To help cover rent, Billy made rag rugs to sell and took in sewing, tasks Joyce had associated with pleasure and satisfaction. But the dire circumstances discoloured her memories of her mother's work, and in later years Joyce described these times as a Dickensian kind of existence.

The Wielands had a neighbour who was particularly kind to the children after Sidney's death. He was a junk dealer, and sometimes brought them toys or books. One book was called *Foxe's Book of Martyrs*, which pictured saints, some of them being tortured. The two sisters spent hours looking at this book, with Joan telling Joyce stories about the pictures. Joyce clearly remembered looking at one picture of a man lying naked on a bed of nails and asking Joan why no one gave him a blanket. But the most dramatic picture for Joyce was that of Joan of Arc because Joan acted out the story. She was so good at the dramatization that Joyce became frightened, feeling she was in another world, where Joan of Arc was standing in flames. It was mysterious that Joan could be Joan of Arc one minute and her sister again the next.

With her friends, Joyce made up dramatic productions. When she was ten the children made a theatre for stage plays in an old garage. They wore aprons with organdie edges for their singing and dancing acts, and used flashlights for spotlights. In a different spirit, they staged "wars" with children from other blocks of the neighbourhood, running down the streets carrying long clothesline props for spears to defend themselves.

During this period Billy frequently had back pains, and when she was hospitalized several times, Joyce knew something was terribly wrong. What she did not know was that Billy had bowel cancer. Joyce ran home from school every day at lunch-time to make tea for her mother and to empty her bedpans. When she discovered blood in the bedpan, Joyce became terrified, and wondered why her mother was bleeding between her legs. As the amount of blood increased, Joyce felt a deep sense of helplessness. One day when she came home her mother was not there. What she had been afraid would happen had happened.

In Joyce's memory, her mother died soon after her father did, but it was in fact three and a half years later, in the spring of 1941. If by then the pain of her father's death had partly healed, the death of her mother opened and enlarged the wound again. As an adult, she would discover that in childhood she had used her imagination to create a richly coloured place where she could escape being an orphan and play imaginary games in which she found her parents again.

At Billy's death, Sidney, the older brother, was of age, which meant that his decisions regarding Joyce would be legally recognized. Joan's foreman at Neilson offered to adopt Joyce, but Sidney wanted the three of them to stay together. Joan agreed, despite knowing that she would be the one who would look after Joyce. The 1941 directory of city residents in the Toronto City Archives lists Joan as the only employed person at 145 Dovercourt — Sidney's name does not appear — which means that Sidney probably did not have a job at the time.[24] Living on only Joan's earnings, they could not afford to stay at their Dovercourt home, and besides, it was the house of two deaths. They packed up a few things and walked out one day, leaving behind the furniture.

Finding an affordable place to live was difficult. They stayed at a flat on Gladstone Avenue for a time, and from there went to another one. Sometimes they moved from rooming house to rooming house, partly because Joan did not want the city's social services staff to know where they lived, as they would check up on whether Joyce was being cared for properly. Also, Joan could not always make the rent payments. Joyce remembered landlords coming to their door to collect rent money Joan did not have, and she claimed that sometimes they left a rented room in the middle of the night when they couldn't pay, and moved elsewhere. By 1942, they had apparently tried to create some semblance of a family unit, as the 1942 Toronto city street directory lists both Joan and Sidney as residents of 12 Shirley Street. The directory states Joan was a cellophane wrapper at Neilson, and Sidney a worker in the moulding department.[25] With two small incomes, they could afford a place together.

What was the impact of the loss of her parents — and the disruptions of moving from place to place — on Joyce's school life? As an adult she remembered spending a lot of time daydreaming in school. Her school reports took her to task for not paying attention, saying that if she'd look out the window less and look at the blackboard more, she would learn better.[26] But during her seemingly useless daydreaming she was absorbing the substance for her creative work as an artist, and the things Joyce learned were not what the teachers thought they were teaching. As an adult, she vividly remembered the pink and green colours of the map of Canada, and chalkboard numbers and letters would show up in some of her paintings. Among those works is her 1961 oil-and-collage painting, *Laura Secord Saves Upper Canada*. She attributed this painting-collage to her search for female role models and a history class. Apparently at the rare mention of a woman in a history lesson, Joyce interrupted her daydreaming to find out who this person was. All her life she remembered the C.W. Jefferys drawing of Laura Secord in the textbook.[27]

Joyce experienced another upheaval when Sidney enlisted and joined the

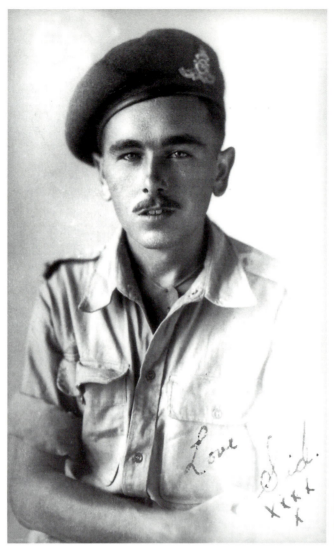

Sidney, Joyce's brother, at age twenty-three in 1943.

army in 1942, the year after Billy had died. Like many young men who went off to the war, he first married his sweetheart, Barb Kerr, one of Joan's friends who also worked at Neilson. When he prepared to go overseas, he insisted that Joan and Joyce live with his mother-in-law and her family — against Joan's will — so the two of them moved in with the Kerrs on Sylvan Avenue in the same part of the city. From 1943 to 1945 Sidney's address is listed in the Toronto directories as 10 Sylvan, but instead of place of employment, the phrase "active service" appears. It is curious that Joan is not listed because she did live with the Kerrs for a time.[28]

In later years, Joyce remembered "Mother Kerr" as "a fat, tough little woman under five feet tall."[29] Her husband, who suffered from a serious neck and head injury received during World War I, had been in a military hospital for a number of years. Eight children, along with several little girls Mrs. Kerr took in, made up the Kerr family, and some of the adult children with families of their own came and went from time to time. Several of the young women also worked at Neilson, and one, Alma, had a dress-making business and worked at home some of the time. Joyce spent quite a bit of time with her; after school she sat on Alma's "big plump bed" and helped her sew. In her diary, Joyce described Alma as "a tiny woman, with slim fingers and pretty small legs, and she always wore high heels, even when working."[30] Interestingly, many years later Joyce would open a gallery named "Alma" as a way of nurturing younger artists.

In this large household that included other women, Joan still took responsibility for her sister. Joan was an intelligent young woman with a love of books and classical music — in her elementary school days she had been introduced to Brahms, Beethoven and Chopin by her friend Grace who was studying piano — and she shared these pleasures with Joyce by taking her to the library and listening to opera with her on the radio. Through Joan, Joyce discovered Black Beauty, Dr. Dolittle and the Beatrix Potter books, which became a lifelong influence. The free library was a blessing because Joan's earnings could not extend beyond basic necessities and a few movies. Joyce used her imagination to come up with spending money. In grade eight she drew pin-up girls and sold them to the boys at school for a dime, a steep price in those days. By the time she was fourteen, she always had summer jobs, and had learned that it was a hard scrabble for everything she got, an attitude that would surface from time to time even when she had enough to live comfortably.

A 1943 diary in which Joyce had written her address as 10 Sylvan Avenue contains brief daily entries the year she was in eighth grade at Brock School, beginning on her thirteenth birthday and continuing till December. "Dear Diary today is my 13th birthday I got lots of stuff. I'm the happiest girl in the world. Everything is good [crossed out] swell. good night" But the next entry says that the day began with an argument as usual — not surprising in a house full of so many people. Or were the arguments between Joyce and Joan?

Although Joan did not like living at the Kerrs, and according to Joyce's diary talked about moving, Joyce liked the arrangement, and it had many benefits for her. Sewing with Alma gave her a sense of pride and self-confidence. She recorded a successful sewing job in her diary. "I sewed Bill's pocket for him to-night and I sewed it good." Bill was Joan's boyfriend at the time and Joyce obviously liked him because she says "I think Bill would be a swell brother." She was disappointed when it seemed that Joan and Bill

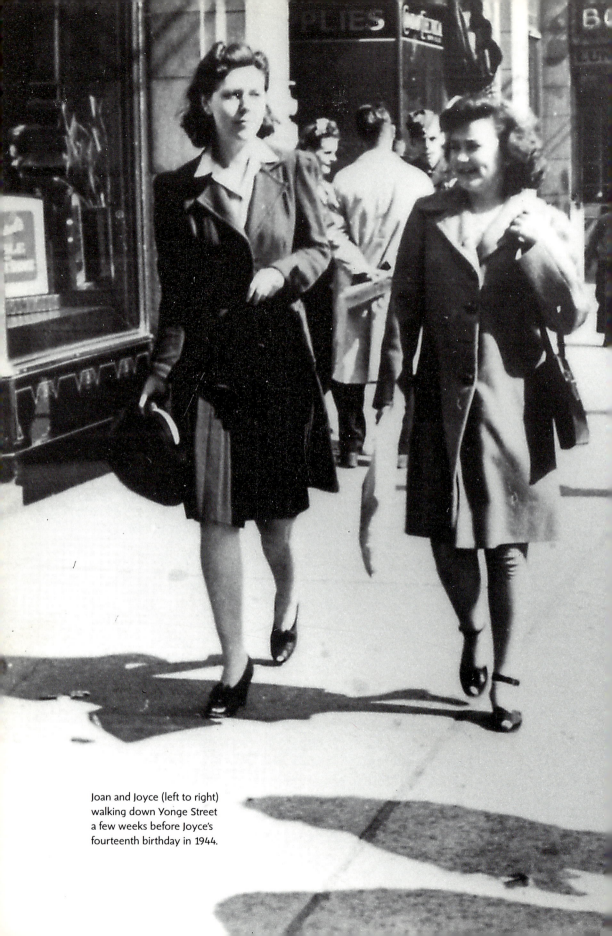

Joan and Joyce (left to right) walking down Yonge Street a few weeks before Joyce's fourteenth birthday in 1944.

would break up, and at one point she tells her diary that "Jo is doing crazy things like Bringing home a pickup." Later she records, "Dear Di Joan has broken up with Bill for shure she will never get a guy gosh we will have to live alone." Obviously, she had strong ideas about how things should develop. She wanted Joan to get married, and then she could live with the couple — achieving some semblance of a normal family, perhaps. When Joan went to a fortune teller, Joyce speculated about whether the fortune would include marriage to Bill. It didn't. The "fortune teller turned out to be corny."[31]

Joyce's most exuberant diary entries are about getting new clothes — a new corduroy jumper — and seeing or making art: "I saw the most wonderful art today it ws marvelous I am happy go lucky wacky — Jo went to the show [movies] although I happily staed home."

Where did Joyce see the "wonderful art"? It might have been on a visit to what was then the Art Gallery of Toronto. From 1930 on, and through the post-World War II years, Toronto School Board students in grades seven and eight were taken to the gallery twice a year to look at current exhibitions. A teacher chosen by the Board talked to the students about the art they were shown. *Centennial Story*, a history of Toronto's Board of Education from 1850-1950, contains a photo of a group of public school students looking at *Pasture*, a 1919 Fred Haines painting of cows in a pasture under a huge sky.[32] On the photo, taken from the back of the room, one girl with long wavy dark hair could easily be Joyce, though, of course, it's impossible to be certain.[33]

As a schoolgirl, Joyce had an opportunity to see how frequently such artists as Horatio Walker painted cows in the rural countryside. In a scene of her feature film *The Far Shore*, Ross and Eulalie try to convince Alfred the art dealer to promote Tom's work, but he tells them he looked at twenty-seven of Tom's paintings, and not one of them had a cow in them, and for that reason he would not be able to sell them. Trees and rocks just didn't draw the same clientele!

Another diary entry mentions that she "painted some great masterpieces to day." The next day she records that she "stayed home and did my homework had some candy and was happy. Joan was with me." And another: "Stayed home Jo did to. I love her ... not so fond of Barb [Sid's wife]."

During her last years of elementary school, her report cards record an A in art and Bs and Cs in the other subjects.[34] Joan was sensitive to Joyce's talents and knew she was an artist, perhaps even before Joyce did. From the time she was very young, Joyce had drawn pictures everywhere, including the walls. Joan loved books, and was infuriated when she found Joyce's sketches in her school books. Nevertheless, when Joyce had completed grade eight, Joan wanted her to attend Central Technical School because of its art program. Barb thought Joyce should attend Kent Commercial School and learn to do

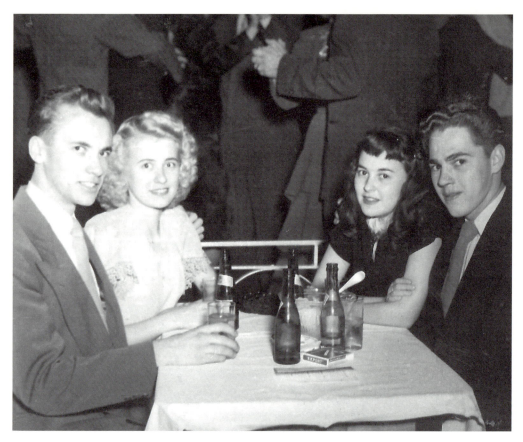

Joyce and David Etherington (couple on right) with John Rathbone and Irene Price at Club Top Hat on November 17, 1947.

office work. But Joan knew Joyce would be hopeless in an office. Barb wrote to Sidney and explained their disagreement, and Sidney agreed with Joan. So in the fall of 1944, Joyce began high school at Central Technical School, the great stone building with a square tower at Bathurst and Harbord Streets.

Joyce enrolled in a dress-design course. To learn to draw the human figure, the students went to Doris McCarthy's class in the art department on the fourth floor. Over the door of the art room, room 401, there is still an archway with a beige plaster relief of Canada geese, seagulls, a rabbit, a bear, whales, a squirrel, a bobcat and a seal. Whether or not she noticed it, Joyce walked underneath this relief of animals native to her country every time she went in and out of the classroom.

McCarthy described the young Joyce as waif-like and neglected. "I remember her as being a dirty little girl that made you just sad, but talented and sweet."[35] She recognized Joyce's abilities, that she was good at drawing, and spoke to her guidance teacher and suggested that Joyce change to the fine-arts program.[36] Joyce was pleased. For the first time since the loss of her

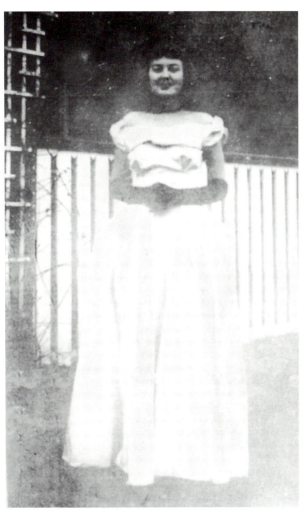

Joyce wearing a pink gown for the Imperial Masonic Lodge Ladies Night Dance in early winter 1948. David Etherington, whose father was in the Masonic Lodge, took her to the dance.

parents, she had a reason for hope about her own life. When she returned to Central Tech for grade ten in 1945, she enrolled in the fine-arts program.

Despite McCarthy's memory of Joyce as neglected, David Etherington, who dated Joyce for a year, remembers her as one of the prettiest girls in the school. He once took Joyce to a ladies' night at the Imperial Masonic Lodge, where his father was Master, and she wore an off-the-shoulder pink dress — he was impressed with how gorgeous she was.[37]

From grade ten on, Joyce had a close friendship with Barbara King (now Barbara King Graham), also in the art program. When Barbara and Joyce met, they knew very quickly that they were "kindred spirits," a term they picked up when they read the *Anne of Green Gables* books together. She remembers Joyce as sad, but "so beautiful, with that skin and that gorgeous hair. She had so much going for her ... I thought she was lovely. She didn't."[38] Joyce once described her high-school self as "the beautiful and unhappy Joyce."[39]

Joyce then lived in East York on Sammon Avenue with her brother and Barb. In November 1945, Joan married Harvey Stewart, who had served in the medical corps during the war. The couple lived with Harvey's parents on Jones Avenue, so Joyce no longer lived with Joan.[40] As Joyce lived in the east end of the city and Barbara King to the west near Harbord Street and Ossington Avenue, the two girls spent a lot of time together riding on the streetcar between their homes and school. In good weather, they walked because they had more time than money for streetcar fare. It was on the streetcar that they shared secrets and talked confidentially, as do any two schoolgirls who are fond of each other. They sometimes became so engrossed in their conversations that they missed their stop. On one streetcar trip Joyce revealed that she had been an accident. It seemed to make a difference in the way she thought of herself because she talked about it a number of times — she had been a "change-of-life baby." In fact, her mother had been forty when Joyce was born, her father, fifty-three.

When Joyce felt comfortable with someone, as she did with Barbara, she by turns, became serious and then funny. She had small, white hands, dimpled like those of a child. On the streetcar, she often did a routine with her hands, turning them in certain ways to create the illusion they were something else. She was mesmerizing. Barbara later learned that it was an old Fanny Brice trick Joyce had picked up — she must have seen Fanny Brice movies. Nevertheless, despite their close friendship, a part of Joyce was sealed off. She never talked about her early life, other than to say that her mother had died, and she never, ever spoke about her father. But she did tell her friend that she disliked living with Sid and Barb and their children.[41] She and her sister-in-law did not get along very well.

The two friends often went sketching in the ravine by the Bloor Street viaduct. Barbara discovered that Joyce craved recognition, and that she was determined to develop her artwork. Perhaps selling a painting for eight dollars to a local cigarette store at age sixteen spurred her on.[42]

Joyce was very intelligent, and she certainly had the capacity to do well at Central Tech, but for the most part her grades hovered around average and were sometimes lower, particularly in grade ten. Those years, as is the case for many teenagers, were difficult for Joyce, according to both David Etherington and Barbara. She was unsure of herself, and often acted "goofy" when she was with people she did not know well. However, by her last year at Central Tech, according to Barbara, she seemed to come into her own, which was when she and David were dating.[43]

An event during her final year at Central Tech evoked difficult memories of her childhood. She had learned firsthand how the uncertainties of the labour market could affect a family when her older brother and sister were laid off work from time to time, and everyone in her house became sad and anxious. She carried a clear memory of herself as a young child wondering why no one would hire Joan and Sid. When several of her grade-twelve classmates told her about a labour strike at Eaton's, she was interested and went with them to find out what was happening. She never forgot what she saw. "Everything looked grim," she recalled, "and it was the middle of winter and those people were walking up and down and looking scared and there were a bunch of students watching."[44] It may be that this experience formed the seed for *Solidarity*, her film about the Dare strike in Kitchener, Ontario.

The same year as the strike at Eaton's, Joyce did something else that could have led her into considerable trouble. The students at Central Tech were a mix of people, ranging from recently returned war veterans, who formed a large proportion of the students, to a group of young men who would now likely be labelled "activists." Out of curiosity, Joyce attended several Communist Party meetings with the latter group of classmates, though she never joined. Eight years earlier the Communist Party had been banned in Canada, and during that era, the Toronto police commission had a history of monitoring public meetings and breaking up any that were suspect. They attempted to keep communist propaganda out of the hands of the public, and outside of socialist groups, anti-communist sentiment prevailed. Attending a meeting of the Communist Party was not something a respectable girl did. However, considering her experience of poverty, Joyce's curiosity was understandable. At this stage of her life, with no parents watching over her, she was less restricted than most young women, free to experiment and follow her curiosity even in supposedly suspect areas.

By this time, Joan and Harvey no longer lived with his parents. His sister Melita, known as Mel, remembered that Joyce often visited Mel's family, and Violet Stewart, Harvey and Mel's mother, became very fond of Joyce. For a short time Joyce lived with the Stewarts during her last year at Central Tech, and shared a room with Mel, who was ten years older than Joyce, Joan's age. Joyce quickly developed a friendship with Mel. It seems that after Joan was married, Joyce no longer felt close to her. In fact, Joyce told Mel she didn't talk to Joan. Looking back, Mel said, "I can understand because Joan had a hard life, and it was hard to get close to Joan. You could get very close to Joyce." She called Mel her sister, told her of her dream to become a painter, and often said to her, "Oh, it's so good to be able to talk to you."[45]

Unfortunately, violence erupted in the Stewart household. "There was this terrible scene where the father tried to kill everybody, so I had to leave there and I went to live with my friend, Mary Karch," Joyce said in a 1986 interview.[46] The situation was so frightening that she simply walked out and didn't go back. Mel also moved out the same day and was married a week later, but unlike Mel, Joyce was without a home. When Joyce's friend Mary Karch told her mother that Joyce didn't have a place to live, Anna Karch asked no questions and said Joyce could move in. Anna Karch, too, became very fond of Joyce and accepted her as part of the family circle. After about three years Joyce felt constrained within the Karch household, but initially the Karches offered the security Joyce needed in a time of crisis.

The relationship with Anna Karch was characteristic of Joyce's experiences with women during her formative years after her mother's death. Joyce was a likeable young girl and had a capacity for establishing connections with women, perhaps suggesting she had a strong bond with her mother as a young child. Even though in later years Joyce felt she had been a burden to Joan, who also considered the responsibility as a burden, without question Joyce's primary bond during early adolescence was with her sister, who appreciated Joyce's gifts and encouraged her. Nonetheless, these other women who cared about Joyce also offered her stability. The Kerr women had been interested in her, taking her to movies, and to some extent played the part of aunts.

At Central Tech, Joyce encountered for the first time women who were artists — Elizabeth Wyn Wood, Virginia Luz and Doris McCarthy. Wood taught sculpture, and when Joyce made out of plaster a woman who appeared be looking up at the sky in communication with God, she got the first good mark of her life, she said.[47] Joyce had a particular appreciation for McCarthy because she was not a typical teacher. She wore flight boots and drove a jeep, though McCarthy claimed that until 1960 she had to dress "like a lady" to teach, which meant wearing gloves and shoes that ruined her feet. However, to keep warm on cold days when she went out sketching, she and one of her friends bought surplus flight uniforms that could be zipped up in the front.[48]

It was not only the way McCarthy dressed that appealed to Joyce; she liked this artist-teacher's spontaneous manner. When McCarthy entered her classroom full of teenagers, she threw open the windows to air out the place as she exclaimed about the "fustiness" of the room. This kind of physical liveliness appealed to Joyce and gave her a firsthand experience of an energetic woman with a life of her own, dedicated to her art.

Not all students were affected by McCarthy to the extent that Joyce was. Her responsiveness to this teacher must have grown from her own desire for a creative life, fuelled by a strong desire for recognition, something she would discover during her personal therapy in later years. Whatever else made up her creative drive, she decided that if McCarthy was what an artist was like she, too, wanted to be one. What she was not conscious of at the time was the imprint women had left on her, and the multitude of impressions and images of her country that she had absorbed — images that would surface many years later in her paintings, quilts and films, and that provided the foundation upon which she would build a large segment of her life's work.

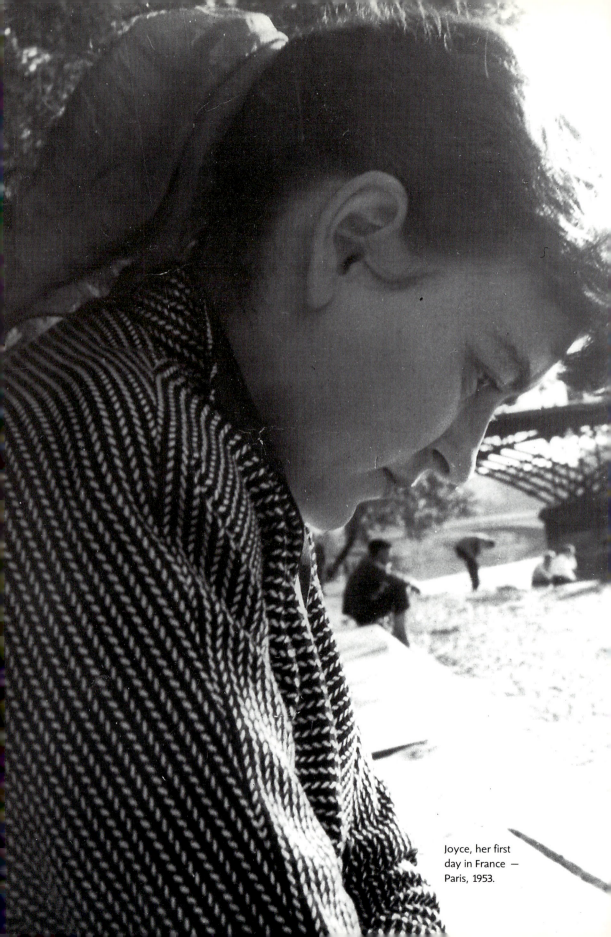

Joyce, her first
day in France —
Paris, 1953.

3

Experiment with life

... the metaphor with which one thinks of one's self has much to do with the way one constructs both one's life and one's art. —A.S. Byatt[1]

WHEN JOYCE graduated from Central Tech in 1948, most Canadians were still trying to restore patterns of normal life after the war. "Normal" for men meant establishing themselves with a secure job, marrying and raising a family. While the returned soldiers had been in the trenches, "home" had represented all that was good and wonderful in life — a beautiful woman at its centre — and the *fulfillment* of their dreams. Under the horrific circumstances of the war, there is little wonder that an exalted concept of the family took on mythic proportions. However, it distorted the role of women in postwar society.

Canada's Liberal government, in its plans for a postwar economy, had set up a six-man Advisory Committee on Reconstruction as early as 1941. Women began lobbying to have their interests represented. Consequently, in 1943, a subcommittee of women was established to consider problems women might encounter after the war. This subcommittee's report, for the most part, was relegated to the women's pages in the newspapers, and the federal government ignored the recommendations.[2] The message was clear. Women were to return to their role as keepers of the home, and were to be content there.

Postwar popular culture, at its height when Joyce was in her teens, represented girls as boy-crazy, with interest in little else in life. The comic strip "Penny's Diary," depicts Penny, a teenage girl, drooling over any "cute" man and becoming dejected when he does not fall in love with her.[3] A 1952 school text, *Just Like Mommy, Just Like Daddy,* published simultaneously in Canada and the United States, portrays Mommy sweeping the sidewalk, picking flowers and waiting for Daddy to come home. Of course, Jane copies her and does everything "just like Mommy." Dick is likewise busy copying Daddy, and comes for lunch when Mommy calls and eats everything on his plate, which means when he grows up he'll be a daddy, "just like Daddy."[4] The difference between what men did and what women did was clear. With this kind of conditioning, there was little room for autonomous young women.

These rigid roles meant marriage was the "route to respectability," an idea "reinforced by social psychologists, politicians, and religious leaders. Those who did not marry were the subject of suspicion, for they were, in a sense, deviant in terms of cultural norms."[5] In fact, some so-called experts went so far as to suggest that being single was akin to having a disease or mental illness. The assumption was that the goal of every girl and woman was marriage, preferably before the age of twenty-five, and if it didn't happen it was her fault.

The Canadian activist and writer Ellen Stafford, who was a generation ahead of Joyce, said in her eighties that during her youth, "Everything I thought, everything I believed, I'd picked up from the lyrics of the pop songs of my time; a foolish girl, eager to play the romantic role of mother, to cuddle a cute little baby."[6] The role Stafford learned twenty years earlier than Joyce was perhaps even more strongly imprinted in Joyce's generation.

Joyce was not a typical young woman in that she had a passion for trying something different. However, she also absorbed notions about women from popular culture, and these two opposing viewpoints gave rise to inner conflict. A few months before she turned twenty-one, Joyce began keeping a journal in a fifty-cent black notebook, as a way of sorting through her thoughts and recording them. On the inside front cover she wrote "Private Notes and Philosophical Jottings" and recorded her place in time: "Age 20 March 6/51."[7] For the five years she wrote in this notebook, she worried over a question that she framed as an either-or choice: marriage or a career as an

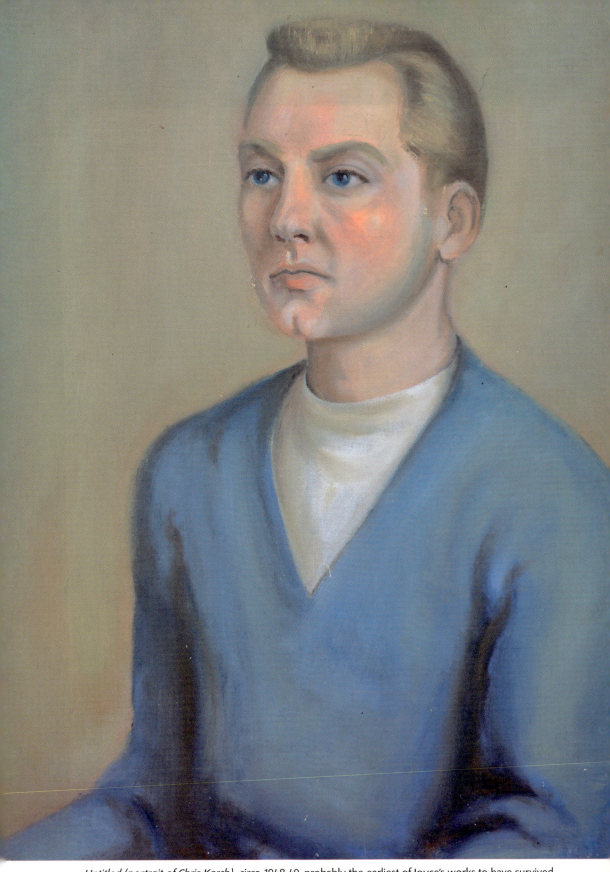

Untitled (portrait of Chris Karch), circa 1948-49, probably the earliest of Joyce's works to have survived.

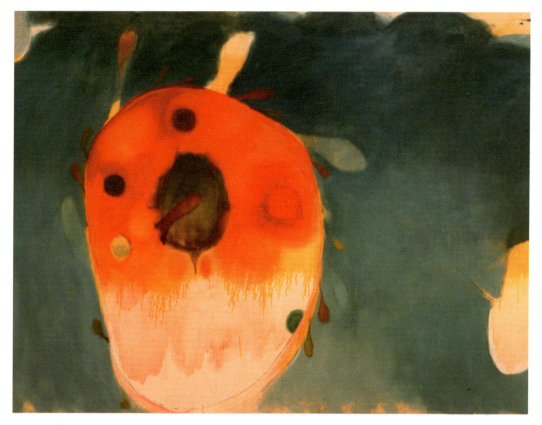

Time Machine Series, 1961.

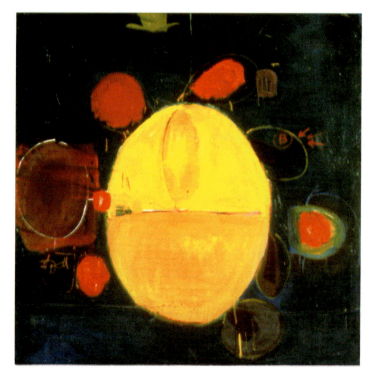

Time Machine, 1959.

artist. Sometimes she deplored her single status. She also thought that if she was going to have children, she wanted to do it before she reached age thirty, and she felt that "A woman hasn't much time really. has she?"[8] This thought must have informed her first *Time Machine* painting four years later.

When she was in her early twenties, she did not yet understand that what she was up against had begun long before the 1950s. Whitney Chadwick described this kind of conflict as an "ideology of sexual difference," forcing women to choose between marriage and a career.[9] A century earlier Berthe Morisot encountered the idea that "Single women were 'excess' human beings who had not fulfilled their womanly destinies. A career was supposed to 'unsex' a woman, leech away her femininity, and render her abnormal."[10] These notions filled Morisot with doubts about her passion for painting, but she persisted, and it was only many years after her death that her contribution to Impressionism was recognized.

Joyce was at a disadvantage without a knowledge of the struggles of Morisot and other female artists throughout history. She often wondered whether she had the necessary stuff to follow her own passion for her art — "I am not strong willed enough for all my ambition. I must train myself. Above all choose my own way in life and stick to it without regret."[11] Around the time Joyce was writing these comments, Doris McCarthy had turned forty and was enjoying the freedom her life choices were giving her, and McCarthy was still Joyce's primary role model.

She had not yet discovered the writers — Colette, Katherine Mansfield, George Sand — to whom she would look for an alternative to the image of woman prescribed by society. But her journal shows that she carefully observed the women around her: her friend Mary, who was a year younger, and Mary's mother, Anna Karch.

Joyce had continued living with the Karches after she graduated. She and Mary formed a close friendship, even though the two were very different. By 1950 Mary had become a switchboard operator at the YMCA, and would later be a secretary there before working for the Steelworkers Union, becoming well known in the union movement. Mary was a tidy, particular person who reined in her emotions, while Joyce's emotional state swung between highs and lows, and she could quite happily keep a room in a state of messiness and chaos.

Joyce and Mary shared their clothes, which was a benefit to Joyce since she had come through high school with only a few outfits. Anna Karch, who did the laundry for the household, knew that Joyce was poor and had few clothes. Nevertheless, she was annoyed when Joyce put on Mary's clothes that had been put aside to be washed. "I washed them and ironed them, and what Mary took off, Joyce put on dirty. I said, 'Joyce, don't you put that on.'

She said, 'They're not dirty, Mary doesn't get them that dirty ...' She used to make me so mad."[12] Despite the minor annoyances, Anna Karch and her family loved Joyce and accepted her as one of them. She was at liberty to live with them as long as she liked, even if she could not pay for her room and board. There is no question that Joyce benefited from the structured and stable family life of the Karches, and particularly from the care and affection of Anna Karch.

Joyce kept in touch with Joan, visiting her often enough to know the kind of life she had, and she did not like what she saw. She perceived Joan's marriage as an unpleasant trap and tried to do what she could to cheer her up. For a period of time she visited Joan two or three nights a week, but seeing her with her "downturned lip" upset Joyce. She wanted to help her sister but didn't know how — Joan acted as though there were no reason for living and had no sense of humour.[13]

Joyce also helped out Sidney's wife, Barb, when she had her third child and Sidney was ill. Again she saw firsthand what happens when a woman is caught in a prescribed role, raising a family with few financial resources. Joyce's diary in the early fifties mentions several times how bad she felt about the lives of her brother and sister. Closely related to her discovery of the impact of sexism was her dawning understanding of the generally unacknowledged class structure in Canadian society. In her diary she recorded her realization that her family was of the lower class, and always would be.[14] Her own clear memory of poverty — and her fear of it — along with seeing her sister and brother caught in circumstances similar to those of her parents, led her to admire the way of life of the wealthy, another admission in her diary. Surely these discoveries gave impetus to her intense drive to hoist herself out of the working class, where she began life, and would fuel her determination to win Michael Snow, whose family came from a "higher" level of society. In later years Joyce would develop friendships with several wealthy people. Her thoughts as revealed in her diary in the early fifties suggest that during this time she became determined to live a life very different from that of her family.

The first summer after Joyce graduated from Central Tech, she worked as a switchboard operator at Percy Herman, a plastics company where her brother-in-law, Harvey Stewart, was also employed. According to Joan, she did not last long there because she frequently connected her boss to the wrong phone lines. When an E.S.& A. Robinson ad appeared in the newspaper, Joan encouraged her sister to apply, even though Joyce had little confidence in her ability to do design work. With Joan's urging, Joyce applied and was hired to design packaging, a job that lasted for almost five years.

Robinson, with its head office in Bristol, England, was one of the major printing firms in Canada and employed more than a thousand people. In the Leaside plant the art department was divided in two groups: one for packaging materials printed on letter press, the other for lithography — calendars, posters and banners. Joyce was hired in the lithography department. This was a company with a friendly atmosphere — a good place to start out. Once her job situation was stable, she paid Anna Karch seven dollars a week for room and board.

Until this time, Joyce had had very little opportunity to travel outside of Toronto. While she was still in high school, she had gone by car with members of the Karch family for a weekend in Chicago to visit Tony Karch, Mary's brother, who was attending George Williams College. By the time Joyce had worked for several years, she had a little money to spend on travel, and in March 1951 she and Mary took a train trip on their own to visit Tony. He set her up with a date one night, a young man named Paul Tegler, and they went drinking in a group and talked about politics, including the possibility of war with Russia. Joyce admitted that she could have fallen in love with almost any of the young men she met that night. Her date, the blond, blue-eyed Tegler, impressed Joyce to the extent that his name appears on the inside back cover of her journal under the heading, "romancing." "Joyce Tegler" also appears there; she must have been trying out his surname on herself.[15]

Evidently she was carried away by her romantic ideas about the weekend; afterwards she wrote that she would sacrifice her "art and ambition for him and support him through school if [he] wanted me, but he is young and inexperienced to know what he wants from life, let alone worrying about women. Am afraid he didn't take to me that much any ways. I was just another girl and good time I am afraid, thats all I was!"[16] By telling herself that Tegler was inexperienced and wasn't really interested, she managed to redeem herself from her own sentimentality and the trap of renouncing her own passions — who she was — for a man. Her responses are not surprising: she was only beginning to explore how she would relate to men. She would have to extricate herself from false notions of romance many times over.

Sometime after the Chicago venture, Joyce and Mary took another train trip together, this time to New York City to visit galleries and explore the night-life — Joyce's introduction to the city where she would later spend almost ten years of her life. She was amazed at the size of everything and noticed that the people were different from those she knew. She and Mary saw the musical *Gentlemen Prefer Blondes*. Joyce also had her "first big art experience," a tour of Rockefeller Center where she was mesmerized by the murals, looking at them until she suddenly realized the tour had gone on and left her.[17] She didn't know how long she had been standing there alone.

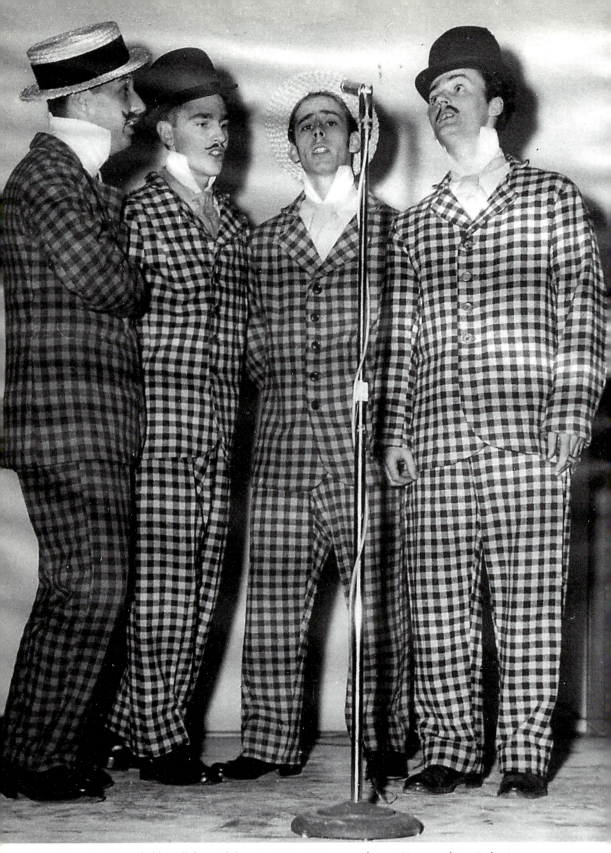

"The Robins" in the early fifties: (left to right) Jimmie Morrison, Don Smith, Don Rivers, Leslie A. Parkes in rented outfits. Leslie A. Parkes' mustache was the only real one.

Back home in the Karch household, Joyce kept ruminating over men. Should she look for a husband or pursue her painting, or could she do both? Doris Anderson, another feminist pioneer, and editor of *Chatelaine* magazine for twenty years, experienced the same conflicts over men a few years earlier than Joyce. In her autobiography, *Rebel Daughter,* she recalled, "I look back in bewilderment on how much time I spent in emotional turmoil over men I can barely remember today."[18] But the reason seems clear when one takes into account the enormous pressure to marry, a pressure Anderson called "formidable."

Joyce's first serious romantic relationship was with another E.S. & A. Robinson employee named Don Smith. Don was dark and handsome, and one of the "Robins," a barber-shop quartet whose members all worked at Robinson.[19]

Joyce thought she was in love with Don, and she experienced mood swings from one extreme to another. "Isn't it strange how a person can change in the space of a day or two." she wrote. "One moment I am in the heights of ecstacy and then suddenly I am down in the depths of self doubt and insecurity. This is a very excellent sign of emotional instability. But I can't control It have no desire to either, it brings excitement into the drabness. Two things thrill me more that anything one is painting and the other is loving with someone I love. Which is the stronger I don't know."[20] One reason for her conflicting emotions was a conversation she had with Don about whether she could pursue her career and still marry. He didn't think that would be possible. "Is it so wrong that a person should desire to travel and paint," Joyce asked her diary. "Can't these things blend with marriage. God I don't know, Don didn't think so." Through the next year, she seemed to have an off-again, on-again relationship with him.

Finally, according to her diary, Don told Joyce he couldn't help her find what she wanted, that she already knew what that was. True, she did know what she wanted, but getting it was a difficult road. She wrote about her fears of not being able to find freedom within marriage, concluding that a career and her work would last longer than love, "unless its with someone who feels the way you do and then career and love can blend together." Where would she find a man who was secure enough in himself to risk marriage with a woman who was passionate about a career in art, and not interested only in a husband and family? "God damn! must not get tide down in this web of convention and marriage not yet!" she told herself. "There is so much to see and do and grab at and to love and to desire and give."[21] As these entries reveal, Joyce was struggling to reconcile her desire to make art with her desire for a man. To imagine that these two goals could be compatible was a revolutionary thought in the 1950s.

Joyce wanted to attend art school somewhere but was intimidated by the cost. Meanwhile, at E.S. & A. Robinson some of the employees organized a life-drawing class and hired a model, which only intensified Joyce's wish for art school because she wanted to study the figure. But her confusion remained: "If I found a smart chap, I would realize just how unimportant I am. I long to look up to the man I love. (to a certain extent) I long for freedom and yet afraid of the insecurity that goes with it."[22] This wish to see herself as unimportant meant Joyce, of course, had internalized the conventional way men and women related to each other — she had seen her mother always deferring to her father.

On the one hand, Joyce wanted her freedom, but she tied herself in knots because she feared life without the security of marriage. Giving up Don evoked her fears — "Life is full of these dread departures into the unknown." However, throughout this period of inner conflict, Joyce continued drawing and painting. In fact, Chris Karch, who was still at home when Joyce lived with his family, has a portrait she painted of him in 1949 or 1950. The painting, a carefully rendered portrait of a blue-eyed, serious young man in a light blue sweater, is slightly damaged and unsigned. In the spring of 1982, at Mary Karch's funeral, Chris reminded Joyce of the portrait, and she offered to sign it if he brought it to her. He neglected to phone her, however, so the painting remains unsigned, possibly the earliest of Joyce's works to have survived.

By the spring of 1951, Joyce decided she wanted more time alone, and it must have been at this time that she left the Karches to live with another friend named Phyllis, whom Joyce mentioned in notes on a small scrap of paper. From Phyllis's place, she moved to 700 Bathurst Street to live in the third-floor studio she had rented since she was nineteen.[23] This house was directly across the street from Central Tech.

Dr. Morris Miller, who had his medical offices on the first floor, rented out rooms on the second floor as artists' studios. George Shane had a self-contained apartment there and took responsibility for collecting the rents of the other artists, who included Walter Kopcz, Chris Yaneff and Gerald Gladstone, although others did move in and out from time to time. Joyce had met Gerald Gladstone through Victor Waterman even before she had rented a room at 700 Bathurst. Gladstone took her to a big Christmas party in 1950, where she and Sheila McCusker first met.

Sheila was a young woman, an Irish Catholic from the east end of Toronto who since childhood had aspired to becoming an artist. She took a commercial art course at Central Tech's night school and hung out with illustrators in commercial art studios. Sheila worked as a secretary for Purdle and Wylie, and went with Jack Purdle to the Christmas party. She vividly recalled Joyce's entrance. "In the door comes this gorgeous woman ... with black bangs, and she's got a white sweater on, pleated skirt, all in white with red lipstick and who the hell is that? Very skinny, but with big boobs ... I was absolutely dazzled by her. She seemed to be totally in command," Sheila said.[24] Sheila's first impression was characteristic of how people responded to Joyce. Sara Bowser recalled that "You met her once, you knew who she was ... She was always strikingly dressed."[25] Joyce and Sheila, who both inhabited a male world of artists, were drawn to each other immediately. After they had talked for a while, Joyce said, "I like you, I think we're kindred spirits." Sheila was startled. Kindred spirits? What did that mean? She had never heard the term before, and she became even more taken with this unusual woman. At the end of the evening, Joyce and Sheila exchanged telephone numbers.[26]

A few days later, Sheila phoned Joyce, who invited her to accompany her to the Art Gallery of Toronto the next Sunday afternoon — Joyce regularly spent Sunday afternoons there. Thus began their friendship, and the regular Sunday afternoons at the gallery. When one of Gerald Gladstone's paintings was exhibited in a show of water-colours at the gallery, the three artists spent Sunday afternoon together at the show and had tea. From then on, Gerald joined their Sunday excursions to look at art.

Joyce suggested that Sheila take the room beside hers when she moved into 700 Bathurst — she knew Sheila wanted to leave home. Sheila did move in, but then discovered that living with someone was very different from simply having a friendship with her, and she did not stay very long. She decided the attic space was too small for two, even though the low rent of $18 a month had appeal.

Living at 700 Bathurst was the beginning of Joyce's experience as the only woman in a group of artists. It was also her introduction to artist parties that lasted long into the night. Cheap wine was the favoured drink, with guitar playing or jazz records filling the silence. Sometimes a party centred around discussions that lasted for hours — talk about politics, music and art. According to Chris Yaneff, they were all rebels and offered answers to what was wrong with the government. Of course, there were also arguments about art; the burning question was, Are you really an artist?[27]

Joyce's new living quarters introduced her to more than parties. She joined a political group, Canadians for the United Nations, which was established by George Shane while he was living at 700 Bathurst. Joyce invited Joan to join the group, evidence that she tried to help her sister make connections outside her family. Most of the time the group met at 700 Bathurst Street, but occasionally they met at someone else's home, including Joan's house on Jones Avenue. To raise money, the group rented an old theatre and showed films, the only place in the city at that time where

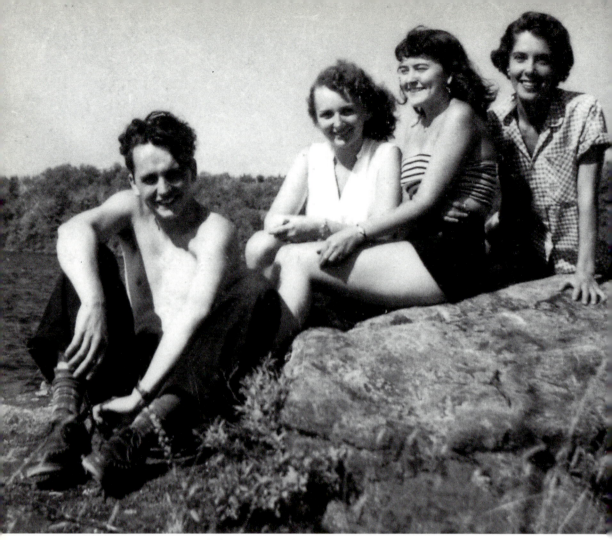

Bryan Barney, Ann Didych, Joyce and Isabel Borhy (left to right) in the early fifties.

movies could be seen on a Sunday. Art shows were another way of raising money. Anne Dydich Robbins, the group secretary, remembered that she, Joyce and others from the UN group visited Group of Seven artists and asked them to donate paintings to raise money. The Unitarian church on Avenue Road lent their building for the art shows, where the Canadians for the United Nations sold the works and contributed the proceeds to UNICEF and other United Nations projects.[28]

Canadians for the United Nations continued for several years. During some of their group discussions, they talked about the unhappiness in their families. But Anne remembered that Joyce did not talk about her family. They discussed the role of women in society, particularly the opportunities that women had had during the war. Because Anne was taking a night course in psychology, she and Joyce and Mary Karch discussed psychology at length, and these three became close friends. They formed the core of a group of women who together searched for ways of understanding themselves. In this group Joyce broadened her grasp of psychology, articulated her own ideas and gained confidence. However, Anne remembered Joyce's intense emotional lows, sometimes caused by job-related problems, but more frequently because of her longing for romance.

Anne also discovered, as Barbara King Graham had earlier, that Joyce had an intense need to be loved. She was not a happy person, but she was a loyal friend. "You could always call on Joyce," Anne said. "If you befriended Joyce, she'd be a very good friend."[29]

That spring, Joyce became increasingly discontent with her job at E.S. & A. Robinson. She felt it was unfair that her boss kept the "creamy" jobs for himself or farmed them out to other men, freelancers at that. She wanted him to let her do these jobs as overtime, but apparently that was not what happened. Finally, she became so angry with her boss for giving her only the "crumby" jobs that she walked out on him.

Meanwhile, she bought a litho printing plate to try out colour lithography for herself. She also made a number of drawings of children, using Joan's children as models, and felt pleased with her accomplishments. By then Joyce's friend Barbara was married and was starting her family, but occasionally she and Joyce would meet. She told Joyce that if she had children, she would not have time to draw them because she would be too busy taking care of them instead. This observation added another angle to the marriage-career dilemma for Joyce to consider. Barbara remembers that Joyce spent time thinking about this, and then agreed.[30]

And yet, she was not sure she wanted to give up marriage and a family. The summer of 1951 Joyce became confused and depressed and fell into one of her emotional lows. On the one hand, she wanted to go back to school and study the figure. She couldn't stand the "thought of marriage right now and children." But in the same entry she blamed her depression on not having a boyfriend. "Everyone else has witty boyfriends who know just what to say and they have manners and don't have such dull friends." She wanted a brilliant man to fall madly in love with her. Even though she still thought about Don, she decided she did not want to marry him because she felt sure that they "would never have anything." She also concluded that life would be dull with him because he would likely sit and read the paper while she did the ironing.[31] And then she blamed herself for being stupid and without talent, fearing she would never have another job again.

The feelings revealed in this journal entry are those of someone whose depression had resulted in a loss of perspective. Joyce seemed to need a romantic attachment to a man to feel her own value. When she felt bereft, her feelings became tangled in longings for a romantic relationship. She also

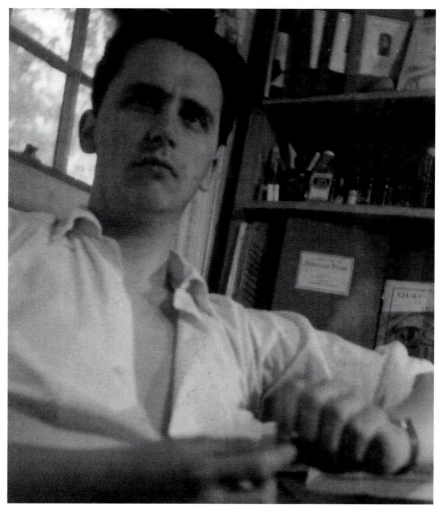

Bryan Barney in the early fifties.

blamed herself and could not recognize that she *did* have good instincts in not wanting to marry a man who thought she could not have her own career within marriage.

Though Joyce felt lonely and needy, in fact she had several circles of friends. There were the graphic artists she had met through her job and life-drawing class. The United Nations group included people who were not artists, and through this organization she expanded her awareness of a larger world. There was also the group of artists at 700 Bathurst, and of course, some of these groups overlapped. She also had her friendship with Sheila McCusker, through whom Joyce was about to meet a man who would play a major part in her life.

Sheila McCusker had travelled to Europe that spring and on the boat had met a tall, dark-haired young Englishman named Bryan Barney. He had come to Canada in 1948 and now lived with his parents in Hamilton, Ontario. On her way back to Canada, she again happened to be on the same boat as Bryan. Sheila liked him, and after she returned home introduced him to her friends in Toronto. One day at the end of the summer of 1951, they met by chance on Queen Street, and Sheila invited him to come with her to the Canadian National Exhibition. She told Bryan she was going to visit a friend who was working at the Ex — Joyce, who was drawing portraits there.[32]

Bryan was an affable, soft-spoken young man, an aspiring writer who had been working in a shoe store in Hamilton. After he met Joyce he began writing letters to her. In February 1952, Joyce recorded in her diary, "I have had two letters from a remote fellow in Hamilton ... an equally remote city. He wrote a poem to me!! To my psyche, I think. Strange how one goes along never dreaming one has anything at all — and suddenly one discovers one has a psyche — and attractive one at that."

In his poem, Bryan said that knowing Joyce had erased his cynicism: "... this apotheosis/of your psyche/has meaning/and that is motivation/ motivation for me to write/for when before/I had desire/it was unallied/by the only true/justification/for existence/which was an ideal/which I now have/perhaps it is illusory ..."[33]

Bryan's letters, in which he called her "Joycelyn," sent Joyce into a fanciful frame of mind. "Here I sit on my narrow couch The date is somewhere in February of 52," she says. "I have found a little comfort and inner peace of late. I live in a dazed little world, devoid of appointments and time. Wander about listening to people through a film of fog. Surely then I am in love with life. I now enjoy small pleasures, easily. I paint and draw, and even find pleasure from it although there is little pleasure to show."[34] One of her projects was a self-portrait, which she called "ghastly," and threatened to throw it out the window except that her landlord, Dr. Miller, would not like that. "He would probably feel it his duty to come up and have a look at me."[35]

Bryan began visiting Joyce regularly at 700 Bathurst. She was pleased. She called him "the chap from Hamilton" and said "he interests me quite deeply now. And he is ever so remote. Sometimes very thoughtful sometimes extremely jovial."[36] They became good friends, and one Saturday they stayed up all night talking and "necking intermittently. We went out for breakfast at 5:30 and then walked all over town. We ended up in front of the parliament buildings sitting on a bench" and watched people on their way to church. "Strange how unreal everything seems so early in the morning after lack of sleep. We must have looked like spring fever victims."[37] By June, they both felt their relationship was "serious," but Joyce immediately began thinking about marriage and dreaded the idea, though they had not yet become lovers. A month later, she wrote that they had gone as far as they could

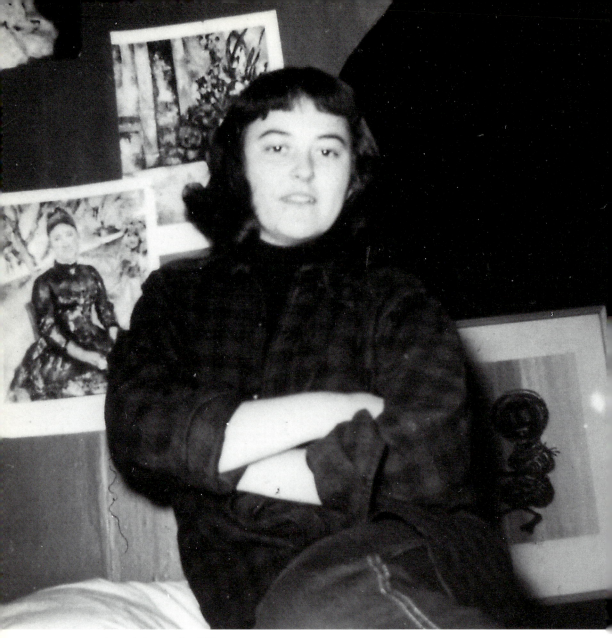

Joyce in her studio, 1953.

"without completing ... Bryan says he does not care and will not let it get in the way." For the first time, Joyce found she wanted the "complete physical contact. I am ready for it, yet there are serious consequences to consider, possibly a child or regrets of some sort. Bryan isn't pushing the frustrating issue so I guess I'll let things go and cut out necking and petting — if possible."[38]

Sometime after that, at the end of the summer or in the fall, they became lovers and Bryan moved in with Joyce at 700 Bathurst Street. Her diary skips from July 1952 to January 1953, so she did not record when he moved in.

However, her entries during the winter indicate that she felt content — "things are beginning to shape and take on a pattern in my existence" — because she had security and warmth from Bryan. "Love is favourable to a good life it is perhaps the only way to lead a balanced and stabilized life. I can see myself working without that threatening sensation over my head. Now I can draw and paint a get a favourable sensation from. Now I can look forward to a quiet life without regrets for I have found my lifetime friend ... I know that we shall work in harmony and complement one another."[39] Though in fact they would live together only a few years, Joyce was right that they would remain lifetime friends, and Bryan would play an important part in putting together her major feature film.

During the summer, Joyce focused on drawing. She spent so much time with Bryan that six weeks went by without her seeing her friends because Bryan's "hermit instincts" were affecting her, she said. She concluded that being "a social bug" was fun but didn't get you anywhere, particularly if you didn't have money. The interest of a man had restored her confidence. "The only way to get anywhere is on your own merit and integrity. This will open all gates of all circles sincerely. Sincerity is the best of all as no one can refuse ones accomplishments. Some day I hope to prove to a lot of people that I am a sincere artist and make them believe me although they are not worth trying to prove anything to. People don't want you for yourself alone — only rarely — you must offer them something ..."[40]

Bryan's "hermit instincts" were related to his aspiration of becoming a writer. He was a grade-eight drop-out, but had educated himself in the topics that appealed to him. His interest in literature led the two of them to read a number of books together, among them, Stendhal's book about love. He introduced Joyce to other French writers in translation, including Gustave Flaubert. Joyce was pleased when she found André Malraux's *Voices of Silence* for $2.19 because she had been wanting to read it for at least a year. She also read Balzac's *Père Goriot*, which she called a social portrait, and the memoirs of the eighteenth-century adventurer Giovanni Giocomo Casanova.

For a time Bryan worked as a copy editor in the advertising department of Caterpillar Tractor, and later in the public relations department of George W. Crowthers in Leaside, which is where he met George Gingras, whom he introduced to Joyce. But Bryan's heart was in his own writing. In her diary, Joyce says he was working on a novel and had written a collection of short stories, which he had not been able to get published. She also said that he read all the time, on the streetcar and even while he was walking down the street.

Their small, two-room space required little housekeeping, though Bryan was more interested in order and tidiness than Joyce was. With only a hot plate in their rooms, they did a minimal amount of cooking, instead eating cheaply at a number of restaurants. At L'Europe, on Bloor Street near Brunswick Avenue, a five-minute walk from where they lived, they could get a complete meal for 95 cents and often ate there. Sometimes they walked to La Chaumière, a French restaurant at Church and Charles Streets, to Tops at Bloor and Yonge Streets, or to Fifth Avenue, which was in the same area. Another popular restaurant was George's Spaghetti House on College Street, and farther south on Gerrard Street near Bay Street was Mary Johns, a favourite spot for artists in the fifties because the food was exceptional and it had the cheapest prices around — customers "could stay alive for sixty cents a day and get fat for a dollar." If you wanted sliced hard-boiled eggs on top of your salad, it cost a nickel more.[41] Joyce loved Mary Johns because of its garish green walls and travel posters, and in later years when the interior was spruced up the change upset her. Eating at these places was more fun than cooking on the little hot plate in their attic home. Besides the food and atmosphere, there was always a chance of finding along the way something else Joyce loved — good book sales.

Living with Bryan gave Joyce a sense of security, and she felt enough at ease to look for another job. At the beginning of the New Year she began working at one of Robinson's competitors, Planned Sales, where she made $40 a week and had her own office. She also designed greeting cards for Austin Marshall, and was making more money than she ever had before. However, she was a bit disturbed that she was not doing any serious work, nor was she reading much, and her mind felt dull. But she planned to go to Europe with Mary Karch, which gave her the motivation to save her earnings. At one point she wondered why she wasn't planning a trip to Europe with Bryan, and then concluded that there must be some reason. She speculated that when she returned, she and Bryan would likely get married.

In later years, Bryan remembered that during that summer, while she was working at her new job, Joyce went "quite off the rails" and would go to work and then leave and wander about town. Apparently she became somewhat disoriented. "I think she just flipped out," he said, and it lasted for a few weeks. Bryan remembered that as a "weird summer" when Joyce was somewhat incoherent.[42]

Joyce's summer "off the rails" is an example of how she gave herself over to whatever feeling she experienced, the emotion of the moment. For her, this was the way to find out what she needed to know about her own life. As we know from her diary, she had made a conscious decision to be this way because it made life more exciting. By entering into a state she created inside herself, she explored her interior spaces that summer, the beginning of a pattern she would follow throughout her life, which led her into emotional places few of us go.

For most of us, parents and siblings act as early socializing forces, teaching us how to make connections with other human beings. According to Dr. John Rennie, who would treat Joyce in later years, "That's sort of the model. What happens when a child loses a mother or father, or both parents? They don't have that model." Most people who suffer this type of loss find a substitute way to form attachments. Some "become athletes or [find] some other way to have the world come to them." Joyce's "emotional ability to form attachments was cut off, truncated, full of frightening images," and her art became her way of connecting to others, a pattern she began when she drew pictures for her dying father.[43]

Bryan understood the implications of Joyce's early experiences. He pointed out that "there was no family to impose any kind of structure on her."[44] From his intimate connection with her in the early fifties, he saw that her approach to life as a young adult was formed largely by this absence. His understanding of the process of forming a personal mythology corresponds to that of Jill Ker Conway: "We travel through life guided by an inner life plot — part the creation of family, part the internalization of broader social norms, part the function of our imaginations and our own capacity for insight into ourselves, part from our groping to understand the universe ..."[45] As we have seen, in Joyce's case social norms and her own self-knowledge resulted in conflict, but the family part was lost, and she gave herself over to a life in her imagination, not only while making art, but in her emotional life as well. She had not learned to separate and compartmentalize the various aspects of living, which is the approach to life of many people. It seems that early on she discovered that for her, life had to be all of a piece — her life and art would be one continuous experiment of her own making.

At the beginning of September, the Karches took Mary and Joyce to Montreal, and waved goodbye to the ship as the two young women sailed for Europe on September 2, 1953. On the Canard Line's *RMS Ascania*, they met a middle-aged anthropologist. Joyce was not pleased that he and Mary got along well because she grew tired of their small talk during the lunches they ate together. To "get away from Scotch war brides and howling children," as well as Mary, Joyce went to the first class deck to read. She acted as though she belonged there, so the stewards didn't stop her. Joyce was not interested in conversations about "panty-girdles, pills and baths," which is what Mary and the other women talked about.[46]

The ship docked at Liverpool, and Joyce wrote to Bryan in the tram between Liverpool and London, saying how thrilled she was by the green, rolling countryside. She also mentioned British seamen and wished she could "build them into a movie."[47] In London they first stayed at the YWCA but didn't like the early curfew imposed on the women, so they found another

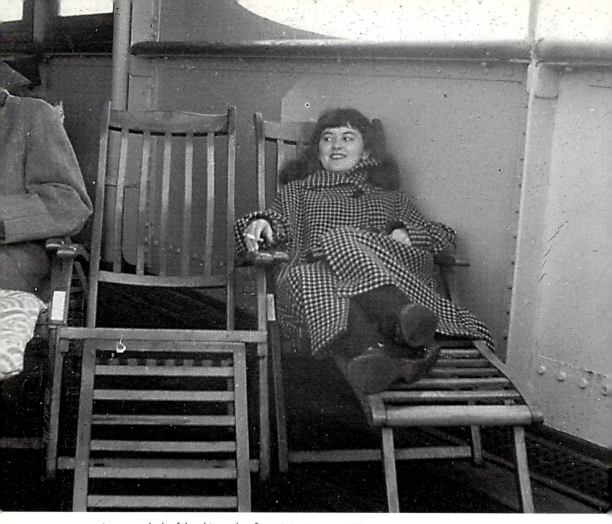

Joyce on deck of the ship on her first trip to Europe, 1953.

place, a bed and breakfast for which they paid fifteen shillings each.

Many of Joyce's letters to Bryan began with an affectionate "Dear Beube," and she also signed them, "Beube." She revealed in a letter dated September 14, 1953, that she was not getting along well with Mary. "I never realized how little Mary and I have in common," she wrote. In the years of sharing a room, had Joyce not discovered how different they were? A large factor must have been that in the two years since she had left the Karches to live on her own, she had become accustomed to a more turbulent life than had Mary, who had remained at home in a structured environment. And Joyce was discovering the old axiom that you don't really know someone until you have been away on a trip with her. She told Bryan, "However, I shall go on making the best of a bad idea." This was only the beginning of their travels, and already she felt she couldn't share things with Mary, and talked to her only when necessary. In another letter she complained that Mary was a chatterbox. Part of Joyce's discontent might have been caused by the lingering effects of her withdrawn state over the summer.

Regardless of her impatience with Mary, Joyce enjoyed the city of London. "The city is so vast that it would take years to understand it. The haymarket is interesting with so many old theatres. And the Festival theatre is beautifully designed." She and Mary spent some time sitting in Hyde Park watching the people. Mary wanted to leave, but Joyce decided to stay longer, getting lost and wandering around for two hours before she found their bed and breakfast.

Before leaving England, they spent three days in Brighton, staying with Bryan's grandmother.[48] In another letter to Bryan a few days later, Joyce gave three addresses where he could send her letters: the Canadian Embassies in Rome, Paris, and also the Hague in Holland. She told him that she would pray for him. "I feel very holy lately and have taken to praying again. Maybe the city of churches and religious art does this to me or maybe I am lonely."[49]

By the time the two arrived in Paris, Joyce seemed to be in a better frame of mind. In a letter to her sister in September, Joyce described sitting on the bank of the Seine in beautiful weather, eating lunch from a bag. She enjoyed the variety of wine available, and how cheap it was, and praised the good food. She was taken by the outdoor cafés and the two-foot bread sticks. "Young people and old people make love in the streets, in the subway and in the parks and restaurants. Their motto is live and let live, I guess. Good idea, though." She fell in love with the French, and could not help comparing them to the English. "I like the way the people eat and shop and cook here. There isn't very much to dislike in the French."[50]

Joyce and Mary stayed in a hotel in the Latin Quarter, the *Mont Blanc*. One night, wearing her nightgown under her coat, she walked into the bar at midnight to get a "lemon citroen." She noticed a man at the end of the bar staring at her. Speaking in French through a waiter, he asked Joyce to dance. Flattered, she agreed, forgetting that she was wearing her nightgown. It took some convincing before he believed that she was not a French prostitute, but a good Canadian girl.

Thomas Ripka, "well-bred, handsome, divorced with a child," was love-struck with Joyce. He told her he was on his way to Australia to work for the Israeli government, but he asked her to go with him to Nice, Cannes and Antibes first. Joyce felt confused. She was afraid of his hardness, but she also thought she could fall in love with him if she allowed herself. Although she could not imagine sleeping with him, the idea of running away with him appealed to her fantasies. In the end, she concluded that she still loved Bryan too much. Nevertheless, she had "a continual dinner date" every night for two weeks, which she thought made the "other girls" at the hotel jealous.[51] After he left, Joyce received a postcard from him addressed to her at the *Mont*

Blanc, saying he thought of her day and night.[52]

In her diary, the only art she mentions seeing in Paris is Marino Marini's sculpture and ceramics by Fantoni, but later she would talk about having discovered the work of Albrecht Dürer on that trip. She brought home some beautiful books from both Paris and Italy. In Vienna Joyce saw the operas she would have heard as a child when she and Joan listened to the radio. Three nights in a row they attended operas: *La Bohème, Aida* and *La Traviata*. She sobbed during *La Traviata*, and blew her nose in Mary's scarf. They had box seats, so she was sure everyone saw how the opera had affected her. In Munich, when they attended Beethoven's *Fidelio*, the smell of dirty feet was so overpowering that Joyce covered her nose with a glove, like a gas mask, and Mary laughed so much the two were nearly thrown out.[53]

By mid-October Joyce and Mary were in Rome visiting the catacombs. She described the monks they encountered as heavy smokers, with "very dirty feet and are continually scratching themselves and eyeing the girls." Her sketch of the monk who was their guide shows a broad, robed figure with a bald head, wide face and no neck, holding a smoking cigarette in his right hand and a candle in his left.[54]

Joyce returned home in November to discover that something had happened to her feelings for Bryan. The two of them were different with each other — "love seems to have left us and flown elsewhere" — and she declared in her diary that they would not marry. They were free people, she said, so perhaps it would be better that way. Even though she didn't think she would ever love anyone as much as she had loved Bryan, lovemaking had become difficult for her. She wished sex could be excluded from their relationship. "I need loneliness most of the time," she said, "so long as there is someone nearby with whom I could talk sometimes."[55]

Joyce concluded that Bryan did not like her any more, and she again became insecure and self-deprecating, calling herself "a social leper." Remembering Paris cheered her somewhat. For her, Paris had been "like a home," and travelling had given her a great feeling of freedom and a sense of dignity within herself, but now that she was home in Toronto, the feeling was gone. She felt lost, had no job and no money, a state of affairs that discouraged her even further. She returned to the idea that discovering herself in art, rather than looking for any "one" person, was the way to self-fulfillment because her ultimate satisfaction was in her art. But Joyce's basic loneliness did not allow her to sustain this feeling. She continued to vacillate between feeling that the answer lay in art and believing that she could find happiness only through love.

Since she didn't have a job, she figured at least she could count on Bryan to feed her. She spent her time working on drawing and sculpture but felt she should be looking for work so she could buy Christmas gifts for her family. She experimented with sculpting in wood, and apparently it was during this time that she made a carved self-portrait relief, which she eventually gave to her niece, Lois Stewart Taylor, one of Joan's daughters. She also drew a portrait of Bryan, which he and Sara Bowser had hanging in their living room in later years, and a plaster plaque of a mother and child, which disappeared.

In the early part of 1954, through one of her friends, Joyce met John Ross, the financial manager at Graphic Associates. This small animation company had originated in 1950 when Jim MacKay, who had been working for the National Film Board of Canada, asked George Dunning, one of his associates, to join him in starting their own company. Between them they had $850 to put into the venture, and they set up at 56 Grenville Street in an office next to the studio of Group of Seven painter Fred Varley. They recruited John Ross, whose father had been president of the Bank of Nova Scotia, and benefited from Ross's experience handling money. The mandate of the company was to provide a "visual presentation of ideas."

MacKay and Ross bought three-acre lots in Kleinburg, where Ross built a house, which became the Graphic Associates office. But the location caused problems. It was too far from Toronto, and the firm's telephone was on a party line, resulting in poor service. One month the company billed only $12 worth of business.[56]

Graphic Associates returned to Toronto, setting up first at 1111 Bay Street and then moving in 1953 to 21 Grenville Street, where the company was when Joyce met John Ross. The drawings she showed him lent themselves to animation — figures of children used to form lettering, for example. George Dunning, the artistic director, liked Joyce's samples and gave her some freelance work. It was likely her new work that prompted her to try some experimental filmmaking on her own in March of 1954. Her diary records that she was working on a plan to make a three-minute film in honour of Isabella, the heroine in Keats's long poem "The Pot of Basil." "It will probably not come off," she wrote, because "I am terrible on Long range schemes."[57] In fact, she never did make the film, but her choice of subject matter tells us something about her at this time in her life.

The poem, set in Florence, Italy, is the love story of Lorenzo and Isabella. Her brothers disapprove of Lorenzo and coax Isabella to consider a wealthy nobleman instead. Isabella refuses, and her brothers decide to get rid of Lorenzo by inviting him to ride into the forest with them, where they stab him to death, dig a hole and bury him. Isabella eventually wastes away, mourning over the loss of her lover.

Joyce may have chosen this poem because it embodies unattainable

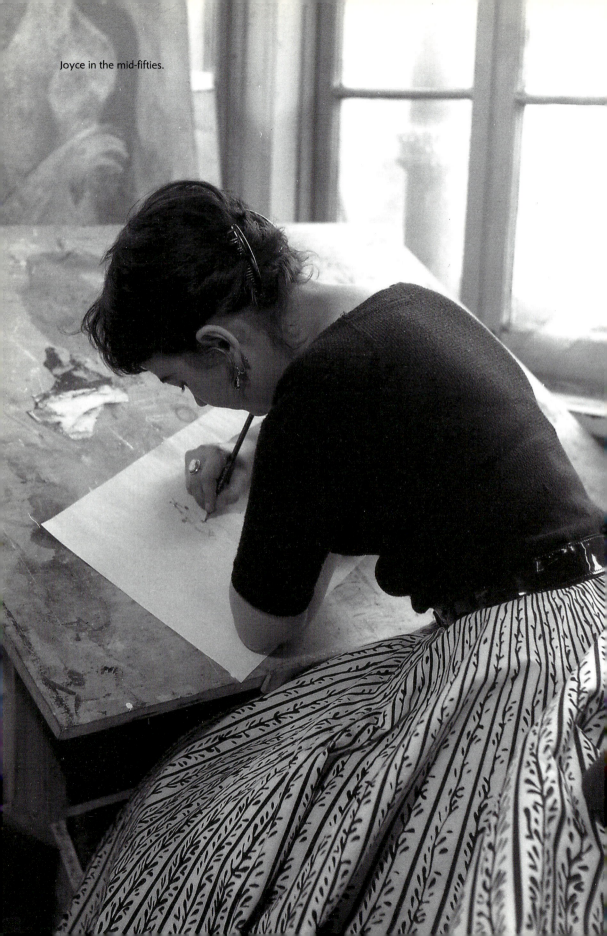
Joyce in the mid-fifties.

romantic love. She herself was caught up in the notion of romance as unfulfillable longing. If in later years she had made this film, perhaps she would have brought to it her sense of humour. However, at the time that she conceived the idea for this experimental film, she would have identified with Isabella too much to do anything but a serious treatment of the story, and perhaps this is one reason she never carried through with the project. Nevertheless, according to Bryan, she was obsessed with the concept and worked on it for a long time.[58]

Joyce continued to do freelance work for Graphic Associates and eventually was hired full-time. At first, she felt insecure and frightened; she thought she did not fit in with the people there. "I've been acting a little strange there and I guess they can't quite figure me out or else don't want to."[59] She lost her self-confidence as she entered this unfamiliar territory in which she was trying to learn new skills. Her first assignment was to animate a picture of Niagara Falls, a task that would be difficult even for an experienced animator. She did not want to reveal that she did not know how to do the job, however, and worked on it for two weeks. The work created so much stress that she "went into a complete flip-out."[60]

She began thinking again about getting away, and reasoned that if she could save $1,500, she would go to Italy for a year to study. Bryan, too, had dreams of going to Europe to write, and she speculated that he would leave first, and she would follow later. But by the beginning of the summer, Joyce had gained some confidence in her ability and discovered she enjoyed working with film. She drew on twenty-five feet of film, then screened it on a projector and was intrigued with the process.

Although she had not experimented with making films until she was working at Graphic Associates, she had attended the films shown by the Toronto Film Society, an organization that rented movies from the Museum of Modern Art in New York. Starting on October 25, 1948, the film society showed movies in the theatre of the Royal Ontario Museum. One of the screenings that Joyce would likely have attended was Hans Richter's surrealist film, *Dreams that Money Can Buy*, inspired by works of Marcel Duchamp, Max Ernst and Man Ray. Richter attended the three screenings and introduced the film. At the same time the Film Society had also hung a small exhibition of works by Max Ernst in the lobby of the museum's theatre.[61] In later years Joyce would credit her life-long love of film to the international cinema the Film Society brought to Toronto.

Along with experimenting with drawing on film footage, Joyce also began doing some wax print drawings and picked up her painting again, something she had abandoned while she trying out other media before her job at Graphic. As she gained more confidence at Graphic, she also began reading more — Malcolm Cowley's books — and went to see *Aida* at Maple Leaf Gardens. She bought a book on the work of Jean Fouquet, a painter born in 1420, and was drawn to Piero della Francesca and Sandro Botticelli, both Italian painters from the fifteenth century. "I like Piero's work ..." she said. "His women seem to carry deep secrets about life in their heavy lidded eyes and sullen sad and expressive mouths ... Piero's eyes will always haunt because they are sad and knowing." In fact, the eyes of the women in Piero's *Baptism* resemble those in the self-portraits Joyce would paint many years later. It was a time of exploration for her — "There are such wonderful painters to discover and rediscover," she said, "such great and wonderful painters to know intimately through their work."[62]

That fall Joyce discovered the pleasure of feline company — a lovely grey cat with green eyes. "A cat can be a joy in a quiet house," she said. She liked watching the cat's movements, and having it sit on her knee as she worked.

The year ended with Joyce amazed at what was happening to her. She had not expected things to turn out this way. "Bryan and I are breaking up house next month. I haven't changed much since I was twenty. Isn't that sad? I haven't grown much (mentally)." Why did she describe herself this way? In fact, she had grown in a number of ways, and 1954 was a particularly expansive year for her. She had done a lot of reading on her own and with Bryan; she had tried a number of new media; she had learned how to work with animation and had continued working at Graphic Associates. Her lack of perspective, as before, arose from the end of her romance with Bryan, and she again doubted her worth.[63]

Joyce recorded a series of crushes on other artists who worked at Graphic Associates: Michael Snow, John Ross and George Gingras. Her sudden interest in these men in the latter part of 1954 disturbed her, but she did not think any of them were as intelligent as Bryan — they were all merely looking for someone to talk to. Eventually Joyce felt much more a part of the group at Graphic and was among the artists who at the end of the day's work headed for their favourite hangout at the St. Charles nearby, or The Pilot at Yonge and Bloor Streets.

Sometimes their work naturally led to having a party, particularly when they were working on ads for beer companies. Since it was illegal for ads to depict people drinking beer, Joyce and her colleagues had to come up with a way to show a beer glass becoming empty without anyone drinking from it. Nor could they portray beer without including food. So the glass of beer with its inch of foam stood on the table, with a tube from the glass leading under the table to where one artist made the level of beer go down, by either drinking it or siphoning it into a bucket. To get the effect just right, they sometimes repeated the exercise several times. Besides the cases of beer that

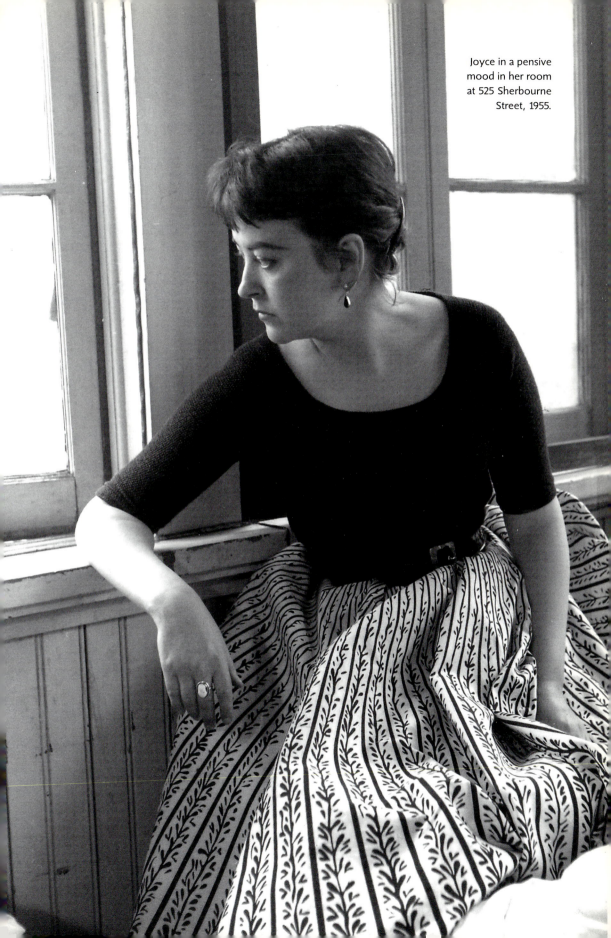

Joyce in a pensive mood in her room at 525 Sherbourne Street, 1955.

had to be disposed of, there was the ham and cheese and whatever else was included in the props, and so the party began. Donna Montague (then Donna Lawson) remembered that "We ate the ham and ate the cheese and everything and two days later we'd get the runs ... I think we did that thing three times."[64]

The artists at Graphic were becoming a tightly knit group, and Joyce's social life was increasingly tied up with the people there. Even though she still admired Bryan, she had become fixated on a young artist — Michael Snow. When Joyce and Bryan decided to go their separate ways, the decision was mutual. Looking back, Bryan recalled that the two of them were "getting on each other's nerves ... I think the experiment was over." He remembered an incident around that time that he associated with their separation. Sometime during the latter part of 1954, he was coming home on the Bloor Street West streetcar, heading east towards Bathurst Street. He looked out the window and saw Joyce, also coming home, walking along Bloor Street, "and she looked just crazy. I think she had big overshoes on or something and her hair was all over the place and it was one of those things — not recognizing her for a moment — then 'That's Joyce!' It was such an eccentric Emily Carr type figure."[65] Despite their initial strong attraction and enjoyment of each other's intelligence and unique perspectives on life, essentially their different needs were not compatible. Bryan was a quiet, orderly person, who needed a calm space for thinking and writing. "Joyce was like a gang of fireworks, all over the place."[66] Something was always going on at 700 Bathurst Street, and crazy things happened that were unnerving to Bryan.

He recalled that one night there was a knock on the door and a Lithuanian man came in and began talking. Joyce seemed to know something about him, but Bryan didn't know why he had come or what on earth was going on. This man had put an ad in the paper for a model, and Joyce had answered it. Bryan and Joyce had difficulty understanding his English, but finally realized that he wanted a model for creating pornographic material, something that Joyce had not known when she answered the ad. The more the man attempted to describe what he wanted, the more flabbergasted Joyce became until the man realized things were not turning out as he had expected, and he scuttled down the stairs. "There was always stuff like that going on," Bryan said, and he had difficulty coping with the unpredictability Joyce created around her.[67]

Nevertheless, Joyce always considered Bryan a friend she could count on. Among Joyce's personal papers at York University's archives is an undated typed note from Bryan, saying that he's working on thinking about her in a more impersonal way, and "it's best that we don't see each other anymore."

But he also said that if she were ever in a tight spot and needed him, she should get in touch. "I really mean that," he added.[68] In fact, she did just that. Many years later, probably in the late sixties, Bryan received a call from Donna Montague asking him to come to The Pilot because Joyce was in an incoherent state and had asked for him. He went, but there wasn't much he could do. Donna took Joyce to her house and called a psychiatrist friend to help her. In Bryan's and Sara Bowser's recounting of the event, they speculated that problems with Michael might have triggered this episode, and Donna agreed. Regardless of the source of the incident, obviously Joyce still felt that Bryan was someone she could turn to, even after the passing of so many years.

During the time Joyce and Bryan lived together, her discovery of Colette had a great impact on her life. Even now, more than forty years later, her friends who knew her during the 1950s all have a similar memory of Joyce — oh, yes, Colette, it was always Colette!

Joyce's diary from the early fifties seems to have been written from the same emotional fire as that of Colette. Did Joyce use *The Vagabond* — she mentions this novel in her journal — as a model for her stormy journal notes? Perhaps she felt a special connection with it for its portrayal of the lives of music-hall artists in Paris in an atmosphere similar to that which would have surrounded her great-aunts Clara and Zaeo.

However, a larger attraction to the book would have been in the problems faced by Renée Néré, not necessarily in the details of her life but in her inner conflict. As the book opens, Renée, a music-hall artist, lives alone, which she experiences as a mixed blessing: sometimes she is intoxicated with the freedom it gives, but at other times "it is a poison which makes you beat your head against the wall."[69] She is also in conflict over the lure of a man so devoted to her that he wants to bestow everything within his power on her. Although he thinks he is giving her everything, he is actually taking what he wants for himself. At the same time, he is so overwhelming in his goodness to her that she feels she would no longer have a right even to her own feelings.

Joyce had experienced Don Smith in the same way that Renée saw Max. He was a good man, too good for her, she knew, and too kind. But there was the other side of the coin — what men wanted from her, and what they saw her to be. Even while Joyce was infatuated with the men at Graphic Associates, she saw their neediness. The response of Max to Renée and the responses of the men Joyce knew had the same binding result for the women. One part of Joyce was clear-sighted enough that she told herself to focus on making art and give up the distractions of looking for a man. But the other part of her knew that she could not go on without a man to give her self-worth and the security she needed.

One of Colette's biographers described her as a "freedom-seeking woman in an age of male dominance."[70] The same could be said of Joyce in the 1950s. She knew that by satisfying her need for a man she would deny herself that freedom. But it was a price she had already decided to pay when she gave herself over to being in love with Michael Snow because of what she would gain. She would incorporate him into her experiment with her personal mythology, and in marrying him she would gain a family.

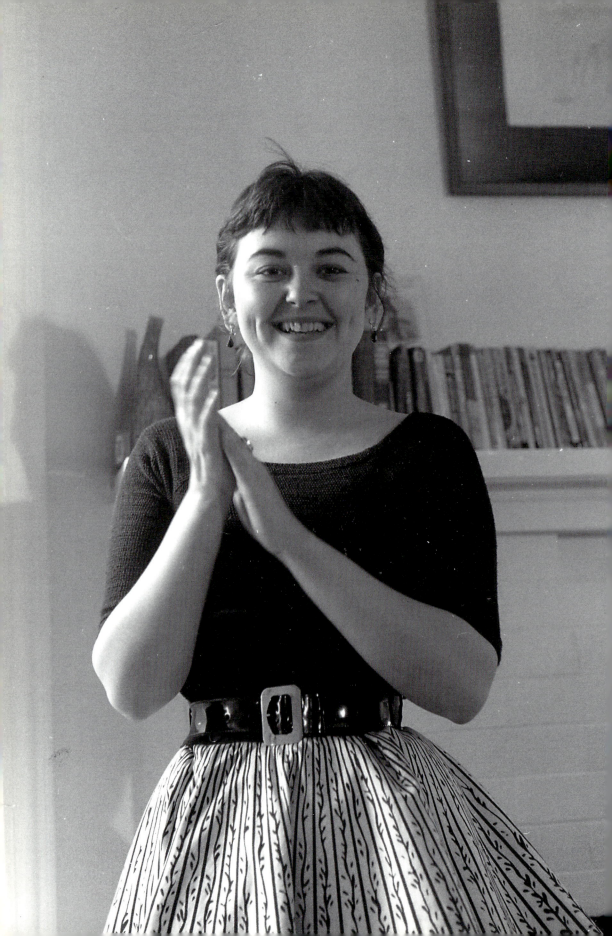

The artist, the lover, the artist-wife

Man pronounced any individual man who showed talent in a variety of arts a "genius" or a "Renaissance" man; any woman who did the same was, naturally, a "dilettante." —Robin Morgan[1]

THE ESTABLISHED PATTERN of behaviour for a young woman in the fifties restricted her way of thinking about her life and undermined her sense of self. If she did not marry young, she easily feared growing old too soon, and in this aspect Joyce was typical of her generation. Just before her twenty-fifth birthday, she wrote, "Age is a fright to me now. Perhaps even as much as it was to Colette in 'the Vagabond' when she leaves her lover and goes to South America."[2] And Joyce wanted "babies, babies, cats, flowers, books, love, drawing, crazy friends, music." To be unmarried meant there was something wrong with her.

Joyce was on her own after Bryan left their Bathurst Street home at the beginning of the New Year. Not having a lover prompted her to write that "drawing and being a bloody brain" was not as important to her as she had once thought. In other words, a man was more essential to her happiness.

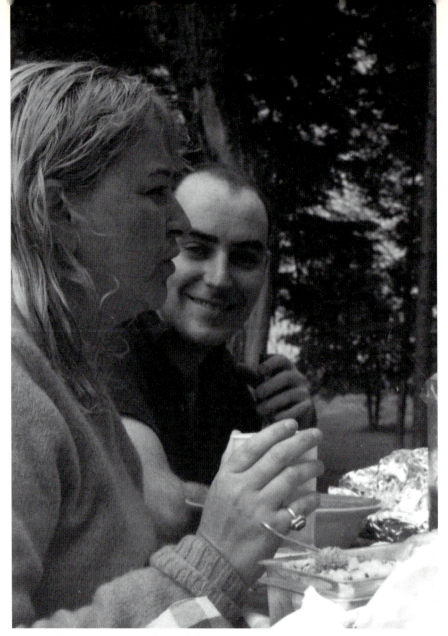

Joyce and George Gingras, probably 1959.

She admitted that she had been in love with "that bastard Mike Snow" for five months, which reveals that her feelings for Michael may have influenced the dissolution of her relationship with Bryan.

At the end of January or in early February, Joyce and Donna Lawson, the redhaired secretary at Graphic Associates, were among five friends who moved to 525 Sherbourne Street, which had been a funeral home for many years.[3] Joyce had a sun room on the third floor, where George Gingras and Donna also each had a room. On the second floor was a common area, and Barry and Doreen Gordon lived on the first floor. Rather than being spooked

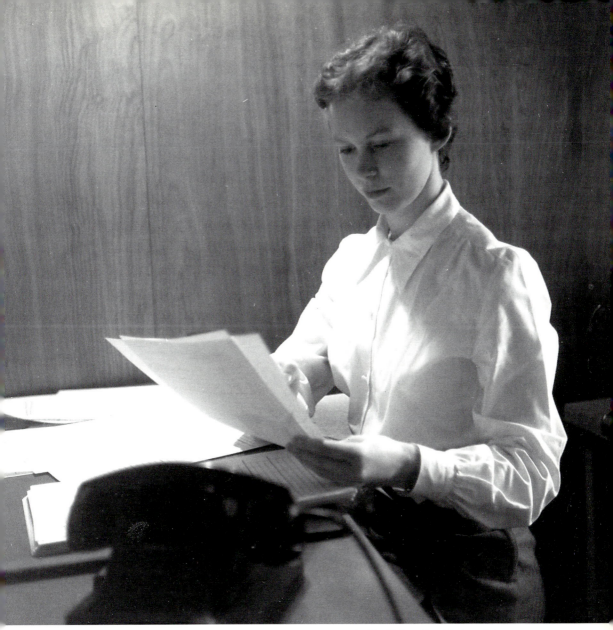

Donna Lawson, probably 1955, at Graphic Associates.

at their house's history, the residents laughed about it, joking they could use the marble slabs for pastry. They also quickly saw the practical benefits — the "No Parking — Funeral" sign to set out front came in handy when they had a party. The three on the third floor were among the group of Graphic's artists who were together constantly, often beginning the day with breakfast at a local greasy spoon, then eating lunch at the St. George. After work they headed for beer at the St. Charles or The Pilot. They developed into a closely knit group, so much so that in looking back Donna thought of it as incestuous, and "so tight it was dreadful."[4]

Within the larger group were smaller clusters of friendships and love affairs. Graham Coughtry remembered Michael's response when he first saw Joyce. He and Michael had come back from spending a year in Europe and had just begun working at Graphic. When Joyce walked past the cubicle where they were both working, "Michael acknowledged that he was interested and they started going together soon after that."[5] Joyce and Michael had an immediate appreciation of each other's sense of humour. They cracked jokes and made funny drawings referring to their job, which they passed around or pinned over their desks.[6]

Joyce, Michael and Graham became good friends and worked on animation projects together. During their off hours, they collaborated on a variety of projects, including two-minute spoofs of ads, with Warren Collins as their cameraman. The three also each borrowed George Dunning's copy of *Picasso's Suite Vollard* by Hans Bolliger, a book that influenced their erotic drawings.[7]

Michael had trouble getting to work on time, arriving as late as eleven o'clock. Eventually George Dunning promoted him to director of the animation department at a salary of $4,000 a year, perhaps thinking that would get Michael out of bed in the mornings. But a few months later the company collapsed.[8] According to George Gingras, Joyce was let go from Graphics sometime during the summer of 1955, and afterwards she found a job with a sign painter on King Street near Sherbourne.

Joyce and Donna, who became fast friends while at Graphic, had in common childhoods drowned in poverty. They both remembered wearing "gum shoes" that were too big and had holes, and stuffing them with newspapers. The two women also shared a mischievous sense of fun, and concocted a variety of antics that struck others as outrageous. At a party given by a newly wed young Southam man, a more proper affair than Joyce was used to, she and Donna horrified the "bourgeoisie" with ridiculous comments, Sara Bowser recalled. "Donna comes in and says, Joyce, doesn't that venetian blind remind you of a pulsating vagina? ... They would keep this up until all the proper folks in the room were gasping ... and they [Joyce and Donna] were just as cool." During these exchanges, they conspired to egg each other on without a crack in their dead-serious expressions.[9]

They decided it was time to take their first ride on a plane, so they flew to Buffalo, New York, one Friday evening for a weekend of shopping. After a night at a hotel, on Saturday morning they headed for the stores. Joyce was wearing a typical fifties flared skirt, and after trying on a crinoline, she left the fitting room without taking it off and walked out of the store with it. "I don't think she meant to, but she came home with a new crinoline," Donna recalled.[10] They had planned to return to Toronto on Sunday by bus to save

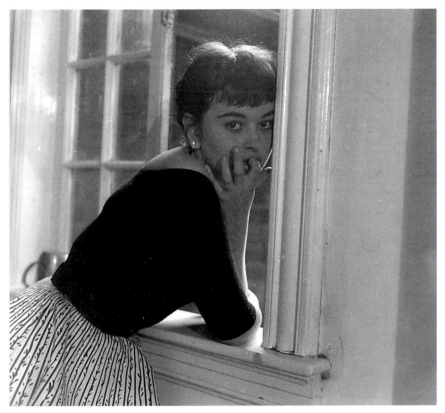

Joyce in her room at 525 Sherbourne Street, May 1955.

money, but the officials at the border detained them because the value of their purchases was too high for a trip of less than forty-eight hours. They had to stay in a hotel overnight, and Donna called her taxi-driver boyfriend to pick them up on Monday morning so they could get to work on time.

Joyce and Donna would remain friends for many years. However, when Joyce asked her to participate in demonstrations or other activities and Donna declined, Joyce held it against her. The two would then keep their distance until another circumstance brought them back together. After Donna married George Montague in 1959, the couple would be among Joyce and Michael's first patrons, helping them in a variety of ways, including an open invitation to use their house when Joyce and Michael returned for frequent visits to Toronto after they moved to New York.

It was at 525 Sherbourne Street in the room with many windows that Joyce and Michael made love for the first time.[11] By then, Joyce was determined to marry him. One of her friends remembered clearly that once when Joyce came to visit — not long before moving to Sherbourne — she stood in the doorway with a hand on each doorpost, saying, "All I want out of life is to marry Michael Snow."[12]

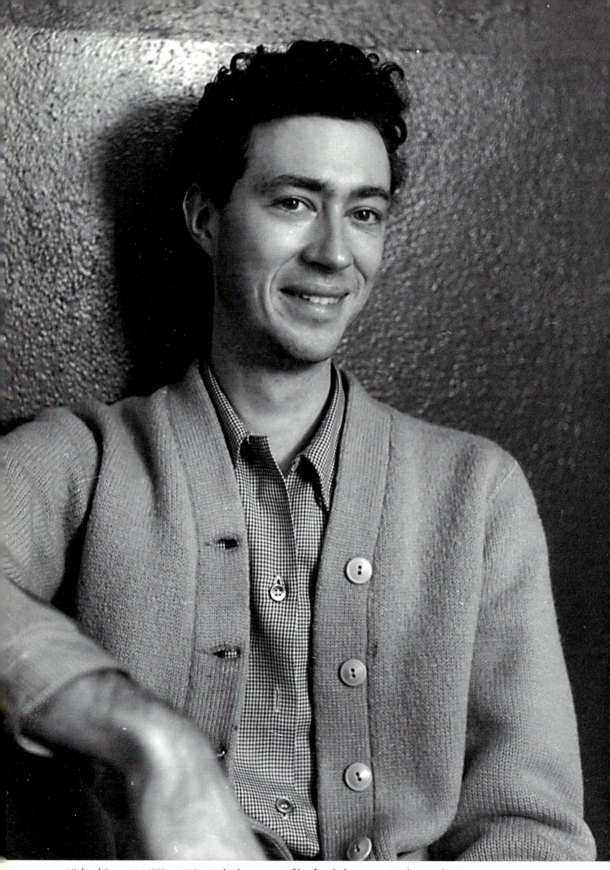

Michael Snow, in 1955 or 1956, in the basement of his family home on Roxborough Drive.

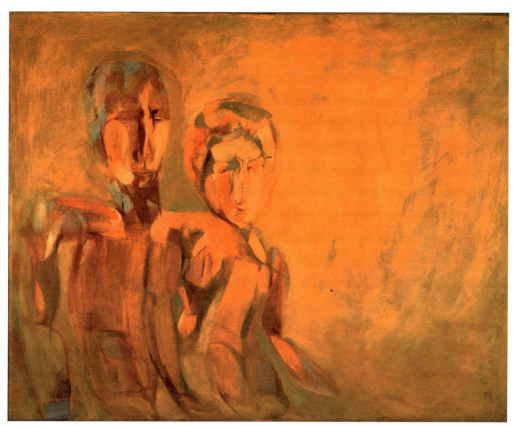

Untitled (Two Figures), circa 1954 or 1955.

Joyce's first impression of Michael had been from a distance as she observed him with friends walking down the street. He was wearing a long black coat down to his feet, "His head worn in the end of long string like a balloon ... Thousands of drawings later Mr Snow and I got married."[13]

Michael excited Joyce. He was a "born lover," slim and handsome with dark wavy hair and a sensuous nose and mouth. In her diary in the spring of 1955, she described him as having "Pale blue slate eyes," which she perceived as "cold and yet glittering if wicked evil and almost passionate. ... The mouth is almost the greatest delight except the eyes murder me." To Joyce, his body was like "a young boy's body and yet too full of sensuous awareness for a boy. Beautiful legs and yet I can't tell him because he knows they are beautiful ... His back is beautiful and delicately molded like a modern sculpture in wood."[14] Of all the men Joyce knew, Michael was the most seductive — even when he talked about art.

She was attracted by the earnest way he talked about modern art and in the same breath admired his own paintings, explaining why they were good. His self-confidence transmitted an electric current, as though everything were sexual. After an evening of listening to music and leafing through a book on Paul Klee — "turning the pages slowly so that I too would understand"[15] — it seemed going to bed was the next logical step.

Although Michael alternated between acting aloof and being charming and seductive, Joyce clung to her experience of his charm. At the beginning, Joyce accepted this kind of relationship with Michael because she wanted to be able to look up to a man. She lost her ability to see that she had placed him in a position of power, and she was caught. Later she would feel betrayed.

In these early years of their relationship, Michael encouraged Joyce in her art work, and she fed his ideas; in later years he would come to count on her opinions. They frequently discussed what each of them was working on. From the beginning they had what one friend described as "a bedrock of feeling together,"[16] based on the respect each had for the creative process. In a climate where women generally were not encouraged to pursue their own lives, Michael's response to Joyce's art was exactly what she needed, and she determined she would hang on to him regardless of what happened.

She had another big reason for wanting Michael: his family. Born on December 10, 1929, Michael grew up in Toronto's exclusive Rosedale neighbourhood and attended Upper Canada College. His was a family of lawyers and engineers. His father, Gerald Bradley Snow, was a civil engineer as well as a lieutenant with the Toronto 48th Highlanders in World War I. Michael's mother, Marie-Antoinette Françoise Carmen Lévesque, was the daughter of Elzear Lévesque, a lawyer and the mayor of Chicoutimi, Quebec, for twenty years. Photographs of young Antoinette reveal her to be seductively beautiful and self-assured, a young woman who dressed with flair, an elegance she cultivated all her life. Michael and his mother adored each other, and she was likely the standard against which Michael measured all other women.

The Lévesque family home was a large brick house on a hill, surrounded by a low stone wall and an imposing line of steps leading up to the house. Antoinette's paternal grandfather was the Honourable Claude Denechaud, a representative for Quebec City for forty years in the province's legislature.

For Joyce, this patrician family was the one she had never had, the one she longed for. She particularly loved Michael's mother for her eclectic taste and elegant style, and would incorporate her into her own sense of herself, something she would come to question in later years. However, at this time she needed Antoinette and the rest of the family and began comparing it with her own.

Her diary entries of November 1955 reveal that she had already built up a fantasy around Michael and his family — he was still living at his family home and had his mother and father to talk to, whereas she had only her brother and sister.[17] Her family paled in comparison to this ideal, regardless of what the reality of Michael's relationship with his parents might have been.

Joyce was distressed because her feelings for Michael were intense, but his feelings for her were not equally strong. She became unsure of how much he loved her when she found out that he continued to sleep with other women, and admitted to what she hoped for: "I could love him even if he were twice as wicked if he would only just give me a small part of himself to hang onto." She felt lucky if they made love even once in a two- or three-week period. "But I am only tumbled right down again to find out that he's been with someone else."[18]

When she found a note from his former girlfriend written in French in his jacket pocket, she felt betrayed. "He treats me as though I were some sort of joke and continually takes advantage of my love for him." Once he told her he loved her, but as soon as she showed him that she also loved him, she felt he became cold and moved away from her. She felt hopeless because he did not love her enough to satisfy her. As in her previous experiences with men, when she felt unloved she sank into despair. She cried over her diary, and if she cried when she was with Michael, she felt that at least moved him to pay more attention to her. If he told her he loved her after she cried, however, she thought he was placating her and wasn't sure if she could trust him.

Joyce felt she had something to offer Michael. "I feel confident that most other women would be a drag to him except maybe the ballet dancers." Michael and Graham Coughtry had phoned the National Ballet and said they were making a film. Under these false pretences, they tried to woo the dancers, but they only got as far as having parties with them.[19] Joyce knew that Michael was trying to seduce these women, and she wondered if he did not realize that though he "wishes to screw all the pretty girls asses" he also had to put up with their stupidities.[20] Clearly she did not see herself as stupid, and wanted him to appreciate her for her intelligence, sensuality and imagination.

Even when distressed, she sometimes saw the difficulties in her relationship with Michael in a broader context. "Why for God's sake cannot we girls be brought up to be humans instead of dependent wretches. We cannot find happiness this way. Its not like in the movies, we don't always grow up and get married and live happily. And this is the truth which kills me a little more each day and disables me little by little."[21] She did not know how prophetic her words were — she fulfilled the "get married" part, but living "happily" would be shattered, largely by the continuation of patterns of behaviour that had already begun. Joyce's overwhelming loneliness, along with Michael's remoteness and interest in other women, set the scene for a

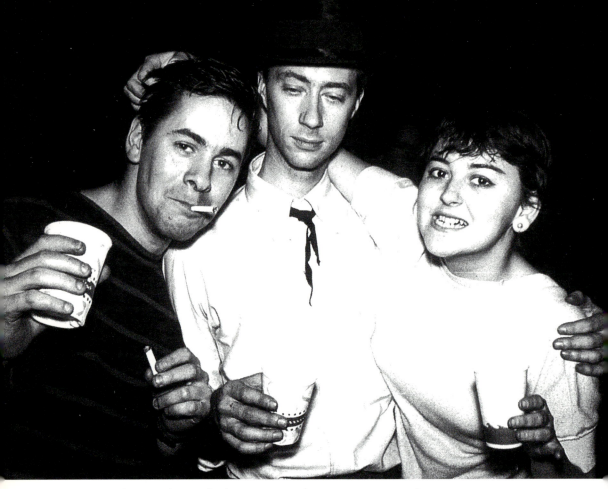

Graham Coughtry, Michael Snow, Joyce at the CBC Scenic Artists Ball
on River Street in Toronto's Cabbagetown in December, 1955.

relationship that, whatever the benefits, was also bound to disappoint her.

Joyce's experience was similar to that of Berthe Morisot who learned that women were conditioned to believe in love, but that false expectations led to disappointments.[22] The writer Dorothy Richardson, at the end of her life, commented on the loneliness that women experience. "When one is within it, one is apt to exaggerate the quality of human 'belongings', particularly whether in the case of 'love' or of 'friendship', or of the two combined."[23] Similarly, Joyce's longings and her fantasy led her to exaggerate what she could get from Michael, indeed, from any man.

One of Joyce's old friends from that time had been surprised that Joyce fell in love with Michael Snow, and even more surprised that she married him. She thought Joyce needed a man who was like a big teddy bear. "Someone big, romantic that would cuddle her up and sort of cradle her."[24] Another friend had a similar point of view, and expressed surprise that Joyce married at all "because she had her own — not demons — she had her own drives and ambitions ... There wasn't a lot left over when Joyce managed to get through life and every day and do and think and vision. There wasn't a lot left over of Joyce to give to somebody else."[25] Joyce ended her 1955 diary wondering whether to close off her relationship with Michael and start over in the New Year by looking for a new man.

Joyce did not entertain her doubts for long. A photograph of her with Michael and Graham Coughtry at the end of 1955 reveal what Joyce and Michael were like, the way their friends remember them then. Joyce's youthful beauty shines; her kohl-lined eyes are glistening; her jaw is set in a spirit of determination. The photo practically vibrates with her life and energy, especially in contrast to Mike's cool, still bearing.

Joyce desperately wanted to know if Michael would commit himself to her, and she thought of a plan that would help her find out. She decided to go to Europe without him. Coincidentally, in the spring of 1956, George Gingras, one of Joyce's friends who shared 525 Sherbourne, had also decided to head for Europe because he and Donna Lawson had been lovers and he wanted to separate from her. Since Joyce and George were both going to Europe — for opposite reasons — they travelled together as far as London, but they were not lovers at the time. George stayed in England, and Joyce went on to France.

France had special meaning for Joyce. In undated notes she wrote that she thought "Joan of Arc's spirit is in France," an idea surely connected to her sister's dramatization of the photograph of Joan of Arc. Joyce believed Joan of Arc, a peasant girl, cared about nature, "the animals and all living things."[26]

Her journal from those months in the south of France reveals that she visited museums, painted, drew, wrote love poems, read books and spent time thinking. "What is it that men are never satisfied with one women for long? I think the only thing I can do is not see him again ... I am sick of life already and I haven't been away from him for one whole month yet. If he misses me I haven't heard yet."[27] She stayed with a friend, Lydie, who owned a bookstore. There Joyce painted and took day trips to galleries. A customer at the bookstore saw her painting and brought her an easel.[28]

She met a man with whom she made love in the moonlight on a hill in Montmartre, but she was disgusted with him because he was inexperienced. In her journal she listed eleven things she did not like about him, and decided she would teach him a lesson — "Do him dirt ... It would be a good summers work. Teach one bad boy a good lesson. It will be tougher than working on Michael. Mike is capable of a little love. Never again will I show my true feelings to a man."[29] In her journal, as in her interchanges with other people, Joyce had what some friends described as a sharp tongue. Some, in later years, tried to avoid becoming the object of her biting comments.

Joyce's France journal seems typical of that of a young artist going to Europe to experience being alone and depressed while reading Proust and Kafka. Besides passages about her depression and wanting letters from Michael, her journal includes pen-and-ink sketches of lovers. She analyzed these drawings by posing as a critic and asking herself questions and answering them. She concludes she is better at drawing women than men. If her journal is any indication, always present in the back of her mind was the question of whether her absence would win Michael over.

Toward the end of May Joyce began living with Denise Dubois, who had a farm in the hilly countryside near the tiny hamlet of Castellet, north of Aix-en-Provence. Joyce loved the place, with its pine and cyprus trees, saying the smells in the air were the "smells of Paradise." She wanted to live there, "even if I take up the study of chickens to do it ..."[30] But when she had a "beautiful affectionate letter from Michael" a few days later, she changed her mind. She was ecstatic about his letter, received on June 7th, and answered immediately. "I filled the letter with flowers and little drawings. I made the letter innocent, charming, mysterious, poetic and nonsensical. It was such fun. I sent him three poems. And he wants a photograph of me in France!"[31]

Another cheerful, newsy letter from Michael, written on a large sheet of tissue paper, reports that the "Graphics Building is now being rented by Chetwynd Films. Animation Equipment was sold to the C.B.C. John Ross I have a sneaking suspicion is going to Europe soon which is where you are if you remember."[32] He mentions that he made a second film for Consumers Gas and when they pay him he might go to New York for four days to "look the place over. Might be nice as we have discussed to open a branch office in New York. Haven't we?" Perhaps the somewhat stilted ending of the letter, with the accompanying drawing, gave Joyce at least some of what she was looking for from Michael: "I embrace you with fervour inasmuch as it is possible over such a long distance all my love Mike." Beside these lines was a sketch of two shores with wavy lines in between to represent the ocean. A man, all legs, stretches across the great body of water and kisses a woman on the opposite shore, with a French flag standing behind her.[33]

With that letter, Joyce decided to hurry home. On June 30, 1956, she sent a letter to Michael at 110 Roxborough Drive: "I am twenty-six today. Denise is making a nice cake for a picnic in my honour." She also said she was flying home on July 11 and would be in Malton at four o'clock in the afternoon and asked Michael to meet her.

Joyce likely felt her scheme of going to Europe had worked because sometime after her return that summer, she and Michael began living together in an apartment above Clean-it-eria Cleaners at 312 College Street, just west of Spadina Avenue. Joyce explored the area, walked up and down

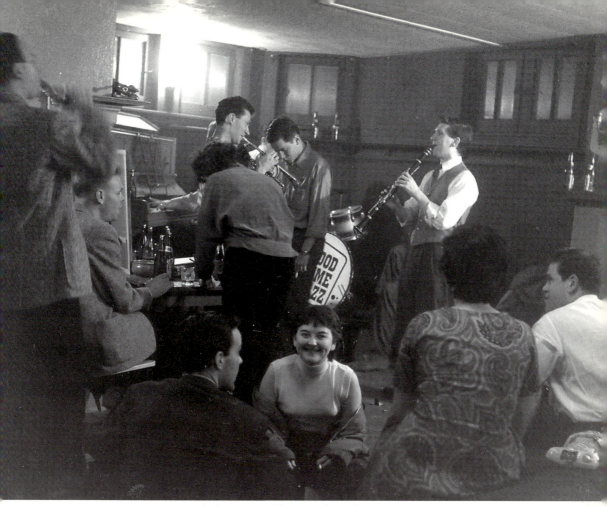

A party in the basement of the Snow family home at 110 Roxborough Drive in Toronto's Rosedale, 1955.

the back lanes and made collages in homage to Toronto's back fences. She also picked up old wooden shingles, which became the raw material for a series of what she called "shamanistic works," most of which were thrown out when they were later stored in the basement at the Isaacs Gallery — Avrom Isaacs's father helped with clean-up around the gallery and thought they were garbage.[34]

Joan recalled that Joyce and Michael went to Toronto City Hall that September and were married, although in recent years Michael could not remember the date. Bob Hackborn was Michael's best man and Marcia Spiegel was Joyce's bridesmaid, the only friends who attended — no family members were there. After the ceremony, the four of them went for a drink at the Walker House Hotel, which was near the Royal York Hotel on Front Street. Hackborn recalled they had a bottle of Chauvanet Red Cap, Joyce and Michael's favourite sparkling red wine. Later, Michael did not recall, but various friends remembered a celebration party at the Snow family home on

Roxborough Drive, with the usual mix of music and dancing in "Mike's basement," a celebration that would have been important to Joyce given her love of parties and her affection for Michael's family. Many of Michael's friends remembered numerous jazz parties there, so the one in celebration of his marriage to Joyce blurs in the haze of memory, partly because the 1950s were made up of a string of parties.

However, among the indistinct memories of music, drinking and crazy behaviour, certain particularly bizarre parties stood out. Sara Bowser, with whom Joyce had a close friendship of more than forty years, grew up in the United States, and arrived in Toronto in 1955 with architect Gerald Robinson, via Paris and Boston where she had been working. She remembered some of those parties clearly, although as a magazine editor she considered herself on the fringes of artists' parties. One hot summer night she had about a hundred people at her small Yorkville apartment for a party that spilled onto the fire escape. To get to those outside stairs, guests had to go through the bathroom.

In Sara's memory, people streamed through the bathroom to get outside, while Joyce was perched on the toilet, talking to them as they passed through. "[The parties] were like that, they were wacky ... And we were always switching boyfriends and it was just kind of a mad house."[35]

These artists both created and enjoyed Toronto's bohemian way of life. In a spirit of friendship, they encouraged one another's artistic endeavours. They came from a variety of backgrounds, and many of their families wanted "better" careers for their sons, even though many would eventually opt for longer-term relationships and marriage. In the meantime, they persisted with their idea of how artists live, which included frequenting The Pilot and the Andore Hotel on the south side of Charles Street, just east of Yonge. Within this group, Michael Snow would become established as king, and Joyce, as his "artist's wife," would become queen bee.

Joyce and Michael's position among the artists evolved this way because they clearly focused on what they wanted to do and understood instinctively how to represent themselves to the media. They "knew how to be photographed, how to present their faces for the camera." Joyce had a "larger than life presentation, which was never pushed too far."[36] If you met Joyce at a party in those days, you would not forget her — her eyes outlined in black kohl like Colette's, dark wavy hair, no-nonsense body language and yet, paradoxically, a kind of endearing girlishness. And she was a good dancer, swinging around with her flared skirt swirling.

When Dennis Burton first met Joyce in 1957, he thought she was strikingly beautiful and immediately developed a crush on her, but he soon found out she was married to Michael Snow. Burton was afraid of her because of her "sharp tongue." He was surprised at how much this "hip chic painter and jazz fan" knew, and how originally funny she could be. He was astonished, too, at her capacity for launching into a "swear-fest," something he had never before heard a woman do.[37] Robert Hedrick remembers that she had a "wicked humour," and was a great satirist. "She was taken as a character," someone who had "a great sense of the dramatic moment" which always "came out slightly amusing."[38]

Once Joyce and Michael had their first apartment together they decorated the walls with their drawings. Joyce began to take pleasure in cooking and her new domesticity. Since they followed the traditional model of the wife looking after the house, Michael was free of most day-to-day chores. However, he kept their finances in order — he was much more organized than Joyce. Neither of them had regular jobs, but they picked up paying work wherever they could.

Many of Joyce's and Michael's freelance assignments were small animation jobs that they got through connections they had made while at Graphic Associates. Often the work was boring and tedious. "It was kind of driving us crazy, except that we were [making] a little bit of money and we decided we ought to go on some far-out trip,"[39] Michael recalled. The "far-out" place they chose was Cuba.

On January 8, 1958, they withdrew $1003.88 from their bank account.[40] Two days later on a mild, cloudy winter day, when Toronto's high of 40°F was almost the same as Miami's low of 39°, they flew to Havana by way of Florida. Their plans had been to start out in Cuba and then go on to Haiti and some Central American islands. But travelling farther would have been too expensive, so they ended up staying in Cuba, spending time first in Havana and then renting a small house on the southern coast in La Boca, a little fishing village. They had not investigated the political situation on the island and were not aware of the guerrilla fighting under Batista's dictatorship. The only violence they encountered was in Havana, where they walked past a theatre in which a bomb exploded about half an hour later.[41] They spent most of their time on the south edge of the island, watching the boats and the fishermen and drawing and painting. They returned home by way of New York City.

Back in Toronto in May of 1958, for $100 a month Joyce and Michael rented an apartment at The Manhattan at the corner of Charles and Church Streets, where they would live until they moved to New York in 1962.[42] The interior of this three-storey, beige-brick apartment building likely appealed to their aesthetic sense — beautiful oak woodwork and tiled walls in the entrance leading to their one-bedroom apartment, the first one to the left at the top of the front steps. They had a large foyer, a living room that led into another

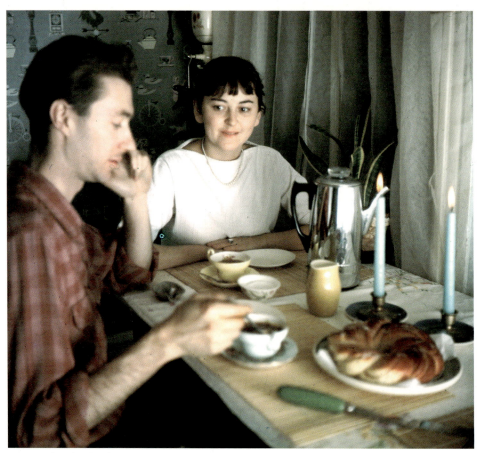

Joyce and Michael in their apartment at Charles and Church streets in 1958.

smaller room, which at first Michael used for painting, and at the back, a bathroom. The kitchen and bedroom were across a hallway that ran the length of the apartment.

In their foyer they placed an ancient Japanese suit of armour made of metal plates connected with pieces of fabric, something Michael's mother had picked up at an auction. The piano dominated the living room and Michael's paintings of chairs hung on the walls. A nude mannequin, a wicker chair and Hugh the cat were also part of the establishment. Very soon after their move to Charles Street, Michael rented a studio above a furniture store on Yonge Street near Dundas Street, and Joyce began painting in the small room Michael had vacated.

Along with painting, Joyce continued freelancing to earn money. She even did a stint at Office Overload for which she was paid $114.30 for a three-month period.[43] Michael, soon after their return from Cuba, began playing in the Michael White Imperial Jazz Band, often at the Westover Hotel, a job that gave him a steady income. For the next four years he would play almost every

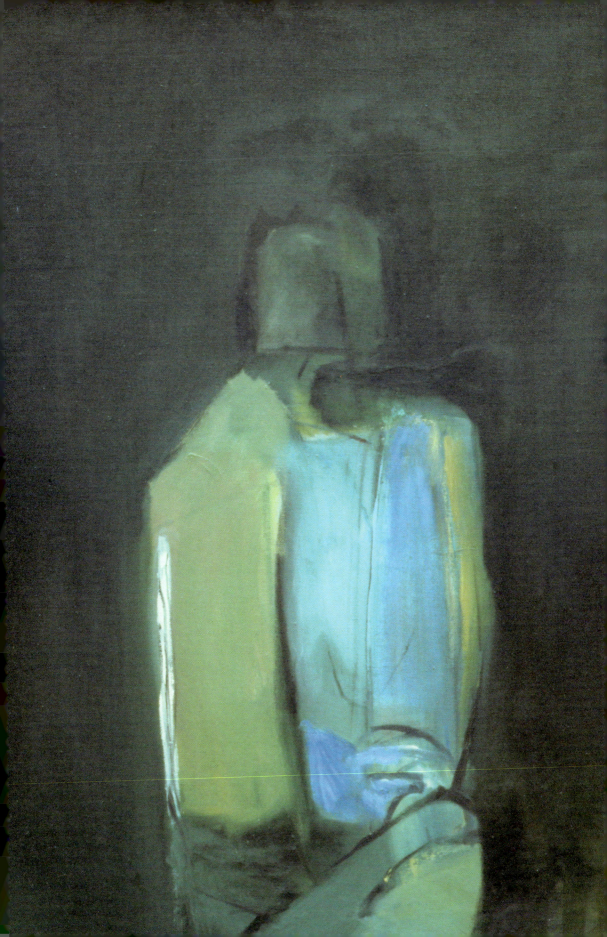

night, something that dramatically changed day-to-day life. Because he was out late, he slept in the morning and painted in the afternoon. Joyce often spent the evenings where Michael was playing, accompanied by one of her women friends.

Jazz had long been a part of the lives of the artists later associated with the Isaacs Gallery. Gordon Rayner claimed that it was jazz as much as art that brought a number of these friends together. One night when he and a few others were playing jazz for the fun of it in Rick Gorman's studio, Joyce arrived. When someone asked who was playing, Joyce said it was the artists' jazz band. And that's how The Artists' Jazz Band got its name.[44]

Through the jazz band Joyce met Sylvia Fogarty, Michael White's wife, who also attended the performances. Joyce and Sylvia became close friends. Sylvia, several years younger than Joyce, grew up in a lively middle-class family, the daughter of Vera Hendry, well known then in Toronto's east end for her involvement in the community and in politics. Her family liked Sylvia's new friend, who was unlike anyone they had met — hair now bleached blonde, with kohl-lined dark eyes and a round face. Like Mary Karch, Sylvia was Joyce's opposite: preoccupied with tidiness, she often put things in order at Joyce's place. According to Sylvia, it was a case of opposites attracting each other.[45]

Sylvia was trained as a commercial artist, but when she and Joyce met she was a filing clerk at the Toronto Stock Exchange. Through Joyce, who knew Jim MacKay from working at Graphic Associates, Sylvia got a job in 1960 working with Film Design, Jim MacKay's small animation company, located in the Flat-Iron building on Wellington Street. The only other person in the company at that time, besides MacKay, was George Gingras, who had worked at Graphic Associates, though other people came and went. Joyce also did freelance jobs for Film Design at the going rate, two dollars an hour.[46]

MacKay remembers hiring Joyce on a rush job for a tea company. He, Joyce and Sylvia were working late on a very hot summer night. They didn't think anyone else was in the building, so the two women stripped down to their underwear. The office was on the third floor, where there was only a men's washroom, and Joyce didn't bother going to another floor to use the women's. The next day the caretaker cornered Jim MacKay and said, "Mr. MacKay, you gotta do something about them girls, they keep using the men's washroom." Apparently the janitor had encountered Joyce coming out of the men's washroom and "nearly had a heart attack."[47] Of course, Joyce was not embarrassed whatsoever — it took more than a janitor or a men's washroom to intimidate her.

When Sylvia experienced a rift with her husband, Joyce invited her to live with her and Michael, which she did for a number of months. Sylvia remembers that one day Michael traced Joyce on the wall of the apartment, which Sylvia thought was the origin of Walking Woman. However, Michael said it evolved from his many drawings of women, and the tracing Sylvia remembers was something he did just for fun to see if there was a resemblance between Joyce and the abstract form he had developed earlier.[48] Nevertheless, many people see Joyce in this legendary image, which first appeared in October 1960.[49]

In Sylvia, Joyce had a friend who enjoyed her riotous sense of humour. "Joyce and I had a lot of nonsense together. Some people didn't — they didn't understand who Joyce was."[50] The two women took their clothes to a Chinese laundry, gave their names as Joyce Snow and Sylvia White, and every week for months they used the same line, "'Here we come for our Snow-White laundry.' We thought we were hilarious and would continue to drive that poor man loony with this nonsense."[51] Prostitutes worked the area, and sometimes when Sylvia and Joyce were out at night, cars drove by slowly and stopped, men trying to pick them up. One night as a car stopped, Joyce strode over to it, and when a roly-poly man turned down his window, Joyce pulled out a water gun full of red ink and splattered him.

Sylvia told another story about Joyce wanting to see the world from a dog's point of view and enlisted the help of Hogan, Sylvia's English bulldog. The two women spent hours crawling on their hands and knees in the park with the dog. They also strapped Joyce's 16-mm Bolex camera onto a wagon that was hitched to Hogan, and followed him as best they could — in an upright position — while he explored the city, in and out of stores, including a butcher shop.[52] Unfortunately, a film could not be made from the footage because of technical problems.[53]

Joyce introduced Sylvia to the St. Lawrence market, where they went on Saturday mornings to buy fresh eggs, fish, vegetables and meats. When they came home loaded with food, they often had a big cooking spree, while Michael, looking on at first, with amusement at their bustle in the kitchen, eventually withdrew to work on some project or play the piano.

The kitchen at the Charles Street apartment had a big, old iron gas stove with a warming oven and a compartment for building a wood fire. Joyce liked this old stove for trying out her favourite kind of recipes, French cuisine. As much as possible, she used only fresh ingredients. By then she was reading Adelle Davis and took her seriously. She and Michael's mother shared an interest in nutrition.

Apparently Michael's mother thought Joyce should have a better stove. She ordered a white electric one and had it delivered. It sat in the foyer without ever being moved to the kitchen. Joyce saw no reason for using it because she liked the old one. In fact, one day Sylvia discovered that Joyce stored her menstrual pads in the oven of the new stove because she could never find an out-of-the-way place to keep her personal things. Buying appliances, or even pots, pans and dishes, was at the time outside of Joyce's range of thought. She didn't go to the store to buy new household items but picked up whatever she needed wherever she could, without spending money.[54]

Joyce's unconventional way of doing things was not affected. She was not just adopting a bohemian style; rather, the way she lived was completely natural to her; it was who she was. On the other hand, Joyce did sometimes fool people with fantasies she turned into stories and told as though they had actually happened. Her friends sometimes differed on the truth of her yarns. One such example is her story about running away to Buffalo to join the circus, which Sylvia thought could have been true. A business card stuck in her journal reads, "in person Joyce Wieland CLYDE BROS CIRCUS The World's Greatest Panoramic Circus Spectacle." It was the kind of thing she would have had printed for a joke.

According to Sylvia, Joyce identified very strongly with Giulietta Masina in Federico Fellini's *La Strada*, a film she went to see repeatedly. She looked like Masina, with her blonde bangs, round face and sad, kohl-lined eyes. In *La Strada*, Masina plays Gelsomina, a fey, waif-like girl who works in a circus. In one scene Gelsomina sits on the sidewalk, feeling abandoned, bent over with her head resting on her knees and cradled in her arms, a scene that echoes Joyce's memory of herself as a child sitting on a curb along the street, dejected, feeling wretched and not knowing what to do. "She had that sad wanderlust, was in her own little world," Sylvia said.[55]

In the 1950s, Toronto had a reputation for being stodgy and dull. Perhaps it was, but a number of artists set off a chain reaction of energy that changed the city. The critic and writer Robert Fulford characterized the 1950s as "the most creative years in the history of central Canada, a time of risk and high ambition."[56] This creative spirit bubbling through central Canada's decorous establishment was sometimes seen as improper, particularly when the artists portrayed anything explicitly sexual. In 1955 Toronto's mayor, Nathan Phillips, did not like the nudes in a show of drawings and paintings that Graham Coughtry and Michael Snow mounted at the Hart House Gallery at the University of Toronto. He thought them obscene and said he would not want his children to see them.[57] It would have taken more than the mayor's comments to stop Coughtry and Snow, however.

By then, Painters Eleven had begun showing their abstract paintings. Although their work was a departure from traditional landscape painting, Painters Eleven was "just another scene," according to Michael Snow.[58] Coughtry, Snow and the others in their circle felt what they were doing was

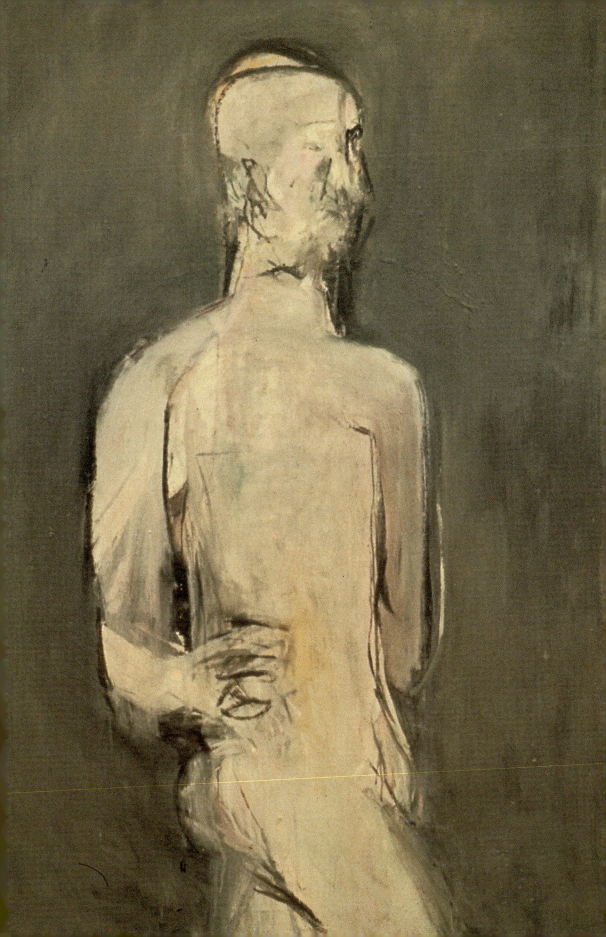

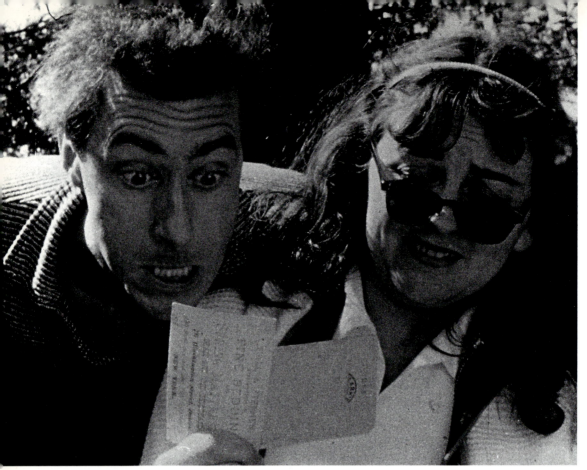

Michael and Joyce in her 1959 film, *A Salt in the Park*.

important. They were also more brash and unapologetic, and were considered renegades.

Some of Joyce's drawings later evoked responses similar to those of Mayor Phillips. Her work was shown for the first time in a group show of The Canadian Society of Graphic Art in 1956 at what was then the Art Gallery of Toronto. The next year she appeared again in a group show, this time at Barry Kerneman's gallery. Opened in 1956, Kerneman's Gallery of Contemporary Art was located at 98 Gerrard Street, in what was known as the Village, an area Harold Town described as "the only real Bohemia Toronto has ever known."[59] Dorothy Cameron worked in Kerneman's gallery, and there noticed Joyce's work for the first time. She opened her own gallery in 1959, and would offer Joyce a show the following year.

Joyce had two, two-person exhibitions in 1959, the first one with Gordon Rayner at Avrom Isaacs's Greenwich Gallery, which began when Isaacs, having graduated from the University of Toronto, joined with a friend, Al Latimer, to frame students' diplomas to make some money. It evolved into a picture-framing business, and when Latimer decided to leave, he sold the business to Isaacs for $1,200. Isaacs stuck with the framing business, which was on Hayter Street, just south of College Street, west of Bay. In 1955, he closed up and went to Europe for several months.[60] After he returned he opened The Greenwich Gallery in February 1956 at 736 Bay Street, just around the corner from Kerneman's gallery.

In a review of Joyce's show with Rayner, Robert Fulford described her two small collages as Dadaist in spirit. "In one of these she stuffs a small feather, a bit of a French calendar, a strip of animation film with eyes painted on it, and the legend clipped from a book, 'The product of an unhappy family life, Marina was fated to be what she became — a sinner.'" Fulford said her paintings were "raw, brilliant and intense, they are also deeply original. Two of them ... are full of confident strength."[61] He is referring here to *Man Turning* (1959) and *Figure in the Window* (1959).

That November Joyce and Michael had a show of drawings at the Westdale Gallery in Hamilton, a gallery run by Julius Lebow. Elizabeth Kilbourn, then on staff at the *Hamilton Spectator*, remembers receiving a call from Lebow, asking her to review the work of a young couple. There in the back room of the gallery she met Joyce Wieland and Michael Snow, "curled up like a couple of terrified children" on an old wicker sofa. According to Kilbourn, not many people besides her came to see the show, which opened on a typically grey, windy November day.[62]

It must have been around this time that Joyce wrote in a notebook about how she and Michael related to each other as artists. She led into her thoughts on Michael by writing about Stendhal, saying if she met a man like Stendhal, she would fall in love with him, but would not get along with him because she was as serious about her own work as he would be about his. "With M. its the same we are both deadly serious about our work — neither of us have what we really need and that is an intelligent but not ambitious person to fall back on. I wasn't as serious when we got married about my work so things seemed fine now we find it a drag both doing the same thing. I am jealous of him he is not very jealous of me."[63] She went on to say that the only thing she had done was a portrait of a man turning, but her slow progress was not for lack of effort. "I try too hard with an eye out for my audience. My only trouble is I want to be famous and rich at 30 years. It keeps going up, next it will be 31 (eternal compromise)." Despite the difficulties, she kept on working and that year she produced her first *Time Machine* painting.

Throughout the 1950s and early 1960s, Joyce made a series of erotic pen-and-ink and pencil drawings. Many of these were exhibited under the title "Twilit Record of Romantic Love" at the Agnes Etherington Gallery in Kingston, Ontario, from December 1994 to March 1995. Although many of these drawings

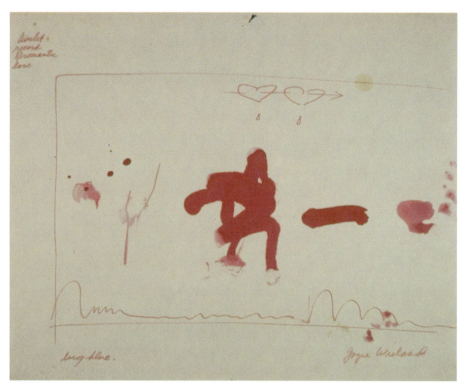

Twilit Record of Romantic Love, n.d.

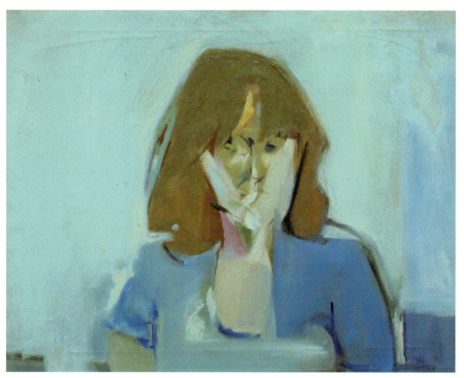

Myself, 1958.

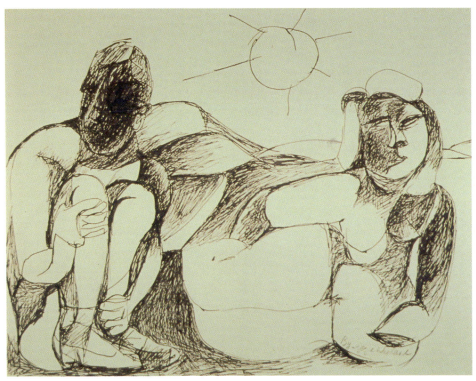

Untitled, n.d.

were undated, it is likely that most of them were from 1954 to 1956, when her relationship with Michael began. These drawings add to the picture of her personal history. She expressed a wide range of emotions, from the playfulness of making love and the thrill and bliss of connection to the beloved, to alienation and distance between two lovers looking in opposite directions.

In one such drawing, the male figure's face is darkened with cross-hatching to the point of obliteration, and he sits crouched to one side of the page while the female figure sprawls in the opposite direction. A sun, drawn as a child would, sits in the sky between them. The connection has been broken between the two lovers, and they turn away from each other.

Woman is a Parasite is about the troubling conflict Joyce experienced in establishing her own identity within a sexual relationship — troubling not just because of her own difficulties, but also because of what she observed in women around her, reflected in her comment at the end of 1955 about girls being brought up as "dependent wretches." As curator Jan Allen described it, "This work posits love as a dissolution of personal boundaries in which woman exists at the expense of a male host."[64] The inner conflict is clear — one that ensues when a woman's personal autonomy must be sacrificed for the sake of love.

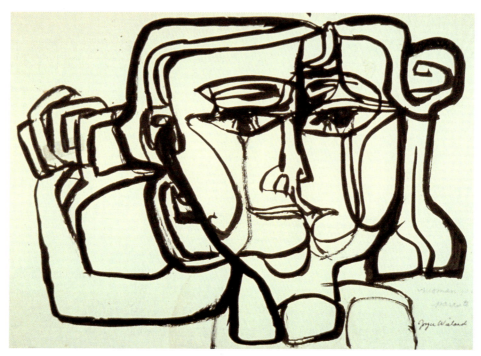

Woman is a Parasite, n.d.

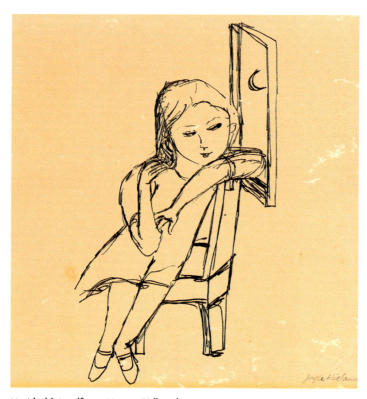

Untitled (Myself as a Young Girl), n.d.

According to her 1950s diary, there were periods of time when Joyce was ambivalent about sex. Her notes about Michael reveal that wanting sex with him was, at least partly, her longing for a sign of his love and an attempt at binding him to her — she needed him. An undated pen and ink drawing of herself as a child, most likely drawn in the early fifties, shows a sad, wistful girl's face in an adult body, sitting on a chair and leaning her arm on the window through which you can see a tiny new moon.[65] This typical image of the young girl waiting for her prince reveals Joyce's romantic side and perhaps how she saw herself in relation to Michael.

During the mid-fifties, Joyce chose to use domestic life and her own sexual experiences as her main subject matter. One of her 1956 works, entitled *Morning*, a somewhat abstract painting in peachy flesh tones, appears to be a peaceful domestic scene, the female figure lying down and the male sitting at the end of the cot. She painted this "sort of about the relationship" before her marriage, she said, a sad painting.[66] *Lunch Time*, also painted in 1956 in a similar style, depicts two figures sitting opposite each other at a table. The one figure, much smaller than the other, sits higher, giving the impression of a child in a high chair rather than an adult.

Of course, in the middle of the twentieth century it was almost unheard of for a woman to represent female sexual experience in her painting and drawing — eroticism as subject matter was a male privilege. Joyce, by representing female experience, risked being relegated outside the realm of serious art; in other words, in the bracketed category of (woman) artist. Yes, she was a good painter, but she was still a "girl," and that meant something different from being simply an artist, which implied "male." There was "the assumption that the male role is inclusive of artistic vocation, whereas the female role is exclusive of it. Artistic aspiration in women, therefore, necessarily induces conflict."[67]

"Woman artist" was a sign of her belonging, even if she was somewhat on the margins among the men. In marrying Michael and adding "artist's wife" to "woman artist," a greater danger lay in how Joyce saw herself in relation to Michael. A number of people remember Joyce as being in his shadow, and only occasionally did she step out from behind him — she regarded him as more important and did not value herself as he did himself. "As strong as she was about doing her work, he was always a little bit better. Joyce's work suffered for that."[68]

Not only was he seen as "a little bit better," but according to Robert Fulford, Michael was the most talked-about artist in Toronto during the late fifties and the sixties. "He was not A Toronto artist. He was THE Toronto artist. That is a hard row to hoe. You get up every morning and down the hall or on the other side of the bed is THE Toronto artist."[69] Fulford went on to

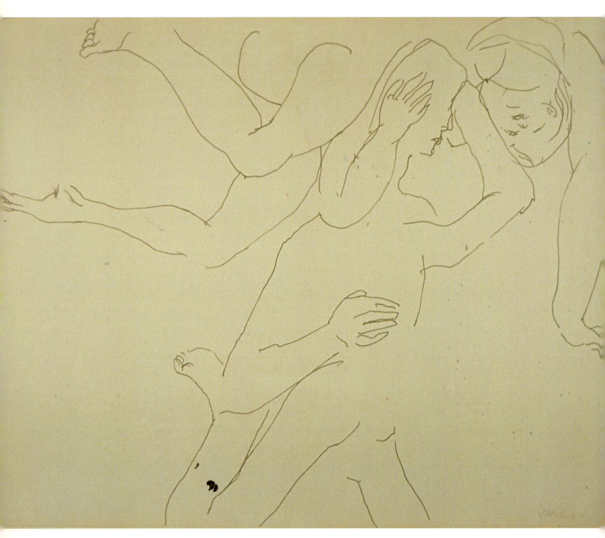

Lovers, 1956.

say that Michael was not just "more impressive than Joyce, he was more impressive than anyone." But if Fulford was right about how Michael was seen — and doubtless he was — what were the reasons behind this concept of him?[70] It was a part of the art world's need to classify artists as "great" — or "not great" — the kind of hierarchy Joyce truly detested. Certainly Michael Snow was a gifted artist, but his elevation was symptomatic of the whole idea of genius handed down through art history, a topic outside the scope of this book.[71]

In Anne Middleton Wagner's conclusion to *Three Artists (Three Women)*, she reminds readers of the complexity of male-female relationships within art, which in reality is a social hierarchy. She urges us to "think more deeply about the representational purposes and ambitions of work by women, and to assess their place in a cultural dialogue."[72] Similarly, we must seek to understand the social hierarchy in which Joyce and Michael worked in Canadian art, and the male-female ranking at play there. Joyce was appalled at the idea of ranking artists, as she made clear in a satirical, fictional interview with an artist named Frank Flunk who made up a prize because he had never received one and duped the world into thinking he was a genius.

In the milieu in which Joyce and Michael lived and breathed — the Isaacs Gallery — women were appendages, Fulford maintained. This gallery circle "was always spoken of as a boys' club, which to a considerable degree it was"[73] — not unlike the atmosphere of the New York Abstract Expressionists. Marjorie Harris, who worked at Dorothy Cameron's Here and Now Gallery during the early sixties, said the men at the Isaacs Gallery respected Joyce "in a grudging sort of way because she was so smart."[74] When asked recently how they regarded Joyce and her work at that time, several of these artists said they liked her — they liked women. "That is not an answer," said artist Ross Mendes. "That's a terrible answer ... She was intelligent, talented, not just ho, ho, ho, please get me a drink."[75] There is no question that the men in the Isaacs Gallery were of their time, when women were groupies and lovers, and men were the artists. Joyce's friends recalled that often at Isaacs Gallery openings women clustered around the star artists, Michael in particular, leaving Joyce to wonder which ones he was sleeping with.

Some of these women worked at getting the "best" men. Joyce was no exception in wanting the man she thought was best, and the reason, she thought, that she was allowed into this artists' boys' club was that she was married to Michael. In other words, Joyce would have felt her marriage was one reason for her success, which would create a shaky foundation for her career and give rise to her guilt.[76] Joyce's experience was similar to that of other female artists throughout history. Wagner's book on Eva Hesse, Lee Krasner and Georgia O'Keeffe, who were each married to an artist and

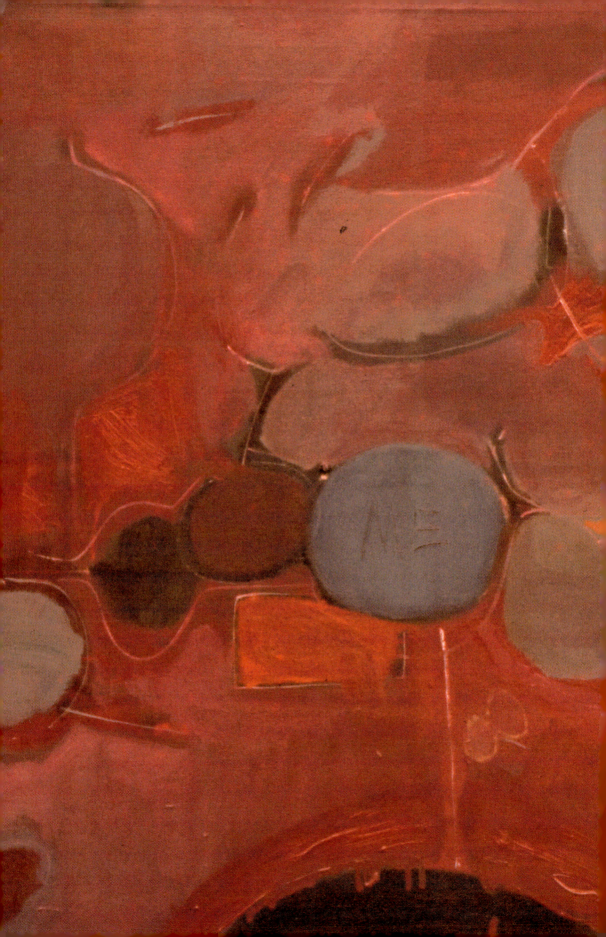

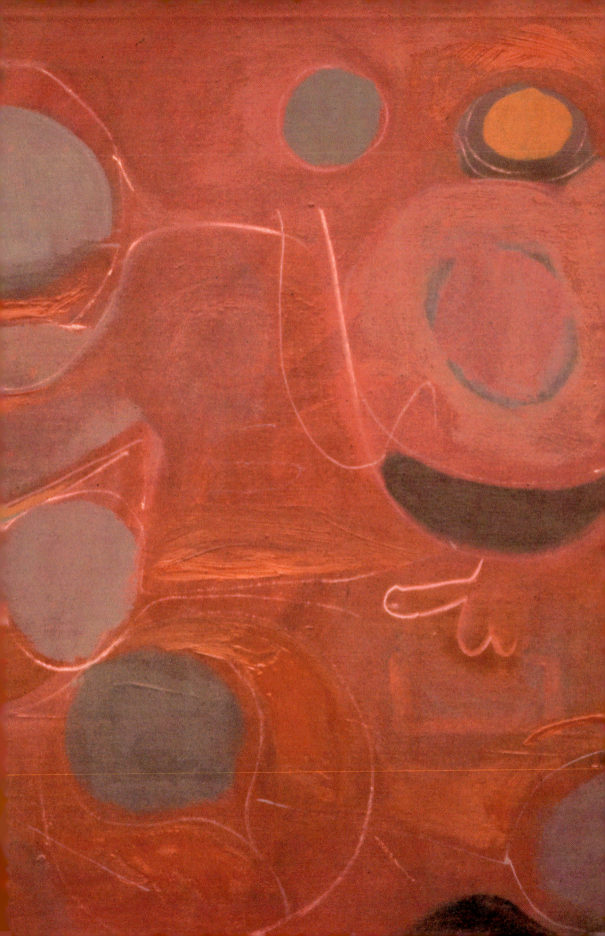

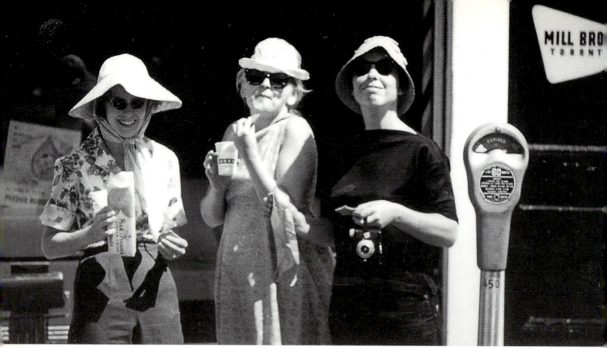

Donna Montague, Joyce, Sara Bowser (left to right) in Hull, Quebec, 1960.

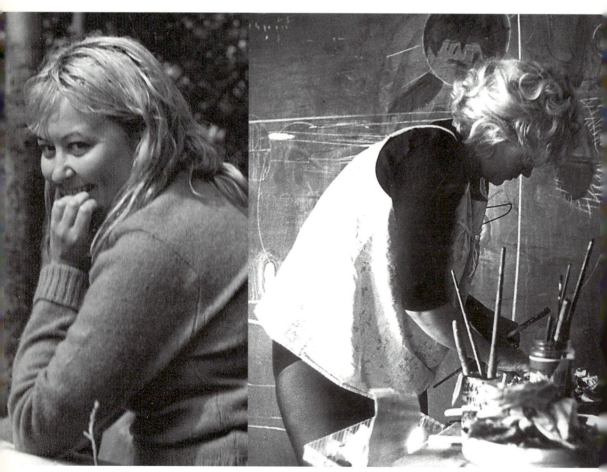

Joyce, probably 1959.

Joyce in her studio in 1960 with *Wall* in the background.

childless, concluded that marriage to an artist was central to women's artistic success. At the same time, Hesse herself asserted, "It is as difficult as it is said to be to be an artist's wife and an artist also."[77]

An example of what Joyce encountered as artist's wife is revealed in a review of the show she and Michael had at the Westdale Gallery. The first three paragraphs of the four-paragraph review, which appeared in the *Hamilton Spectator*, were about Michael, his drawings and his music, describing him as a talented musician and his drawings as exhibiting "fine draftsmanship and wit." A brief paragraph at the end adds, "Just to complete the picture, his wife, Joyce Wieland, also leads a dual life. Not only is she an actress, but her witty and amusing drawings at the Westdale Gallery indicate her growing stature as an artist."[78] How did Joyce respond when she read this review? Although she had conflicting feelings about her identity and how good her work was, she would also have known she deserved better and would doubtless have seen how skewed the review was.

Joyce had continued painting at home for several years after getting married, while Michael rented a separate studio. By the end of 1959 or the beginning of 1960, Donna and George Montague were living at 17 Prince Arthur Avenue, about a kilometre north-west of Joyce and Michael's apartment. Behind the Montagues' house stood a coach house, a small building that no longer exists. They offered it to Joyce as a studio, and she would work there until she and Michael went to New York in 1962.

George Montague, along with several other people, had bought a house and some land in the Gatineau Hills, not far from Ottawa. The summer of 1960, Joyce and Donna packed paints, canvases, books and household items and drove in the Montagues' Ford convertible to the Gatineau house for the summer. While Joyce painted, Donna read.

The two women drove to Ottawa's Byward Market almost every day to shop and have coffee; then they would come home and cook. If Joyce and Donna were feeling lonely in the evening, they went for a drive through the Gatineau Hills in the convertible with the top down and the radio blaring, the two of them singing and laughing.[79]

Some weekends, Michael and George took the train from Toronto to Ottawa and the women picked them up, then dropped them off at the train station at the end of the weekend. One week Sara Bowser came for a visit, bringing with her books to read. The three of them dressed up and went out for dinner at the Chateau Laurier one evening. They sat in the white dining room, which included a white piano, had a cordon bleu dinner that ended with baked Alaska and then headed back to the house in the hills.

Donna remembered those weeks as wild, and a lot of fun. At the end of the summer, Joyce gave Donna her painting *The Kiss* in return for the use of the Montagues' place, where she made many paintings for her first one-woman show, scheduled at the Here and Now Gallery on Cumberland Street in September 1960.

On Sunday evening, September 18, there was also a showing at Here and Now of "unusual films realized by a new wave of swell guys," according to an invitation written in Joyce's hand. Her name was the only woman listed among the seven men that included Warren Collins and Michael Snow. Besides the summer's paintings — one titled *Twilight in the Gatineau* — the show included some of her drawings of lovers, rough Dadaist constructions of wood combined with pieces of tin, and a cloth construction, a forecast of the direction she would go in the next decade. The Gatineau paintings, in soft blues, lavenders and greens, formed a contrast to the rough objects of urban origin constructed of cast-off materials.

This show was mounted sometime after she had already shown with Gordon Rayner at the Isaacs Gallery. Dorothy Cameron could not remember whether she invited Joyce to join her gallery, or whether Joyce asked, but Isaacs claims that Cameron "lured her away." There are varying accounts of what happened next, but a letter Cameron wrote to Joyce made her feel that this dealer was out of sync with her work. In the letter, dated June 6, 1961, Cameron told Joyce that she lacked discipline and did not take her painting seriously, dissipating her energy in "amateur film-making and journalism."[80] Cameron admitted that she did not like her "neo-dada stuff" but admired her paintings. She was heartbroken to lose her — she really wanted to show Joyce's work.[81]

Cameron had bought one of Joyce's pieces, "a little wooden board like a shingle [that] had a nail in it, right through a pink bleeding heart, very feminine and vulnerable." She thought the piece was about Joyce and Michael.[82] After Cameron's letter, which left Joyce feeling betrayed, she decided she wanted to show with Isaacs, who claimed that "Mike Snow and Bob Hedrick came to me one day and pleaded with me to reconsider and take Joyce on." That is what he did.[83]

It would be interesting to know at what point in her move between the two dealers Joyce created her very funny, loosely drawn cartoon strip, featuring Here and Now Gallery. It appeared in the second issue of *evidence* (undated, but likely published in 1961), a little magazine featuring poetry, photos, comics and other writings by artists and their friends. Joyce's cartoon strip opens with a truck, "Here & Now Gallery" written on its side. It had just driven over a cat. A man saying, "The market has crashed sob!!!" is carrying a briefcase labelled "Brief," which has also been flattened by the truck. Many different character types appear, from a woman pushing a pram (the baby says, "Wa! Wa!" and the mother says, "Wa! Wa! yerself") to strange-looking

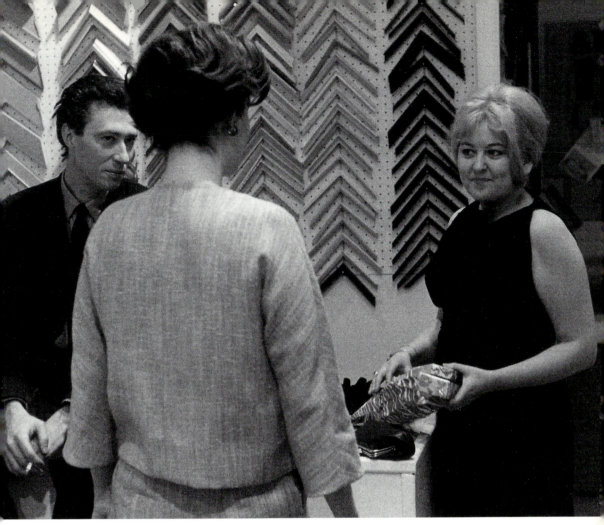

Michael, Sheila Gladstone, Joyce, 1960.

people saying, "I'm starved for art." One woman with a very long nose says "Art isn't what it used to be," and a bearded man replies, "Yes it is — at the Here & Now Gallery." Prime Minister John Diefenbaker says, "We must sell more art to help unemployment," and a spy walks past carrying a bag marked, "There and Then." The ending portrays a figure sitting in despair, saying, "Oh! God art hasn't saved me," with a painting on an easel in the background. Joyce wrote the hours of the Here and Now Gallery at the bottom of the cartoon.

In the late fifties, Joyce read Emil Ludwig's biography of Napoleon Bonaparte, and she wrote a somewhat scattered profile of him, published in the first issue of *evidence* in late 1960. She recalled that because Napoleon was such a powerful figure, she became him for a short while after she read the book. She used him and Josephine in some of her work. *Josephine's Last Letter to Napoleon* (1961) is written in an illegible script, "agitated, tight and curled," and spaced unevenly. "It is gestural writing echoing through mime the

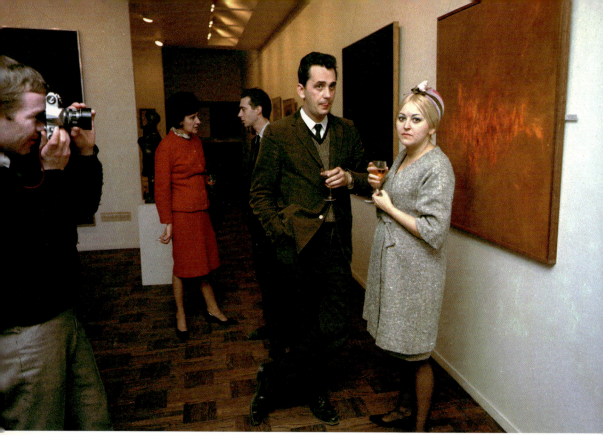

Joyce and Bryan Barney, with Arthur Coughtry photographing them at the opening to Joyce's show at the Isaacs Gallery in February, 1962.

desperate emotions of Josephine in a last letter before she died."[84] Joyce must have created this letter from the reservoir of her own imagination because Emil Ludwig clearly states that "no one knows if she ever wrote to [Napoleon]."[85]

What did Napoleon mean for Joyce? In the first place, having come from Corsica's lower middle class, he rose to become emperor of the French. In his heart he remained a Corsican and cherished his origin in a romantic way, not unlike the way Joyce talked of her parents and her childhood.

Her essay on Napoleon hinges on his contradictions. Joyce explains his ruthlessness as one such paradox. "Many people chastise Napolean [sic] for killing people needlessly but, how hard it is to do good without doing bad."[86]

The creative uses to which she put her readings on Napoleon demonstrate how, already in this early stage of her career, Joyce instinctively pursued fertile subject areas, whether it was people's lives or their ideas on love and spirituality. She stuck with a subject until she had sifted from it the substance that provided grist for her art mill, then moved on when something else caught her imagination. This pattern of relentlessly following each obsession would become her lifelong way of nurturing her creative work.

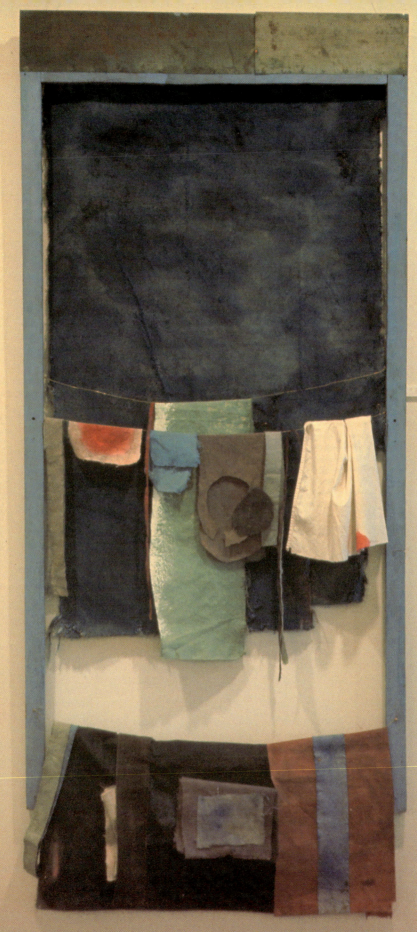

The Clothes of Love, 1960-61.

The Napoleon essay also reveals her sense of humour and irony, qualities that saturated her work in the late fifties and early sixties, particularly the constructions of "little machines to bring back famous literary personages. They were pieces with wood, paper, cloth, wooden dials, and antennae."[87] These Dadaist pieces, along with other works by Joyce, were at the forefront at the Isaacs Gallery at the beginning of 1962, first in the Dada show and then in Joyce's own exhibition.[88]

The invitation for the Dada show was an adaptation of pages from a mail-order catalog, likely Eaton's, featuring men's jackets, overalls and "inner suits," otherwise known as long thermal underwear.[89] Photos of the heads of artists in the show were superimposed on the catalog models, although Michael Snow was represented only by "snow" circled in the words "snow suit," appearing under a boy dressed in a snow suit for $11.43. Joyce was pictured in a sleeping bag underneath a display of guns and part of a badminton set. Her *Napoleon's Grave* appeared in this show, "a rag dummy in a soap box coffin surrounded by fresh roses and burning candles daily renewed by the artist."[90]

Three weeks later a solo exhibition of Joyce's paintings, drawings, collages and constructions opened.[91] It was at this exhibition that *Laura Secord Saves Upper Canada* (1961) was shown for the first time, a collage that originated in her childhood memory of history class and her discovery of the story of Laura Secord's role in the War of 1812. The point of view of the painting is from the air, with the spiral representing the circuitous route Laura Secord took to warn Lieutenant FitzGibbon of the American army's plans. The chalk-like numbers in the painting were also part of her school memories, and the paper airplanes reminiscent of those thrown by students when they were supposed to be learning.[92]

The Clothes of Love (1960-61), one of her first cloth works, was also part of this show. It could be described as fabric collage, with pieces of cloth hung on wires, as though she got the idea for the work while she was doing her laundry. But the cloth pieces, of varying sizes and textures, have Joyce's drawings on them, as well as paint. Her other early cloth work, *Heart On* (1961), resembles a bed sheet, stained red, with cloth hearts glued on; a cloth collage that calls to mind Joyce's description of her childhood experience tending her mother when she had bowel cancer.

She showed a number of drawings of lovers, too. Av Isaacs remembers those drawings as gentle and poetic, from a woman's perspective, "something most of us male chauvinists had never thought of — what a woman's point of view was." But they shocked many people, men and women, because women weren't supposed to think about eroticism, and they certainly weren't supposed to make erotic drawings. One man came

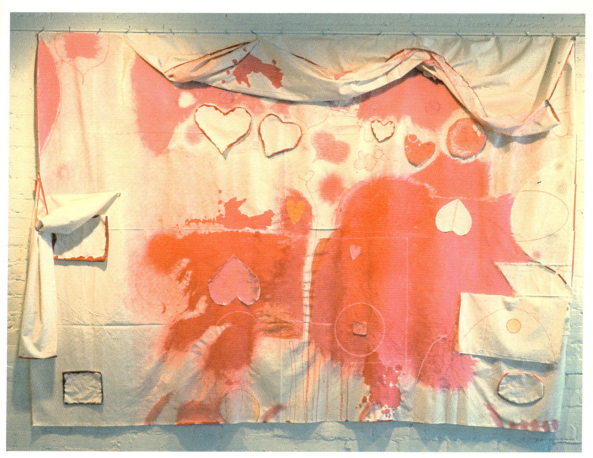

Heart On, 1961.

into the gallery and said he couldn't possibly look at Joyce's drawings because there was a woman there at the same time. The woman was Joyce, though the embarrassed man did not know she was the artist.[93]

That October, Hart House Art Gallery at the University of Toronto mounted a show of Joyce's and Michael's drawings. The invitation, written in Joyce's hand in a script with a flourish, described the exhibition as a "conjugal retrospective of drawings by Joyce Wieland and Michael Snow." Again Joyce exhibited pieces with erotic, romantic and domestic themes. But she also exhibited works having "a mild literary overtone."[94] This was the last time they had a two-person show together, and it was the last time Joyce showed her work before she and Michael left Toronto to live in New York City.

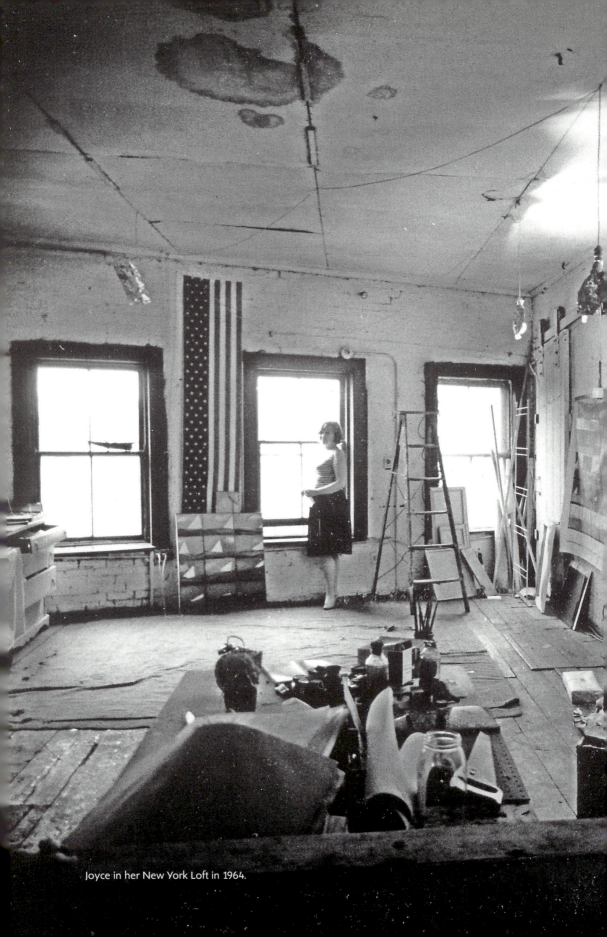

Joyce in her New York Loft in 1964.

5

A Canadian in New York

We influenced each other, and made wonderful films.
However, when it came to my work affecting anyone it
was never mentioned. I am forced to talk in terms of
influence etc. because that was one of the manifestations
of the discrimination. Yet when books have been written
to document this movement my work is relegated to a
woman's place, small that is. —Joyce Wieland, in
conversation with Debbie Magidson and Judy Wright.[1]

WITH THE DIN and vibrations of New York swirling around her, Joyce sat
alone at her kitchen table, having lived in Lower Manhattan for two years.
She was making a film and had assembled a variety of objects — a camera,
glasses of water, plastic pink roses, plastic fern-like leaves, a purple teapot,
rubber gloves, a toy boat, mirrors, a magnifying glass, lenses. With her table
and objects she created a set, and she used herself as the sole living "object"
in this new film, except for her cat, which appeared only fleetingly.

Seven years later, she would have a conversation with her close friend
Hollis Frampton about making this film, *Water Sark* (1964–65). Frampton, a
filmmaker whom Joyce had met in New York, was born in Ohio in 1936 and
died of cancer in 1984. His grandmother, who raised him, taught him to read
at age three by using an old typewriter. By the time he was six, each Saturday
he took his wagon to the library and filled it with books to read. When he

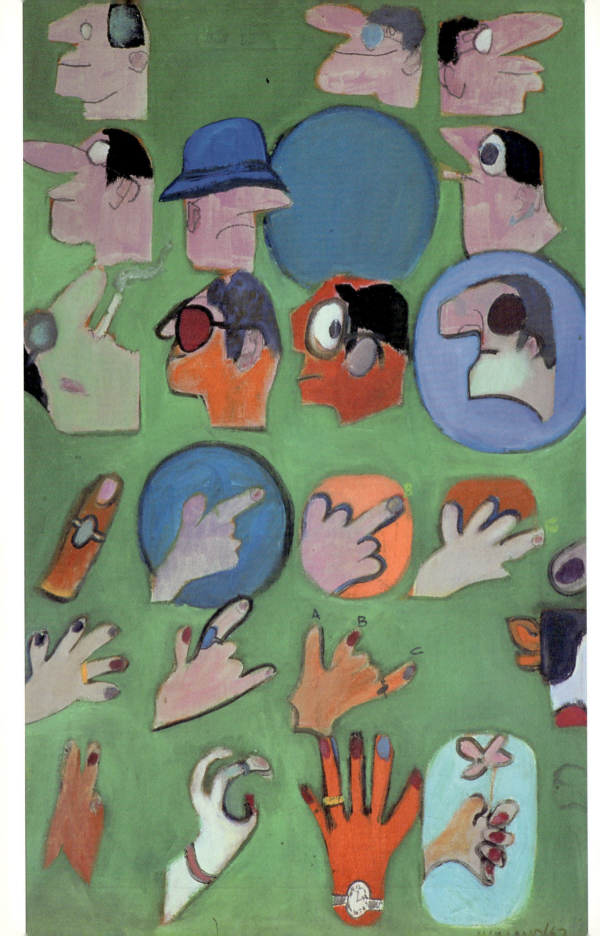

was nine, his uncle gave him a Brownie box camera, some film and a developer for Christmas.

Had he grown up in a later era, Frampton, who hardly ever spoke, probably would have been diagnosed as autistic. However, in his tenth year, the results of a test showed his mental age to have been that of an eighteen-and-a-half-year-old. In school he was in classes for gifted children and eventually won scholarships for the Cleveland Museum of Art and the Phillips Academy in Andover, Massachusetts, where his classmates included the painter Frank Stella, the sculptor Carl Andre and composers David Behrman and Frederic Rzewski. Despite his brilliance, he never received a diploma from the Phillips Academy because he intentionally failed the required American history course, even though his average was the highest in his class.[2]

Frampton was the kind of person for whom Joyce had a strong affinity and understanding — they had in common a life of roaming in the space of the imagination. Their conversation, taped sometime in 1971, is remarkable because it reveals two artists/filmmakers' thoughts about the creative process from very personal points of view. The feeling in their voices, the pauses and the exchanges show that the two felt comfortable with each other. Frampton's intelligence and breadth of knowledge gave Joyce something solid on which to base a creative interchange, as she tried to articulate her thoughts about her work.

In that conversation, Joyce called *Water Sark* "a desperate self-portrait." She called it "a drawing film," meaning it was an extension of her drawings. By using the camera as a pen or pencil, she was saying "I can do this and so can you ... you can make a film from very little. It's also connected with all the domestic arts, and done at the table, which I've been doing for twelve years. The kitchen table has been the core of all my art since I was a child. The kitchen table I did everything on ... and I drew when I grew up and I drew on that table and I made films on that table. ... It's like some kind of altar."[3]

This film, a rendering of the intimate process of making a work of art, became an expression of surrender to the ecstasy of the imagination. Why, then, did she call the film a "desperate" self-portrait? One reason is that she was exploring aspects of what would later be called feminism, before the introduction of the notion that domestic matters were valid subject matter for women's art. Women isolated within the four walls of their kitchen were desperate. In that sense, *Water Sark* was a desperate female expression. There is also another reason, related to Joyce's specific personal history. It seems likely that for her, life in the imagination originally resulted from feelings of desperation and later led her to discover a power over experience that she at first did not have in her traumatized childhood. That the pain and

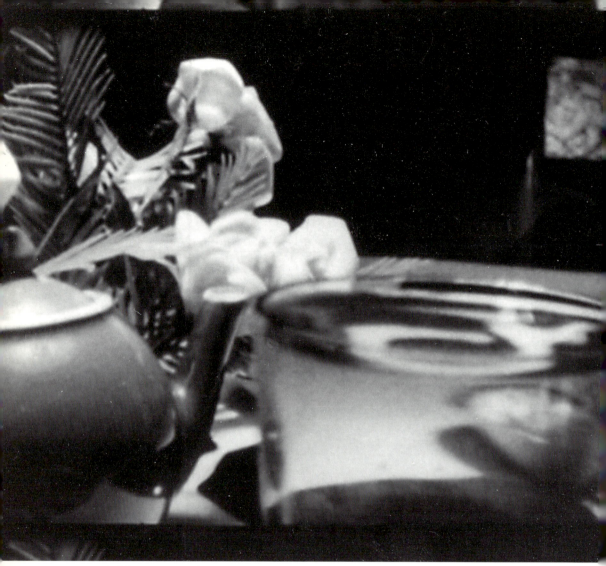

Still from *Water Sark*, 1964-65.

desperation did not stop her is evidence of the strength from which she worked throughout her career. Along the way she would create key works that would both reveal who she was and provide new ground under her feet on which to develop her imagination further in the use of a variety of media. *Water Sark*, a sixteen-millimetre, fourteen-minute colour film that she made in 1964 and 1965, was one of those key works, and she would return to elements from this film in other works of art, among them, her lithograph *Facing North — A Self-Impression* in 1974 and *The Far Shore*.

In some ways, *Water Sark* is anything but desperate. It is most playful, an explosion of erotic and sensual images and light, with subtleties of colour that are reminiscent of sea shells. It is a film that links colour with emotion, "if colours could have emotions," said her former student and friend, Jamie Erfurdt.[4]

This play with the movement of form and colour evokes a sense of being high. In fact, Joyce did use drugs when she made that film, something she talked about in her conversation with Frampton. Even the title is a part of the playfulness of the film. "She liked playing with words and 'sark' was a nonsense word she liked and vaguely associated with an ancient word for boat, and which she playfully substituted for almost anything."[5]

Joyce possessed what writer Jeanette Winterson described as a "supreme confidence," and "a capacity to recognise in one thing the potential of another, and the willingness to let that potential realise itself ..."[6] In the film's title, Joyce was doing exactly that with words. By choosing this name, she transformed herself into a creature exploring itself at home, looking through water, through glass. But for all its playfulness, the film communicates an underlying feeling of disturbance and chaos, something like a microcosmic earthquake.

Water Sark opens with the sound of running water and an image of pinkish red paper cut-out letters reading, "Corrective Films" — the name Joyce used for her film company — in front of a round, white paper lampshade.[7] Amid an unsettling screeching noise, Joyce comes into focus holding her camera. Water falls into a glass; then the glass constantly moves and tips. The purple teapot pours water into a glass; a plastic pink rose rocks up and down. Accompanied by banging and grating sounds, the objects shift, tip and pulsate; the lampshade swings underneath the glass instead of above it, and the usual points of reference are lost, though the liquid, pink forms have a sensual beauty. As the banging stops, Joyce's blonde hair appears behind the camera, and then she seems to be sitting in a tub of water playing with camera lenses. A tiny toy boat is suspended with a string — it is not floating in water as one would expect, but is being gently pushed by a rubber-gloved finger, so that it swings back and forth. Joyce pans down her own body, and we see her breasts, first in a haze, and then in focus, and as the camera moves down, for a split second the form of her body appears pregnant.

After the camera moves to a window and through it glimpses a roof in the background, it moves back to the kitchen table and the banging resumes. Joyce plays with a magnifying glass in front of her right eye as it opens and closes. The magnifying glass moves to her lips, which also open and close, and the magnification distorts her face into a grotesque image. As the sound quiets, a floating balloon appears briefly, then the profile of a breast in isolation. A cat's face is shown in the magnifying glass. The whole thing trails off into "Corrective Films" again. The film evokes the sense that something is completely out of control and turned upside down, and Joyce's description of it as "desperate" appears apt.

Joyce's comments to Frampton about *Water Sark* reach far in two directions of her life, into her past as a child in her parents' home, and forward into her subsequent work and her life as an artist in New York and afterwards. In *Water Sark* she traversed the boundaries of what she had done before, and transformed into visual images the approach she adopted in her early twenties of experimenting with her life to develop fantastic visions, "fantastic" in the sense of fanciful and phantasmagoric. She used her housewifely prison — she imagined the film to be made by a shut-in who had to create it on the premises — as a solid base from which to launch her explorations, like Colette locked up by Willy to make her write. Of course, she was not literally imprisoned in her loft, but neither had she escaped from the place she felt she had been ascribed simply because she had been born female. And as the woman of one particular body, she explored its territory and in a sense travelled a long distance there to create luminous images of colour and texture without leaving her kitchen.

Joyce's perspective in this film — asserting the validity of making art from whatever she had in her own space — ascribed value to ordinary objects and her kitchen table, the domestic. Whatever activities occurred on or around the kitchen table were worthy of exploration to see "how much you can find out about next to nothing."[8]

Though the film grew out of the personal, that Joyce dared to make *Water Sark* as she did shows her uncompromising expression of her vision, despite the art world's disregard for the domestic. When she showed the film to Shirley Clarke, the highly regarded New York filmmaker liked it so much she "helped Joyce launch it with a positive critical review for the Film-Makers' Cooperative catalogue."[9] The welcome Clarke gave her into the avant-garde New York film circle when they met for the first time made an enormous difference for Joyce, giving her a feeling of belonging, something she did not experience among New York painters.

From Joyce's kitchen table, we can now backtrack to trace events leading to her move to New York, and her life in the first few years there. In the early sixties, Joyce expressed mixed signals about wanting to leave Canada, and the memories of her friends about whether she wanted to go are contradictory — she wanted to go, it was her idea; no, she did not want to go, it was Michael's idea. According to him, it was his idea. "She was really quite afraid, which was justified," Michael said.[10]

By the end of 1962 the two of them were familiar with New York's art world. They knew about Marcel Duchamp's anti-art pieces. The third and last issue of *evidence* featured Duchamp on the cover, and came out just before the Dada exhibition at the Isaacs Gallery.[11] On Joyce and Michael's frequent visits to New York, the vitality of the city and its artists seemed alluring, with the excitement of new possibilities.

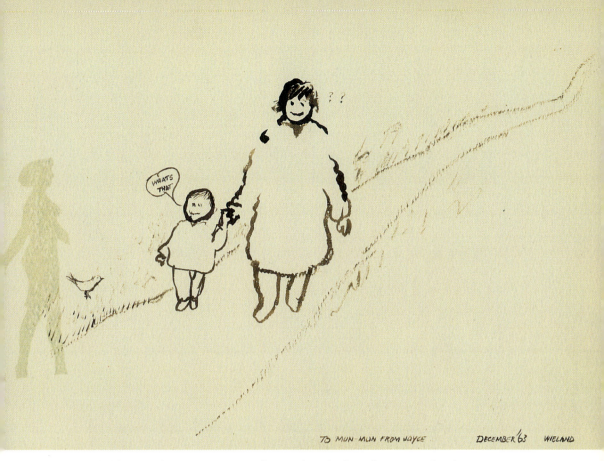

Untitled (Joyce and Munro Ferguson walking, with Michael's Walking Woman), n.d.
Munro asks "What's that."

Joyce and Michael had been friends of Toronto filmmaker Bob Cowan, who went to New York as a student and lived there for a number of years. On one of their visits to New York, they drove late into the night and arrived at Cowan's place so early in the morning that they slept in the car until they thought he would be awake. That day he showed them around the city.

When the pair went to New York again in the summer of 1962, they looked around with the possibility of living there in mind. On that visit, they stayed with Betty and Graeme Ferguson in their large Upper West Side apartment at 924 West End Avenue near 105th Street. Joyce and Michael had known Graeme when he was a filmmaker in Toronto — he had moved to New York in 1958. The following spring, on a trip to Alaska, Graeme had met Betty Ramsaur, a strikingly beautiful, dark-haired woman who had grown up there and was working at an airline check-in counter in Anchorage. They became friends. He told her about people he had met in Africa when he was filming there, and since she could get free airline tickets, she decided she would like to go on safari. On her way, she stopped in New York and called Graeme. She didn't get to Africa because she and Graeme decided to marry,

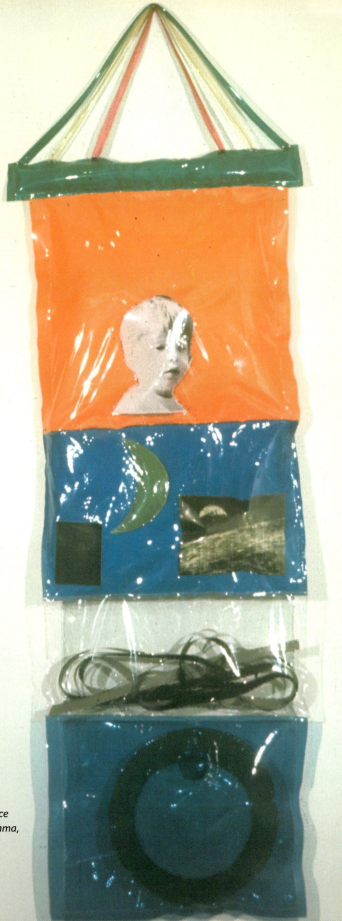

*The Space
of the Lama,*
1966.

and they settled in New York. The next year their son Munro was born, and two years later, their daughter, Allison.

When Joyce and Betty first met, they had an exchange that would symbolize their lifelong friendship. Joyce admired Betty's sleek sealskin bag, and thought the buttons on it were beautiful. She pointed out to Betty what made them so appealing, and Betty took them off and gave the buttons to Joyce.[12]

When Joyce and Michael decided to move to New York, Graeme and Betty invited them to stay at their place until they could find a loft. They accepted the invitation and in late 1962 moved into the Fergusons' four-bathroom, five-bedroom apartment — some of the bedrooms had originally been built as maids' quarters. As it turned out, Joyce and Michael did not find a loft until after the New Year. During the several months they lived with the Fergusons, Joyce and Michael became fond of two-year-old Munro, a blond-haired, dark-eyed child.

He was just learning to talk, and Joyce thought his words sounded Asiatic. Munro also loved rice. In fun, Joyce and Michael decided Munro was the reincarnation of the Dalai Lama and dressed him in Indian cotton dyed saffron yellow and asked his help in finding a loft. They scouted the city to look at lofts and then returned to the Fergusons' apartment and asked Munro, as an oracle, whether or not to take a particular place. It was a game they all enjoyed. Four years later, Joyce would call one of her plastic see-through hangings, which included a photo of Munro, *The Space of the Lama*.

During this time, Joyce and Michael enjoyed bantering and punning with each other, something at which they both excelled, and Munro drew out their playfulness. Michael played word games with him, calling objects by the wrong names. Once they pretended it was snowing in the apartment and ripped open a pillow and threw feathers around. Joyce took Munro with her to museums to look at art, and engaged him in conversations about paintings, beginning when he was only two but continuing as long as the Fergusons lived in New York. Sometimes as they stood in front of a painting talking, people visiting the gallery gathered around them to listen.

Joyce wanted a family, too, and wondered why, after all this time, she had not become pregnant. In December, shortly after they arrived in New York and even before they found a loft, Joyce had a medical appointment for tests in the gynaecology department of the New York Hospital. Again in March 1963 she had further tests, and underwent a tubal insufflation, an extremely painful procedure used in those days to unblock the fallopian tubes by blowing air into them. It was an excruciating experience, and Joyce told Betty Ferguson she would never do it again. It seems the procedure did not give Joyce a clear diagnosis.[13] Joyce also went into therapy to explore what she thought might be psychological factors preventing her pregnancy. She speculated that perhaps she was too much a child herself to become pregnant, and in later years, when she spoke of her infertility, she remained vague about the reason she never conceived.

Although some of her friends have questioned whether she really wanted children, Michael felt sure that she did, that it was part of her very domestic bent. But he also claimed that having children "was not talked about very much," and that he did not want children.[14] However, Jo Haines, who, with her husband, Paul, lived next door to Joyce and Michael's first loft, had a clear memory of Joyce telling her that Michael wanted a child, and that whenever Michael and Joyce were having difficulties "there was always this question about her wanting to have a baby but couldn't."[15] Joyce loved the children of her friends, and many of them, now adults, have memories of time spent with her. Munro remembers Joyce as a person who had a child very much alive inside her, the kind of grown-up whose natural playfulness made being with her a lot of fun.[16]

Whether Joyce and Michael followed Munro's oracle or their own hunches, several months into 1963, they rented a loft for fifty dollars a month at 191 Greenwich Street in Lower Manhattan, where the World Trade Center now stands. Finding lofts was difficult because they were not advertised — these were commercial buildings. In fact, living in these places was illegal, which is understandable as they had no heat or plumbing. Artists rented them, ostensibly for studios, but then lived in them because they were so cheap. The loft Joyce and Michael found was filled with ships' gear and "looked like a ships chandlers shop."[17] Outside the building was a small sign indicating that the musician Steve Swallow lived there, and a band of gypsies hung around, begging, "Give me a quarter to dye my hair red."[18] According to Paul Haines, Joyce was the one who first discovered the loft. He remembers that she knocked on the door and said she was looking for a loft for herself and her husband, who "played piano just like John Coltrane played tenor."[19] She didn't tell him they were Canadians, nor did she tell him she was a painter. Paul told her a loft was available next door, and that was the one she and Michael moved into.

This was a derelict part of the city. Rose Richardson, a friend Joyce met through Donna Montague, visited them in 1964 and remembers that Joyce and Michael seemed nonchalant about transients in the area, even though once a burning mattress was thrown out of the window in the building next to them.[20] Joyce and Michael had to install plumbing themselves and put in a shower and toilet and sink. They tried keeping warm in winter with a coal stove — the coal was delivered by a man carrying it up steep stairs in a sack on his back. The walls were bare brick, painted white, large windows at the two ends of the long narrow space let in abundant light. The floor was of bare wood. At one end was the living space — a bed, a table and a few chairs, and a corner that served as a kitchen. Their furniture was mostly cast-off stuff they found on the street, or built from wooden packing crates that had been put out for garbage pick-up outside shops in the area.

Michael's stencilled *Walking Woman* also lived in the loft — he built a coffee-table cut out in her shape, stencilled her on the white enamel cupboard door beside the stove, and put her on wallpaper and drapes and on the kitchen table. At the opposite end of the loft was Joyce's studio; Michael's studio was on another floor.

Her new home, so different from Toronto, held a great deal of fascination for Joyce. She enjoyed the view of the Hudson River with its boats. And she had her two cats, Dwight and Peggy — the Peggy who would later star in one of her films. The Haines also had two cats, named Theo and Red Dog. Joyce quickly became friends with her new neighbours, and she and Jo explored the area, which included the Fulton fish market. Across the street was Treflick's, a pet store that sold — or rented — circus animals, and Joyce worried about how the animals were treated. Michael remembered often hearing strange animal noises, and seeing an elephant on the street one day.[21] Beside Treflick's was a plant store, with many beautiful plants sitting on the sidewalk, and farther on, Jack's Electric.

In Jo, Joyce found a friend who liked her imagination. The two of them devised a fantasy scheme for saving the world, beginning on Wall Street. Joyce suggested that the problem with New York's businessmen was that they lacked decent nutrition. She and Jo saw their strained faces, their hands clutching briefcases. They imagined calling themselves "Goodie Two-Shoes," making nutritious snacks, including "cookies disguising brewers yeast" and loading them into a cart for distribution in the business district.[22] Bringing these men fruit, flowers and little poems surely would have some impact on how they ran their business! Joyce celebrated the Two-Shoes idea in a hanging she made, *The Hall of Hearts* (1966), which she dedicated to Jo Haines. But Joyce did not stop with the fanciful. She also wrote a letter to Senator Robert F. Kennedy protesting a bill that would allow the use of non-nutritive additives in candy.

For all the silliness of the Goodie Two-Shoes scheme, Joyce's awareness of the consequences of what one eats placed her way ahead of her time. She bought vitamins in bulk and made sure she and Michael each had a saucer of pills to swallow every day. She would use her pet name for Michael, saying, "Now Teddy have your vitamins."[23] In some ways, Joyce was the typical wife of the time and took good care of Michael, making sure his diet included nutritious meals. She shopped at Sherman's health-food store nearby, and

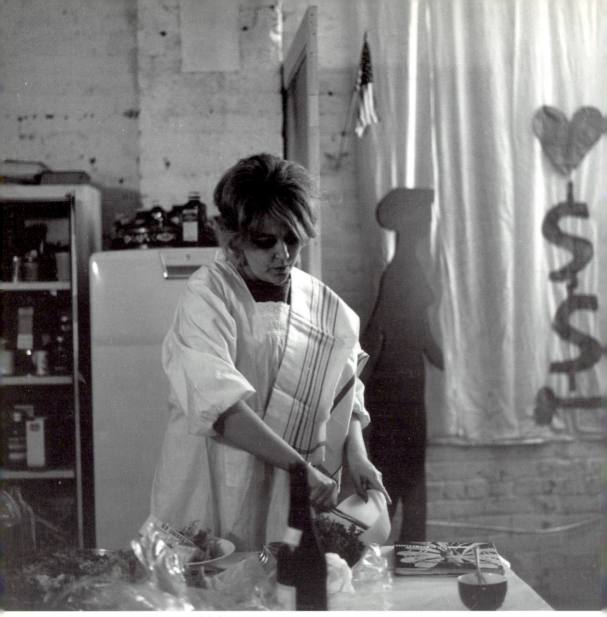

Joyce in the New York loft in 1963.

went to the Washington market in search of organic produce. Once, she and Jo Haines took her motor scooter to New Jersey to visit the organic farmers. In undated notes, she wrote about how awful white bread was, saying it did not even look good. "It is a pappish thing which [people] stuff in their mouths along with other things to numb themselves with." She added, "A glass of Pepsi to wash down a chili burger — a delight but quickly over. Good food gives a lasting sensation of well being spiritual and physical ..."[24]

Joyce loved to cook. Many Sunday mornings Joyce and Michael invited a group of friends and served them her small cardamom pancakes with maple syrup. Paul Haines remembers that Joyce had "an extraordinary presence ...

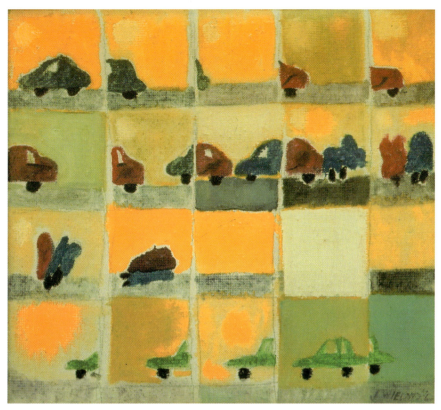

Car Crash, 1963.

that felt very good."[25] At these breakfasts, their friends enjoyed Michael's dry sense of humour, bouncing off Joyce's more ribald jokes.[26] Their New York friends also noticed how much these two Canadians swore; New Yorkers did not swear much.[27]

Joyce and Michael spent many evenings listening to jazz and smoking pot with the Haines. They also enjoyed listening to jazz in clubs, but the expense of cover charges meant they could not go often. Sometimes they did go to Max's Kansas City bar, where painters gathered. And after they met the experimental filmmakers, Joyce and Michael spent many evenings watching films.

Joyce enjoyed visiting the ship museum on South Street, looking at the models of ships and other artifacts on display. On her walks to Battery Park she watched the ships in the Hudson River. She and Michael often went for walks together as well and had conversations about what they were each working on. "It was important to us that we be working on our own thing," he said. "I think it was pretty unique ... that we were both pretty good and we were both working on different stuff."[28]

Living in this new environment spawned a prolific phase in Joyce's

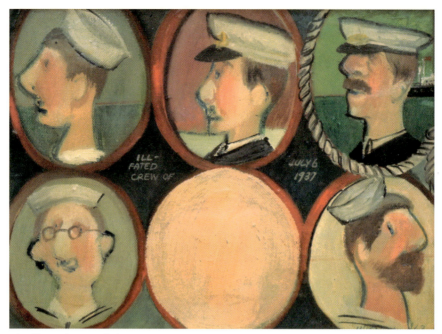

The Ill-Fated Crew of July 6, 1937, 1963.

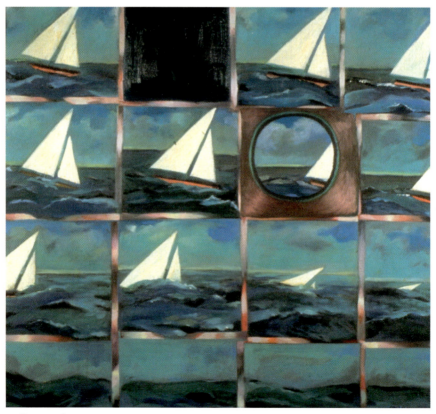

Sailboat Sinking, 1965.

painting. She painted a series often called "the disaster paintings," images of boats sinking and planes crashing. With the transition from the safety of familiar Toronto to New York, it seems her fears and insecurities surfaced, which she translated into these visual images. One such painting was about a disaster that occurred the same year her father died — *The Ill-fated Crew of July 6, 1937*, painted in 1963, which is surely a metaphor for her family, who indeed were ill-fated with his death. At first these paintings were based on her own difficulties in dealing with loss, Joyce said; but later they expressed her social and political awareness. She discovered what she called an "American fascination with disaster and grotesque happenings" in the media.[29]

Joyce was able to use disaster as subject matter, and at the same time her sense of humour burst through in such collages and paintings as *Necktie* and *The New Power*, both painted in 1963. *Flicks Pics #4* (1963) also combines humour with tragedy. Between two columns of ships and sailboats are a row of caricatured penises that look like missiles, at first erect and then in gradual states of sinking.

Though many of Joyce's paintings at that time were influenced by New York, she never showed them there. She and Michael both returned often to Toronto for their exhibitions at the Isaacs Gallery, and to visit friends. Les Lawrence remembered that when he and his wife, Wendy Michener, were away for part of a summer, probably in 1963, Joyce and Michael stayed at their house, an arrangement that shocked that respectable neighbourhood because Michael was into playing jazz. One night they had a party with a house full of people, centred around a long table covered with food and candles. Their friends had brought their saxophones and other instruments, so the noise on that summer evening was tremendous. Lawrence, who was home on this occasion, recalled that at one point "one of the neighbours arrived in shorts, clearly about to make one of those statements like 'Stop this!' or — I don't know what he was going to say. He opened the door and walked in and at that point there was some long-haired guy coming down the stairs with a saxophone and other people milling around, some of them with instruments making all this noise, and he looked around and shook his head and walked out again. He just didn't have the tools to deal with whatever it was that was going on."[30]

Joyce and Michael also frequently returned to Toronto for visits at Christmas. On their 1964 trip home they had an accident in their Volkswagen near Alexandria Bay, New York. The car skidded off the highway and hit a post; Christmas gifts were strewn all over the road and the car was beyond repair. Joyce was not hurt, but Michael, unconscious, was taken to the Edward John Noble Hospital in Alexandria Bay where he spent Christmas Day. He had to have his head stitched up and was in the hospital for four

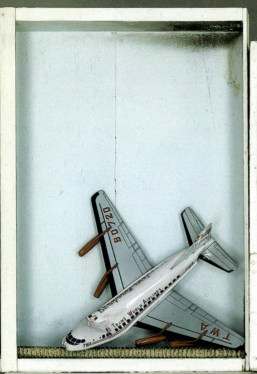
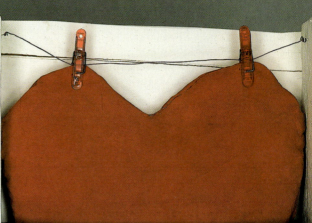
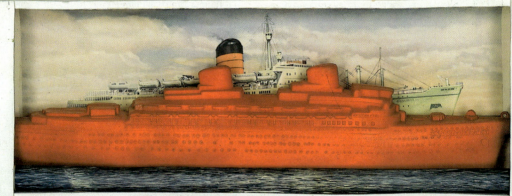
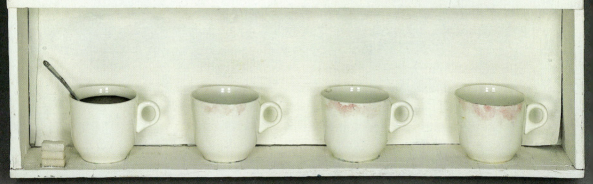

Cooling Room II, 1964.

days.[31] After disposing of the Volkswagen, they gave up having a car while they lived in New York.

Joyce's first show at the Isaacs Gallery after her move to New York was in late 1963. One critic in reviewing this exhibition made an important point about Joyce's work: "She refuses to be pigeonholed; and she leads a life that absolutely defies it."[32] Joyce showed in Canada at least half a dozen times during her nearly ten years in New York — she did not attempt to find a gallery there. The ruthless, cut-throat nature of New York's art world frightened her, and she did not want to become part of it. But it was not only fear that made her pull back. She did not like what she saw happening to women who tried to "make it." She felt these artists became hardened, snobbish and tried to elbow out anyone by whom they felt threatened. And they were unhappy. One woman she knew was obsessed with getting into one of the "good" galleries, and just when she got her foot in the door the gallery went out of business. The artist was devastated. Those women who did achieve a measure of success — Grace Hartigan, Joan Mitchell and Helen Frankenthaler, for example — did so "because they had cast themselves — and were being cast by critics — as disciples and followers of the innovative male founders of the ... Abstract Expressionist movement."[33] Joyce was not willing to be the art disciple of anyone, let alone the men in the club of New York's art world. She was not willing to give up who she was, the point from which she expressed her vision.

Much of Joyce's work in the mid-sixties — the soft sculptures constructed of clear plastic, stitched into pockets and pouches and stuffed with photos and small objects — echoed her work in film and animation. She enjoyed the variety of materials available for making art, particularly clear plastic because of its luminous quality and availability. She credited New York artist Claes Oldenburg and his large, soft sculptures as an influence, but there is no question that Joyce's use of materials and subject matter was completely her own, related to her personal life and vision. Her work at this time reveals that for her there was no division between paintings, quilts and films. She moved back and forth between her media with ease.

The short step from stuffed plastic to quilts was a natural progression, and she deliberately chose this soft medium. Her friend Jacqueline Park, who had also moved from Toronto to New York, said, "Some people make compromises with their vision, but Joyce — I don't think it's a matter of what they call integrity. I think she couldn't be anybody but what she was and she couldn't see anything but what she saw and I think that's what made her such an original. She didn't make any compromise. If she took it into her head to do something, she did it. And not only that, but after she moved to the States, it seems to me it got worse. I mean, she went from conventional,

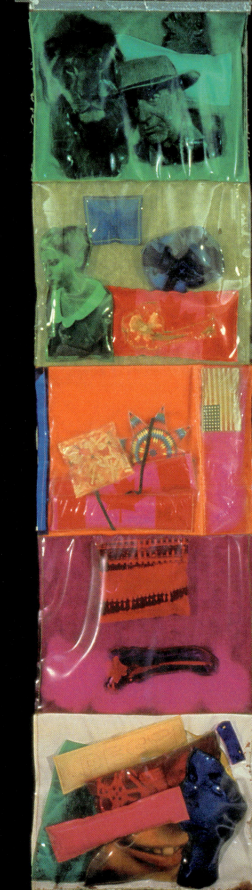

Stuffed Movie,
1966.

respectable media, like oil paint, right back to Titian, to quilts. Quilts! What is that?"[34]

In her choice of subject matter as well as the fabric medium, she was stating unequivocally that domestic interests deserved a place in art. She did not join the women's movement fermenting in the United States while she lived in New York, but she felt she was helping women through her work.[35] According to art historians Rozsika Parker and Griselda Pollock, "Any association with the traditions and practices of needlework and domestic art can be dangerous for an artist, especially when that artist is a woman."[36] Joyce was willing to risk the danger of not being taken seriously, even though she inhabited an intense "guy world," as she had in the Isaacs Gallery circle in Toronto. She did not want to do "guy work." She dared to bring her traditional female fabric medium into the realm of "real art" and included her domestic interests, her kitchen, her house and herself in it, along with what these represented, themes she so brilliantly developed in *Water Sark*.

By continuing her statement of the domestic in fabric, she became a pioneer in the medium. She was ahead of the revival of quilt making, which generally did not take place until "the early seventies concomitant of the general renewal of interest ... as an early feminist model of communal women's work."[37] Joyce's first quilts predated by five years the explosion of women's work in many media at Womanhouse in Los Angeles, California, which opened to the public in January 1972 around the same time that the Toronto-born American artist Miriam Schapiro began making quilts. Joyce's quilts were her contribution to what Parker called the "subversive stitch" by which women have "managed to make meanings of their own in the very medium intended to inculcate self-effacement."[38]

Aside from philosophical motivations for making quilts, there were other reasons for Joyce, which were tied up with her sister. By the late fifties, Joan had started making quilts — she had taught herself to sew when her children were small — and Joyce liked what she was doing. Joyce had started using cloth in some of her works a number of years before she moved to New York, and as she explained it, "there was this thing about her doing cloth and me doing cloth."[39] For Joan and Joyce to work together would have been a challenge because of their history within their family. One of Joan's daughters, Lois Stewart Taylor, said that even though Joan talked about "the good things," she was also bitter about her childhood. Taylor thinks the relationship between the two sisters had improved once Joan was in charge of Joyce. Joan "had a lot of animosity toward Joyce" because of Joyce's preferential treatment in the family and after they were on their own, Joan "learned to really love her as a sibling, or even a daughter."[40]

When Joan began making quilts, Joyce encouraged her to sell them as a

Michael and Joyce, her hand held in a position characteristic of Napoleon, in New York in 1964. The Statue of Liberty is in the background, centre.

way of making an income, but Joan gave them away instead. Joyce decided to design a quilt and hire Joan to do the sewing, partly to help Joan out and partly because it saved her time. Joyce's first quilt was made for Donna and George Montague's son Michael when he was five years old. Joyce did the design and basted the pieces the way she wanted them and Joan finished it.

When Joyce designed *Film Mandala* (1966), again she hired Joan to do the sewing, and Joyce's exploration of the quilt medium was launched, in partnership with her sister.[41] For the next eleven years, Joan, and often her daughters, did most of the sewing on Joyce's quilts, including the large commissions that required solving structural problems, the kind of work Joyce turned over to Joan because she had a more practical mind.

Eventually Joyce and Joan would have enough of quilt making. The last one they would make was *Lens* (1978-79). This was an excerpt from a poem by Anne Wilkinson, the letters of the words formed in fabric, stuffed and stitched on a fabric background. Wilkinson, a southern Ontario poet, was virtually self-taught, and Joyce loved her writing for its warmth and expression of emotion and use of imagery. Joyce used the first lines of Wilkinson's "Lens": "The poet's daily chore/Is my long duty;/To keep and cherish my good lens/For love and war/And wasps about the lilies/And mutiny within." Joyce's work in quilts would finish as it began, with the camera and film as subject matter.

After a few years of living on Greenwich Street, Joyce and Michael moved into an eighty-foot loft at 123 Chambers Street. This was also an industrial area with some of the oldest shops of Manhattan, just west of City Hall and City Hall Park. To the east was South Street and the South Street Seaport, where one could go in the early morning to buy cheap fish. South Street ends at the South Street Ferry slip at the south end of Manhattan; at one time ships docked there from all over the world, bringing cheeses, teas, coffee and herbs.

Chinatown, too, was within walking distance, and offered inexpensive foods. To the north-west was cobblestoned Duane Street with interesting old buildings and fruit markets, an area now completely renovated. At midnight the hand trucks could be heard clattering across the cobblestones as the merchants moved in fresh fruit to sell the next day.

Shops on Chambers Street sold electronics, handbags, clothing, and on one corner was a shoemaker. Some shopkeepers were suspicious of artists, but Joyce won over many of them and they came to enjoy talking to her.[42] In 123 Chambers were a variety of people and enterprises. Joyce and Michael lived on the third floor, and on the sixth floor lived Eugene Lion and Jo Lechay, who also became their friends and who now have a performing arts company in Montreal. Between these two lofts, on the fourth floor was a mail-order book business and on the fifth another painting studio. The first two floors were occupied by a company that manufactured and repaired boat propellers. Across the street lived a photographer, Marilyn Rudd (now Marilyn Schwartz) and the musician Roswell Rudd, who was then her husband.

When Joyce and Michael moved to Chambers Street, as had been the case in the Greenwich Street loft, there was no plumbing — no kitchen or shower or toilet — and no gas or electricity. Friends who were "underground" electricians wired the loft and tapped gas lines so Joyce and Michael could have access to heat and light. Whether or not they knew it, these artists living illegally in Lower Manhattan's lofts during the sixties were not the first ones to steal utilities. In the previous decades, such artists as Bill and Elaine de Kooning, when they first started out, also bypassed electrical meters with ingenious wiring and tapped into telephone wires to avoid phone bills.[43] For Joyce, living with these elements of secrecy, including covering the windows with black cloth, made the New York years more exciting.

The kitchen area — and the entire loft — had few non-essentials, but Joyce did have a blender for whipping up their high-energy shakes. Michael also had his piano, which he often played when he was at home, and good sound equipment for listening to music. The space was arranged similarly to the previous loft — a living area at one end and Joyce's studio at the other. When she began working on quilts, this is where she kept her bolts of fabric and her old treadle Singer sewing machine that she had electrified. Michael had rented a loft on Canal Street for his studio. The shared loft also had a filmmaking cubicle where they kept their equipment.

With few furnishings, they could more easily disguise that they lived there if inspectors came. A specially devised peep-hole in the door allowed them to look out without being seen, in case the inspectors knocked. If they suspected anyone was checking up on them, they did not answer the door and kept very quiet until they heard the footsteps go away. They also carried their bags of garbage a number of blocks away from their building to avoid being detected — they had heard of people being apprehended while they were disposing of garbage.

Joyce's friends remember the Chambers Street loft as homey and comfortable. The floor was painted a gunmetal grey, and the brick walls white. The kitchen table was the focus of the loft. Sitting there with Joyce for tea, she gave her friends a feeling of warmth and light humour, and yet behind it all there was a "sad gaiety about Joyce. There was always something that was on the verge of tears," and various friends puzzled over what this was about.[44]

Although Joyce enjoyed this industrial area, she was also frightened, and

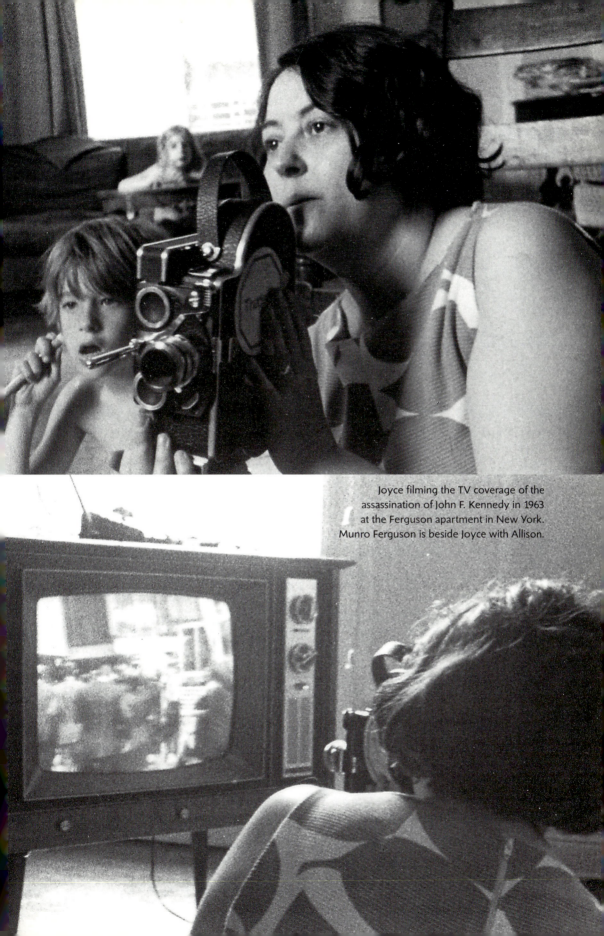

Joyce filming the TV coverage of the assassination of John F. Kennedy in 1963 at the Ferguson apartment in New York. Munro Ferguson is beside Joyce with Allison.

was aware in general of the violence in the United Sates. Only a year after they had arrived in New York, President John F. Kennedy had been assassinated. She had spent days in front of the television with Betty Ferguson in the Ferguson apartment, and like many Americans, Joyce was stunned and distressed. She sat in front of the television set and filmed off it, but never made a film with the footage.

Several years later Joyce was accosted outside their loft. As Michael remembered the incident, she was just outside their building unlocking the door when a man grabbed her. Joyce yelled and Michael came running down the stairs and her attacker disappeared. To Joyce it was an invasive experience, and she told someone the man had pulled out a chunk of her hair. Afterwards, she burned the clothes she was wearing, as well as her new shoes, and went to bed for a week. She did not call the police.[45] Another time someone broke into their Chambers Street loft and stole some sound equipment. This kind of incident, and living in a rough neighbourhood in general, made Joyce extremely wary and often afraid. In Toronto she often went out for a walk at night when she was working and needed a break, but in New York walking alone at night was out of the question.

Nevertheless, New York gave her entry into the world of experimental filmmaking. It happened this way. Filmmaker Bob Cowan, the friend with whom they had stayed when they were considering moving to New York, invited Michael and Joyce to attend an informal film screening at his apartment.[46] There they met the twin brothers George and Mike Kuchar. The Kuchars, more than ten years younger than Joyce and Michael, were born in Manhattan's lower east side and grew up in the Bronx. They had spent a lot of time watching television as they were growing up, and listened to crime drama on the radio. They had already made a film at age fourteen, the same year Joyce and Michael had married. When they met Cowan, they had been intrigued by this Canadian gentleman, and they were even more fascinated when they met two more Canadians named Snow and Wieland. Little did the Kuchars know the impact they would have on these two artists from the North.

The Kuchars' films were a revelation because they opened up the possibility of film as an art form for Joyce and Michael. Joyce was particularly impressed by their style, by their use of irony and caricature. Also, the Kuchar brothers made their films about whatever interested them, with very little money. They and their friends worked this way because they loved it and freely learned from each other and even acted in each other's films. Joyce immediately sensed that these experimental filmmakers were very different from the painters she had met and observed. The sometimes nasty competitive spirit among painters did not figure among the filmmakers, and she felt comfortable with them.

Among the filmmakers they met was a couple introduced by Bob Cowan, Ken and Florence Jacobs, who often screened films at their place on Ferry Street near the Brooklyn Bridge. In 1966 Ken and Florence also moved to Chambers Street, only a block west of where Joyce and Michael lived by then. Once the two couples became acquainted, they saw each other almost every week and became close friends.

Joyce's interest in film had started long before she lived in New York, and it was she who had introduced Michael to non-Hollywood foreign films through the Toronto Film Society when they were still living in Toronto. He remembers that at one point in New York "we recognized that she was disappointed that I was interested in film." Michael feels it wasn't so much a competitive thing but "just a kind of wanting to clarify your own self, and we were both pretty strong ... in a creative sense."[47] It is easy to understand that in her vulnerable position as artist's wife, Joyce wanted her own realm, and when Michael took to filmmaking, she must have seen that as an infringement on her territory. No wonder, then, that she went even further into her domestic subject matter, which male filmmakers would be incapable of using because it was foreign to their experience.

Around this time Joyce gave art lessons to the young daughters of her friend Jacqueline Park. The two girls, Ellen and Sara Jane, took the subway or bus from their home in New York's Upper East Side to Joyce's loft in Lower Manhattan. She taught the girls to use oils, pastels and charcoal. Ellen Rosenfeld, now a jazz musician, and Sara Jane Arnold, a painter and architect, both remembered that they made collage boxes. "We would soak burlap in glue and water to line the boxes, then paint them," Ellen described. "I put cardboard creatures in a bed structure with cotton balls. I will never forget those boxes."[48] Sarah Jane recalled working with "fabrics, paint, lots of Elmers glue and the act of folding. Joyce was big on hearts and folding them ..."[49] Joyce left a big impression on both girls, and from her they developed their sense of aesthetics.

For Joyce, teaching gave her a chance to enjoy how children experience the world. Whatever longings Joyce had for a child must have been most intense during the sixties, when she was in her thirties and many of her friends were having children. Florence Jacobs remembers that when she was pregnant, for a time the doctor ordered her to stay in bed. Joyce came to visit, brought food and told her to be sure to rest and follow the doctor's orders. She remembers Joyce as extremely generous and caring.[50]

In the mid-sixties, Joyce made a small object that suggests she was trying to come to terms with not being able to conceive a child — a beautifully painted cigar box into which she had placed a folded, quilted construction. She called it *Josephine Box*, a reference to Napoleon's wife. Nestled into a section of the quilt are three stuffed figures, the largest one about three inches long, the second slightly smaller and the third smaller still. The figures are penises — they each have two red balls — but they also look like babies covered with a tiny red-stained quilt with a red heart.[51]

This box appeared in a film by Ken Jacobs, in which Joyce had a role. She played Love's Labour in *The Sky Socialist* (1965-67), and had the responsibility of keeping "the Brooklyn Bridge in tip-top shape."[52] In the film, she wears workman's pants, an oil can tucked into her belt, pliers hanging out of one pocket, and wrenches in the tool loops. And she goes around making repairs to the monumental bridge with Scotch tape. But in one scene, Joyce sits on a park bench and holding the small box, she lifts the tiny quilt and looks at the figures underneath. Jacobs described Joyce in that scene as "looking out on life and being somewhat separate from it ... her aging coming through and her longing."[53] In this film, Joyce revealed her unique ability to be both amused by and distanced from the predicament of experiencing her own longings.

Her 1963 oil painting *Heart-Break* shows four hearts, the first one whole, with a tiny sailboat — enclosed inside a round lens — riding on its right side. The second heart has no boat, but a tiny crack appears in the top centre. In the third heart, the crack has grown longer, right down the middle, and the fourth heart is completely broken apart. The year she painted the hearts she had learned from her medical tests that it was unlikely she would have children. But there was also something else that gave her great sorrow.

During the New York years, she was still passionately in love with Michael, but "there was the occasional other woman,"[54] as he put it. Eugene Lion remembered coming upon Joyce in her loft and she was crying. He asked if he could help, and she said "'The only person who can help me is Michael, if he stops.' Something like that — this is now over thirty years ago, so I'm giving you the gist of it."[55] They were both very discreet about Michael's other women, Lion recalled. "She did not get too specific, but she let me know he was cheating on her and it hurt her. She loved him dearly." Perhaps moving from partner to partner was common — certainly the male's prerogative to have whatever women he chose was part of the whole society. But Lion, like other of Joyce's friends, questioned Michael's right to continue his behaviour when it was clearly hurting Joyce. As early as 1955 Michael had told Joyce he was "amoral," and her response to that in her diary had been, "oh shit! What can we get out of life?"[56] According to Ray Jessel, "Joyce stood it because she adored Michael, but she only stood it I think because she had (for a long while, anyway) the strength to laugh it off ... But the hurt was always there between Mike and Joyce ..."[57]

Many people thought Michael and Joyce seemed suited for each other, beyond the romantic notion of "being meant for each other," and even described them as soul mates. However, some of Joyce's friends wondered whether Joyce actually enjoyed her sex life. It might be a legitimate question. In 1983 she would write in her journal that she stiffened and resisted a man at a certain point in making love, "but not with George [Gingras] and strangely enough not with Mike in the beginning and before the end."[58]

However, there is no question that Joyce and Michael shared an intellectual curiosity, fed each other's imagination and enjoyed each other's wit, banter and wordplay. They sometimes looked at each other's work, not necessarily as a regular practice, but spontaneously when they felt like it. According to Michael, they simply went about doing their own work and got together at suppertime, talking about what was happening like any other couple. To his credit, Michael was not typical in that many men at that time did not want a wife who also had a career. Joyce was a "confirmed artist" when they met and "really couldn't stop it." Michael liked her work and saw no reason why she shouldn't continue.[59] Still, his pursuit of other women fitted an attitude traditionally based on the male right and the artist's need for a muse. For this he had plenty of role models in the history of art.

There were often long periods of time when Joyce was not in touch with her sister and brother, and Joan wrote letters, wanting to hear from Joyce. In August of 1966, Barb, Sidney's wife, died of breast cancer. Sidney found looking after his large family alone and earning enough to support them extremely difficult.[60] The following spring he asked Joan for help, and Sidney and the three youngest children began living with her. He met another woman and the two were getting along well together, giving him some hope about starting a new life. One Friday evening they were cooking dinner together and he planned to introduce her to his children afterwards, but that didn't happen because the same evening he had a fatal heart attack.[61] Joyce returned to Toronto for her brother's funeral.

David, Sidney's oldest son, now a successful forensics specialist on the Toronto police force, had just turned twenty-one and was about to be married. Because he was of age, he could legally take custody of the family and prevent the children from going to foster homes. It was a repetition of what had happened to David's father twenty-six years earlier, except now there were more children and no war to fight in Europe. Although he was the legal guardian, his mother's sisters helped out in looking after the younger ones.

For some reason unknown to both David and younger brother Glenn, Joan, without discussion with anyone else, decided to keep Glenn with her, and that summer Joyce invited him to New York for a month to stay with her and Michael. Was she considering adopting him? There is no evidence that she ever revealed her thoughts about it if she did contemplate the idea.

Children have a way of observing adults and revealing things grown-ups might not notice or speak about. The point of view of an eleven-year-old provides an interesting picture of Joyce and Michael in their loft, for Glenn retained some clear memories of living with them.[62] To him, climbing the stairs to their loft seemed to take forever. There, he discovered a toilet with a pull-chain mounted on a platform. He slept on a bed built on top of a cupboard, with a ladder to get to it. He concluded that Joyce and Michael liked things high, because everything was high where they lived.

Every day Glenn went with Joyce to buy fresh fruits and vegetables, and frequently fish. When she cooked fish, it was not some small frozen thing, but a salmon "three-quarters the size of the table." The meals were always huge, though there were only three people to eat everything.

At that time, Joyce was working on *Rat Life and Diet in North America* (1968), so the loft was full of gerbil cages, as many as ten or fifteen, according to Glenn. She filmed the gerbils over a period of six months. The movie screen was always set up at the end of the loft, and at night, Glenn lay in his bed and watched as Joyce worked on the pieces of the film, the retakes, then the final version.

Glenn also remembers Michael's big piano, and that he allowed him to play it. Sometimes Michael played his trumpet at the same time and the two made "free-spirited music" together. Other times they had long conversations. It seemed Joyce and Michael and had a lot of fun together, but Glenn noticed that they had "two separate worlds and the only time they went away from those two worlds was when they were together in their house."[63] Not only did they have two separate worlds, but they each had separate ideas. Though they never had fights in front of him, they sometimes argued and talked about whether they should do one thing or another. Glenn observed that Joyce felt she had to prove something, and he thought that was why she worked so hard on her films.

Even though Joyce and Michael respected each other's work in many ways, Glenn's perception that they lived in two separate worlds was accurate, and the distance grew as Joyce expanded her understanding of women's place in a male-dominated society. *Water Sark* had revealed that her view of herself in the world was changing. Though she had always worked from a female perspective, her outlook had been focused on herself in relation to the male. In *Water Sark* she gave herself over to her imagination and ventured beyond her earlier point of view, farther into her own self. In doing so, she was opening herself to feminism, though at the time she did not use that term.

Interestingly, the film preceding *Water Sark* was about wieners. In *Patriotism Part I* (1964), animated wieners leap on a man who is sleeping in bed. "They

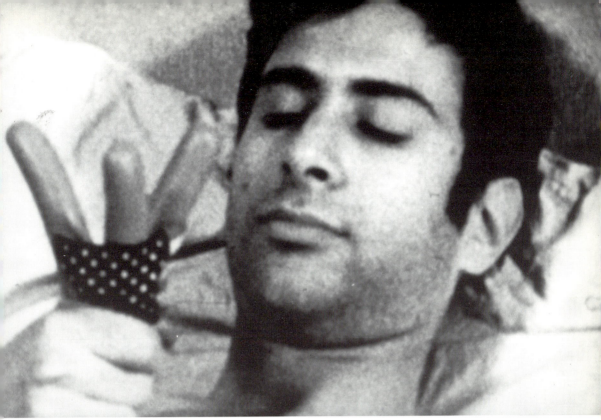

Still from *Patriotism II*, 1964.

march up the bed in military formation and perform all kinds of drills while he's asleep and then they all have their fight and fuck each other and go under the covers and he wakes up and finds all these things around."[64] In their patriotism, the wieners also wrap themselves in an American flag, a symbol of male, political domination. As Joyce gradually made a shift away from using phallic images as subject matter, she also began thinking more about Canada and its relation to the United States.

Rat Life and Diet in North America (1968) was Joyce's first film with a political reference in which she developed a point of view on Canada, as a safe place for those wanting to escape repression. She had been reading an article in *Scientific American* about how crowded conditions affect mice, that they become vicious — and she thought that crowding must affect people the same way. These ruminations prompted her to create *Rat Life*.

The "rats" in the film, who are actually gerbils descended from the Ferguson children's pets, escape from their cage and evade those who held them prisoners, the cats. On their way they have many adventures, including breaking into the house of a millionaire and stuffing themselves with rich foods from his table. They arrive in Canada in time for cherry season and have a cherry festival and celebrate with a flower ceremony as well. There they will live in peace and grow their own organic vegetables.

The narrative of the film, with the winsome little animals standing in for humans, is beguiling. This was Joyce's arena for creating her own counterpart to her much-loved Beatrix Potter stories, this one a simple tale that encapsules a strong political statement. The year after she made the film, Jonas Mekas declared that after seeing it eight times, he still thought it "the best (or richest) political movie around." And also one of the most original.[65]

Joyce's use of the camera in the film gives the scenes the effect of paintings. Close-ups of a domestic environment, a teapot and fruit, are populated by the gerbils nibbling among wine glasses, fruit, cakes, flowers and china. The kitchen table again plays a dominant role. But in this film we are introduced to an additional player, the country of Canada, which was, in Joyce's mind, female, particularly in its position beside the United States. At one point in the film she shows us the American flag rolled up into an obviously phallic shape, but the Canadian flag is flat and the meaning is reinforced by the text, "Canada, which is 72% owned by the U.S. Industrial complex." Exploitation of Canada, particularly its land, is a theme she would explore, and would go to great lengths to develop in the first half of the seventies in her one and only feature film.

During the late sixties she was in a panic about Canada, "an ecological, spiritual panic about this country." This land painted by The Group of Seven was losing its soul to "old shoes and hamburger buns in those lakes" — to commercialization.[66] Her panic would motivate her to make the country the subject of most of her art for the ten years following its Centennial, and to photograph the country on a train trip from Toronto to Vancouver in early 1968. Canada was her lodestone, drawing her back like a magnet, and whether or not she had yet started talking about returning, it seemed in her heart she had already come home.

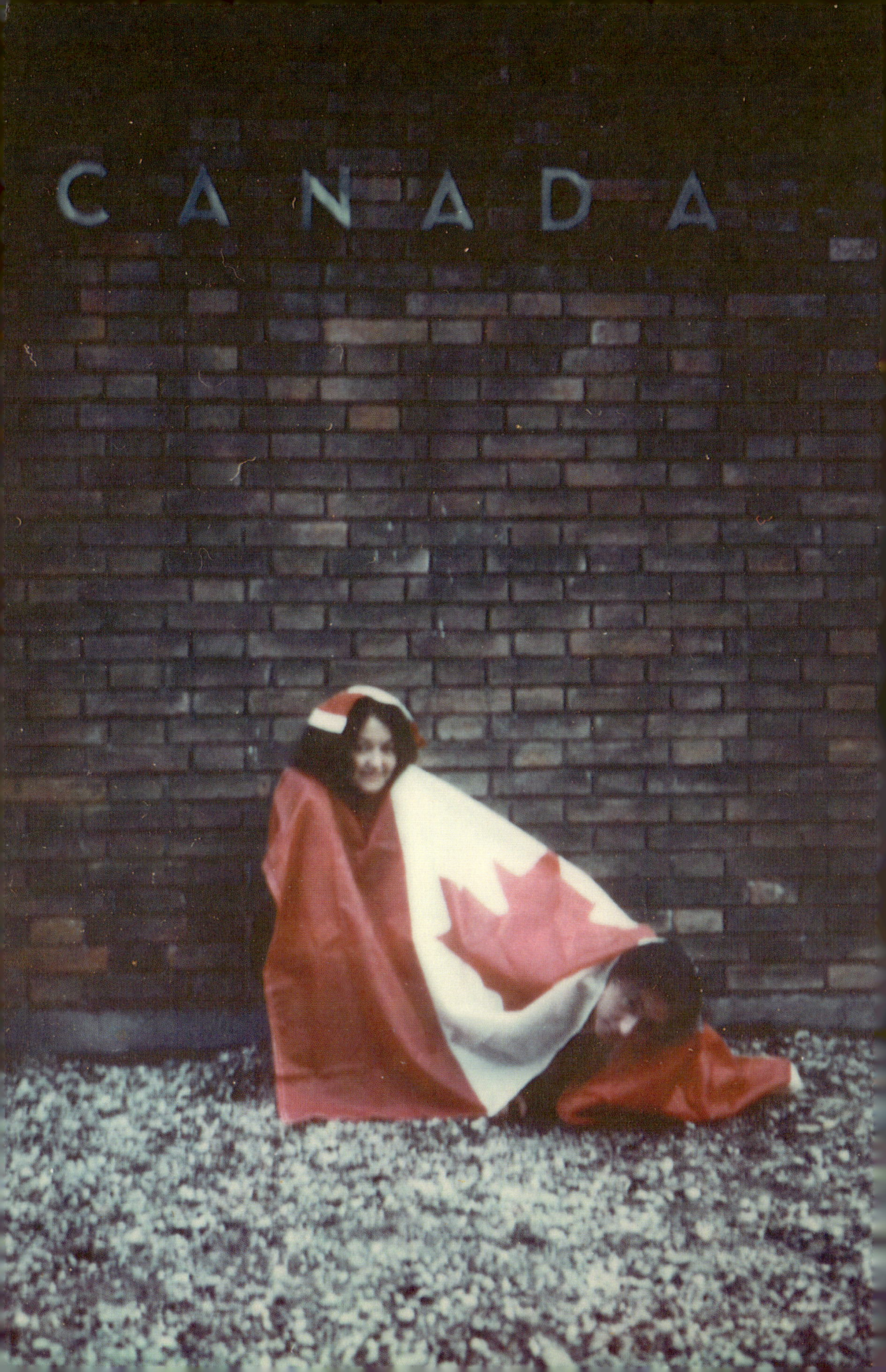
CANADA

6

The true patriot returns

By the late 1960s ... only a few women had been bold enough to paint essentially from their experience as women. In fact, denying they were women seemed to be the women artists' passport to professional acceptance and success. —Maria Tippett[1]

FOR JOYCE, 1967 was the year of *Bill's Hat*, her multimedia performance that one reviewer described as stretching "one's perceptions to just below the pain threshold."[2] Besides waking up people's senses, did *Bill's Hat* also modify people's perceptions of Joyce? By Canada's Centennial year, she was the country's most successful (woman) artist. She had had four solo exhibitions in Canada, and her work had been displayed in nearly twenty group shows. Not only that, but she was a part of Canada's most famous artist couple. What was not yet known was the intensity with which her life was bound up with the country, and how her work would give a visual manifestation to the fervent nationalism of the period.

Spirited celebrations took place across the country — Canada was one hundred years old. This was also the year that Prime Minister Lester Pearson set up the Royal Commission on the Status of Women; an event which, as a

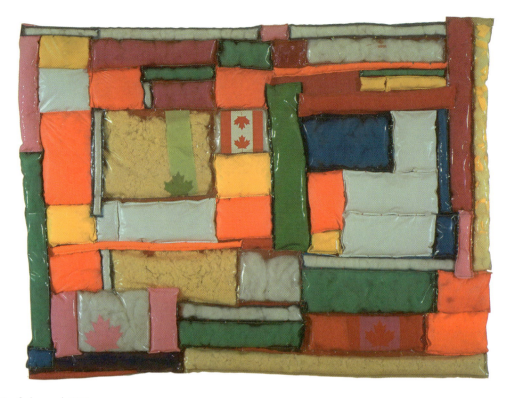

Confedspread, 1967.

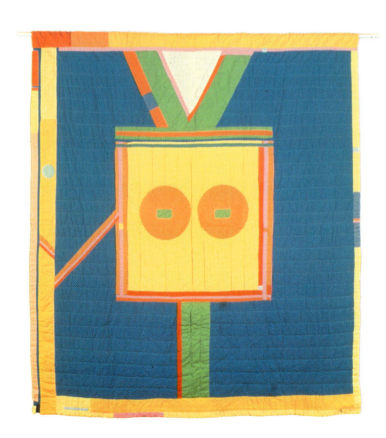

*The Camera's
Eyes, 1966.*

milestone for women, was perhaps of greater consequence than the Centennial.[3] The rise in nationalism coincided with women's push through the barriers of a male-dominated society. Joyce would become a voice for both movements.

In fact, with all of her activity, she seemed to be Ms. Centennial in 1967 — she was fully engaged with a schedule of shows that required her to travel frequently between New York and Canada. To begin with, in the spring she had another show at the Isaacs Gallery. She came to Toronto again in August for the first performance of *Bill's Hat* at Toronto's festival of experimental film, the Cinethon at Cinecity on Yonge Street; and returned once more when it was performed at the Art Gallery of Ontario. She also returned for Expo 67 in Montreal, as both she and Michael showed their work there.

Joyce usually stayed with Donna and George Montague when she visited Toronto, but when she came for her Isaacs show she stayed with Diane and Abe Rotstein. Diane was a biologist and Abe a political economics professor at the University of Toronto. They were both nationalists and had much in common with Joyce. From the Rotsteins, she learned about Canadian economics, and she fed these ideas into her work. At the end of March the birth of the Rotsteins' second child was imminent. One morning during breakfast, as Joyce was eating her wheat germ and praising its merits, Diane went into labour as she sat listening to Joyce and watching her eat the stuff, which did not appeal to Diane. As Joyce's wheat-germ discourse developed, Diane's labour pains intensified. Later, Diane joked that watching Joyce eat wheat germ brought on her labour. As a biologist, Diane understood the properties of such things as nutritional yeast and wheat germ, and although Joyce was long on enthusiasm, her "biology was off," as Diane put it.[4] Nevertheless, Joyce enjoyed her own discourses on food, and included references to them in her work.

Her Isaacs Gallery show of paintings, plastic hangings and quilts was described as "vintage Wieland," which implies that she offered something unique — images that grew out of her own particular vision. In his review, Harry Malcolmson went so far as to say that Canadian art had two parts: "Joyce Wieland in one section and the rest in the other." He explained that other artists "have a masculine aggressiveness even when they are humorous."[5] In other words, in Canadian art in 1967 there were the male artists and then there was Joyce — unapologetically female. Although Joyce deserved the praise in this review (a number of reviews at the time described Joyce's appearance as much as her work), it also reveals how few female colleagues she had in the Canadian art world.

At the Isaacs show, Joyce's recent work in film was reflected in such constructions as *The Camera's Eyes* (1966) and *Film Mandala* (1966). Some of her clear, plastic hangings referred to the Vietnam War and commented on the meaning of the Americans' actions there. *Betsy Ross, look what they've done to the flag you made with such care* (1966) is the title of one work, in which red lips spit out a piece of the American flag to which a small band-aid has been applied. Not only did Joyce portray the American flag as stained by the country's aggression, but in choosing her title she deftly told the story of a woman's work being desecrated and disregarded — by alluding to the well-known legend that Betsy Ross made the first American flag. By way of contrast, the show also features *Confedspread* (1967), another colourful, stuffed-plastic piece, predominately red, with green, yellow and blue stuffing and featuring the maple leaf — another kind of statement about a different country.[6] If people thought stuffed plastic hangings strange, they would be even more nonplussed by *Bill's Hat*.

Joyce had won a $1,000 commission from Cinecity's Cinethon, which gave her a chance to try something completely different from the films she had made. She explained *Bill's Hat* in an Art Gallery of Ontario press release in November. "The opening sequence shows the story of the mythical Birth of *Bill's Hat* (the hat of Brotherhood and Love). The wood nymphs of the upper Hudson River Region in solemn ceremony bring forth from sylvan glades the wondrous, friendly furry crown — of commonness. The whole film (and slides) are non-art portraits of people in which they do what they want with this hat — and therefore, act or stand in front of my camera. It's only love: therefore it can't harm you."

An account of the origin of *Bill's Hat* formed part of a fascinating conversation Joyce had with Wendy Michener, Joyce's close friend, a journalist and art critic.[7] Joyce's friends liked wearing her old racoon-fur hat, and it looked different on each person. This gave her the idea of traveling around the United States and Canada to give many people a chance to wear her hat. Very quickly she discovered that people revealed their personality by the way they responded to her request that they put on the hat. Some didn't want to wear it. Others sniffed it first and then put it on, as though they were afraid of bugs or a contagious disease. "The really square and inhibited ones just stuck it on top of their head, like a chef's hat." Joyce photographed many people wearing the hat, hundreds, she claimed, and captured a diverse group — Jack Bush, Jean Sutherland Boggs, Judy Lamarsh, A.Y. Jackson and Timothy Leary among them.

In their conversation, Wendy sensed there was something Joyce was not saying, and she persisted with questions. Joyce hesitated. "I don't want to get into that because that involves maybe something I can't talk about" — an unusually timid response for someone who had made dozens of lover drawings.

"Really?" Wendy replied.

"Well, you know, it's like a pussy, and it's going out and bugging the whole world." She spoke in a small, naughty-sounding tone of voice, and the two of them giggled.

"It's a pussy hat because it's so furry," said Wendy.

"Yeah. A female thing. I realized half-way through what it was all about. Me being friendly, me and my hat." And from there the conversation turned to Joyce's description of filming what she described as the birth ritual of the hat.

The setting of the opening scenes was the country home in New York State of Jacqueline and Ben Park. Children dressed in summery cotton nightgowns and stepping lightly as though they were walking on air, frolicked through the woods carrying a large sheet stretched between them with the fur hat lying in the middle. As the sun's rays streamed through the trees, the children flapped the sheet up and down to bounce the hat.

"So these magical children with the wonderful mother ... I wanted them to be innocent and I wanted it a ritual. That's how they bring forth the hat on a blanket and they have this ritual of throwing it into the air ... and then they go down deep into this grotto and then they lay out the white blanket and put the hat on it and then the one little chubby girl asked them all to move in [close to the blanket], but no one knows why. They're all moving in and staring at this hat. I guess it's some kind of birth ritual. It's hard to talk about it. That's what's so good about it. It's on film and it's beyond words." This conversation, along with the AGO press release, reveal Joyce's wistful pantheism, her yearning that all things be beautiful and loving; and her romantic notions about mothers and children.

However, this idyllic film was only a part of the whole performance of *Bill's Hat*, which included an altar with a hundred candles and pots of flowers. From the ceiling hung a pillow shaped like a heart. A woman lay silently on top of a piano with the hat on her belly. Besides the fifty-minute movie projected on a screen, four simultaneous slide shows featured the "hundreds" of people wearing the hat, and some of those sitting in the audience had small, hand-held projectors that projected images on the backs of others. Strobe lights did for the eyes what the sound did for the ears, music from two live bands, Stu Broomer's Kinetic Ensemble and The 25th Hour, a rock band that included Joyce's nephew, Keith Stewart. Apparently the two bands produced "a writhing welter of sound."[8]

Joyce wanted the audience to give themselves over to this environment. Wendy thought the music and Joyce's concept clashed, so Joyce tried to convince her. "First of all ... just sit on the music and it'll just carry you through the whole experience and naturally you're going to be watching the film, and you might miss some things. ... You might be looking at the slides ..., you might just get involved with one of the musicians' faces. ... So you're going to miss things. In other words, it's not a bourgeois experience where you're given something and there it is, your money's worth ... one film and there it is. Most people miss half the things in a film. ... You're going to miss things. Isn't that too bad! You're going to get other things ... Sometimes you're going to get the whole thing."

It's not surprising that Toronto audiences didn't know what to make of *Bill's Hat*, since they were not used to such a mixture of sights and sounds. Joyce claimed that Torontonians were hungry for this kind of thing, but that might have been wishful thinking, considering the audience sat quietly the whole time, hardly a sign of giving in to the experience.

With her shows in Canada behind her, Joyce returned to New York, but she kept tabs on what was happening in Ottawa. In December Prime Minister Lester Pearson announced he would retire, so a Liberal leadership convention would be held in the spring to elect a new leader. As Pearson's minister of justice, Pierre Elliott Trudeau was a possible candidate. He became known in English Canada partly because John Diefenbaker, who had a Conservative "country lawyer" appearance, criticized Trudeau's clothes for their "foreign influences and God knows what other deviltry." Even among Liberals, Trudeau at first did not seem a serious contender. However, a short time after Pearson announced his intention to retire, Trudeau brought before the House a bill to reform divorce and "several amendments to the Criminal Code liberalizing laws on abortion and homosexuality ... Trudeau made the changes his own by telling the television cameras outside the House, 'The state has no place in the bedrooms of the nation.'"[9] Joyce approved. She did not yet know that Trudeau would become a part of the film she would begin that winter.

In January, Joyce had a retrospective at the Vancouver Art Gallery and decided to travel west by train, accompanied by Wendy Michener and Rose Richardson. She took her camera, and filmed hours and hours of footage out the train window to capture the winter landscape as they went.

"[I] got on the train with the Bolexes and tape machine, and as soon as we got past Lake of the Woods the snow started, and it was the most idyllic, exquisite trip I think I've ever taken in my entire life. As soon as we came to the Prairies, it was just this vast glacial winter and then into British Columbia where the trees were heavily laden with snow and I photographed every day all day from the train window. I used every possible combination of the camera, fooling around with exposures, using different film stocks, different camera speeds."[10] Joyce fell in love with the land, but she had no idea what she would do with this footage.

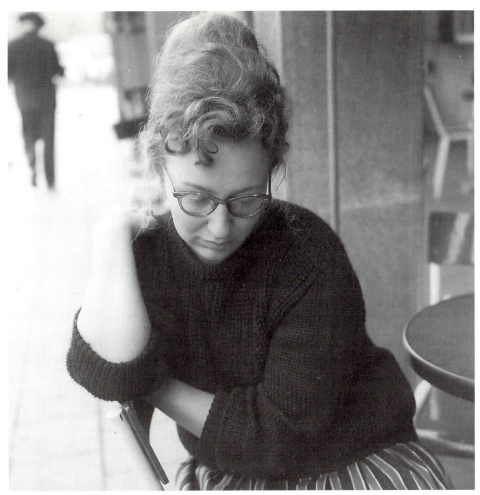

Wendy Michener, 1960.

At the Vancouver Art Gallery, Wendy and Joyce taped a conversation about many of the individual pieces in the exhibition, which included forty-six paintings, drawings, constructions and plastic and cloth hangings dating from 1958 to 1967. One of the first quilts, *Square Mandala* (1966) had a special meaning for Joyce because she felt it expressed something that came from her centre and the depth of her mind — she believed Carl Jung's concepts of symbolism. The vibrating, narrow bands of colour reminded her of "the colour inside my head ... That really has to do with my soul." Joyce achieved the specific colours she wanted by working with unbleached cotton, which she shrank with boiling water and then hand dyed. For a pure white colour, she used Egyptian cotton.

Another piece in the show was an ink drawing called *Air Pollution Sketch for "This City Now" Mural* (1967).[11] Joyce felt this project commissioned by the Art Gallery of Ontario was the best cartoon type work she had ever done. "I did

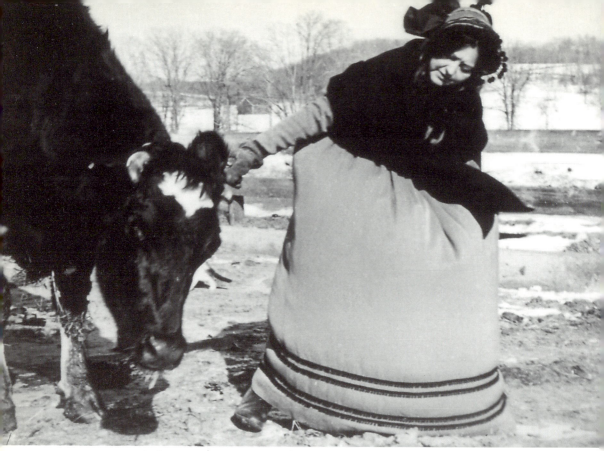

Joyce in the late sixties in Upper New York State reenacting Laura Secord's legendary trek with a cow during the War of 1812.

about seven or eight hundred drawings to get to that. All for $250!" she said. This cartoon was her working drawing, which she then transferred onto a wooden fence in the AGO exhibition, "This City Now," a show intended to explore in a variety of media the problems and pleasures of city life.

The cartoon included a number of situations, one of which was a couple having a picnic at a place marked "Picnic Area" beside a lake. Smoke pours out of the chimney of the Sunshine Chemicals Company near the tiny knoll where the man and woman are sitting, and the woman says to the man, "Eat your sandwich before it gets dirty." One fish in the water cries for help, and another says, "barf." Joyce dedicated the cartoon to the women who had influenced her thinking about the environment, our food, and ecology — Rachel Carson, Adelle Davis and Jane Jacobs. These topics infused much of her work at a time when few people thought about these issues.

When Pierre Trudeau ran for the Liberal Party, Joyce, like many other Canadians, was taken by his wit, charm and intelligence. And he was a strong federalist. She became interested in Trudeau in the same way she had become preoccupied with Napoleon nearly ten years earlier.

In March 1968, Joyce and Michael received a phone call from Mary

Mitchell, a great-great-great-grand-daughter of Joyce's heroine, Laura Secord, and a Canadian playwright then living in New York. She suggested they organize themselves in support of Trudeau, which they did, and called themselves Canadians Abroad for Trudeau. Within a short time they created a "bogus movement" for him in New York, a movement they knew didn't really exist.

It took Mitchell and Joyce only two weeks to organize a cocktail party in Trudeau's honour. They invited a hundred Canadians. Sixty people showed up for the party on the eleventh floor of the Columbia Pictures Corporation Building. Lloyd Burns, then president of Screen Gems International and a Torontonian who had lived in New York for ten years, acted as host for the evening. Trudeau himself was not there, but he sent a special filmed greeting, which was shown after a screening of a televised interview of Trudeau conducted by the writer Pierre Berton.

The Liberal leadership convention was held in Ottawa in the first week of April. Mitchell suggested to Joyce that they attend. They did, and Joyce took her camera. Somehow, she managed to get one of the best seats in the press section of the Ottawa Civic Centre and was close enough to study Trudeau's face. She filmed him for five hours before the moment he became leader of the Liberal Party. Throughout that time, when she ran out of film, people from the CBC press corps and others passed film to her, providing her with as much as a thousand extra feet of film to keep shooting.[12] Joyce had no idea what she would do with the footage, but she was having a good time and indulged in scrutinizing every aspect of Trudeau's face and gestures. She was fascinated by him, "a guy who seemed fantastic, who acted like he didn't want power and was an intellectual."[13] But Joyce had missed something, for her own film footage revealed the facial expressions of a man relishing his climb to the most powerful position in the country.

On the return trip from Ottawa to New York, Joyce and Mitchell were still discussing Trudeau and reading about him. Joyce mulled over his ideas about reason and logic in politics. When she read that he touted reason over passion in government, she jokingly told Mary she would make a quilt about "reason over passion." Though Trudeau himself was cool and utterly reasonable, he aroused a great deal of emotion and passion in other people. He was Joyce's ideal subject matter. She compared him to Napoleon and, placing their pictures side-by-side, concluded that they even looked alike. The Napoleon comparison was not just part of Joyce's imagination. According to Trudeau's biographers, "he saw himself as a kind of statesman-general in the mould of Napoleon."[14] Joyce screened her Trudeau film footage with Michael and Hollis Frampton, and then put it away with the landscape footage. She still did not know what she would do with all this.

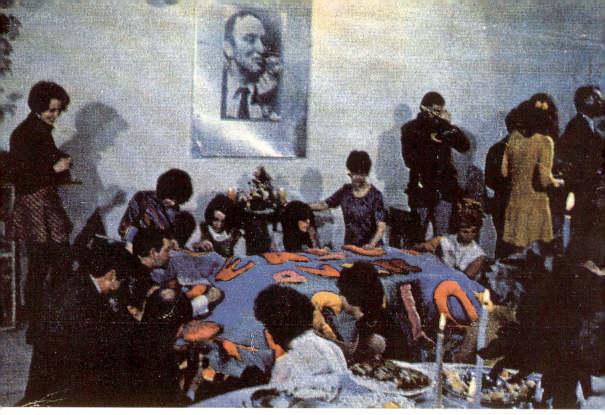

The quilting party for the Trudeau quilt, New York, May 1968.

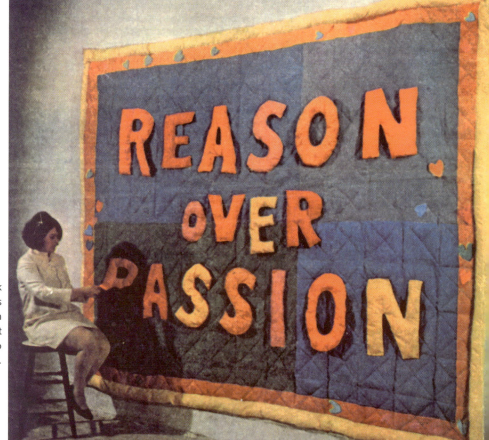

Joyce in New York in the late sixties with the English version of the quilt she gave to Trudeau.

Joyce carried through on her idea of making a quilt about "reason over passion," and on one of New York's beautiful spring days, she hosted a quilting party at her loft on Chambers Street. The invitations for this event were made of see-through pink plastic pockets stitched together with thread and holding a small sheet of paper that read "You are cordially invited to a quilt-in for Prime Minister Pierre Trudeau's Art Quilt Gift Wed. May 21, 4:30." Earlier she had constructed a quilt of hand-dyed cotton in reds, yellows and tones of blue. Inside the back of the quilt, she had stitched private messages to Trudeau, which included quotes from Machiavelli.[15]

By the time of the party, Joyce had machine-stitched the background of the main part of the quilt. A dozen of her guests sat around it, stitching on the letters and tiny hearts. On the wall above the quilters, which included both men and women, was a blow-up photograph of Trudeau playing with a carnation. Many people stood around chatting and sipping Beaujolais, while Ray Jessel, an American who had lived in Toronto from the mid-fifties to the mid-sixties and one of the writers of the Broadway hit *Baker Street*, provided live entertainment on the piano. In the background a projector ran continuously, showing Joyce's film footage of Trudeau at the Liberal convention. Press releases had brought members of the Canadian press, the CBC, and *Time* magazine.

The climax to the afternoon was a ritual. With burning candles placed around the quilt, Joyce's guests threw flowers at it and sang a song written by Jessel. "Who is the man for Canada? Trudeau! Trudeau! Who's got a plan for Canada? Trudeau! Trudeau!"[16]

After filming the western part of the country, Joyce wanted to film in the East. This time she would go by car. With Rose Richardson driving, the two travelled from Toronto to Nova Scotia in June, after Richardson picked up Joyce in New York.[17] Joyce filmed out the car window with her hand-held camera.

Their stop at Cheticamp, Nova Scotia, was a high point in the trip because there Joyce discovered a cooperative of Acadian women who were experts at hooking wool rugs. She loved the colours they used — brick reds, pale blues and white. She decided that someday she would make designs and have this group of women render them. In fact, she would return in 1970 to commission *Eskimo Song — The Great Sea* (1970-71), a piece that would appear in her 1971 show at the National Gallery in Ottawa.[18]

Richardson remembered that one morning in Nova Scotia they got up very early to catch a ferry and saw a spectacular sunrise. They spent much of their time driving around the countryside. From Cape Breton, they came back through mainland Nova Scotia and New Brunswick and returned by way of the Gaspé Peninsula in Quebec and down along the St. Lawrence

River, stopping by the old Denechaud Seigneury in Bertier-en-Bas that had belonged to Michael's mother's family.

After her trip to the East, Joyce realized what all this was about: a "sandwich" film with one part of the country in winter, the other part in summer, into which she would insert Trudeau.[19] Thus, *Reason over Passion* (1967-69), a ninety-minute film, evolved as she spent night and day editing the footage.[20] But Joyce had a technical problem. She had filmed Trudeau with a small lens because her zoom lens had been broken, resulting in medium-shot footage. She rephotographed the Trudeau footage, some in black-and-white and some in colour. At first she was "hysterical" because the result was not what she wanted. However, she did have "a truthful portrait. I showed the [rephotographed] footage to different people and some said, oh, that man is a swine and to other people [he was] fascinating. So I edited it and the whole thing of myself came into it, myself as the third person ... the land, the leader and myself."[21]

By rephotographing Trudeau's face, Joyce achieved a grainy effect and in a sense the face became part of the Canadian landscape, but her film footage also reveals the man and his masks. Perhaps Joyce saw his face as a public persona, and she was trying to unmask him. Ironically, Joyce, with her passion and her unpredictable imagination fuelling her work, was championing someone whose reason overpowered passion. Here was a contradiction typical of Joyce: she railed against the cold intellectual approach, but at the same time was attracted to Trudeau for his place of power and use of wit and intellect, not unlike the way she often felt about her husband.

As Joyce worked on the film, she began fantasizing, what if she were Leni Riefenstahl making a propagandist film?[22] At the same time she told herself that she — and no one else — was making the film, which gave her a sense of responsibility, of being at a distance and yet being a part of the film, being a part of Trudeau as a character and a part of the land.

In the taped conversation between Joyce and Hollis Frampton about three years later, Joyce admitted that Trudeau wasn't as "concerned and impassioned" about Canada as she had thought. Frampton pointed out that as a result she was in a "serious political dilemma, a position other artists have taken in relation to political figures." He continued in this vein, saying that artists must struggle with their illusions, and for Joyce it was Trudeau with his "plastic policies," and that in a way her film would outlast Trudeau because the thought she had injected into the film meant "there are permanent values which inhere in the work which have survived their pretext completely ... What we've been talking about in a way is a commonplace in the history of art, something that Ezra Pound is fond of quoting, a little couplet to the effect that the bust outlasts the throne, the coin, Tiberious. Your film has already, at least in your own mind, outlasted the pivot."

"Not the country," Joyce replied. She seemed quick to assert that Canada would survive. This conversation took place in 1971, and today one wonders whether Joyce would now say that the film outlasted at least the heart of the country, though its physical boundaries still exist. But Joyce saw the film as totally Canadian, while Frampton saw it as equally related to literary art because of its use of language, the 537 permutations of "reason over passion" and Joyce's face mouthing the words of the Canadian national anthem, as though she were teaching Canadians their song or a child to speak. This audio tape, besides revealing Joyce's thoughts at the time, is striking because of the strong resonance in her voice, a quality missing in recordings in the 1980s.[23]

When *Reason over Passion* was screened in New York, Joyce was disappointed that the "avant-garde establishment more or less advised her to return to short pieces rather than to attempt to compete with the major figures of the structural film movement who were by then producing feature-length avant-garde works."[24] However, it was well received at the Cannes Film Festival's Directors Fortnight series. In the late eighties, filmmaker Kay Armatage would call it a "classic of Canadian experimental cinema."[25]

Despite all the work Joyce had done in support of Trudeau, she was still not finished with him. On November 8, 1969, she and Michael hosted a party for him in their loft, where Joyce had staged the quilting party. For this event, she went to great lengths to serve Canadian foods — tourtière (a French-Canadian meat pie) and Canadian cheeses, including Oka, made by Quebec monks. Eugene Lion and Jo Lechay's sixth-floor loft was used for dancing. Eugene remembered that he and Jo were both interviewed before the party in the interest of Trudeau's security, and the night of the event the prime minister arrived with his bodyguards. Eugene described Trudeau as charming, and after taking some time to look at the women, he chose one and began dancing.[26]

On this special evening, Joyce panicked in the middle of the dancing party because her cat, which had a habit of attacking people's legs, had escaped the closet where it had been locked up for the night. For a cat that liked human legs, it was the opportunity of her nine lives. Joyce asked Jonas Mekas to find the cat and lock it up again, which he tried to do by crawling across the floor between people's legs. He was the one who had locked up the cat in the first place when he came early to help prepare for the event.[27]

It was at this party that Joyce gave Trudeau the French half of the pair of quilts, *Reason over Passion/La Raison avant la passion*. Later, when someone asked

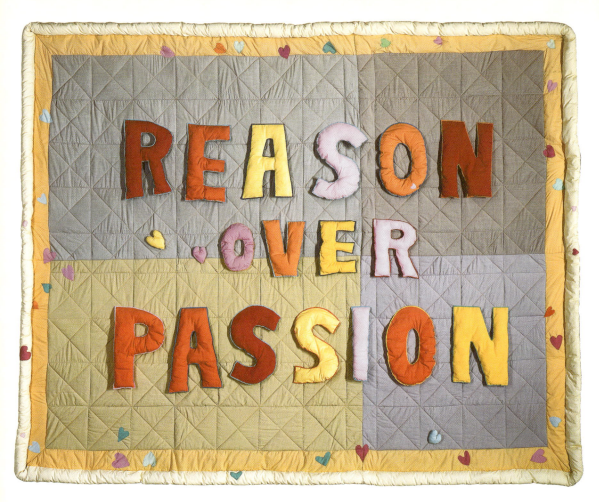

Reason Over Passion, 1968.

him about the quilt and his ardent supporters in New York, he replied, "Reason over passion; that's the theme of all my writings." Joyce was pleased to have yet another quote and concluded that he took it all seriously.[28] In later years, when Trudeau was married, legend has it that his wife Margaret tore the letters from the quilt when they were having a fight, "presumably in an effort to re-arrange her husband's priorities."[29]

Joyce, with Mary Mitchell, organized at least one more nationalistic event. For New Year's of 1970, calling themselves Les Activistes Culturels Canadiens, they took "New Year's Greetings" to the Canadian Consulate. They managed to enlist thirty-five or forty people to occupy the Consulate's tenth floor premises on Fifth Avenue to create something like a New York-style happening. Aaron Grafstein, a Brooklyn man, dressed in a poorly fitting Mountie suit, stood on the street outside the official Canadian travel bureau, which was in the same building as the Consulate, singing "O Canada." "The policeman on the beat came to investigate the disturbance, but found himself posing for Joyce Wieland's pictures, smiling and standing beside Mountie Grafstein."[30]

Joyce and her friends declared the little plot of grass in front of the Consulate part of Canada, Betty Ferguson recalled. As with all the events during which they "misbehaved," the point was to draw attention to Canadian culture. "She loved Canada and there was no way to love Canada more than to not live in it. I mean, if you live somewhere else you miss home."[31] Indeed, for all her love of the country, she could already see that the fight against United States imperialism was almost impossible to win, unless by some miraculous intervention. She admitted that as the struggle became tougher, her fraternizing with "continentalist-minded Canadian government leaders may have to stop, and the Activistes' demonstrations might get to be less amusing."[32] This was not the first time, nor the last, that Joyce Wieland's words would be prophetic.

After the Trudeau party, sometime during the winter, Joyce received a phone call from Pierre Théberge, then the Curator of Contemporary Canadian Art at the National Gallery of Canada in Ottawa. Théberge had admired Joyce's work for several years, and he wanted to curate a show of her art. When he took his idea for a Wieland show to the director of the National Gallery, Jean Sutherland Boggs, she was enthusiastic.

"I just about passed out," Joyce said years later about Théberge's phone call. "I said, well, I'll have to think about that [in a defensive, sparring tone of voice] ... I thought this must be a joke or something. He said, when will you tell me? I said I'll call you back in a week."[33] Joyce accepted. They began working on "True Patriot Love/Véritable amour patriotique", a show that more than fifteen years later Théberge would call "the most beautiful show I ever did."[34]

For Théberge, the impetus to do the show was his belief that Joyce "was a terrific artist." He thought her work should be shown, and "that the National Gallery should recognize her." He was not curating the show just because Joyce was a woman, but as he later said of the lack of recognition for women's work, "It sure took a long time, I mean, poor old Emily Carr, she had a show with somebody in the 1920s ... but to be the first [living] woman to show in the National Gallery in 1971, wow! That took a long time, [but] I had no political agenda at all."[35] Théberge was right that a change of attitude towards the work of women took a long time — Joyce was the first living female artist given a solo exhibition at the National Gallery. And change continued very slowly, for in the decade following "True Patriot Love", only six exhibitions at the National Gallery were the work of female artists, while there were twenty-seven shows by male artists.[36]

Joyce was ready for this show in that she had within her a passion — equal in intensity to Trudeau's reason — to develop a body of work about Canada, and the drive to create objects that would articulate her vision. In her cloth works she had moved from personal subject matter to the political; from the first made in 1966 for a child to one for the man who would be "king."

From the time Joyce first began thinking about her show, she decided she wanted to make a book instead of having a traditional catalogue for *True Patriot Love*. She explained to Théberge what she had in mind, and the two of them went to the Queen's Printer to look at government publications. As Théberge remembered, "She wanted to do something that would look official … that would be like a government book, whatever that is."[37] In other words, a parody in book form of the whole idea of "official" in government. As Joyce looked at the government books, she came upon *Illustrated Flora of the Arctic Archipelago* by A. Erling Porsild (1901–1977).

Joyce's memory of finding the book was fresh in her mind even years later. "First of all, I loved the gold lettering on the red covering and I kept saying I want that cover. I want a book that looks like that. [Théberge] said you can have a book like that, they can just remake it … I said, can I have a flag in the front and a pocket in the back, and he said, everything, and the tissues over the pictures … I got what I wanted, and I loved that cover. They still had the materials available to make that maroon cover."[38] It seems more than coincidental that the book Joyce was drawn to for its appearance turned out to be about Arctic flora. She had been reading everything she could find about Arctic animals, insects and flowers.[39]

Joyce took a copy of the burgundy book back to New York with her and spent a lot of time looking at it. "I just played … and I photographed and rephotographed a lot of images until they became quite dense."[40] In the finished book for *True Patriot Love*, a four-by-eight-inch silk Canadian flag was attached to the inside front cover, and a photograph of the knitted flag with its knitted maple leaf from the show appeared on the first and last pages. Most of the text on the title page is covered with a photograph of Joyce's *O Canada* quilt. Over the original year of publication, 1964, Joyce crossed out "64" and penned in "71."

She placed her own images on top of the text throughout, and in some cases the original pages were completely covered; in others, whole pages of text and illustrations were left intact. On some pages she wrote in the margins around maps indicating sites where certain flora grow in the Arctic. She used paper-clips and sewing pins to attach some of the small pieces of paper and photographs onto the original pages and photographed them that way, making her method of working very obvious.

The centre spread of the book is the working drawing for *Arctic Passion Cake*, with detailed notes about colour and explanations of the objects

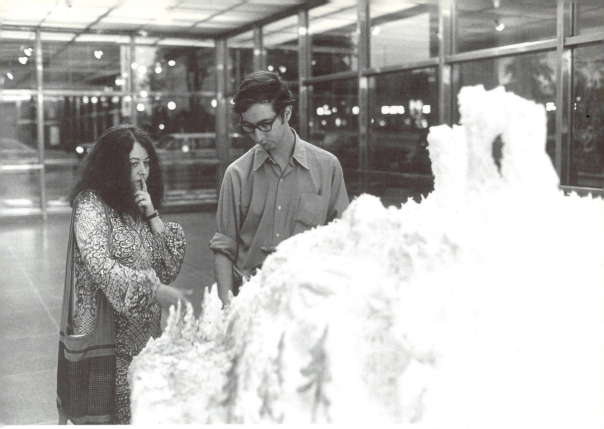

Joyce and Pierre Théberge with *Arctic Passion Cake* at the National Gallery of Canada, 1971.

involved in both French and English. Photos throughout the book depict a variety of subjects — manuscript pages of Joyce's story outline for her feature film; Tom Thomson with his dog; Colette's face; the Ottawa Parliament buildings in winter; a single, wrinkled maple leaf lying in the snow, photographed through a round lens; details from *Arctic Day* (1970-71), with its coloured pencil drawings of Arctic flora and fauna — a snow goose, caribou, arctic hare, otter and penguin among them; the front part of a snowshoe track and some animal tracks; a quote from Thoreau ("To love nature was to worship freedom, To believe in nature was to rebel."); dried flowers; Joyce re-enacting Laura Secord's walk with her cow in the War of 1812; close-ups of details from Joyce's pieces in the show, so grainy that the images can hardly be delineated; a tiny photo of land between Ottawa and Montreal; a tiny photo of a detail of Napoleon's coat and vest; tiny photos of Canada geese taking off; a detail of *O Canada Animation* (1970) — the 71 mouths forming the words to the national anthem, which were embroidered in red lips and white teeth, with a single thread laid across the side of the mouth.

All together, the book is an exquisitely beautiful collage, showing the artist's love for life and her country. Joyce described the book as having the richest interplay of all her work because it was about the film she was then

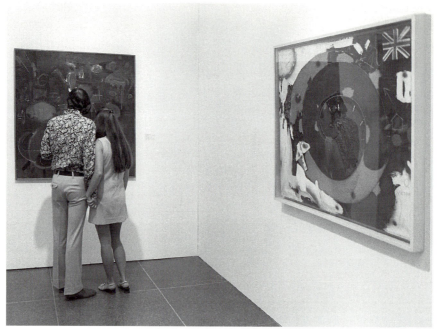

At the opening of "True Patriot Love." The couple is looking at *War Memories* (1960). *Laura Secord Saves Upper Canada* (1961) is on the right.

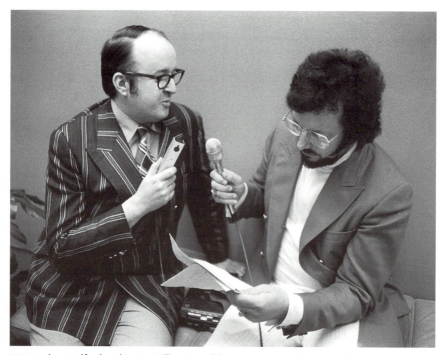

Critic Robert Fulford and Artist William Ronald interviewing each other at the opening of "True Patriot Love."

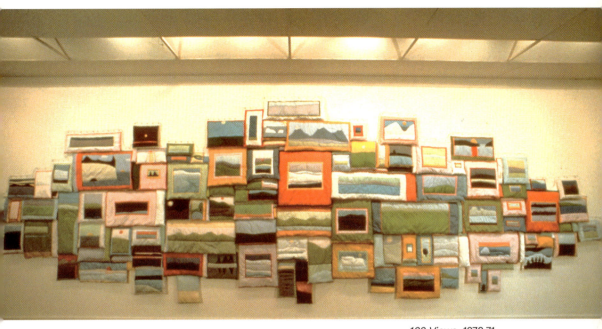

109 Views, 1970-71.

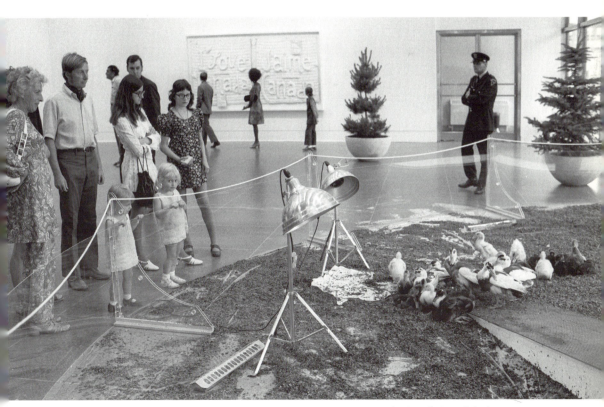

The installation of ducks.

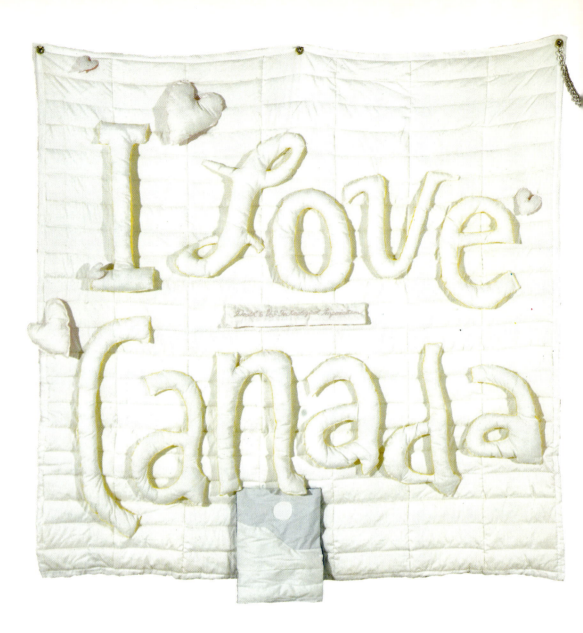

working on, which became *The Far Shore*, about the work she had done to that point, and also about her work at that time.[41]

One of the last pages is made up of credits thanking the people who helped her prepare her exhibition, all in Joyce's handwriting, with tiny hearts and flowers drawn all over the page. Throughout the book, nearly all her handwriting is in both French and English.

It was appropriate that Joyce's show, featuring her work from 1960 on, should open on Canada Day and be on exhibit for more than a month as part of Ottawa's 1971 Festival Canada. The exhibition was like a great collage about Canada that filled the first level of the Lorne Building, which then housed the National Gallery. That evening she invited her friends to a special dinner,

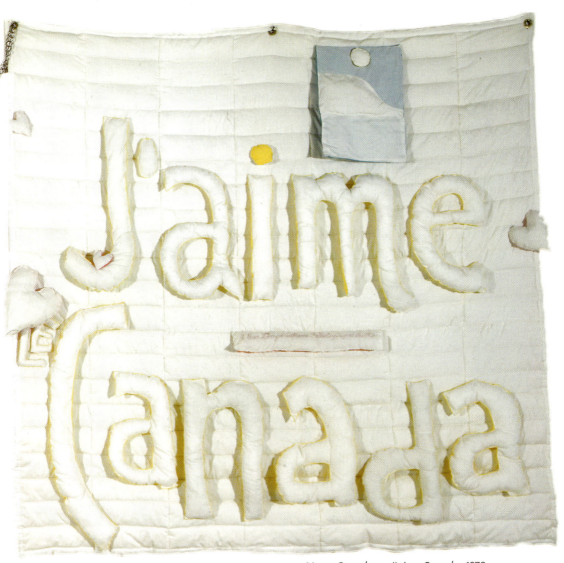

I Love Canada — J'aime Canada, 1970.

a meal that featured organic Quebec lamb and organic vegetables, strawberries and cream and maple sugar leaves.

At the public opening, people of all ages, from babies to the elderly, came to see Joyce's quilts, which were being shown in a museum for the first time. Her cloth works were a poetic expression that symbolized a "warm" medium for a cold, northern country. She hoped Canadians' sense of humour would let them enjoy the woodsy-smelling Sweet Beaver perfume, which contained nothing from a beaver, but was given its name just because Joyce loved the animals. She did not know what people would think of an installation of twenty-four ducklings and four adult ducks with a blue plastic pool of water in a cordoned-off section of the gallery. As the taped sound of the loon's call drifted through the air, Joyce wanted everyone to understand that this show was her way of giving Canada to Canadians.

Pierre Théberge certainly understood what was behind it all because he went out of his way to make sure the show was mounted as Joyce envisioned it. When she had asked that live ducks be part of the exhibition, and even read about how to look after them, Théberge did some research to find out where they could get ducks. They ended up renting them from a duck farm. The farmers must have had a sense of humour because they thought the idea "just outrageous and funny." And Joyce was amused that a curator of the National Gallery, who had a very clean job, got up early every morning to feed them.[42] When the show was over, the ducks went back to the farm and their fated end on someone's table. Joyce had also suggested the possibility of putting cows in the park nearby, but had settled for the idea of sheep in Confederation Square Park across the street. Théberge sent a letter to the National Capital Commission requesting permission, saying the National Gallery would take responsibility for the fencing and care of the sheep. However, a reply came back saying that because of "barnyard odors where people enjoy their lunches" and the damage to grass and scattering of hay in the area, the request had to be denied.[43]

Inside the gallery, on a large wall in the same area as the ducks, hung *109 Views* (1970-71), an irregularly shaped fabric assemblage more than seven metres long and three metres high, made up of small, brightly coloured, quilted Canadian landscapes. On the wall next to *109 Views* hung *I Love Canada — J'aime Canada* (1970), two quilts in two languages linked by a metal chain. The symbolism of this work is unlikely to be lost on anyone, either then or today.

Another outstanding cloth piece was *The Great Sea* (1970–71), a hooked wool hanging in two parts, one in English and one in what Joyce called "Eskimo language." It was for this piece that in 1970 Joyce hired the women she had met in Cheticamp while on her trip to Nova Scotia in 1968. The text, which is an Inuit song, reads in the English translation she used on the hanging, "The great sea has set me in motion/Set me adrift/And I move as a weed in the great river/ The Arch of sky/And mightiness of storms/Encompasses me/And I am left/Trembling with joy."[44] This piece is predominantly white, with a few delicate bits of colour; a filmy, white cloth hangs over each part giving the impression of looking through a snowstorm. In the book Joyce made for the show, the song appears in Inuit symbols on page one, in French on page two, and in English on page three. These lines could have been written by Joyce herself and have the same spirit as the two paragraphs by Pierre Théberge, which appear in English and French at the beginning of Joyce's book.

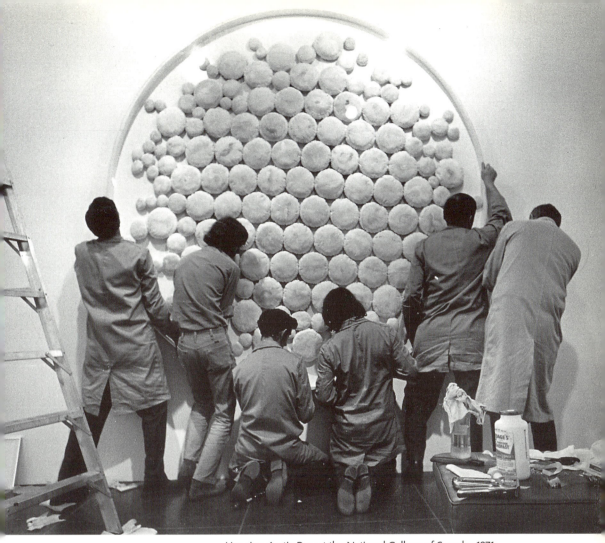

Hanging *Arctic Day* at the National Gallery of Canada, 1971.

From one ocean to the other, Joyce Wieland crosses a Territory in search of a land of which the vital breath would be that of the North wind, of the trees which grow to the great sun, of the animals which inhabit it, and of the white of winter and the snow which falls; of a nation of which the breath would be that of all the peoples which compose it in all the energy of their myths and their history, of a soil which the reality would be that of the wind which passes over the flowers in the fields.

The Water Quilt (1970–71) and *Arctic Day* (1970–71) hung side-by-side in the gallery, both of them white with only a bit of soft, delicate colour. *The Water Quilt* is made of sixty-four tiny square pillows joined by a thin rope attached through grommets. Onto each cushion has been photo-printed a section from *The Energy Poker Game*, a book by James Laxer on Canada's natural resources that includes a warning about an alleged plot by the Americans to take over our water resources. This quilt, remarkable for its delicate beauty

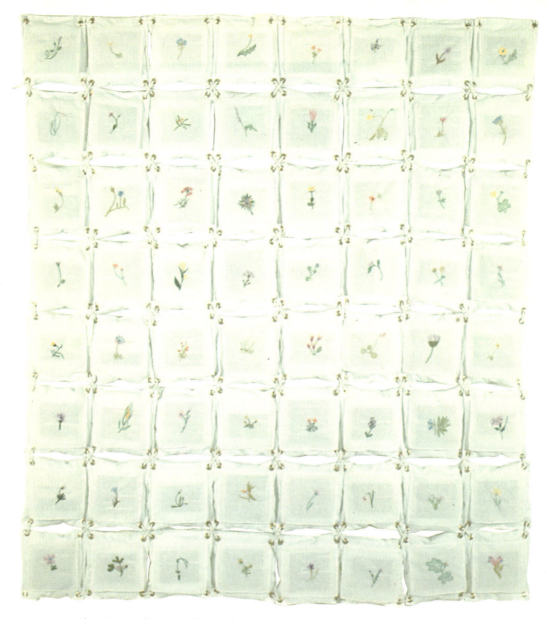

The Water Quilt, 1970-71. (Right) detail.

combined with its message of dire consequences, is another example of Joyce's prophetic vision, for in the late nineties private Canadian companies began applying for licences to export water. The federal government asked provincial governments to place a temporary ban on bulk water exports, but at the beginning of the twenty-first century the country continues to be in danger of losing its sovereign rights to its water.

Covering *The Water Quilt*'s texts about the threats to Canada was a flap hanging over each pillow, onto which an Arctic flower had been embroidered. With the flaps rolled up, the texts can be read. In later years,

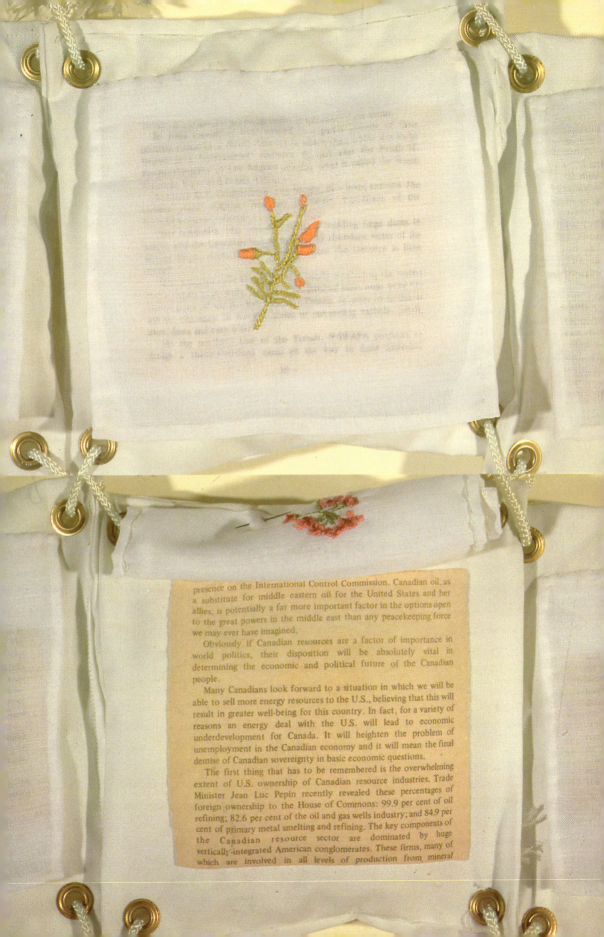

presence on the International Control Commission. Canadian oil, as a substitute for middle eastern oil for the United States and her allies, is potentially a far more important factor in the options open to the great powers in the middle east than any peacekeeping force we may ever have imagined.

Obviously if Canadian resources are a factor of importance in world politics, their disposition will be absolutely vital in determining the economic and political future of the Canadian people.

Many Canadians look forward to a situation in which we will be able to sell more energy resources to the U.S., believing that this will result in greater well-being for this country. In fact, for a variety of reasons an energy deal with the U.S. will lead to economic underdevelopment for Canada. It will heighten the problem of unemployment in the Canadian economy and it will mean the final demise of Canadian sovereignty in basic economic questions.

The first thing that has to be remembered is the overwhelming extent of U.S. ownership of Canadian resource industries. Trade Minister Jean Luc Pepin recently revealed these percentages of foreign ownership to the House of Commons: 99.9 per cent of oil refining; 82.6 per cent of the oil and gas wells industry; and 84.9 per cent of primary metal smelting and refining. The key components of the Canadian resource sector are dominated by huge vertically-integrated American conglomerates. These firms, many of which are involved in all levels of production from mineral

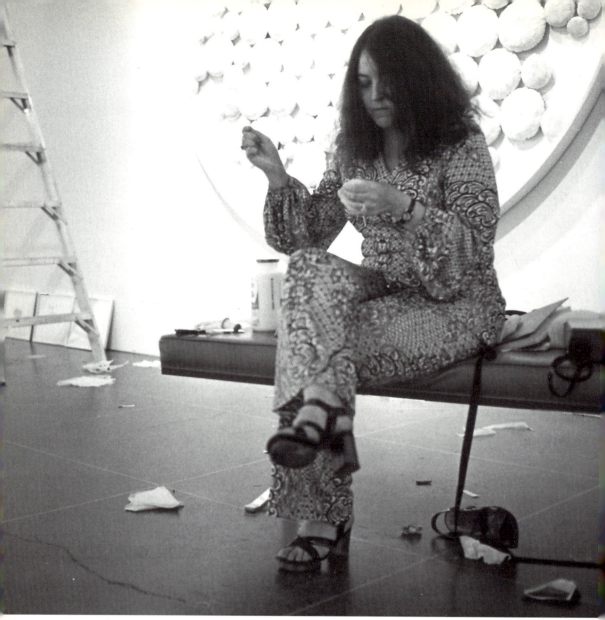

Joyce sewing an *Arctic Day* pillow at the National Gallery.

when the quilt hung at the Art Gallery of Ontario, Joyce took great delight in opening the plexiglass case of the quilt and changing the flaps. Of course, the security guards were always aghast until she explained who she was.

Joyce's choice of medium for her message placed her squarely in the tradition of other female artists who had, as Rozsika Parker noted, made "meanings of their own in the very medium intended to inculcate self-effacement" — including the suffragists of the early 1900s in Britain, whose art society was called Suffrage Atelier and who used their banners in political demonstrations.[45]

Like *The Water Quilt*, *Arctic Day* is also made up of tiny white pillows, 163 of

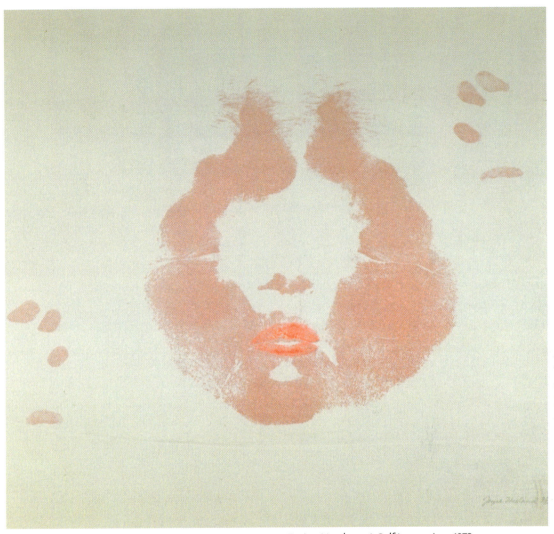

Facing North — A Self Impression, 1973.

them, all round and assembled on a large, round plywood base, with the larger ones in the centre and the smaller ones around the edges. The backs of the pillows are bright pink to produce a rosy glow. On each cushion is a soft colour pencil drawing of either an Arctic landscape, or an animal, bird, fish or flower.

For Joyce, the physicality of Canada and her sentiments about it were all one. She even found a way to give the national anthem a physical manifestation in two media: lithograph and fabric, a hard medium and a soft. She pressed her lipstick-coated lips into the stone as she formed the words of the song. As Michael Pantazzi observed, this was "the closest possible contact with art ... You can't get any closer than that. It was at the same time interesting and enormously imaginative. She came up with the darndest things like that. She didn't care two hoots, like so many artists do, what will happen next. It just came."[46] She made the lithograph during a three-month teaching stint she and Michael had in Halifax at the Nova Scotia College of Art and Design in the fall of 1970.

Joyce had also attended the Halifax Fall Fair and looked at the work of knitters and embroiderers. She hired Valerie McMillin to knit four Canadian flags and Joan McGregor to embroider lips for the *O Canada* hanging. To create her design of the lips, Joyce stood in front of a mirror and sang "O Canada" and traced the outline of her mouth for the different syllables on muslin, seventy-one mouths in all. McGregor also embroidered the last letters of the English and French generals James Wolfe and Louis-Joseph de Montcalm just before the Battle of the Plains of Abraham in 1759. This piece reflects the same awareness of Canada's historic dual nature as the double quilt joined with a chain. It also brings down to size the work of army generals and their battles by transforming their original letters into needlework created by women in their homes.

Joyce's set piece, *Arctic Passion Cake* (1971), was translated from her rough drawing into a large, six-feet-in-diameter construction by the parliamentary pastry chef, Jan Van Dierendonck. The Arctic, with its snow geese and wounded polar bear, was at the top of the three-feet-high styrofoam cake covered with white icing. The tree line was represented by a row of fir trees. Between trees lay the mate of the polar bear, a woman suckling their children, French and English beavers. Around the bottom were the crests of the provinces and their official provincial flowers, as well as petit fours, "stones" from the Canadian Shield.

For six weeks before the show, the gallery's conference room had been set up as a workroom. A taped video of the preparations shows tables piled with boxes of supplies, and rolls of fabrics and tools.[47] A young man pins odd-shaped pieces of fabric onto small puffs of cotton. Joyce and her sister, Joan, work at stitching together the fronts and backs of the small *Arctic Day* pillows that will line the edges of the hanging. Théberge and his staff come and go, as does Michael Snow. Once the pillows were all assembled — they were all stitched to twill tape, which was stapled to the plywood backing — installing the glass and mounting the large circular piece on the wall required six men.

By the time of the exhibition, Théberge and Joyce and Michael had become friends, something that is obvious in their exhibition correspondence, which is full of jokes and good humour. Michael was in Ottawa with Joyce for a month before the show to help with the preparations. During this time Théberge conducted an interview with Joyce,

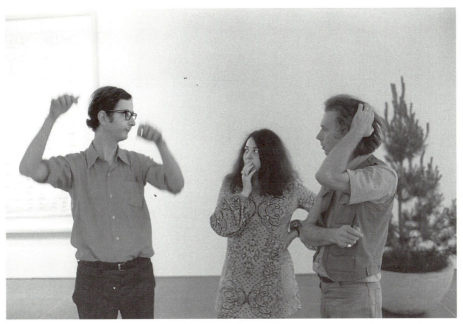

Pierre Théberge, Joyce and Michael discussing the installation of the 1971 exhibition in Ottawa.

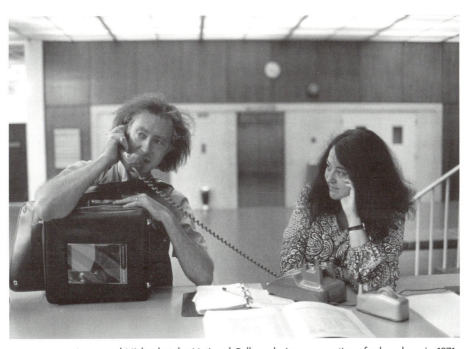

Joyce and Michael at the National Gallery during preparations for her show in 1971.

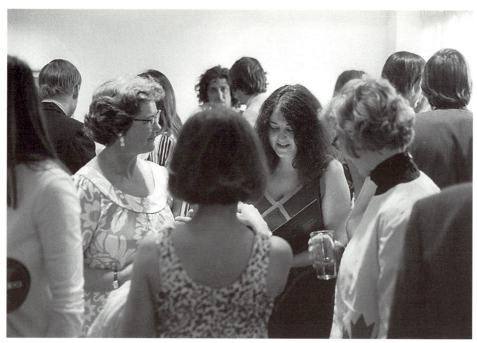

Joyce reading from her *True Patriot Love* to some of her guests at her 1971 exhibition in Ottawa.

asking questions in French with Michael translating and Joyce responding in English. This interview was printed on a large sheet of paper, folded and inserted into the paper pocket of Joyce's exhibition book, along with a map of Canada detailing its hundreds of lakes and rivers, a booklet of bibliographic information, and an essay on Joyce's films.

Joyce traced the origins of her feelings for her country to her years in elementary school, when the teacher often pulled down the map of Canada, printed in beautiful shades of pinks and greens, and moved the big pointer from one part to another across the huge space. It landed on such words as Keewatin, Hudson's Bay, and at the bottom, a tiny point, Toronto. Toronto meant Joyce and her home, and "Dominion of Canada," printed in a big arc across the top, meant all these other places where she had never been in this vast, mysterious space. This map became a space in her psyche, so much so that she saw the country "as a direct extension of myself ... What is done to it is done to me."[48] On her train trip from Toronto to Vancouver she made her adult exploration of Canada, and was amazed at how "the land cries out to be discovered through art."[49]

Even then, in 1971, Joyce saw that perhaps Canadians no longer directed the fate of their country, and in that admission she expressed an awful truth. Still, she wanted to hold out some hope for this extension of her own self. She admitted in the Théberge interview that she did not see a solution to American imperialism engulfing Canada. However, if there was one, it would come about if Canadians wanted to change what was happening, and for that reason came together. At the same time, she also saw that the solution would be different for different people and at different levels. The energy generated in the coming together of all these people would be a way "to release the country from its fate."

Théberge questioned her because he understood that she saw her work as being about the end of Canada. "Maybe it is the end of Canada, but I won't stop this work ..." Joyce maintained, and she described her idea for *The Far Shore*, which at that time she called "True Patriot Love." By at first giving the film the same name as her 1971 Ottawa show, she revealed that the film would be to Canadian cinema what "True Patriot Love" was to wall art. As she claimed she would, she continued working on her concept of Canada; a few years later she further developed her thoughts about what could be done to generate a feeling about our country. To start with, individuals needed to learn about the whole of Canada, and once they did, their knowledge would spread to others. "Then maybe people can take responsibility for this place ... Unless you can be responsible to the piece of land you're standing on and relate to the nature of it, not just a city, if you can start to do that, then you can start in the most intimate regional way to be responsible for what you are. I feel that's something all of us can do."[50]

It is ironic that despite Joyce's nationalistic fervour, at the opening of her show a group of artists held a demonstration outside the gallery and distributed a leaflet entitled, "True Expatriate Love?" They objected to Canada Council grants being given to artists living outside of Canada. Joyce was stunned. How could they demonstrate against her when she had poured her heart into this exhibition for the country? Furthermore, she already knew she wanted to return to Canada to live so she could do the work she felt compelled to do, something she admitted in the Théberge interview.

Another irony is that while she was living in New York she began reading Canadian history and the writing of Canadian nationalist Mel Watkins. Perhaps these interests were at least partly triggered by civil rights demonstrations and protests against the Vietnam War. These events had sparked many discussions among Joyce and her friends, and she had participated in a number of marches and demonstrations, including the historic 1963 civil rights March on Washington, not long after arriving in New York. Her work definitely showed that although her residence was in New York, very soon after moving there she had turner her face more and more to the North. She had begun the process of choosing Canada. She seemed to know intuitively the truth of Margaret Atwood's claim, "This country is something that must be chosen ... and if we do choose it we are still choosing a violent duality."[51] This duality merged with her own psyche, and Joyce, living in the heart of another country that increasingly encroached on her own, discovered — and in a sense created for herself — a Canada she dreamed of, and from within developed her own vision of what it meant.

Joyce and Michael had frequently discussed the idea of returning to Toronto to live. As it was, they were in Canada for months at a time. Joyce was clear about what she wanted to do, but Michael felt he had "more to lose than she did ... in terms of a career" by returning.[52] A New York friend felt there was a constellation of reasons why Joyce, particularly, wanted to return to Canada, among them that "life here was too painful for her," meaning that Michael had interests in someone else, and Joyce felt the answer was to get away from New York.[53] In fact, Michael was having a "steamy" affair with an influential art critic, according to one account.[54] Joyce knew the woman was Amy Taubin. When I asked Michael about it, he shifted uncomfortably in his chair and said the Kuchars' version was exaggerated, and he didn't think it was something to "name names over."

There were other reasons Joyce wanted to return, aside from the lure of Canada itself. Something had happened among her filmmaking friends that certainly was a large factor in her desire to leave. Joyce had gained much respect in avant-garde film circles, something that Jonas Mekas recognized in one of his regular film reviews in New York's *the village VOICE*.[55] However, with time, these filmmakers became absorbed into the museum establishment and sold out to a star system, which replaced the non-ranking community of artists that had so attracted Joyce. As one writer said, "No single event contributed more to the narrowing of focus than the founding of Anthology Film Archives in New York City in 1970."[56] When a selection committee was formed to set up this new canon, a definitive film collection, Joyce's work was excluded. According to Mekas, some members of the committee, including himself, voted to include Joyce's films, but the decisions were made by majority vote, and the few who were in favour of including her were outnumbered.[57]

Joyce was hurt and disappointed by this rejection. She had worked on films with both Michael and her close friend Hollis Frampton, who were both included in this star system, a system she disliked because the group became a "boys' club" and worked against the friendliness that had once characterized the community. "We were once very intimate in New York," Joyce said of the filmmakers, "sharing each others films, tapes, shadows, and conversations ... I doubt whether we shall all see each other that much again, even though we were part of a Movement. I didn't know that I was part of a Movement until for me it was over."[58]

The founders who formed the Anthology Film Archives were all men, as was their selection committee.[59] Even so, it seems strange that only male filmmakers were included in the canon — even Shirley Clarke was excluded, a highly regarded filmmaker who had helped raise money for the Anthology. When it came to the idea of recording avant-garde film history, her work, and that of other women, was deemed unacceptable. "Since their [the founders'] policy was never to give out reasons of choice or rejection, I never had a clue, and had to surmise that none of my works were classics ... Shirley Clarke, Storm de Hirsch, Joyce Wieland — our films are not classics ... It is really a wonder that any woman filmmakers have managed to survive."[60]

All along, the filmmakers with whom Joyce had worked acknowledged that they influenced each other. However, when it came to Joyce's work "affecting anyone it was never mentioned ... When books have been written to document this movement my work is relegated to a woman's place, small that is."[61] Joyce knew that her subject matter, which she chose deliberately, "put me in a strange way outside the movement I was a part of. The men in that movement, including my husband, were no more enlightened than any other men at that time. They failed to treat me as their equal as an artist. It was simply this, that even very civilized men compete, and they only cared to compete with each other."[62] Not only that, but she perceived that film critics, as well as some of the filmmakers, "wanted only one thing at a time" in a film. It was not her way to give that little. She gave many things in films: humour, political comments, feminism, thoughts on domesticity and ecology — without crowding her medium. And she wasn't "going to check my sense of humour and what art is at the door for a bunch of people who lived by theory alone, and I don't want to live in a world that they would create."[63]

Even though Joyce eventually made peace on a personal level with what had happened, from a historical point of view, establishing an anthology of men's films skewed the picture — just as art history texts in the past had excluded female artists. By the time the Anthology had been officially established at the end of 1970, when Joyce was hard at work on her show in Ottawa, she had likely already decided to return to Canada.

Only a few months after the show ended, Joyce and Michael bought a house in Toronto, across the street from CPR tracks. They took possession of 137 Summerhill Avenue on a typically grey, mild November 16th in 1971. This oddly shaped house, which still stands on the corner of two streets at the end of five row houses, surrounded by trees and bushes, cost around $30,000.[64] In keeping with her love of light, a sunporch with glass shelves filled with plants became her studio.

Joyce was relieved to be back home, and the first thing she wanted to do was go tobogganing. She had been away long enough that she felt she understood the creative process of other artists who had lived in exile,

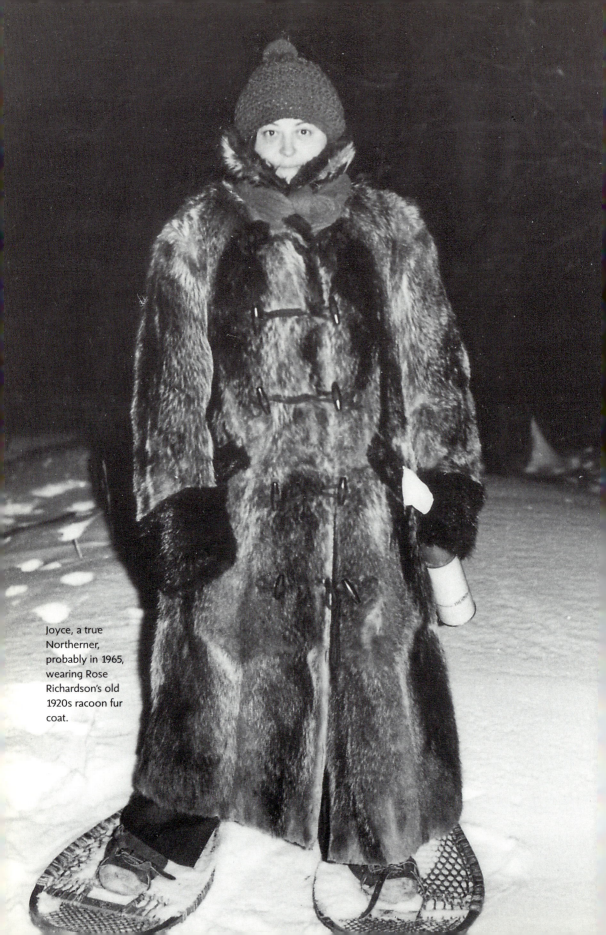

Joyce, a true Northerner, probably in 1965, wearing Rose Richardson's old 1920s racoon fur coat.

particularly the writers James Joyce and Gertrude Stein. She, too, aspired to using "regional" subject matter that had universal meaning, especially in the new film she had in mind. She could not have chosen a more Canadian subject than Tom Thomson, her inspiration for a new feature film that would consume her for the next five years.

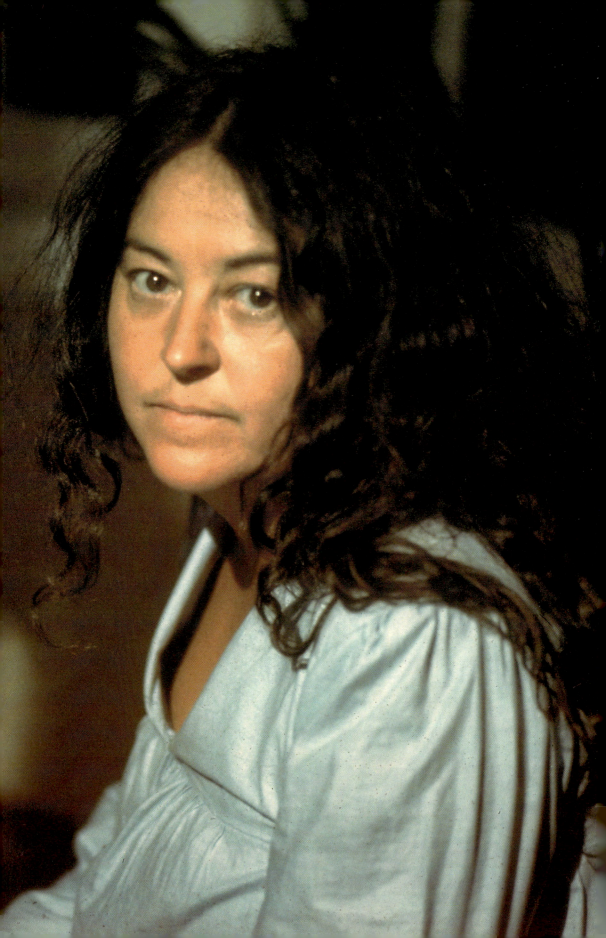

7

Voyage to the far shore

All my films are intensely personal. I am not a film theoretician. With my film The Far Shore I tried to sum up many of the things that I love about film. On another level it was a film about Canada made for Canadians and the world. —Joyce Wieland[1]

LAND had special significance for Joyce Wieland, especially Canadian land, which for her held mythological meaning. She said more than once that she identified with Canada as female, just as nineteenth-century writer Anna Jameson had, who saw "the land as a passionate woman."[2]

In 1970, while she and Michael were teaching at the Nova Scotia School of Art and Design in Halifax, Joyce became preoccupied with looking for a summer place in Nova Scotia. Why in Nova Scotia? Because Scots had settled the province — she was part Scottish — and were "rugged," "individual" and "inside" themselves, qualities she liked.[3]

Joyce and Michael also went to Newfoundland that fall. One day they rented a car and drove through the wilds. Joyce persuaded Michael to drive up a certain lumber road, which eventually disappeared into rocky terrain. They kept going anyway because it was almost impossible to turn around.

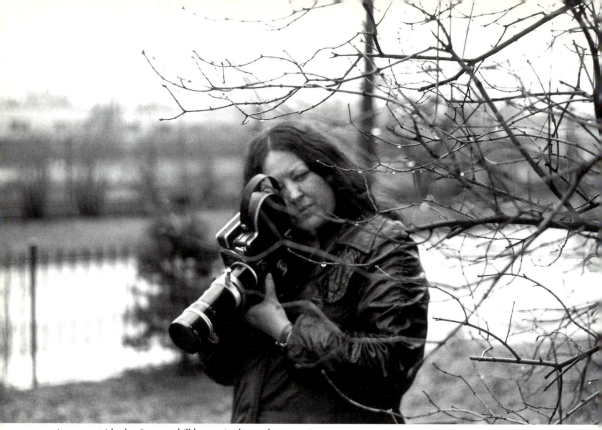

Joyce outside the Summerhill house in the early seventies.

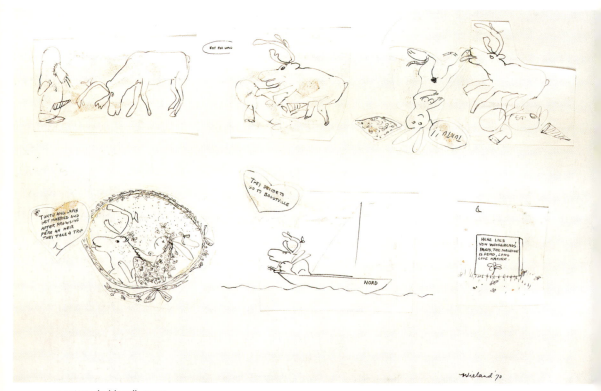

Aqui Nada (detail), 1970.

Finally, the car got stuck. It was wedged in at the axle, and they couldn't move. Miles from any human habitation, they had no choice but to start walking, and on their trek to get help they discovered that the land was "beyond-belief beautiful." After several hours, they reached a fishing village where they encountered a man who was over ninety years old. He found someone who could pull out their rented car with his truck.

On their way back to rescue the car, Joyce ask the driver whether any land was for sale nearby. As it turned out, he and his brother owned property in the area where the car was stuck. "I think we must have stayed there a day," Michael said, trying to recall the chain of events. "I seem to remember sleeping in some cabin."[4] They leased two acres on one of Newfoundland's many capes, and in the summer of 1971 they bought land. Later they built a small one-room cabin that had no running water or electricity. This would be their secret summer place, to which very few friends and family members would be invited and other people were never to know where it was. Joyce fell passionately in love with this piece of Newfoundland and invested it with her mythology of herself and Michael.

By the end of 1971, having bought both a house in Toronto and a piece of her "New-found-land," Joyce had firmly planted both feet in her native country and city. During the time she and Michael had lived in New York, Toronto had substantially increased in population, from 1.6 million in 1961 to 2.1 million in 1971, spreading its urban sprawl farther and farther.[5]

That same year, Toronto's first artist-run centre was born, an event that coincided with the city's political reform movement. David Crombie became Toronto's mayor in 1972, the year a women's collective formed, which became The Women's Press. The women's movement had been launched, with "consciousness-raising groups ... forming far faster than tupperware parties," said Doris Anderson, whose *Chatelaine* had been published for years before the 1972 launch of *Ms.* magazine in the States[6] — just as Joyce Wieland had preceded Judy Chicago.

Joyce joined one of those consciousness-raising groups, a gathering that writer Marjorie Harris's children called "the laughing and crying group." It was the first time these women had talked openly about sexuality. They also discussed men because many had husbands who were well known and more powerful than they were. "All of us were living in the shadow of men," Harris said.[7] Of course, Joyce knew all about that.

Joyce's return to Canada also coincided with a surge in nationalism — the time of the New Democratic Party's Waffle movement and economic nationalism — including cultural nationalism, a term defined by culture critic Susan Crean as "connected to a political idea, a vision of Canada as a self-sustaining culture and a society that values its artists and understands

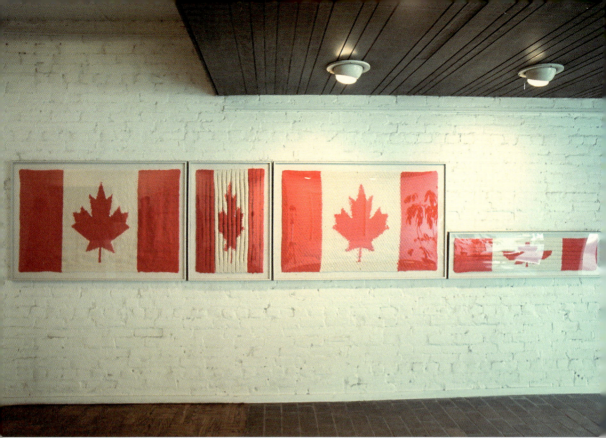

Flag Arrangement, 1970-71.

the importance of art, imagery and memory."[8] Joyce's show in Ottawa had revealed her own nationalism, which meshed with that of a group of artists in London, Ontario, who felt the need for a national organization to look after artists' economic and legal rights.

Among the proponents of a strong regional cultural nationalism were Jack Chambers, Greg Curnoe and John Boyle. About five years younger than Curnoe, Boyle grew up in a working-class family in London and had no formal training in art when he began painting. He looked up to Curnoe, who had attended the Ontario College of Art in Toronto but returned to live in London. In Toronto Curnoe had encountered the idea that a Canadian artist could be successful only by going to New York or Paris. But he did not agree with that idea, nor did he like living in Toronto. Curnoe deliberately chose to establish his career in Canada — at home in London — with the same fervour with which Joyce returned to Toronto.

In 1970 Boyle articulated the cultural nationalistic sentiment of many artists in a manifesto called "Refus Continental," published in *20 Cents*, a small magazine, which, in the spirit of things not being quite what they seem, sold for 25¢.[9] The London artists expressed the worry of many nationalists who were dismayed by American imperialism. Curnoe and Boyle believed that the life and culture of Canada were embedded in the small regions of the country, and they made the reasoned decision to remain in one of those regions.

In the same spirit of nationalism was a Centennial year incident that helped set in motion the formation of an artists' organization. Jack Chambers asked for a fee for the use of slides of his work in an educational package the National Gallery of Canada had put together for schools, since he depended on his art for a living. The National Gallery did not want to set this precedent and at first refused, so other London artists began negotiations for the use of their work in reproduction in every form. The following year, in 1968, Chambers with other artists officially organized the Canadian Artists' Representation (CAR). However, the first national conference of CAR was not held until the early spring of 1971 in Winnipeg, a meeting that both Joyce and Michael attended. At this first meeting, the delegates established exhibition fees and copyright royalties, and museums were given until January 1973 to comply.

Joyce was in complete agreement with the premises of CAR. The artists' spirit of nationalism fed into the feature film she was developing. She received "a sense of moral strength from those [London] men. So I wanted to join up with the forces of regionalism and nationalism; I wanted to be a part of whatever that impulse was to protect the country ..."[10] Still carrying the concepts for her feature film in the back of her mind, within months of arriving home she leaped into action in support of the very nationalism she wanted to weave into her film.

Writer Susan Crean remembered that in the spring of 1972, Joyce phoned and asked her to come to a meeting at the Isaacs Gallery because something had to be done about the appointment of an American curator at the Art Gallery of Ontario. Most of the more than three dozen people who came to the meeting were members of CAR. They felt that nothing short of real dramatics would make the public aware of the situation at the AGO. The artists objected to hiring Americans who, after a term at the AGO, went on to more prestigious positions, a pattern that would continue into the 1990s.

On a sultry June 15, 1972, twenty artists, including both Joyce and Michael, roped themselves together outside the Isaacs Gallery to protest the appointment of Richard Wattenmaker at the AGO. Their point was that an American curator would not have a knowledge and understanding of Canadian culture. Some of these artists went on to form the Committee to Strengthen Canadian Culture, and continued a campaign against Wattenmaker's appointment. On the first day that he reported to work, which happened to be July 4, American Independence Day, Joyce was among the demonstrators who marched past the United States embassy to the

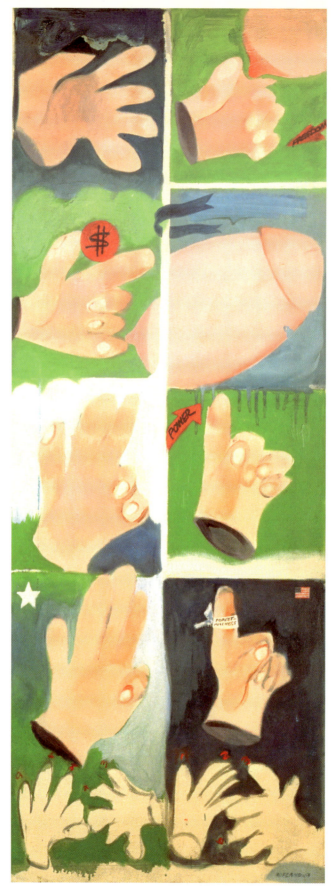

*The New
Power,*
1963.

gallery's administration offices with photographer "Michel Lambeth dressed in an Uncle Sam suit in the lead."[11] Lambeth and a delegation asked to meet with William Withrow, the gallery's director, and they also wanted to meet with Wattenmaker to give him a letter of resignation to sign. Wattenmaker agreed to meet with one group spokesperson only, but the demonstrators refused the offer. Meanwhile, Lambeth and the poet Jim Brown chained and handcuffed themselves to filing cabinets. The secretary-treasurer of the gallery, Michael George, warned that he would call the police, which he did; the police removed them.[12]

Michael Pantazzi, now Associate Curator of European and American Art at the National Gallery, remembered that around the same time, at a special event at the gallery, probably an opening, Joyce stood at the door dressed in slacks and a rain jacket with a zipper, as though she were officially receiving people. She and the others with her in "proletarian costume" had a cardboard box from which they pulled out red buttons saying "CLOSE THE 49TH PARALLEL" in white lettering. They gave everyone a button; some guests wore them and others didn't, as "Wattenmaker, looking quite composed but very still with his wife holding his arm, [walked] among the guests ... Everyone was having a wonderful time, both participants in the anti-Wattenmaker pact and those looking at what was going on."[13] No wonder that years later the AGO security guards jokingly asked Joyce if she was behaving herself when she came to visit the gallery!

One can imagine, despite his exterior composure, how Wattenmaker must have felt. Joan Murray, who at the time was Curator of Canadian Art, remembers that he had one of the buttons "and wrote somewhere 'Close the 49th Parallel with them down there.'"[14]

Besides protesting American curators, CARO (the Ontario branch of CAR) members also objected to an AGO board of directors made up of only business people — no artists and other cultural workers. CARO artists were relentless in their pressure on the AGO, and in the fall Joyce was elected to the board, the only artist, and the first one ever, among twenty-seven board members. To attend the meetings, Joyce countered the board members' impression of her and her ilk as rag-tag hippies by dressing like a proper lady, including hat and gloves. But even that did not work. The next year at the annual meeting, by means of proxy votes, those in power prevented any more of the CARO-type nominees from crashing the board, and Joyce's term was at an end.

Around the time that Joyce was participating in the AGO protests, two events occurred that would have an impact on her life and work during the seventies: she read *White Niggers of America* by the late Quebec writer Pierre Vallières, a former leader of the Front de libération du Quebec (FLQ), first

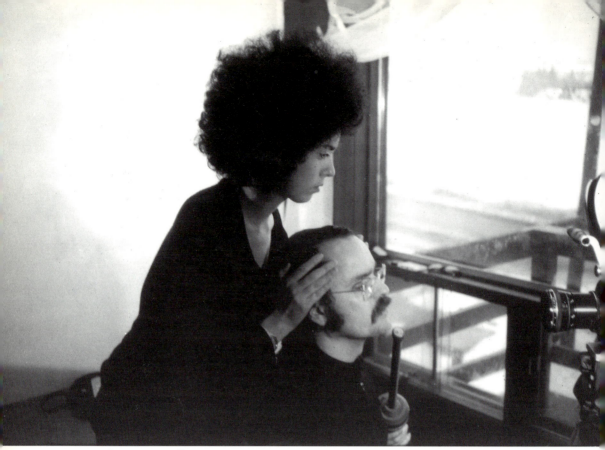

Filming Pierre Vallières, 1972.

published in English in 1971; and she met Judy Steed, who at that time was working for *W-5*, a television show for CTV in Toronto.

Judy grew up in Ottawa, where her father, the late John Burke Ewing, was the chief surgeon at the Ottawa General Hospital and the head of the surgery department at the University of Ottawa. Because of his profession, Dr. Ewing lived in a different social circle than that of his original family in a farming community in the Kingston area. Thus Judy's childhood experiences more or less straddled class lines. She saw firsthand the struggles of the working class when, as a teenager, she worked for her father and interacted with his patients, many of them working-class French-Canadians. At age seventeen, Judy left Ottawa to study literature and philosophy at the University of Toronto and continued living and working there after university.

After seeing Joyce's exhibition at the National Gallery, she suggested that CTV do a feature on her. CTV sent someone to interview Joyce, but as it turned out, did not want to use the material. Judy was free to take the clips, and with some follow-up interviews, she made *A Film about Joyce Wieland* (1972).[15] This is how the two women became acquainted.

At Joyce's suggestion, Judy also read *White Niggers of America*, a largely autobiographical social history in which Vallières characterizes the working class as colonized people and describes the hopelessness of their existence when their attempts at improving their lives fail. Joyce's poverty as a child and Judy's childhood in a doctor's family meant they each understood Vallières's book from opposite experiences, but Judy, because of her work with her father, was very sympathetic to the history of French-Canadians. Judy proposed a feature on Vallières for CTV, but again, there was no interest. She wanted to pursue the idea anyway. Thus Joyce and Judy began their first collaboration.

On a February 1972 weekend, the two women rented the equipment they needed and drove in Judy's red Volkswagen through a snowstorm to Mont Laurier, Quebec to interview Vallières. While Joyce filmed, Judy held the microphone and Danielle Corbeil, a translator, held Vallières's head in position as Joyce focused the camera on his mouth while he spoke. Joyce had used the image of lips in several media before, including her own mouth in both *Water Sark* and *Reason over Passion*. This Vallières film, which Joyce called a "mouth-scape," was made up of details that embedded several levels of meaning into the images: the close-up of the mouth with crooked, encrusted teeth tells us this is a poor man, while the movement of bright red lips underneath a moustache gives a visual image to the idea of "voice," an opportunity usually denied the poor. He delivers, in French, monologues on the Québécois, the "white niggers of America," and on women, two colonized groups. Subtitles are printed in English.

A "hidden" significance to the Vallières film lies in his association with Trudeau in the early sixties. Vallières had been living in Paris, and when he returned in March of 1963, he was offered a job writing about world affairs for *La Presse*, a Montreal newspaper. He also began working for *Cité Libre*, a magazine founded by Quebec intellectuals in 1950. By the fall of 1963, Vallières became the editor of the magazine, and he wanted to turn it into "a weapon for Québécois workers."[16] However, on the editorial board was one Pierre Elliott Trudeau, who with his associates, did not want the magazine to become an advocate for separatism, what Vallières called a "revolutionary separatism, a working-class separatism."[17] Of course, the editorial board disagreed with this philosophy and Vallières resigned by the following spring. Vallières felt that Trudeau abandoned the common people, the Québécois proletariat, to align himself with imperialists. And here lies the contradiction of the two Pierres Joyce used in her films. She sided with the under-dogs, but maintained her admiration and fascination for such men as Trudeau, who had attained power.

The Vallières film, as Joyce described it, "was a one-shot affair … and shows the whole process of making the film, camera breakdown, Vallières pulling

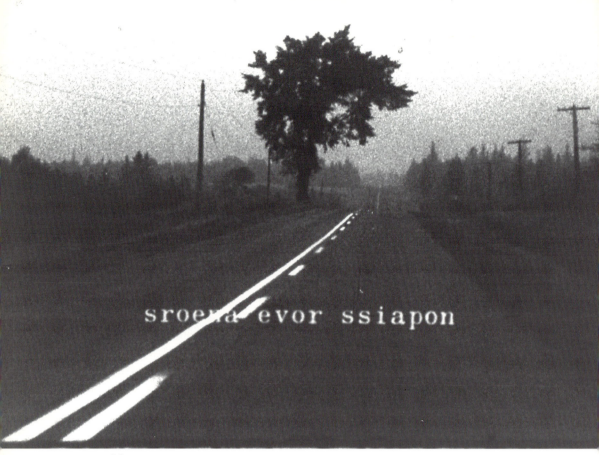

Still from *Reason over Passion*, 1967-69.

away after shots, and the final emptying of the camera ... I had over fifty feet in the magazine so I turned the camera around on the tripod and had it look out the window at the snow while it emptied itself."[18] It was not just happenstance that she concluded the film with the winter landscape. It was her intuitive understanding of the landscape as part of the Canadian imagination, which points back to *Reason over Passion*.

Joyce had combined a landscape film with a "face-scape" in *Reason over Passion*; now she had done a "mouth-scape," and her next film would be a "foot-scape" at a workers' strike — *Solidarity* (1973). In the spring of 1973, Joyce with her camera and Judy with her tape recorder went to Kitchener, Ontario, where the workers at the Dare cookie factory, mostly women, were on strike for better wages and decent working conditions. Five thousand people had come out in support of these workers, who often had to work in temperatures as high as 130°F.[19]

In the same way that Joyce had focused on the details of the mouth of Pierre Vallières, she now took close-ups of the feet of the striking workers: women moving their feet to the rhythm of the chanting, "Don't buy Dare cookies," the sandal strap across the back of a bruised heel, reflections of more feet in puddles. These images communicated the plight of women mistreated in the workforce, with the word "solidarity" overprinted throughout the film. As she let her camera roll, perhaps she remembered the Eaton's strike she attended in downtown Toronto when she was a teenager.

After making *Solidarity*, Joyce got up before dawn on summer mornings to work on two other projects: photographing birds outside the window of her Summerhill house and writing a script for a feature film loosely based on Tom Thomson. With her camera, she used "rolled-up papers to make these strange irises, and I made other irises out of paper and cardboard ... It was the life of birds at the window when dawn's coming and the light is changing."[20]

Joyce had also won a commission for a wall work for the National Science Library in Ottawa, and during 1972 and 1973 she designed a large quilt and hired quilters to create *Défendez la terre/Defend the Earth*, a work intended "to give warning to students who go there to do research ... Defend the earth against the god-damn chemicals."[21] She was pleased with the results of this new commission. Working with fabric was familiar territory; however, writing a script for a feature film was another matter, and she was floundering.

Joyce persisted because she had carried the seed of the idea for this film for many years. At age twenty, she had seen the Gorky Trilogy at the Toronto Film Society screenings. This trilogy, based on the autobiographical works of Russian writer Maxim Gorky, who was orphaned at a young age, tells his life story.[22] It evoked in Joyce a desire to make a film that had to do with a country.[23] However, at that time she had not yet worked with film, and she did not even know whether making a film would be possible. During her last few years in New York, she had become fascinated with the Group of Seven painters and Tom Thomson. More than half of Thomson's paintings depict the far shores of lakes, an image of mystery and longing, something that resonated with Joyce.

Typically, when an idea took hold of Joyce, she researched and read and talked about it, milking it completely. The Tom Thomson obsession was no exception — his mysterious death made his story even more appealing. Her desire to tell a story about a country fused with her obsession with Thomson and with concepts from films she had made in New York. She began thinking of this new film as the third part of a trilogy to complete the work of *Rat Life and Diet in North America* and *Reason over Passion*, and as a means of encompassing what she knew about making art.

Joyce also wanted to tell a story about love in a certain time period — 1919. She wanted to create an "emotional history" that included both French and English Canada.[24] She found the idea for her characters in her in-laws, a

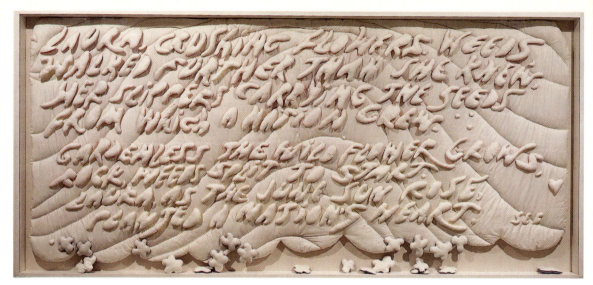

Laura Secord, 1974.

talented French-Canadian pianist and an English-Canadian engineer who, according to Joyce, eloped.[25] The flourish she added to the story — eloping — is not quite what happened. Michael's parents became acquainted in Chicoutimi when Bradley Snow was there. When he returned to Toronto, he invited Antoinette Lévesque for a visit with his family. With her parents' permission, she came to Toronto and while she was there the two married without a formal wedding.[26] Joyce, however, preferred her own story in which the pair eloped.

In Joyce's 1971 story outline of her film, she imagined British Columbia artist Emily Carr in love with Tom Thomson. Later she dropped Carr from the script, but she kept the idea of two artists as lovers.

"Nightmares in Dreamland," the title of one of the chapters in Susan Crean's *Who's Afraid of Canadian Culture*, is an apt description of the making of *The Far Shore*.[27] In this book, published the same year Joyce's feature film premiered, Crean details the history of filmmaking in Canada. Like many visual artists, Canadian feature filmmakers thought they had to go to the United States to be successful, with the exception of those who were content to make shorts and documentaries for the National Film Board (NFB). The NFB, established in May 1939, had become Canada's feather in its filmmaking cap because of its excellent social documentaries, documentary drama, animation and direct cinema. For a period of time in the early sixties, the NFB produced dramatic feature films, but continuous debate on whether this was an appropriate mandate adversely affected support for and production of these ventures.

As a result of pressure from within the NFB, Ottawa set up the Canadian Film Development Corporation (CFDC) in 1968 to support feature

THE FAR SHORE

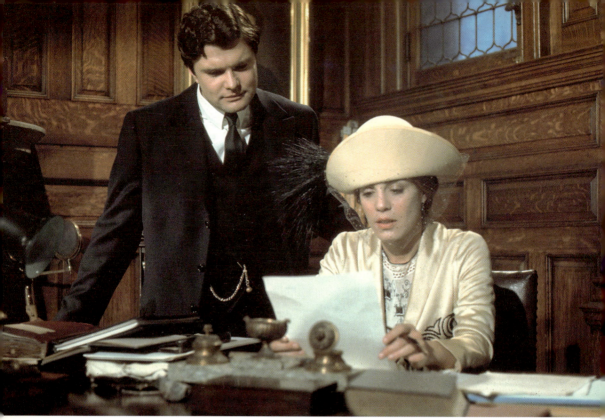

Ross (Lawrence Benedict) and Eulalie (Céline Lomez) in *The Far Shore*, 1974.

filmmaking. With government support available, Canadian feature films seemed more possible.[28] However, after an initial peak, feature film production dropped off. The idea had been that private investors would team up with the CFDC, but in the short time span of two years, funds from the private sector had not been forthcoming. Further complications lay in the distribution system, which is another saga in the history of Canadian-American relations, explained by Crean in her book.

Joyce had submitted a film outline to the CFDC in 1970 and it was rejected, but she was determined not to let that stop her. The year following her 1971 show at the National Gallery, she set up an office at 137 Summerhill and had letterhead printed, which included a logo of a tree resembling Tom Thomson's iconic tree in his painting *The West Wind*. Judy Steed had agreed to work with her, and they spent a year writing and mailing letters to dozens of potential investors, making follow-up phone calls, and whenever possible, going in person to offices of businesses to make a case for the film. They visited every floor of both the Toronto Dominion Centre and Commerce Court in downtown Toronto, but 90 per cent of the businesses were not interested.

Along with working on the script, Joyce had been drawing panels of scenes with dialogue pencilled in, a unique approach at that time for feature

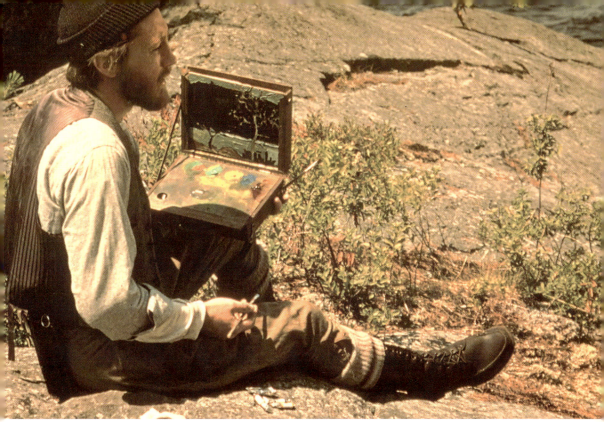

Frank Moore as Tom, the Tom Thomson character, in *The Far Shore*.

filmmaking, but a method that seemed natural to her because of her experience in animation. When she realized she could not write the script herself, she offered the task to her friend of many years, Brian Barney, who by then was a scriptwriter for radio and television. Sara Bowser, who was married to Barney until his death in July 1996, recalled that Joyce showed up at their place one day with a shopping bag full of "notes."[29] These notes must have been the twenty-one-page story outline she had originally developed. Joyce was relieved that Barney agreed to take on the project.

This, briefly, is the film's story. The exquisitely beautiful Eulalie Berthier, a pianist, is to marry a Quebec politician, but he breaks off their engagement. When she meets Ross Turner, a tall, well-to-do mining engineer, he falls in love with her and proposes marriage — a beautiful, charming woman would do credit to him in his position. Eulalie agrees to marry, though she does not love Ross, and she goes to live with him in Rosedale in Toronto.

Ross has mining interests in northern Ontario, where the Tom Thomson character, Tom McLeod, who is in love with the land, spends much of his time painting. Ross and his business partner, Cluny, take Eulalie with them when they go north. There she and Tom become acquainted. She discovers they are kindred spirits and increasingly Eulalie dislikes spending time with Ross and Cluny.

While Cluny, Ross and Eulalie are staying in a lodge in the area where Tom is painting, Ross announces suddenly that he must return to the city to look after some business. Eulalie refuses to return with him. As a compromise, Ross suggests that Cluny stay with her. Cluny, boor that he is, would be sure to take advantage of her. To escape these men, Eulalie jumps into the lake, fully dressed, and swims through the water to meet Tom.

Of course, the two men are startled by Eulalie's behaviour, suspect her intentions, and set out to find the lovers. By the second day, they spot the pair in Tom's canoe on the lake. Cluny has his gun with him and shoots at the canoe. Ross tries to stop Cluny, but he shoots again and kills both of them.

With this story in the hands of a scriptwriter, Joyce and Judy searched for a producer, someone who would be good at raising money. During the summer and fall, two producers were hired but after a few months they moved on to other jobs.[30] Finding a producer was a big problem. However, in the middle of all the difficulties, there was some progress — Barney's script was ready by the end of November, and in December Joyce and Judy submitted it to the Canadian Filmmakers Development Corporation with an application for $100,000 and a commitment to raise matching funds for a total budget of $200,000.

In January 1974, the CFDC replied that the film deserved a total budget of only $115,000. Joyce and Judy were disappointed because that amount would not cover the costs. They reasoned that if they could raise more money themselves, perhaps they could impress the CFDC enough that it would raise its offer since the corporation liked the script, and wanted the film to be done well. But they had to have a producer who could convince private investors that this was a good investment.[31]

Making feature films was not something many women had tackled. In English Canada, only two women before Joyce had done it.[32] She was into a tough game. Between January and April, two more producers came and went without raising any money, but somehow Joyce and Judy found the courage and determination to push on. Things were not going well at the beginning of 1974. In their wildest dreams they would have seen shooting by the year's end, but based on immediate evidence, chances were slim. In the name of their company, The Far Shore, Inc., they again set about raising money themselves. An actor named Larry Dane was hired as producer, and he persuaded the CFDC to raise the total film budget to $300,000, half of which would be raised from private investors. This was their first real breakthrough, but after six weeks, like the other producers, Dane left.

When Joyce saw the budget climbing — the CFDC regarded the film as a period piece and wanted it to be done as such — the size of the project frightened her. Still, greater than her fear was her desire to become a successful feature filmmaker, even though working with this much money and a big crew was as far from the process of making her kitchen-table films as the equator was from the North Pole. But an infusion of private money raised her spirits.

Phyllis Lambert, daughter of billionaire Samuel Bronfman, invested $20,000.[33] She had been living in Toronto for a year, and during that time met Joyce through the Isaacs Gallery. The letters Joyce wrote to Phyllis at that time reveal two things: Joyce was barely coping with her anxiety about raising enough money for the film and she was already fond of Phyllis, though she hardly knew her. She took great care to keep her new friend informed about the progress of the film.[34]

Famous Players put up $50,000 and Baton Broadcasting came in at half that, which was also the amount *The Toronto Star* invested. The architectural firm of Webb, Zerafa, Menkes and Housden invested an undisclosed amount, and there were also a number of smaller investors.[35] Several supporters hosted events to provide publicity for the film. Boris Zerafa, an art collector who still feels that the arts are vital to the life of this country, read the script and liked it. He felt women were not recognized enough and appreciated Joyce as an artist, which is the reason his architectural firm invested in the film. He hosted a dinner at his house for his family and friends to raise awareness of the project.[36] Joyce and Judy staged a variety of publicity events to raise funds, including a lecture at York University and a party in a Forest Hill home. Critic Robert Fulford remembered attending one such event. Although Joyce was at the party, instead of speaking about the film herself, she played an audio recording of what she had to say. Fulford could only conclude she was too shy to speak in person.[37]

Being without a producer was still a problem, but Judy and Joyce pushed on with the work of casting and finding the rest of the crew. They felt pleased when they found Eulalie after many trips to Montreal — Céline Lomez, who at age twenty-three had played a stripper in *Gina*, a film by Denys Arcand. Lomez was different from the other actresses they had interviewed, unconventional, very beautiful, a woman Joyce described as a little animal because of her spirit and the way she moved. Lomez liked the story immediately and was impressed with the research Joyce had done on Tom Thomson's life. And she was taken with Joyce herself. "At one point she [Joyce] gave me a little moonstone" — the name Eulalie means "moon." "I really liked Joyce, she was … earthy, her long braid down her back. I thought she was more Eulalie than I could be, almost. She was inspiring."[38]

Frank Moore was cast as Tom McLeod, the Tom Thomson character. Moore remembered that to get acquainted, Judy, Michael and Joyce came to his apartment. After Moore played his guitar and sang, the four of them

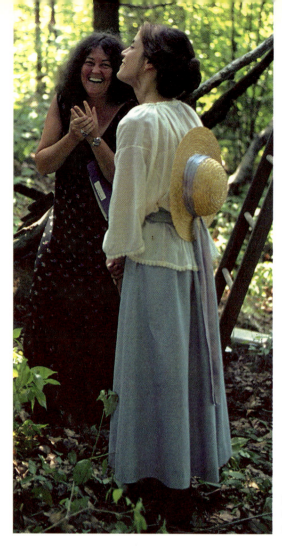

Joyce with
Céline Lomez
(Eulalie).

chatted for a while. He noticed that Michael was sympathetic to Joyce's work. "My impression was that this was Joyce's project, but Michael was supporting her, giving his two cents."[39] According to Moore's observations, Joyce and Michael were getting along well then. Also, during a shoot in Toronto, Lomez noticed that one morning when Joyce came to work she had a glow, like a woman who had spent a night making love.[40] Intimacy with Michael would have given her the self-confidence she needed.

Lawrence Benedict was hired to play Ross Turner, Eulalie's husband, and Sean McCann was chosen as Cluny, Ross's friend and business partner.[41] Besides finding the right actors for the roles, Joyce and Judy had to hire a crew and fill the two key positions of production designer and cinematographer.

Joyce had seen the work of Richard Leiterman in a film called *Wedding in White* and liked the camera work. Leiterman recalled that at their first meeting, he discovered Joyce was a smaller person than he expected, with little hands. He also noticed that she had a "wonderful face, round ... and a soft quality, a soft way of speaking."[42] Leiterman appreciated her approach because she knew how she wanted light to fall on objects, what colours she wanted, the time of day, and all kinds of other specific details, and because she used the work of such artists as Vermeer, Fragonard and Chardin as sources of inspiration. Joyce and Leiterman liked the idea of working together.

Through Sara Bowser, Joyce had met Anne Pritchard, an experienced production designer. The first time she came to Toronto to discuss the film, she stayed with Joyce and Michael at their house on Summerhill in a bedroom decorated with a giant stuffed beaver, which Anne disliked. Joyce was pleased that Ann accepted the job. Anne returned to Montreal and began work on the drawings for the costumes.

To write the music for the film, Joyce hired Douglas Pringle. Pringle knew Michael and Joyce because he had sometimes played with the Artists Jazz Band. He and Michaele Jordana Berman, a painter, were living and working in a large studio on Jarvis Street near Adelaide.[43] Berman was working on her large whale paintings, teaching herself the technique of airbrushing at the same time. She painted daily in her studio, and Joyce and others in *The Far Shore* would drop in. Frank Moore remembered spending a lot of time in their studio, just because of the atmosphere, playing music with Pringle and watching Berman painting a whale on the beach, huge, the size of an entire wall.

Moore sensed the special feeling articulated by other people who worked on the film. "We were all operating on some cosmic level ... there was a feeling we were all meant to be together doing this," Moore said. He believed that feeling came primarily from Joyce, and this attracted "like souls" and "like hearts."[44]

Richard Leiterman understood what Moore meant. "I think there were some extraordinary forces in there that led us into the places — the marvelous scenes. To me, at that point in my career, she did not articulate like ... the maker of a feature film." Leiterman remembered that sometimes while they were on location looking for a spot to shoot a scene, they would come upon the right place, and they just looked at each other and knew it was right. They drew strength from being in those places. He described the experience as "metaphysical."[45]

During the summer of 1974, Joyce made a number of trips to Algonquin Park in search of the right location. However, there were no suitable buildings there to use as Ross's cabin, so shooting the summer scenes had to be postponed. Judy spent days driving around Rosedale in Toronto looking for a house that would be appropriate for Ross Turner's home. Judy knocked on many doors, but no one wanted a film crew in the house. Finally, at one place the husband of Toronto singer Maureen Forrester opened the door. He suggested the house where they used to live, then owned by the Best family. As it turned out, Sandy Best knew Michael Snow because they had gone to school together. The house was about to be renovated, so in the meantime it could be used for filming. This house on Rosedale Road was exactly right — they could never have afforded the cost of building a similar set, and they borrowed furniture from The Grange, at the Art Gallery of Ontario. They had crossed another huge hurdle.[46]

In July, The Laidlaw Foundation's Dr. R.G. Nicholas Laidlaw gave a reception at which Joyce announced the production of the film as a "what-if" story about Tom Thomson. "What if Tom Thomson ... had met an irresistible French woman pianist?"[47] This was only the beginning of Laidlaw's support for Joyce — he would have a place in her work and life for years to come. Despite some successes, the frustration remained that they had been without a producer since April. By August Joyce decided to rehire Chalmers Adams, who had the job briefly earlier on. Things were looking up by September, when enough investors had come through that they began to plan for a November shoot.

In searching for an assistant, Joyce had sent a copy of a draft of *The Far Shore* to Pierre Théberge's brother, André Théberge, a young filmmaker who lived in Montreal. When the script arrived, he was about to leave for a trip to Europe, so he took it with him. He read it in his small hotel room in Paris and was "totally taken" by it. When Joyce phoned and asked if he would come to Toronto to work with her, he agreed. At age twenty-eight, this was his first experience working in English Canada.[48]

Théberge, who now has his own film production company, called Productions Magellan Inc., arrived at 137 Summerhill on Thanksgiving weekend in 1974. He helped Joyce for about five weeks, completing the storyboards and working against the November 18 deadline, when filming of the interior Toronto scenes and the winter scenes would begin. The outdoor summer scenes and those set in Algonquin Park would be filmed the following July. Later on, Joyce redrew the scenes for the July shoot in colour. Altogether, there were over two thousand remarkably detailed small drawings, now in the collection of the National Gallery of Canada.

Théberge became immersed in Joyce's daily life and thoughts, living with her and Michael, sleeping in their basement and swallowing the dozens of vitamin pills she gave him. They went together to eat at the Copenhagen Room near Yonge and Bloor Streets and spent many evenings talking about fantasy, books and travel, with Dwight the cat sleeping or prowling about the house and Michael playing the piano. Joan, Joyce's sister, was also at 137 Summerhill during that time, doing the shopping and cooking while Joyce worked on her storyboards. Théberge remembers that Joan brought a calm, practical mind to the household — Joyce was "full of fancy, talking about angels and stuff like that ... Joan was a good presence in the house."[49]

Some of the scenes were rehearsed and taped on video. Keith Lock, a young filmmaker who lived in Toronto, video-taped these rehearsals, many of which took place at Betty Ferguson's farm, including Tom and Eulalie's water scenes. They all stayed in Ferguson's rambling house for close to a week while working on this early stage of the film. Lock cannot recall whether he got paid, but remembers Joyce as special, the kind of person for whom you would want to do things.[50]

In November, both Céline Lomez and Anne Pritchard arrived from Montreal to begin shooting. Lomez lived in a donated room at the Windsor Arms Hotel, where she immersed herself in Debussy. To keep herself in the spirit of the period, she used no electric lights in her room, only candles. Fresh flowers arrived in her room daily, and before the shooting began, Joyce gave Lomez a bottle of "aged cologne unearthed from some grandmother's chest."[51] The Windsor Arms Hotel also donated a room for Anne Pritchard.

The plan was to film the winter scenes and those in the interior of Ross Turner's house and the painter's shack, a replica of Tom Thomson's cabin built for $6,000 in the Rosedale Valley ravine in Toronto. This ravine, which begins at the Don River, threads north-west through the city as far as Yonge Street and more or less ends in Ramsden Park, is part of the network of ravines that gives Toronto its parks and trees. Placing the shack in this ravine offered the big advantage of being close to the house used as the home of Ross and Eulalie. The shack had been designed and built in sections, and then constructed on site in a very short period of time. People who walked their dogs in the ravine stopped by to find out what was going on — they were astonished to see a cabin that had not been there the last time they had been through.

According to a typed schedule for *The Far Shore*, the very first shoot was on November 18 on Baldwin Street in Kensington Market outside a fish store, a part of the Remembrance Day sequences in the film. This schedule includes a brief description of scenes, and lists the props and costumes for every day from Day One to Day Fourteen, Thursday, December 5. Interestingly, Day Two included shooting the restaurant scene in the Franz Joseph Room in the Walker House Hotel on Front Street, which was where Joyce and Michael went for drinks after they were married at City Hall twenty years earlier.

Joyce worked hard to help the actors prepare for their roles. One of her influences was the music of the French composer Claude Debussy (1862-

1918). Frank Moore remembered that before they started shooting, Joyce invited him to her house, and they just sat and listened to Debussy and "zoned into the music."[52] She had also arranged for him to go to Camp Kandalor on a ten-day wilderness trip to learn how to swim and paddle a canoe. The idea was to get him to a point of feeling comfortable and completely natural in Tom Thomson's Algonquin Park environment. He also learned to play the ukulele.

On his own, Moore decided to spend a night in the cabin in the ravine. He thought it would be romantic to read there by candlelight and sleep in the cabin. He did not realize that the filming equipment was stored there at night, and he barely had enough space to get into the tiny cot. Surrounded by big metal stands and lights, he had a miserable night because he was cold and slept for only a few hours.

The next morning he and Lomez were to do some scenes, and Moore was in rough shape. He saw Joyce and Leiterman consulting, and they came to him and said, "Frank, how do you feel about doing the mandolin scene today?" He had not rehearsed this part for a few weeks because he had been told the song would be recorded in the studio and he would just be miming on the set. When Moore told them he was not up to it, they walked away, and he could see them in their consultation again, Joyce with her thumb and finger on her lip, her characteristic posture when she was thinking hard, probably wearing her blue denim shift down to her ankles.[53]

Joyce and Leiterman returned to Moore and "impressed upon me that they felt it was incredibly important that we do the scene ... that we just do it live." The look in their eyes, that they believed this was the thing to do, convinced Moore. He and Lomez did the mandolin scene, a one-take performance. "They'd been right to insist on it," Moore said. "That's the kind of thing that would happen, and the way it would happen. When I saw the belief that was in their eyes — you just had to go."[54]

Sometimes it was not clear what Joyce wanted. She often described the essence of what a scene was to be rather than how to get there. Her way of directing almost by osmosis, as Moore put it, was sometimes too vague to give an actor what he needed. For Moore, confirmation of his acting sometimes came from Leiterman — from Joyce he got what the scene's essence was to be and from Leiterman, whether he was getting it.

It is not surprising that Joyce had difficulty in communicating what she wanted. This was her first directing experience. In other aspects of the film, her rigorous research stood her in good stead: her investigation of Tom Thomson, her search for the objects that characterized the period, and her study of paintings as a basis for texture and colour.

Her investigation was fuelled by an obsessive curiosity — Judy Steed

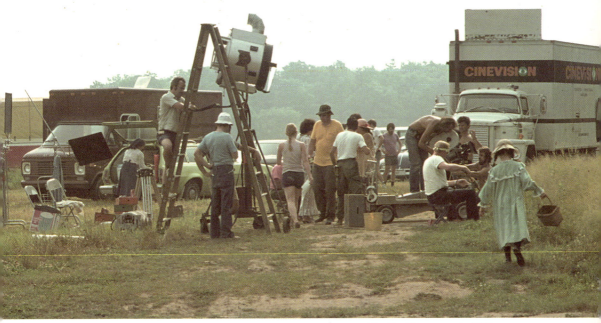

The Far Shore crew in 1975.

characterized Joyce as having an "entrepreneurial strength combined with an artistic vision." Judy was also convinced that Joyce "wanted to make a break into mainstream film ... that she had a big ambition of becoming a big-time filmmaker."[55] If Judy was right, then that drive was likely one of the things that kept Joyce going.

The filming process was overwhelming to Joyce. It was so much more complicated than what she had experienced in making her small experimental films. In fact, according to Théberge, the film "became a machine she couldn't control." Théberge stood right behind her during the filming to provide her with the backbone she did not have in such a situation. Théberge remembered that on the set in the cabin, the actors had rehearsed their parts the day before, the lighting had been discussed and the set was prepared, and when Leiterman said he was ready, Joyce simply stood there, vibrating with excitement and unable to speak. So they tried it again. The cameraman was ready, and in a small, quiet voice, Joyce managed to say, "action," instead of the loud "ACTION" typical of a film director. At the end of a scene, "she was so taken and fascinated and in love literally with all that was happening — this vision of hers was actually happening — she would totally forget, she'd forget to say 'cut.'" Finally, Théberge, as always, standing close to her, became her voice when it came to "action" and "cut."[56]

Leiterman thinks Joyce didn't want the scenes to end because they were so beautiful, and she wanted to spend hours with each one. Sometimes "with

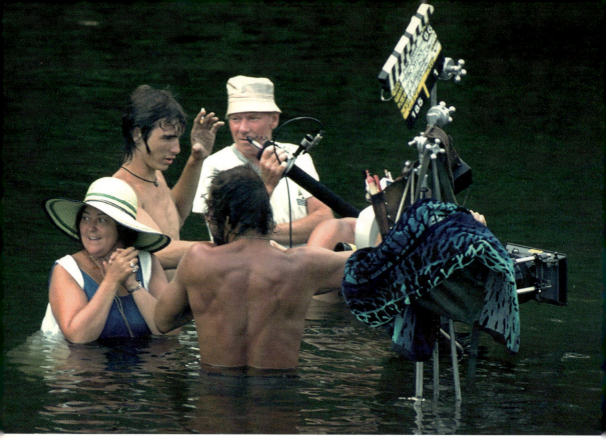

Joyce with the Camera crew, 1975.

a sigh she'd kind of turn and say 'I guess we gotta do something else now.'"[57]

It seemed she could hardly believe that what she had envisioned for five years was at last taking form. But there were parts of her original vision that were abandoned because of lack of money, and some ideas just didn't work. For example, she had wanted to open the film with an airplane flying overhead from which love notes would fall and land at Eulalie's feet. In a scene where Eulalie is playing the piano and Tom is standing listening, his arms folded, he gasps and puts his hand over his chest; Joyce had wanted to use animation to show cupid shooting an arrow in Tom's heart because at that moment he fell in love with Eulalie. In another scene, when the lovers come out of the water, Joyce wanted Eulalie to make a noise like a bird — "a wild Canadian bird" — which was to be the sound of love, but it did not work.[58] Joyce had also wanted to portray the lovers near the end of the film winding through the forest with the woodland animals gathering around them to pay homage to their love, an example of her "pantheist mind."[59]

Some of the crew noticed when Joyce's lack of experience with feature films created difficulties. Sometimes they told her, "you just don't do that" in a feature film, when she wanted to try certain things. However, Théberge believed that Joyce's ideas would have worked, and the real reason they were

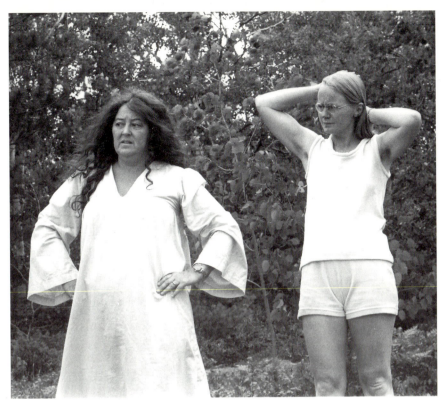
Joyce and Judy Steed during the filming of *The Far Shore.*

rejected was that they were "outside convention."[60] Perhaps his point of view came from firsthand experience of the creative process, which includes moments when an artist flounders in attempting to discover the way to go. In retrospect, Anne Pritchard, the production designer, wondered what the film would have been like if Joyce had been able to work on *The Far Shore* in the same way she did her small, experimental films, instead of trying to adopt the conventions of feature films.[61]

For the cast and crew of a feature film, the impression that the director doesn't know what she's doing is disconcerting. Furthermore, according to Larisa Pavlychenko, who was the photographer hired to document the making of the film, Joyce and Judy discussed changes and worked through disagreements on the set.[62] This, too, would have undermined confidence in Joyce.

After the turn of the New Year, sometime in January, Joyce held a screening of the film footage for the investors, who apparently liked what they saw. However, the costs for the film had run way over budget. Joyce was under enormous strain because without money the film could not be completed. She entered the hospital in late January "for an unstated illness brought on by the strain."[63]

Aside from money problems, there were at least three concrete reasons for Joyce's stress and illness during that winter and spring: criticism of her ability as a director, her difficulties with the producer and her relationship with Michael. Joyce's way of making art was the complete opposite of the way feature films are made. When shooting is in progress, there is little time to stop and try this and that, to follow a different idea because it might be interesting, to stop off and dream a little and change things. She had an organic way of working, but it was not possible to direct a feature film that way, with a crew around her and actors moving through their scenes all needing her direction. Nor did her way of working fit into a finite budget, which is the reason the budget got out of hand. As Michael explained, "Joyce didn't have the discipline and finding the discipline nearly killed her."[64]

Another complication was that Joyce was working in an era when men had the prerogative to direct women, and not the other way around. In many fields, from education to business, from science and technology to the arts, women experienced not only men's attempts at keeping them out of traditionally men-only jobs, but blatant sexual harassment.[65] Filmmaking was no exception.

Joyce was told a number of times she should let someone else — a man, of course — be the director of the film. As Joyce and Judy perceived the situation, men became insecure when they did not know where the power lay in the working relationship of the two women. A basic criticism was that the film needed more conflict in the love relationship, but Joyce had an answer: that was a man's idea of what a relationship should be.[66]

Eventually Joyce's inexperience, along with the criticism, led her to wonder whether she should listen to these other voices, and she questioned her directing ability. Feeling unsure of themselves, one day over coffee Joyce and Judy talked about whether to let another director take over. Very quickly they realized this was Joyce's project, and she, with Judy, would see it through to the end. Later, Joyce felt ashamed that she had even considered giving over the film to someone else.[67] However, she had known all along that the reality of the power structure meant that to get attention and respect, the film would need a male executive producer. Larry Dane had supported Joyce as director, and his stamp of approval when he was producer had carried some weight with the CFDC, which had helped to get the film this far. Still, Joyce and Judy did not like the implication of all this. "Getting a male in on it means you gotta' be small, weak and dependent. The stronger Joyce is the less appeal to the male figures," Judy said at the time.[68]

The producer during the first shoot, Chalmers Adams, was among those who suggested to Joyce that she hire another director.[69] Not only that, but a number of his actions created an enormous amount of frustration. In an interview dated February 26, 1975, Judy and Joyce explained. After the first shoot, the producer told the editor to begin cutting the film even before Joyce had seen the footage. In the interview Judy said, "We were never able to look at all the film because when they started to cut a reel, they had broken everything down. They'd taken it off the cores ..." It took more than a week to put things back together so they could look at the footage. But "two reels they cut we could never do anything with and those scenes are awkward." There was only so much time and money, and they could not afford to take the time required to reclaim the footage.[70]

Joyce realized she could not work with a producer who tried to take over, and Adams was let go. It is clear from the taped interview that during this time Joyce was dispirited. This was not the way she wanted to work, and it seemed that in English Canada there was virtually no support for women who wanted to make films. She must have felt that the whole project was in jeopardy, and in fact, it was, because she had gone over budget.

All along, the CFDC had wanted an experienced executive producer because neither Joyce nor Judy had experience in feature filmmaking. That spring, after having been without a producer for a number of weeks, the late Pierre Lamy, the highly experienced producer of the film *Kamouraska*, agreed to take the job. He brought with him a production manager, Louise Ranger. Ranger remembered that the financial problems were very serious "and they wouldn't finish the film if they didn't reorganize the production part of it."[71] Lamy drew up a new budget because the situation was impossible as it was. They needed an additional $100,000. The CFDC had confidence in him and promised $50,000, and he managed to raise matching private funds. Lamy decided shooting could resume in July.[72]

Ironically, while Joyce was grappling with situations of gender-bias, the United Nations declared 1975 International Women's Year. Many galleries — large public galleries across Canada as well as small artist-run centres and commercial galleries — featured the work of women artists. At the National Gallery, for example, Mayo Graham curated "Some Canadian Women Artists," a show that included artists not shown before at the National Gallery. Graham, in her catalogue essay, cited Joyce Wieland's 1971 exhibition as an example of the change in attitude towards women's work, a change that she said emphasized women's previous invisibility. "If one thinks of the major figures in Canadian art, two women stand out: Emily Carr and Joyce Wieland. For both of them, the process of becoming, and being accepted as, an artist was difficult."[73] Joyce would have seen this as an understatement if she had read the essay. Because she was caught up in *The Far Shore*, her work did not appear in exhibitions that year.

As the film "office" spread throughout their house, tensions between

Michael and Joyce began surfacing. In later years, Michael would admit that he was uncomfortable with having Judy at the house. But he also said that the film would not have been made if it had not been for Judy. "Judy was more an ideological zealot, which Joyce never was. [Judy] was on the pushy side," and she had the necessary discipline. "But I found it a little bit uncomfortable but I didn't have the right to be uncomfortable [because] what was being done was a fine thing."[74] In other words, he thought it was great that Joyce was making the film, but he wasn't happy with what was happening to his domestic life.

In fact, after the film was finished, one article said that "The last few years ... have been very difficult for her husband, Michael Snow. He has had to assume many of the mundane household chores." The journalist went on to say that despite the difficulties over doing laundry, the couple respected each other.[75] True, they did, but the apparent connection between Joyce and Michael, observed earlier on by Moore and Lomez, was somewhat tattered, and it seemed that Joyce was not absolutely sure she could count on Michael's love.

Jo Haines remembers that at one point racoons had moved into the house and were upsetting Joyce because she thought they were "peeing in the walls." She wanted them removed. "Mike was not good about taking care of fundamental [household] things," Jo said, and it seemed the two of them could not work together on how to get rid of the racoons. Jo saw the situation as a "metaphor that things weren't getting solved."[76]

It became obvious, however, that Joyce and Michael had to find a solution to the stress *The Far Shore* was causing at their house. In the past, the arrangement had always been that Joyce had her studio at home and Michael rented a studio elsewhere, but this was no longer working. Joyce looked around for a house in the east part of the city, and with the help of artist Charles Pachter, she found a place on Queen Street East. The house was purchased for $29,500, with the legal title held by Joyce Wieland and Michael Snow, Ltd., a company they had formed several years earlier, even though they kept their personal earnings separate within this formal arrangement.[77] The house was specifically for *The Far Shore* office. According to Michael, they would "theoretically stay together but we would have the two places."[78]

Joyce took possession of 497 Queen Street East on an unusually cold April Fools' day in 1975. Her nephew, Keith Stewart, lived in the house while he did major work on it, including putting in new wiring and plumbing. A month later, she threw a party at Beaver Lodge, which is what she called the house.

Moving the film office relieved some tension, but it also raised questions for Joyce about what having her own house might mean for her relationship with Michael. With her energy already stretched thin, she developed a

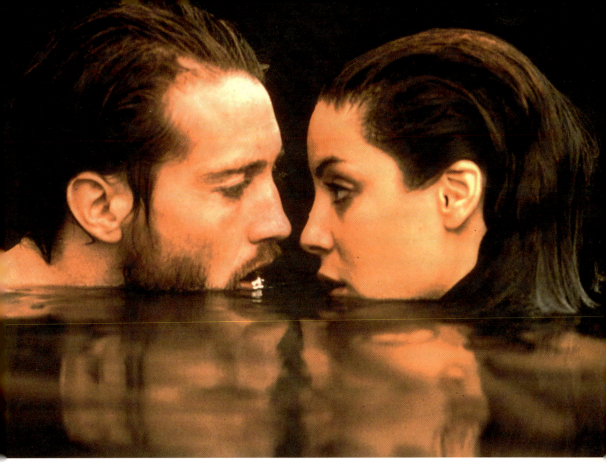

Tom (Frank Moore) and Eulalie (Céline Lomez) in *The Far Shore*.

problem with excessive vaginal bleeding, and her doctor recommended a hysterectomy. She must have been terrified, given her girlhood memories of her mother bleeding before she died. Not only did the bleeding evoke her childhood trauma, but the prospect of surgery opened up the pain of something she already knew: she would never have children. She became extremely depressed and often cried. Her friends were worried about her.

Joyce had surgery in May. Betty Ferguson and Michael were at the hospital with Joyce when she went into the operating room. Betty waited till Joyce came out of surgery, but, according to her memory, Michael had left by then.[79] During her recovery, Joyce at times was overcome with weeping. She went into a dramatic "death-bed scene with Mike where she was trying to keep him with her," Judy Steed recalled. Joyce seemed helpless and in a "panic trying to hang on to him."[80] While she recovered, Michael, her friends and others associated with *The Far Shore* visited her in the hospital. One day while Michaele Jordana Berman was there, Michael came to the hospital to see Joyce, carrying a bunch of dandelions. It seemed to be his way "of being cute, of being affectionate — a jar full of dandelions."[81]

During the winter of 1975, Judy and Joyce had continued their search for the right location for the summer shoot, an environment similar to Algonquin Park with a suitable building for Ross's summer place. They travelled by snowmobile across the frozen Skootamata Lake to look at summer homes and with some help found an old hunting cabin, which turned out to be exactly what they needed, near Cloyne, Ontario, about a hundred kilometres north of Belleville.

By July, when the second shoot was scheduled to begin, Pierre Lamy had set up the new budget, with his production manager, Louise Ranger, in charge of it. After filming in the Rosedale ravine again, the crew went to Lake Skootamata. It was everything Joyce and Judy could have hoped for, with a mixture of sunny days and cloudy, rainy weather. They held to a regular daily work schedule. Some of the crew stayed at the lodge, and others had rooms at a country motel not far away. But after the first few days "we started getting into the swing of things there and it developed a life of its own." Sometimes most of them slept at the lodge instead of returning to the motel, enjoying the congeniality that developed among the crew.[82]

Ranger spent her evenings assessing the day's expenses, including such details of how much film had been used, how much time scenes had required, whether the day's shoot went overtime, and if so, how to cut time the next day. The scene near the end of the film, the two lovers in the water, for example, had to be shot in two hours because of the budget. At the same time the crew was trying to keep away boats full of curious people wondering what was going on.[83] Water scenes, in general, can take a lot of time, Ranger explained, and in a tight budget, something else must be given up if one part requires additional time. The crew must be paid for their time and the production manager must account for everything — you can't lose a minute. This is the kind of pressure that Joyce found stressful, but "she would find solutions even if sometimes it was hard," Ranger said. Joyce was disappointed about some things because "she was not allowed to do everything she wanted to do because of the budget."[84]

By the time July 24 arrived, the shooting had been completed. In an August 6, 1975, memo to the investors, Joyce and Judy reported that they had completed shooting on time and on budget. From August to November the titles and the sound editing were done, and by December the rough cut had been completed.[85] It had been an extraordinary year for Joyce, having been thrown "from pillar to post," and it was not until later that she would realize the severe consequences.

The film premiered on August 5 at Ottawa '76, an international film festival at the National Arts Centre Theatre. A party followed at the home of Dennis Reid. In Toronto, on September 23, the film opened at the Towne Cinema with a party afterwards at the Art Gallery of Ontario. Joyce bought

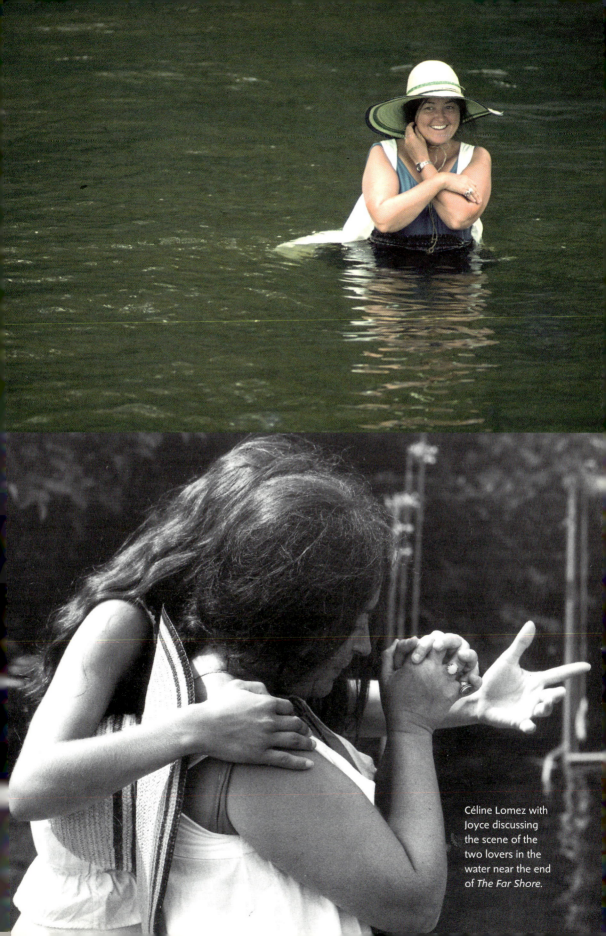

Céline Lomez with Joyce discussing the scene of the two lovers in the water near the end of *The Far Shore*.

herself a new scarlet and cream coloured satin evening gown. And she managed to find 1920s Silver Dart Cadillacs to chauffeur the cast from the Towne to the gallery.[86] A tightly orchestrated schedule of the gala included pipers leading the cast and crew from their cars into the gallery over a red carpet. In a ceremony honouring the film, the cast and crew were presented, and at the end Joyce was introduced, and immediately a fiddler played a fast gig and Alan Withrow asked Joyce to dance.

In the year leading to the completion of the film, numerous articles about it had appeared in magazines and newspapers, creating a sense of anticipation. One reviewer said people wanted it to succeed for "the sake of both Canadian cinema and Joyce Wieland."[87] He added that it didn't.

Critic Robert Fulford described the film in 1976 as articulating Joyce's "sensibility in detail for the first time." He summarized the qualities in her work, which she expressed in *The Far Shore*: innocence, naive and sentimental charm, sexuality, melancholy romanticism, blatant symbolism, parody, ecology and art. Fulford also said that Joyce shrewdly attached her own narrative to the myth created by the Group of Seven artists who, in revolt against European art, painted the Canadian landscape. He called the film "a triumph of Wielandism."[88] But "a triumph of Wielandism" did not mean it succeeded as a film. Twenty-five years later Fulford said the problems in the film made it extremely difficult to watch, and it appeals primarily to people interested in Joyce Wieland's work.[89]

Another film critic, Lauren Rabinovitz, in a theoretical analysis, pointed out that the film shows "how the woman experimental filmmaker has attempted to use melodramatic form for feminist ends."[90] The film clearly conveys Joyce's intuitive understanding of the history of the relationship between men and women from a feminist perspective. For example, in one scene Eulalie photographs wild flowers. Ross takes the camera from her and asks her to pose while he photographs her, thus placing her in a submissive position, and himself in a position of power.

From a feminist perspective, in the context of the time, the film made its mark, but it was not accepted by movie-goers in the theatres. Writer Susan Crean said Joyce had turned the feature film on its head and was "messing around with convention in ways that the audience didn't necessarily follow."[91] Crean was right, and some critics thought the marketing was partly to blame because audiences expected a more typical feature film. Clearly, audiences did not care about Joyce's silent movie techniques and that she was paying "homage to D.W. Griffith's cinematic irises as a bridge between scenes."[92] Nor did the painterly quality in the memorably beautiful scenes make up for an unsatisfactory script and what some critics described as stiff and awkward characters. The run in the theatres was brief.

Joyce took the film to the 1976 Edinburgh Film Festival. The festival program notes described *The Far Shore* as "austerely beautiful" and "accessible yet divisive." The split arose between those who found the film "deeply affecting in its simplicity and passionate romanticism" and those who thought it "naive and badly acted."[93] Lauren Rabinovitz stated that the audience response was hostile, and Joyce dropped the idea of taking the film to other film festivals.[94]

Joyce was devastated. Perhaps worse than the film's commercial failure was the rejection of her attempt to give Canadians their own mythological film about their land, which the artist painted and the mining engineer exploited.

When she had an opportunity, Joyce expressed in a practical way the statement her film had made about the land. In early spring of 1976 she pulled her work from a show called "Changing Visions: The Canadian Landscape," an exhibition at the Art Gallery of Ontario sponsored by Reed Paper Company, a subsidiary of Dryden Chemical Company. This company had been dumping mercury into the Wabagoon and English River Systems, making the fish toxic and consequently endangering the livelihood of the native people there. Joyce told the press that "Cleaning Reed's reputation is not our [artists'] job."[95] What an irony that a show of Canadian landscape would be financed by a company polluting rivers!

Protests against pollution, her nationalism, *The Far Shore* — it all fit together. She claimed the film was her *"Reason over Passion* with people."[96] But it is also true that *The Far Shore* is her *True Patriot Love* of 1971 with people.

The ending of *The Far Shore* was the first time in her work that she portrayed tragedy with such harsh, grim finality. After the shooting, we see the canoe overturned and Tom's dead, floating body. Of Eulalie, we see only her hat floating on the water.

Joyce repeatedly said she worked from her personal experience. We can read the finality of what happens to Tom and Eulalie as symbolic of a shift within her, the beginning of a realization that her personal mythology was breaking apart.

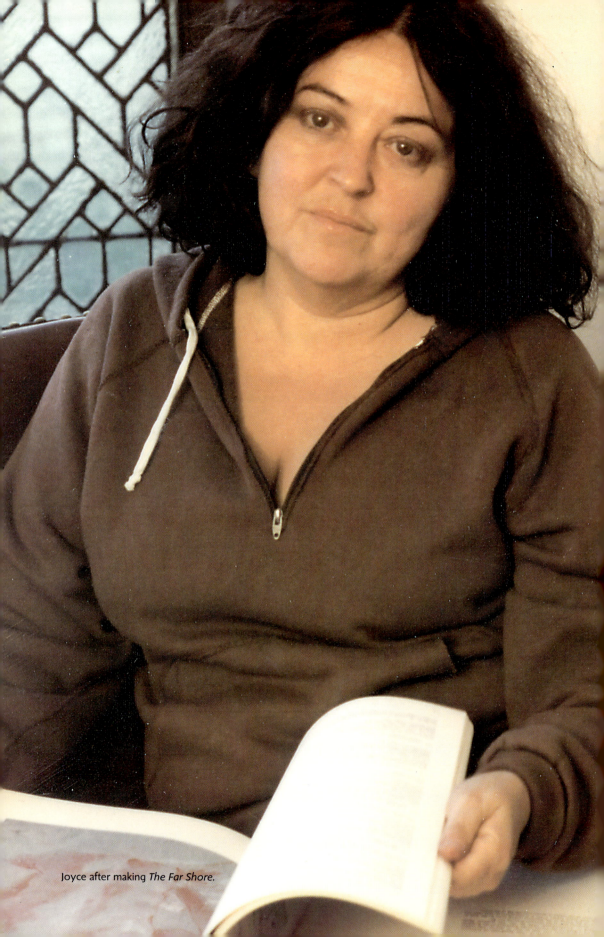
Joyce after making *The Far Shore*.

8

End of life as she knew it

I made some self-portraits a couple of summers back. They were painted up very close and when you get far away, they're a whole different thing. I really wanted to find out what I looked like. One is my Scottish self and one is my English self.

Drawing has always been with me. More and more it had become a form of meditation. My color drawings are very sensual and spiritual at the same time. —Joyce Wieland[1]

MAKING *The Far Shore* was probably the first time in her creative life that Joyce could not take off into her imagination without constraint and still accomplish what she had set out to do. I believe this aspect of those years, as much as the gruelling work of raising money and other pressures, is what depleted her "basic energy," as she put it — living outside her imagination was too painful, and nearly impossible. That the film won several awards — for cinematography and art direction — did not make up for how drained she felt.

Joyce repeatedly told people that making the film nearly killed her. Five years after she had finished it, she described the experience as a "form of madness" and a "very dangerous extension of energy; my energy got where I almost couldn't get it back."[2] She also admitted that when she was touring in

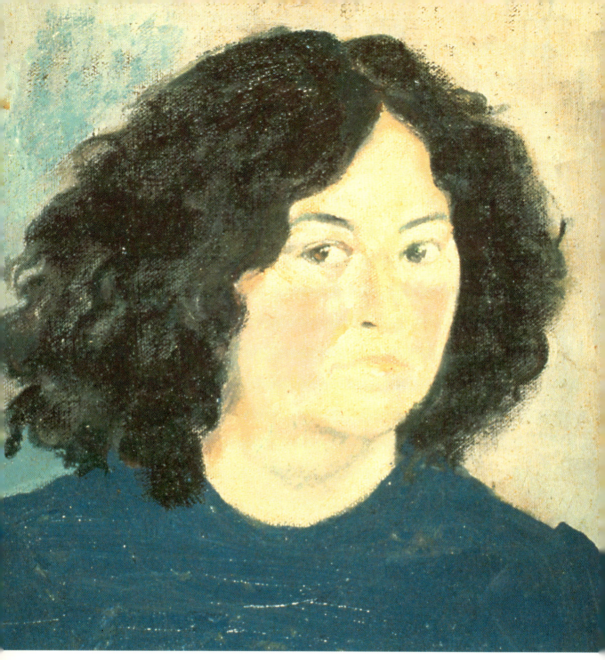

Self-Portrait, 1978.

1978 with *The Far Shore* she sometimes despised the film because of what it did to her.

So why, even before this movie was released, did she begin work on another feature film, while at the same time telling people she wanted to return to her painting? Perhaps she had not yet realized the extent of the depletion of her energy. In January 1976, before *The Far Shore* was completed, Joyce and Judy had rented an office for a film based on Margaret Laurence's novel *The Diviners.* They bought an option on the screen rights from Laurence for $8,000 and set up an office at 24 Ryerson Avenue, a building called Artists' Alliance, bought by Toronto artist Charles Pachter in 1974. He lived on the third floor and rented out the rest of the space to artists and writers, including a first-floor gallery, the Artery.

Pachter, as Associate Producer, raised $140,000 from private investors as seed money for the film.[3] Pachter was excited by the idea of working on *The Diviners*, but years later he would admit that "I didn't know what the hell I was doing," and in retrospect didn't think Judy and Joyce did either.[4]

Judy had wanted to continue a filmmaking partnership with Joyce. They made several attempts at having a script written, and Judy even flew to Hollywood to talk to a prospective director and to explore casting ideas. But a Hollywood-type scenario did not suit their way of working. Judy also soon realized that Joyce had neither the energy nor the passion for it.[5] Furthermore, *The Diviners* was not Joyce's story. After a year and a half, the time limit on the option to the film rights ran out, and in the spring of 1978, *The Diviners* project quietly died.[6] Judy went on to pursue a career in newspaper journalism.

The year *The Far Shore* premiered, Joyce painted a self-portrait, holding a paintbrush, with mountains in the background giving a feeling of solidity to the picture, but her expression is one of fear and uncertainty. With the eyes looking to the side, the portrait is remarkable for its resemblance to an ink drawing of herself as a child she had made years earlier. At a time when making a feature film had drained her, at a time of self-assessment, she returned to her identity as a painter.

In the summer of 1978 Joyce painted more small self-portraits. In several of these, the artist's head is turned to the side, but there is one in which she looks directly at the viewer; she is introspective and vulnerable. These portraits use what writer Marsha Meskimmon called "sober self-portraiture techniques," which challenge the objectification of women. Joyce's self-portraits, which were an exercise in personal exploration, even in their simplicity carry "positive assertions of women as subjects rather than objects in representation."[7]

In all of these self-portraits, the set of the mouth conveys determination, even defiance. But maintaining the fierce determination with which she began her career was difficult during this troubled period of her life. Not only was her energy drained, but the difficulties between her and Michael, which had surfaced during the making of *The Far Shore*, continued. The failure of her feature film and the possibility of losing her husband filled her with fear.

Sometimes when she was in distress, she phoned a friend. Painter Helen Lucas one day responded and rushed to the Queen Street house to find Joyce completely distraught and crying. Helen held her. She understood the state

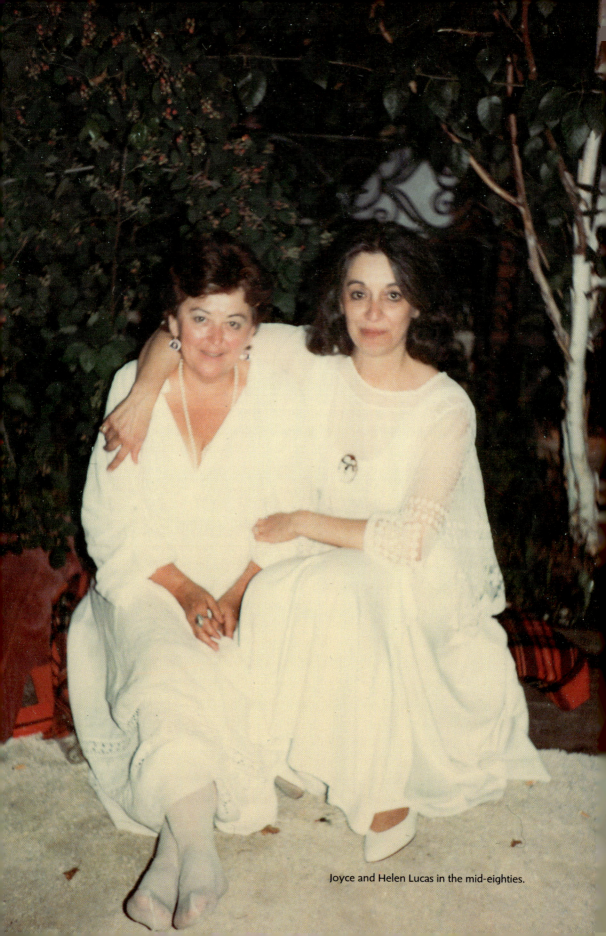

Joyce and Helen Lucas in the mid-eighties.

Joyce was in because of her own anguish when she left her marriage. A week later, Joyce phoned Helen and invited her to a roast-chicken dinner as a thank you.[8]

By then, Joyce had gained a lot of weight. A consultation with a doctor the previous year had revealed that she was eating 145 grams of fat a day — sixty per cent of her diet, twice the recommended amount. Because she was at risk for cardiovascular problems, the doctor suggested a different way of eating and an exercise program so that she could gradually lose forty pounds during the following year.[9] Changing her diet was not easy because Joyce loved rich foods, including chocolate, which was often her downfall. Later, when she got a car, she would sometimes at night drive to a Laura Secord candy store — she knew what time the Laura Secord stores closed. For the rest of her life she went through cycles of gaining weight and dieting.

During the late seventies, Joyce kept thinking about going to the Arctic. Perhaps this desire intensified when she was doing research on caribou for a $32,000 Toronto Transit Corporation commission she had won in 1975, which she called *Barren Ground Caribou* (1978). Her starting point for the large quilt was a comparison of the subway to the Altamira caves in Spain. In contrast to those caves, the subway system was in the "deepest bowels of technology." Like the cave drawings, which were "for magical purposes," Joyce wanted to bring the caribou into the subway as a reminder of the natural world.[10] She imagined businessmen, carrying briefcases, walking past these caribou, and young children holding onto the hands of an adult, asking questions about the caribou as they walked past.

Joyce phoned her sister, who by then lived in Owen Sound, Ontario, and asked her to quit her job to work on the quilt, which she did gladly because she enjoyed quilting. Meanwhile, once Joyce had completed her caribou research, she drew the animals and had enlargements made to be used as patterns for cutting the fabric pieces, which were stitched together and stuffed. This project had enormous technical problems, and as in other large commissions, Joan was the one who found solutions.[11] The quilt took her seven months of full-time work, with help from her three daughters. Joyce paid her about $10,000.

When Joan had the quilt ready to be fully assembled, Joyce did not have a large enough space. She traded art with Charles Pachter for the use of his large studio. Some of Joyce's friends volunteered, but she also hired women to help with assembly. "We laid it down and at one point there were twenty-seven women around it trying to flatten it down ... I had to hire someone to sleep with the quilt because there's no way you could insure it. All these windows — it was on the ground level and you could see in, and I had a lot at stake because this was a $32,000 work. So the only thing I could think of

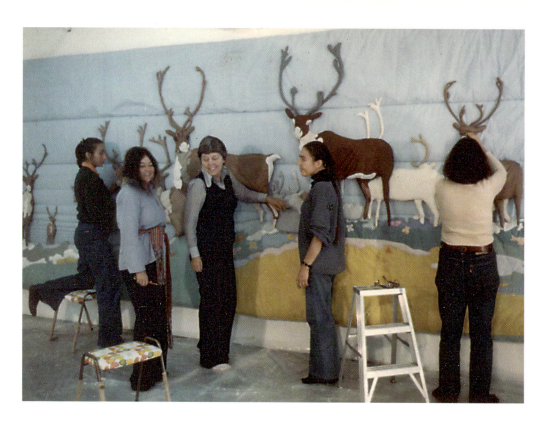

Snapshot of Joyce with friends finishing *Barren Ground Caribou.*

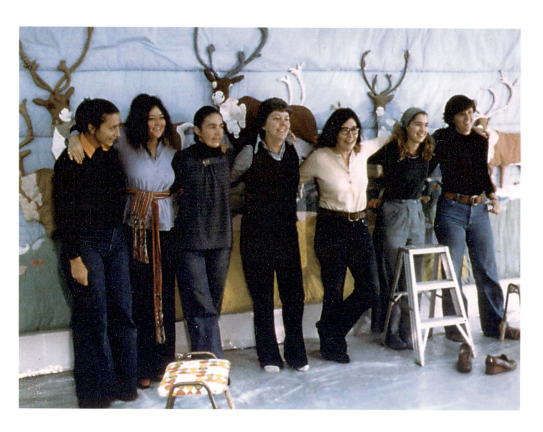

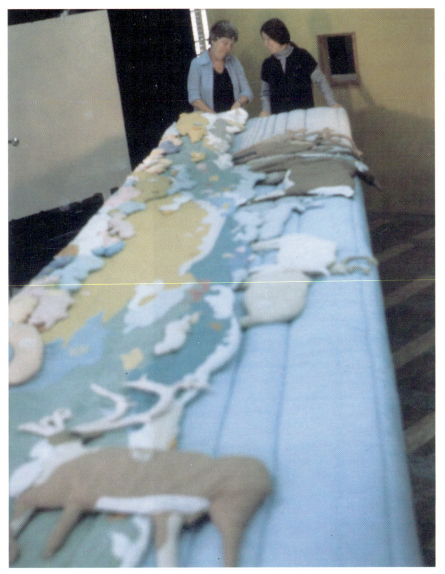

Snapshot of Joan Stewart Prowd and Allison McComb working on
Barren Ground Caribou, 1978.

was to hire someone to stay there."[12] She supplied the two women she hired
with a hot plate and coffee, and they would come at eight o'clock in the
evening and stay through the night.[13]

When *Barren Ground Caribou* was complete, Joyce hired a large flat-bed
truck to take it to the subway station. The quilt, with its seventeen caribou
— one of them has pink antlers! — standing in a variety of positions in the
Arctic tundra still hangs in a plexiglass case at the Kendal Avenue exit of the
Spadina subway station.

Not long after completing her commission, Joyce went to Cape Dorset in
the Arctic for a few weeks early in 1979.[14] She had never before experienced

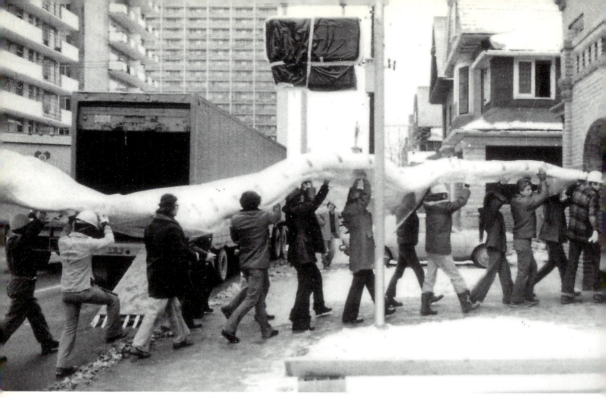

Carrying *Barren Ground Caribou* into the Kendal Avenue exit of the Spadina subway station.

the prismatic light of the Arctic — she saw rainbows around the edges of objects. She wanted to meet an Inuit artist, so she looked through drawings the Cape Dorset co-op had bought from the local artists and was fascinated by Soroseelutu's work. Joyce hired a translator and asked the artist if the two of them could work together. Soroseelutu agreed, and Joyce went to her house, only to feel very uncomfortable there, like an intruder.

Joyce had preconceived ideas of how she wanted to work, hoping she and Soroseelutu could draw each other, but very quickly she realized her ideas would not work — she could not surmount the cultural differences. However, Joyce did draw Soroseelutu, and made prints in the lithography studio there. But the prints were not the most meaningful part of the experience. Her discovery of Arctic light was the transforming part of her trip. She described experiencing its radiance and mystical quality as connecting something inside herself — her own inner light — with something outside in a "kind of union," providing an opening to explore her own spirituality.[15]

When Joyce returned to Toronto, she had to face the difficulties she had left behind: her marriage was in trouble. In a February letter to Phyllis Lambert, Joyce said she was "in the pits lately ... And that I'm repulsive I might just get out of here ..."[16] One can only surmise that she meant she might get out of 137 Summerhill. As was true twenty years earlier, her

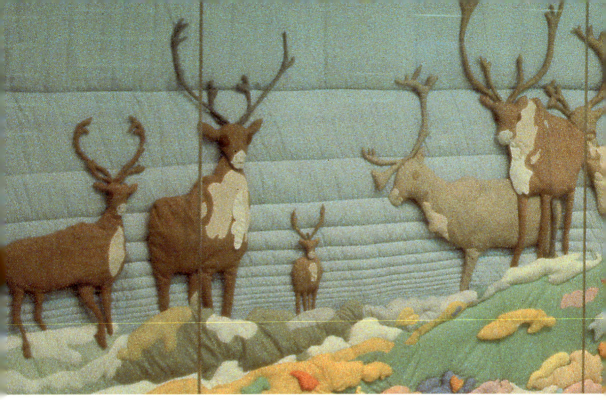

Barren Ground Caribou (detail), 1978.

feelings about herself plummeted when she felt Michael had rejected her.

By then Joyce would have known that he had a mistress, Peggy Gale. He had met Gale, fourteen years younger than Michael and now a writer and art critic, when she was working at the Art Gallery of Ontario as a tour guide in the late sixties. In later years, he would admit openly that during his marriage he had a number of affairs, that if he felt attracted to a woman he would try to sleep with her. He added, "I've caused a lot of trouble."[17]

Michael also said the Queen Street house purchase in 1975 had been a sign of "part of us coming apart." He remembered that they discussed "that it might be a good idea for us to have two separate places that were complete, not that we were totally separating, but that we would try that."[18] Looking back, he felt that in the years after *The Far Shore* their life had become "barren," as they went through the motions of married life — "whatever balancing acts we were involved in were working before," but weren't anymore.[19]

For Joyce, this explanation would have sounded hollow. His rejection pained her so deeply that she was never able to recoup a part of the inner core of the person she had built. Judy Steed said that what Joyce experienced was "like a fault line in her soul that goes back to the primal abandonment ... that was opened up again and she couldn't mend it. She was terrified of being alone, of being left as she had been as a child, after her parents died."[20]

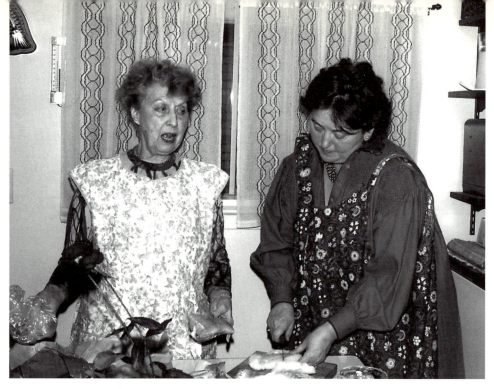

Antoinette, Michael's mother, and Joyce making bouillabaisse in 1982.

Joyce had managed to live with the pain of Michael's infidelities for years because she needed him and loved him. However, learning that Gale had become pregnant tipped her over the edge. That the man she loved would have a child with another woman was for Joyce, who was infertile, the ultimate rejection. She could not live with him any more. She asked Betty Ferguson to help her move out, taking only her clothes and a few of Michael's drawings and paintings. She had gradually moved many of her other things to the Queen Street house during the previous months.

Not long after Joyce left, Gale moved in with Michael at 137 Summerhill. Eventually she and Michael would be married and, after two miscarriages, have a son. In later years, Gale acknowledged Michael's "roving eye" and admitted she was surprised that Joyce put up "with his shenanigans all those years."[21]

No one now remembers exactly when Joyce moved out, but likely it was in early May of 1979. Betty only recalls noticing that the lilac bush at Joyce's house was in bloom when they moved Joyce's clothes.[22] In photographs from the Snow family Christmas gathering in 1978, Joyce appears unhappy, and she did not attend the 1979 Christmas dinner. Just before that gathering, Michael told his sister he would be coming to Christmas dinner alone. That was the first the family knew of the separation. He explained to his niece, Su Rynard, then in her late teens, that he and Joyce had stopped loving each other.[23]

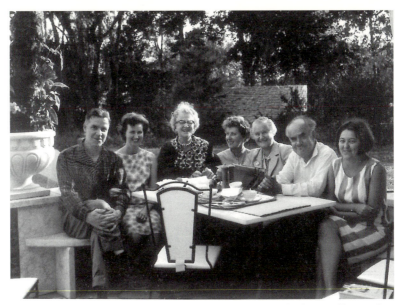

Michael's family in 1966, Claremont, Ontario, at the home of his mother and her second husband, Roberto G. Roig. Left to right: Roderick Rynard, Denyse Rynard, Rhoda Wilson (Bradley Snow's sister), Antoinette Roig, Dimple Snow (Bradley Snow's sister), Roberto G. Roig, Joyce.

When Betty asked Joyce why she had left instead of asking Michael to leave, she replied that she did not want to upset his life.[24] Feeling she could not stay was extremely painful, and even more so when she learned Peggy Gale had moved in. Joyce loved that house with its sunroom and glass shelves full of plants and the living-room wall full of books. "The house was small and 'cottagy' and had a huge, huge tree in the front ... She took a lot of pride" in it.[25] She wanted to cling not only to the house, but to what she and Michael had: the intellectual curiosity they shared, the fun they had — for example, burping contests when they were driving somewhere — and the way they nourished each other. In the early years of their marriage, Joyce's uninhibited creative flow of ideas and rolling emotion had inspired and fascinated Michael, and she had introduced him to the world of film; he in turn had introduced her to aspects of the art world she might not otherwise have accessed. "We used to have these dialogues," Joyce said. "We made each other" as artists, Joyce remembered them saying to each other at their separation.[26]

Not only was Joyce losing her life with Michael, but she was also losing his family, including his mother. She saw in Antoinette what she wished for herself — a special place in Michael's heart, privilege, style, elegance. In a 1973 piece of correspondence from her New York therapist, responding to what Joyce had said about her mother-in-law, he pointed out that people

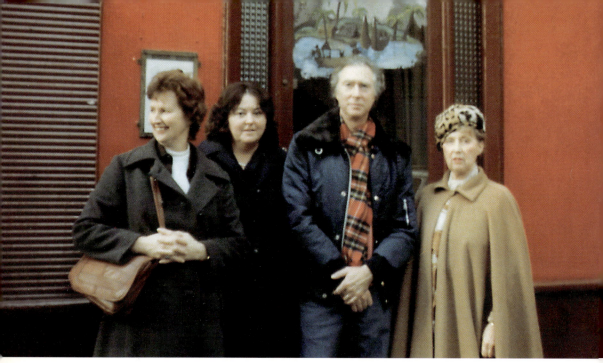

Denyse Rynard (Michael's sister), Joyce, Michael and Antoinette in Paris in 1978.

often invest in another their own unacknowledged wishes and then maintain a close association with that person who embodies what they themselves want to be.[27] In other words, instead of claiming for herself the qualities she wanted, she experienced them in her mother-in-law. If this was true, no wonder the separation from Michael shook the foundation of whatever part of his mother she had used in her own creation of herself.

Joyce also loved Michael's extended family, a lively group of as many as twenty-five people of all ages, from the elderly to newborns, that gathered for holidays and birthdays, with much coming and going. She loved this "sense of age" in the family.[28] For all of us, the embrace of an extended family offers security and a sense of place, and this family loved Joyce, which made the breakup even more painful.

Her marriage had offered some financial security, but that spring she had two new sources of money, which made living on her own feasible. In April the National Gallery of Canada purchased the storyboards from *The Far Shore* for $27,400.[29] She also applied for, and received, a $14,000 Canada Council grant that year.[30]

Joyce's closest friends have often seemed at a loss for words to describe the extent of the pain she felt about her separation and divorce. For any person with Joyce's complex emotional make-up, adjusting to living alone upsets the psychic balance. She made herself sick with eating donuts, much like writer Margaret Laurence turned to alcohol after her separation from her husband.[31] In fact, with hindsight, some of her friends thought that perhaps the illness that would become obvious later had already begun to make inroads during that time of stress, as the mythology of her marriage broke apart. Joyce needed an anchor, something that Michael had provided, because it was in her nature to propel herself into an emotional space that could become frightening. Without a partner, it was much more difficult to remain rooted in reality. And as in any close connection with an intimate partner, a separation causes a multitude of feelings to come to the fore. Joyce's hurt expression in a photograph taken around that time reveals how close to the surface her pain was.[32]

Another part of this picture was that, as early as 1974, Joyce had been in therapy with Dr. Mary McEwen. In a National Film Board documentary about McEwen, directed by Pat Watson, Joyce said Dr. McEwen sensed that she was tired of holding her relationship together, and the marriage was not good for her. Knowing this, and yet feeling sure she still loved Michael, created tremendous inner turmoil. She also discovered that she had placed Michael on a pedestal, having learned this from her mother, who had elevated her father.[33]

It's clear that Joyce felt conflicted about her relationship with Michael, and that they each had a different point of view about their marriage. Whatever the contradictory feelings on both sides, they did not cut themselves off from each other when they separated. They visited each other after they were no longer living together; the attachments remained, and the divorce would take another ten years. What to do about their Newfoundland place would become the most difficult part of the settlement.

Despite Joyce's upheavals, over the years she would create for herself a beautiful home that was uniquely her own. The house, which she continued to call Beaver Lodge — an acknowledgement that Canada was built on the killing of beavers and the sale of their furs — is in the area of Toronto called Corktown. Corktown is bounded by Lakeshore Boulevard on the south, The Don River on the east, Shuter Street on the north, and Berkeley Street on the west. The community newspaper, *Corktown News*, describes the area as "Toronto's oldest neighbourhood established by John Graves Simcoe, first Lieutenant Governor of Upper Canada, in 1793."[34]

Joyce was interested in the history of Corktown and of her place, a house with high ceilings at the end of a row of houses built for brewery managers around 1900. Directly north of Beaver Lodge, behind the houses on the opposite side of the street, is Fee Place, with "five tiny houses in a row running parallel to Queen Street." Likely these were homes for servants of the brewery owners or managers living in the larger houses on Queen Street. Canada Post at one time knew this little street as "Queen Rear."[35] With her irreverent sense of humour, Joyce probably enjoyed the nickname for Fee Place.

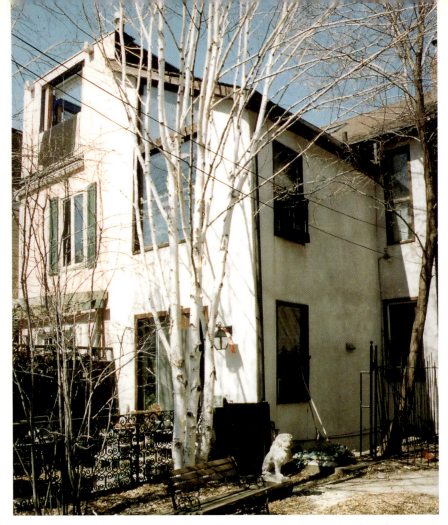

The back of Joyce's house on Queen Street. She loved the birch trees she planted.

That part of Queen Street had been primarily low-income residential in the late sixties and early seventies, with a neighbourly feeling. Later, when the district became somewhat run down, the neighbours banded together to clean up the area.[36]

Vijay and Georgia Nayyar, who live just to the west of Joyce's place, remembered meeting Joyce, and feeling happy to have a friendly neighbour interested in the area. Over the years, the Nayyars would become fond of Joyce and a neighbourly friendship developed between them.[37]

During her second summer on Queen Street, Joyce hired Munro Ferguson to help her with her work around the house and garden and in the studio. As in New York when Munro was a child, they often had long conversations, sometimes about art. Munro, who became a cartoonist and animator, remembered that they had a series of conversations that summer about post-modernism. Was it just a fad or was it an evolution into something else? Joyce had an appreciation for the diversity in art that accompanied post-

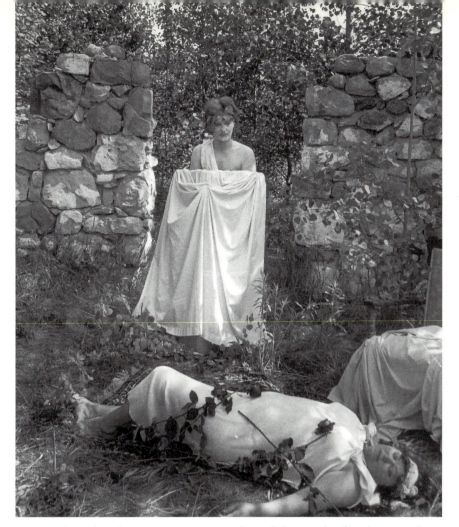

In the early eighties, Munro Ferguson and Pascal Sharp made a film about Napoleon. Eo Sharp played Napoleon and Joyce, lying on the ground, was Josephine.

modernism. She was also interested in the "revival in representation ... She was very turned on by historicism and a renewed interest in the ornament," and "the rejection of abstraction." She talked about it in terms of rejection of the old-boy art movements. Based on those conversations, Munro saw her coloured-pencil drawings in the context of Joyce's rejection of modernism and "her flowering as an artist as an expressive individual ... returning to representation, broadening her range of possibilities," and picking up on what she felt was lasting in post-modernism.[38]

As the familiar personal anchors fell away, Joyce needed something that would help her reconstitute herself, for she had broken apart and was now looking for a way of healing and starting a new life. She had let her wavy hair grow long, and it was usually tangled. Soon after leaving Summerhill, she "had her long, wild claustrophobic hair cut short." This gesture was symbolic of changes she wanted to make in trying to start over.[39]

She focused on two aspects of her life: her spiritual quest, which included building on her experience of the Arctic light; and finding a man to live with her. She went to Buddhist gatherings; she joined a group led by Alexander Blair-Ewart to explore spirituality. She also explored Anthroposophy, which is a Christianized offshoot of Theosophy, a system of thought founded by the social philosopher Rudolph Steiner.

As she looked for companionship, it is not surprising that she turned to someone she knew well and with whom she already had a history, her old friend and former lover, George Gingras. George grew up in Sudbury and at age eighteen had come to Toronto to attend the Ontario College of Art, where he met Michael Snow. He and Bryan Barney had both worked for the same packaging company and became friends, and one day in the fall of 1953, he went with Bryan to meet Joyce at Paul's Ranch House on Bloor Street at Sherbourne. Through Joyce, George was hired at Graphic Associates and became part of the close circle of friends there.[40] George and Joyce also travelled together in the spring of 1956 when he went to England and she to France.

According to George, when Joyce and Michael were living on Charles Street and he was living close by on Isabella Street, Joyce would show up at his place two or three times a week. During the late fifties and until Joyce went to New York, she and George had an extended affair — she was tired of sitting through the nights of jazz when Michael was playing his gigs.[41] When George decided to marry Leah Koman, he put an end to it. That was in 1961, the year before Joyce and Michael went to New York. For the next eighteen years, George and Joyce seldom saw each other — until 1979.

By then George and Leah Koman had been divorced for several years. Joyce still cared about George and wanted to see him again, and the two began corresponding. By then George was working at Jim MacKay's Film Design, and in a letter told Joyce, "You'll be glad to know I've quit drinking ..."[42] He was right. Knowing this would have given Joyce some hope about a relationship with him. That summer, when George had an apartment in Toronto, she sometimes stayed at his place.[43]

When Joyce was planning to go away in the summer of 1980, she asked George to look after her house while she went to St. Michael's Print Shop on the Southern Shore of Newfoundland to conduct a feminist workshop. During this time she lived with fourteen women, an experience she compared to living in a nunnery. "It's so gentle being with these women strolling down paths in the woods and making supper."[44] In her letter to George, she wrote of pining for him and his lovemaking, and signed the letter, "Horney Sister Joy."

While she was in Newfoundland, she also went to her beloved hideout with Michael and a friend. In another affectionate letter from Joyce, she tells George to "use the house and be comfortable there. I like to think you are there and having Markie there — But you have to do what suits you dear." She ends the letter with "Flaccid pasta to you — and JOY too and much meditation and prayer sent on backs of Seagulls you will get the picture when you G look up at the Gulls over the house — all gulls speak and convey messages from the sea to Lake Ontario."[45]

In a letter dated ten days later, George said he had stayed at her house overnight and had defrosted the fridge, cleaned the kitchen, cut the grass and fixed the rotisserie, and that his son Mark had also stayed over. "The future I'm sure holds much dancing for the two of us."[46] It seems they both liked the idea of renewing an intimate friendship.

Joyce asked George to move in with her, and when she returned to Toronto they began living together in September. He was very different from Michael in that he was a man without connections. According to one friend, George was a link with her early life in poverty; they talked about their experiences of the working class.[47] For a time she had a fantasy that she, George and his son, Mark, would become a family — Mark sometimes spent weekends with Joyce and George. They talked about making films together.

In 1980, she put on a big party for Mark's tenth birthday, and her friends came with their children. Contrary to most parents, Joyce kept urging the children to have more cake and ice cream, so much so that at least one of the children vomited.[48]

George and Joyce sometimes took Mark to Betty Ferguson's farm, south of Guelph, Ontario, to go horseback riding and spend the weekends there.[49] She even told a journalist that a second marriage might be in her future. "I'm really happy with domestic life," she said. "It's nice having someone around who cares."[50] Joyce again, with her fantasies, had set herself up for a disappointment.

Until that summer, Joyce had given perhaps only a half-dozen lectures on art. She had taught a course called "Legitimizing Canadian Content in Art" at the Nova Scotia College of Art and Design in Halifax ten years earlier. In 1980 Joyce began teaching a course, "Painting Your Visions," at Artsake, a small art school in Toronto run by artists. Kathy Dain, who already had a Bachelor's degree in Fine Art, remembers that she and others who signed up for the course "were not so concerned about our visions; we wanted to meet Joyce ... We wanted to know this woman who had done it ... She was the number one woman in the country and we wanted to know who she was."[51]

At the beginning of the first class, Joyce came to Kathy and quietly said, "I've never taught before. What do I do now?" Kathy suggested she could have everyone there introduce themselves and say why they wanted to take the course. And that is how Joyce began. Kathy, who became a close friend, learned from that incident that Joyce knew how to get from someone what she needed at a given moment, partly because she had an innate sense of people and their strengths. Though Joyce did not know this at the time, Kathy came from a family of teachers and knew something about teaching.

After that initial insecurity, Joyce created an atmosphere for students to learn to draw and paint in their own way. Joyce's students got what they wanted — besides painting and drawing, they got to know Joyce because the course led to a routine of going to the Peter Pan restaurant on Queen Street after classes for dessert or salads.

While she was expanding outward in the area of teaching, her work was shifting. She pulled inward, into her own interior world, as a result of the major changes she had experienced and the reassessment of her personal life.[52] She continued to focus on her series of coloured-pencil drawings about her experience of Arctic light and what it taught her, drawings she described as "a tumult of creatures and objects in flight or gently swimming between sunrise and sunset, embraced in pale rainbows of Arctic light."[53] The drawings grew, not from wanting to depict certain subject matter, but from a desire to express "a kind of Impressionist visual experience."[54] They also reflect her personal life — she put George into some of her drawings and paintings, many of them erotic. They reveal her sense of humour, a deep sense of joy and pleasure, and a connection to what she felt was the energy of the cosmos.

Her mystical sense of the natural world was not new in her work. It is evident in *The Far Shore*, which warns of the industrialist's heavy hand winning out over the artist's hand. In these new drawings she left behind the warnings and gave over her love of the earth to paper and pencils.

Joyce believed that love was the basis of everything, including art. She agreed with Jesuit philosopher-palaeontologist Pierre Teilhard de Chardin's (1881–1955) idea of love as energy, as "a property of all life" that embraces all matter.[55] Among the books on religion she read was his *Hymn of the Universe*. A chapter titled, "Christ in the World of Matter" describes a vision given to him when he looked at a pictorial representation of Jesus Christ in a church. The picture itself dissolved, and the space around it "radiated outwards to infinity." This was the kind of language Joyce used in talking about Arctic light. In Chardin's vision, the entire universe became vibrant, and while everything was flowing together in this vision, he could still see objects clearly and individually. The garments Christ wore were luminescent, made of matter, "a bloom of matter, which had spontaneously woven a marvellous stuff out of the inmost depths of its substance ..."[56] She would use Chardin's words as the title for her show.

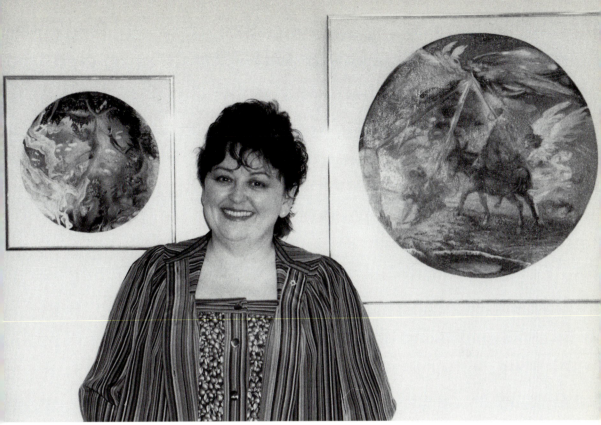

Joyce at her "Bloom of Matter" show.

Joyce claimed that, as an Inuit carver finds the animal in the stone, in doing these drawings she found images in the light on her paper.[57] Perhaps she did, but she projected them there from the depth of her soul, weaving together her pain and her strengths, the personal and the mystical. One thinks of the spiritual as serious business, but as is true of much of her work, these pencil drawings are full of her sense of humour, some of them downright funny, as well as erotic; naked, laughing goddesses cavort and glide on the wind or swim in a light-filled atmosphere that could be air or water, often accompanied by deer or other animals.

For Joyce, art was healing. The late British Poet Laureate Ted Hughes once said, "Every work of art stems from a wound in the soul of the artist ... When a person is hurt his immune system comes into operation and the self-healing process takes place, mental and physical. Art is a psychological component of the auto-immune system that gives expression to the healing process. That is why great works of art make us feel good."[58] These drawings made Joyce feel good, and she made no apologies for them because she knew they could also make others feel good.

However, she also knew that in Canada's art world, "it's against the rules to be totally enthusiastic ... I think it's sad that people aren't allowed to celebrate their works as they come along."[59] Joyce wanted to celebrate her

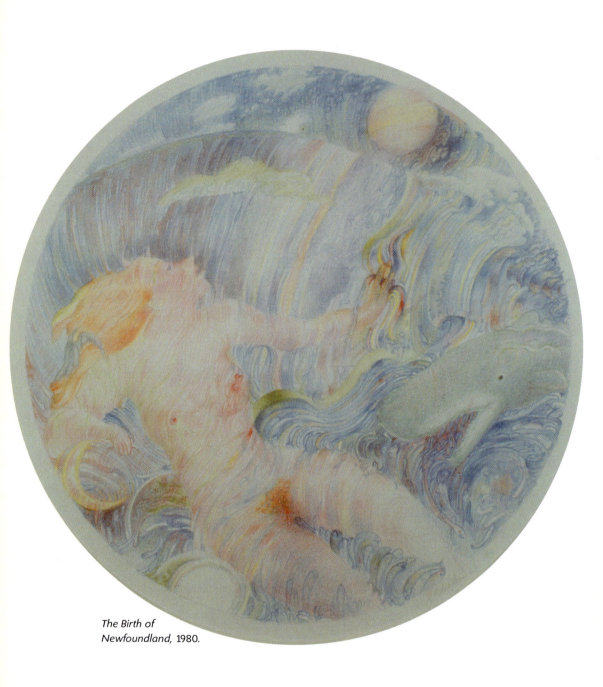

*The Birth of
Newfoundland, 1980.*

opening for "A Bloom of Matter" at the Isaacs Gallery in the spring of 1981. Sara Bowser contacted a wine company and arranged to have wine donated, and her friends baked cookies to serve to her guests. When a hungry, down-and-out man came in off the street and helped himself to cookies, Joyce was pleased.[60]

For "A Bloom of Matter," Joyce created a total atmosphere with an arbour entrance of spring flowers — daffodils, hyacinths and tulips. The walls were painted a soft rose colour, and the floor was covered with richly patterned rugs.

The soft, pastel images made some people uncomfortable. Years later, Jessica Bradley, Curator of Contemporary Art at the Art Gallery of Ontario, would recall that she, among others, had been resistant to the drawings because they were the complete opposite of what many feminists wanted in art at the time.[61] They "posed a problem in terms of Wieland's canonization as Canada's quintessential feminist artist."[62] Were these drawings in a circular format created by the same feminist artist who had boldly dared to inscribe a female point of view as valid subject matter for paintings, quilts and films? Yes, this was the same artist, and she knew what she was about. She was spreading her mythology outward and inward at the same time, outward into the cosmos to encompass more than the northernmost country of the North American continent, and inward in an attempt to explore ways of giving images to a search for mystical experience.

The first drawings were simple, with sometimes only one figure; they then progressed to become "more complex in concept, figuration and prismatic colouring."[63] The invitation to the show featured *The Birth of Newfoundland* (1980), a drawing of a nude female figure riding on top of ocean waves. A tiny heart appears on the left breast of the nude and a little fish swims to her genitals. From the right side, a smiling whale swims into the round drawing. This was the Newfoundland of her dreams.

Victory of Venus (1981) is one of her most erotic drawings, depicting couples having sex. The oval space is covered all over with her drawing, except for the left edge, where the drawing trails off to leave a blank space. Joyce once explained that the blank was an opening to allow the spirit to enter and leave the drawing.[64]

Joyce also began painting images in oils that were in the same spirit as the pencil drawings. Her favourite, she said, five years later, was *The End of Life as She Knew It*. "That's my boyfriend George. The woman is holding on to the earth and the rabbit's been pulled off the earth and the lake is being sucked out. It's a wonderful painting. This is the Goddess of the weather."[65]

The End of Life as She Knew It depicts everything familiar as dislocated, a scene of complete upheaval and disorientation. She was still the same woman who,

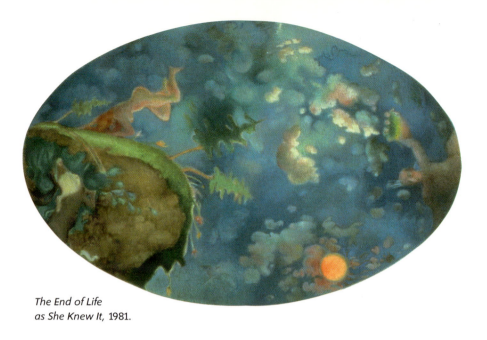

*The End of Life
as She Knew It,* 1981.

thirty years earlier, had lived to experiment with life by simply turning herself over to whatever storm was erupting inside herself. The title is a complete give-away. Her life as she knew it had ended, and she was still clinging on, like the figure in the drawing, holding on to the earth with her hands, her feet in the air. She once said about her work that "I like to go where there's so little to go on that you're just hanging by your fingernails."[66] That's exactly where she was in her life and her art in the early eighties.

Several months after her "Bloom of Matter" show was over, Joyce began some major renovations on her house, spending at least $30,000.[67] She hired her architect friend of many years, Gerald Robinson, to design the changes. "The neighbours think I'm mad as I've never stopped fooling with this place," she told Phyllis Lambert in a letter. "G. Robinson designed my kitchen cupboards — 1912 style."[68] She got something out of the kitchen remodelling that she had always wanted — cupboards built to suit her height.

For the main part of the first floor, a long, narrow room with a high ceiling, Robinson's design with Tudor influences included carved wooden arches on the ceiling and shelves of wood high on the wall. The detailed woodwork was carved by shipwright Anson Holmes. Later she found a long, narrow, 1850 table that fit the space perfectly to create a dining area. She commissioned six mahogany chairs, built by two craftsmen, David Hendricks and Bill Evans. At the opposite end of the long room, in the living-room area, the same hand-carved motif outlined bookshelves on the end wall. On one side of the shelves was a window with glass shelves, and on the other, a cupboard with a glass front matched the window.

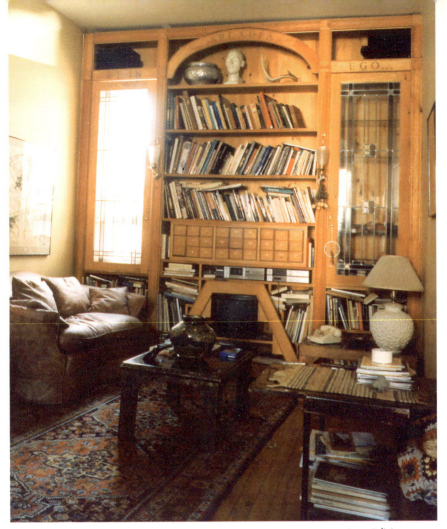

Joyce's living room.

In the centre arch above the bookshelves are carved the words *Et in Arcadia ego*. This inscription appears in the painting *The Arcadian Shepherds* by the seventeenth-century French painter Nicholas Poussin, who lived in Rome.[69] In the painting three shepherds look at an ancient Roman tomb with the four words inscribed on it. One shepherd traces his finger over the words, which mean, "In Arcadia I (Death) too am present." Another shepherd leans forward to see, his arm resting on his knee. A serene-looking woman draped in gold and blue flowing robes places her hand on his shoulder, as though to calm him in the face of this disturbing message. This reminder that Death is always present — not something the shepherds want to think about — gives a sombre feeling to an otherwise bucolic painting in warm colours, its sky in shades of blue with white puffy clouds, parts of it reminiscent of some of Joyce's paintings of sky.

Joyce filled the shelves below this inscription with her beloved books on art, a source of her wide knowledge of Western art history, particularly that of the seventeenth and eighteenth centuries. In a book that Joyce must have read, Katherine Mansfield, one of Joyce's role models, wrote a section in her journal entitled *"Et in Arcadia Ego"*: "To sit in front of the little wood fire, your hands crossed in your lap and your eyes closed — to fancy you see again upon your eyelids all the dancing beauty of the day, to feel the flame on your throat when Bogey held a buttercup under your chin ... when breathing is such delight that you are almost afraid to breathe — as though a butterfly fanned its wings upon your breast."[70] Mansfield, who was ill, continues in that spirit. It's the writing of someone aware of her mortality, an awareness that Joyce also had, informing her art and her life.

Beginning in the seventies, Phyllis Lambert had become an important figure for Joyce, despite their different lives. Joyce admired what Phyllis accomplished — she created what has been called "the international Mecca of architecture" in Montreal.[71] They had in common the experience of living in the United States for a number of years, and they both returned around the same time, at the beginning of the 1970s, because "Canada was a more decent place," and "this was a place where we could do things."[72]

Like Joyce, Phyllis was a small woman, not much over five feet tall, but her presence was much larger. When I met her to speak about Joyce, she wore a black shirt tucked into black pants. As she sat in a Chinese restaurant on Ste.-Catherine Street in Montreal, eating vegetable dumplings with spicy sauce, at one point she surprised me by pulling out of her pocket what is usually considered a man's handkerchief, bright red. At that moment I knew why Joyce liked her.

Phyllis remembered that when she met Joyce there was an immediate bond between them. After Joyce and Michael separated, it seemed Phyllis became a kind of "Mike-substitute"; Joyce came to rely on Phyllis because of her friend's clear sense of direction in life.[73] And yet, at times Joyce felt shaky about her side of the friendship. A June 1981 letter reveals both her desire for a friendship and her insecurities about Phyllis, who apparently had invited Joyce several times to go with her on a cruise. In this letter Joyce tells Phyllis she wants to go with her on her boat "since you invited me 2 years in a row (1 year 1 year) Am I too late to come this time?" Joyce wanted to "sit around with you when you are taking it easy. I find this comforts me, though we are different, *very different* [underlined in original] in certain ways — we are the same in others."[74]

In the same letter Joyce told Phyllis that she was going with Mike to their "hide out just to see it once more once more — you'd love this rare wild spot could be there is nothing like it in the universe to put it mildly." She signed off the letter with "Your Schmaltz who is a great alternative to the great

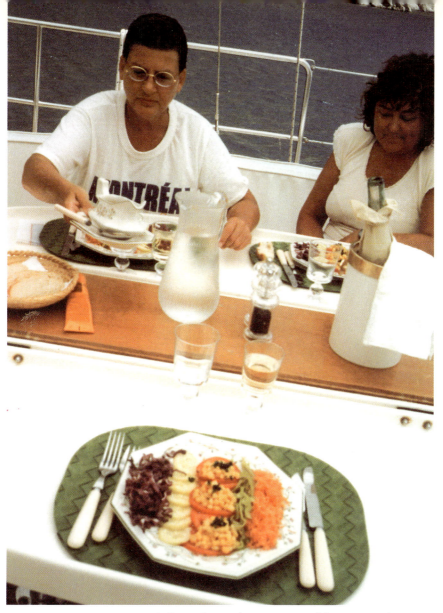

Phyllis Lambert and Joyce on one of the cruises in the 1980s.

minds of the world." On the second side of the last page of the letter she added more. "Sometimes I feel, you feel Im not good enough for you — this is what disgusts me about myself. Your association with the (to me) mysterious Powers of architecture Make me feel that my work is powerless passive, illegitimate more later of this But you are working in a mans world totally dominated by what men have done — for myself I'm burrowing to the roots of femininity Im a pioneer Phyllis, what I come up with can't be judged — here to fore histoire. friend always harmless anyway [small drawing of a heart] Please don't hurt me by looking down at me at this tender stage of my life."

Joyce went on Phyllis's cruise around Greece and Turkey in July. A French crew, three men and one woman, looked after the boat, which Joyce described as comfortable with a generous deck, where a table stood, covered with a cloth for meals. Candles or lanterns and music from the radio made the evenings around this table magical. This was also where they had many conversations and looked at maps to plot their course. As was true of her table in her kitchen, this table for Joyce was a favourite spot on the boat. Joyce started a journal in a beautiful book of handmade paper, called "Journal of Greece & Turkey, July 1981," but she wrote only a few pages.

They arrived in Athens on July 6. When they visited a temple of Aphrodite, Joyce picked up wall fragments and shards, something Phyllis remembered clearly. "... I said, Joyce, you know you're not supposed to do this. I think with anybody else on earth I would say quite categorically, look, this is just impossible, you can't do it. But there was such a childish delight in Joyce doing this ... Her bag was bulging with these things and some guard came along and said you've got to empty all of that out." She did, but in her journal she says she kept one wall fragment and one shard.

Joyce had trouble realizing that the cruise was not just a dream. "Am feeling unreal as this is something I felt I'd never do and to do this under such marvellous circumstances is really too much." The food was amazing, and she loved Phyllis's company, which was "so unusual and wonderful I can't relax as I feel it can't be true." And Joyce thought the area near Cnidus in Greece looked like her cape in Newfoundland.

Once when they went swimming, Joyce became terrified because Phyllis disappeared for a while. As she searched for her, she began thinking about Australian director Peter Weir's movie *Picnic at Hanging Rock*, in which girls from a private school mysteriously disappear while hiking in the wilderness.

Joyce went into "a strange panic." Later, it was Phyllis's turn to be frightened. Joyce records that on one of their hilly climbs Phyllis was alarmed by six or seven wild goats and was afraid they would attack her. However, Joyce thought they were "sweet and curious and lovely," with horns like unicorns, so she helped Phyllis calm down.[75]

The two women enjoyed long conversations about common interests. Phyllis once recorded on paper what she remembered about one of their conversations about light and sound at Joyce's house on Queen Street in November of 1980. Their discussion arose because of the way Joyce used lattices in windows with resulting patterns of light, and also because of the way Joyce combined found objects to create miniature environments, almost like small architectural settings. In their conversation, Joyce's thoughts seemed disjointed, but they made some kind of emotional sense. How are libraries related to thickets? Light filters through leaves on trees, spaces with light, like on a mountain trail — "We're animals that way." And in libraries people need soft light in an environment with ionized air. "Dead air makes your eyes hurt." In the wild, on a mountain trail, that won't happen![76]

Phyllis reminisced about how sometimes the two of them had fun just being silly. They'd give each other different names, like Louise and Dorothy, and then take on the character of whatever they thought suited the names they chose. "I had silly times with Joyce," Phyllis said, and now "there's nobody with whom I can have silly times."[77]

When Joyce had begun painting in oils again in the early eighties, one day musician Marie Lynn Hammond received a phone call from her. Hammond had long admired Joyce, from the time she was a student at New School of Art in Toronto, which was run by some of the Isaacs Gallery artists, and Joyce came to speak there. Hammond had also seen Joyce's show in Ottawa in 1971. When she received this call from Joyce, she thought, "Oh, my god, this is the goddess calling me!"[78]

Joyce knew that Hammond was a friend of Nicholas Laidlaw and called her to ask for his phone number because she had painted a small oil painting she thought Laidlaw might like. Hammond gave Laidlaw Joyce's number, and as a result, he visited her studio. Sure enough, he bought *Wild Rose of Newfoundland* (1982).[79] This tiny painting is unique among Joyce's works, a rendering of wild roses held in a glass of water — the glass reflected in the table's surface and a few petals on the tabletop — against a background of a large cloud-filled sky with a few dark fir trees in the landscape.

Perhaps it was during this studio visit that the idea was conceived of Joyce painting Laidlaw's portrait. The relationship of these two was complex. It seemed Joyce had romantic interests in Laidlaw, though he did not, and of course, she was drawn to his wealth. According to Judy Steed, Joyce knew how to generate excitement in certain people of means, and Laidlaw was one of these, for he gave Joyce a tremendous amount of financial support — Laidlaw loved art and could afford to buy it. Also, she saw him as a poet and a lover of music. She spent hours with him in the ten-month period of painting his portrait. "It's a chance to really look at somebody. It starts to make you feel weird. You start to see the cells, the blood pumping through the cheeks. You sort of 'osmose' the person, absorbing him so you can put him out again."[80] By the time she finished the portrait, she felt she knew the essence of the man. Again, as was true many times in her life with many people, she formed a bond with Laidlaw through her art, something that she contrived to continue throughout the eighties with further commissions.

By the winter of 1982, the happiness Joyce had originally experienced living with George Gingras turned into disappointment and annoyance. According to George, Joyce acted "peculiar," and they had arguments over "nothing."[81] But Joyce's side of the story was that she asked him to leave because he was too difficult to live with when he had some drinks. Given their personalities, the arrangement could not have worked, but in her intense need for someone to live with, Joyce had not allowed herself to see that problems might arise. George moved out in February 1982. Joyce was on her own, and she had to adjust to another change in her life.

Her friend, Helen Lucas, suggested that Joyce place an ad in the personals column in the newspaper. Helen had done so several years earlier and had met seven different men. The first one she met, Derek Fuller, became her husband, and two of the others married two of Helen's friends. It was an impressive result, and Joyce decided to try it.[82]

She had a number of responses, but she was not as fortunate as Helen. One man she arranged to meet in a restaurant was not someone with whom she wanted to dine. She headed for the washroom and disappeared through the restaurant's back door.[83] She tried the ads again, for in 1987, in her appointment book for January 12, she jotted, "Black hair King Edward — Brown suit, grey overcoat." The next day at 7 p.m. — "Blue-grey suit, light brown overcoat, grey hair, gold glasses."[84] Her search was in vain.

She began reaching out to more women for friendship after George left, some of them her students at Artsake. She also maintained a close connection with Phyllis Lambert that year, who continued to be supportive by buying some of Joyce's work. It's interesting that Joyce sold her favourite, *The End of Life as She Knew It* (1981), to Phyllis for $4,500, and asked her to make out her cheque to Wieland & Snow Ltd.[85] This drawing had been shown at the Isaacs Gallery the year before, and selling it without going through the gallery was something that would have incensed Av Isaacs had he known about it. This kind of transaction would eventually contribute to the rift between them a number of years later.

In July, according to Phyllis Lambert's "Summer Notebooks," she took Joyce with her again on another cruise to Turkey. That same year Joyce experienced a lull in creative work. However, she did complete her *Venus of Scarborough*, a female figure sculpted in flowers at the Guild Inn in Scarborough.

That December she was thrilled to find out that she would be named Officer of the Order of Canada. She received a package in the mail from Ottawa and threw it out because she thought someone was playing a joke on her. However, when she received a phone call about the honour, she pawed through her garbage and found the documents. There was cat food on them! When Joyce told Kathy Dain what happened, Kathy sensed that Joyce had thought this honour couldn't possibly be hers because she hadn't gone out to fight for it.[86]

Joyce asked her nephew, Keith Stewart, to be her escort at the Order of Canada ceremony the following April in Ottawa. The day after the awards ceremony, Jean Sutherland Boggs gave a special dinner in Joyce's honour. She gave Joyce a wreath to wear in her hair when she arrived, and Joyce, as a token of appreciation, had also brought one for Boggs. Later, Joyce reported that at the dinner Pierre Trudeau talked with her about Goethe's experiments with light and Teilhard de Chardin and the spiritual aspects of art. But he also said to her, "Ah, your quilt's the quilt that caused the breakdown of my marriage."[87] Apparently the gossip that had circulated when the Trudeaus' relationship was unravelling was true, but Joyce was not at all offended that Margaret ripped up her quilt because she interpreted the gesture as a message about putting passion over reason.

Perhaps seeing Trudeau reignited her obsession with him. She wanted to paint his portrait and wrote letters to him asking for his cooperation. He always replied, saying he was too busy, perhaps later.[88] Nicholas Laidlaw's portrait had been unveiled just two months earlier, two weeks after Joyce's investiture, and Laidlaw sent Trudeau a photo of his portrait and recommended that he have Joyce do his. In July, Joyce herself sent Trudeau another letter asking him to tell the United States to keep its hands off Canada, and in a P.S. she wrote that she still wanted to "immortalize" him sometime and paint his portrait.[89] It never happened.

As it turned out, 1983 was a pivotal year for Joyce. Not only did she receive one of the highest honours in the land, but she also created some of the most powerful paintings of her career. That year also marked a finality in Joyce and Michael's separation — they updated a number of legal documents to reflect the changes in their lives. Her house was still registered in the name of Joyce Wieland and Michael Snow Ltd., though they had already dissolved the company; they were both still listed as joint tenants at 137 Summerhill. That spring and summer, these legal documents were revised to reflect their separation. Michael's car insurance policy was changed to include Peggy Gale, and her name was added to the mortgage for 137 Summerhill and Joyce's name removed.[90]

Joyce did not have much resilience when it came to these legal matters dealing with the separation. Stella Kyriakakis, whom Joyce hired that spring as an administrative assistant, saw close-up Joyce's difficulties. Stella had just completed a six-month contract with Dennis Reid at the Art Gallery of Ontario while his secretary was away. Joyce hired Stella by telephone because "she said that anyone who's good enough for Dennis is good enough for her."[91] She remembers that whenever Michael visited, Joyce became depressed. Often she handled her depression by buying a bag of French pastries and having Stella sit in her kitchen with her to help her eat them.

Stella became more than a secretary, as would be true of most of Joyce's assistants. She became a confidante, chauffeur, and all-around mainstay. For Stella's part, Joyce became like a second mother. She encouraged Stella, who felt she could tell Joyce everything about her life and Joyce would not criticize her or get angry about what she did. "It was always about being true to your heart and your spirit and pursuing your spirituality and following up on your emotions. She was really big on love and connectedness with the world and with animals and nature … She was always very generous." When Stella left home and set up her own apartment for the first time, Joyce gave her extra kitchen gadgets and cups and glasses. When she cleaned out her closets, she gave Stella bags of clothes for her mother.

Stella recalled that during the two years she worked for her, Joyce acted as though she did not know how to manage a house. She seemed helpless, even in relation to the smallest details. For example, if she wanted to know how much postage to put on a letter, she told Stella to call Av Isaacs and ask him. On her days off, Joyce often called her and might ask where her coloured pencils were. "I did not have anything to do with where she put her supplies, so how on earth would I know where her pencil crayons are? And why is she calling me at 8 A.M. or whatever on my day off?"[92] It seemed odd that an artist so capable and creative could also need so much help with looking after routine tasks. Stella did not understand the extent of Joyce's dependency on her. Her memory of working so closely with Joyce day after day and seeing her difficulties seems to confirm what, in hindsight, some of Joyce's friends said about how early in her life Alzheimer's disease began affecting her.

Stella set up files, organized Joyce's prints and drawings, took care of correspondence, paid bills, and tried to find teaching jobs and lecture appointments for her. Joyce said she wanted to teach and lecture, but she was also reluctant, and often did not want to go once the arrangements were made, particularly if the job meant travel. Stella remembered that once they had arranged a trip to Japan to lecture at an art conference, and Joyce cancelled the day before because she could not handle the stress. She felt too overwhelmed by the thought of flying to Japan to lecture to a room full of strangers.

Around that time Joyce again consulted a doctor as well as a nutritionist. The medical report showed that by then she weighed 189 pounds. She was eating almost a thousand calories a day beyond the energy she burned, and the diagnosis showed that her heart was at risk, as was her liver. Hair analysis revealed that she had a high level of chromium in her body. The report included a question as to whether the source was paints and suggested she avoid direct contact with them, a recommendation that she could hardly follow since she was painting again. But photographs from that time do show her wearing surgical gloves in the studio. The medical report also indicated a high level of stress and that she was not looking after her teeth, so she was a candidate for periodontal disease.[93] But summer with its holidays was not a time when Joyce wanted to pay attention to her eating habits. However, she joined Weight Watchers in the fall and over a period of four months lost twenty-four pounds.

That was the summer she and Michael were sorting out how they would use the Newfoundland place, since neither one was willing to give it up. According to a letter Joyce wrote to George Gingras, she spent time there at the beginning of the summer, left when Michael came and then returned after he left. Oddly, Joyce gave her friends the impression that she went to Newfoundland with Michael, as though they were cohabiting, which, according to him, was not the case.[94] That summer Michael's partner, Peggy Gale, was pregnant with a son who would be born in November. Was Joyce in her imagination trying to get back at Peggy and Michael? She once joked with a friend that now that Peggy was the wife she could be the mistress.

Despite her wry humour, she was bitter about Peggy's pregnancy. Sara Bowser said that was one of the few times she was worried about Joyce. "I was really scared about Joyce. She took that harder than anything … She felt that it was simply so unjust."[95] That Michael would have a child that was not hers was so disturbing that once when she saw the baby with Michael and Peggy at a public event she went to the washroom and threw up.

From time to time Joyce became preoccupied with thoughts about babies. In undated notes for a grant application, she wrote that her work is changing, and the change has to do with babies, their innocence and the colour of their clothing next to their delicate skin. She had been looking at babies for three months, she said, but "staring at a baby or child leads people to be suspicious of you." In a dream she recorded, she was carrying a baby that belonged to someone in her family. As she walked down a hill, there was nothing to hold on to, and she became frightened of sliding down the hill and dropping the baby. But she wanted people to see her and think it was her baby.[96] She also had a dream in which she met Michael's baby and he smiled and knew who she was.

Over the years she had enjoyed her nieces and nephews. Joan's daughters remember that one Christmas when they were young, Joyce brought them a big box full of musical instruments — cymbals, whistles, maracas. Joyce was special to them because they considered her their "crazy aunt."[97] She sketched the children of a number of her friends, something she had started doing when Joan's children were small.

However, Michael's child was different, and encountering him ruptured her psychic balance, even though before he was born she thought she had

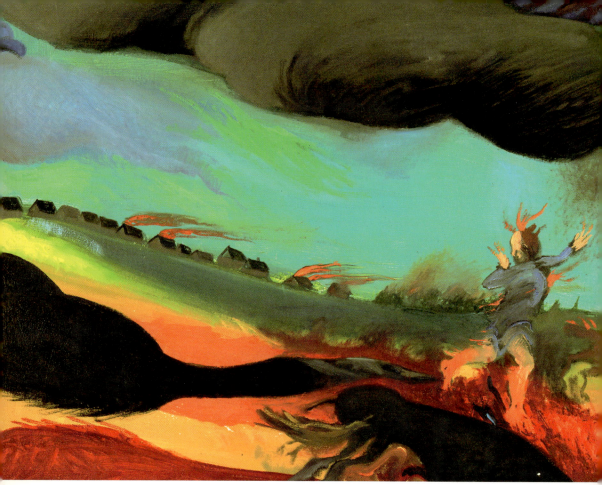

Experiment with Life, 1983.

absorbed the idea that Michael would have a child without her because she could talk about it with him "without a bad effect on myself."[98] She was in psychotherapy during that time and struggled to make peace with what was happening; but despite her best efforts to find the root of these difficulties, she could not reconcile herself to the reality of Michael's new family life.

In the midst of her emotional turmoil, Joyce was working on new paintings, among them *Experiment with Life* (1983), a painting she had begun in 1982, and *She will remain in the phenomenal world filled with ignorance with her sheep, and not go with him* (1983). The first one, in which a woman flees a burning town, is frightening. In the second, the disturbance is more subtle. It seems bucolic, with a pond and sheep in green fields. A naked female figure holding a shepherd's staff is in conversation with a nude male figure with wings and with a missing right hand. It's the faces that reveal that the scene is not as lovely as it first seems. The woman's face is distorted, with a crazed expression, and the man/angel's face is demonic. All is not well between these two characters, whoever they are.

Paint Phantom (1983-84) is one of Joyce's most powerful images. Two

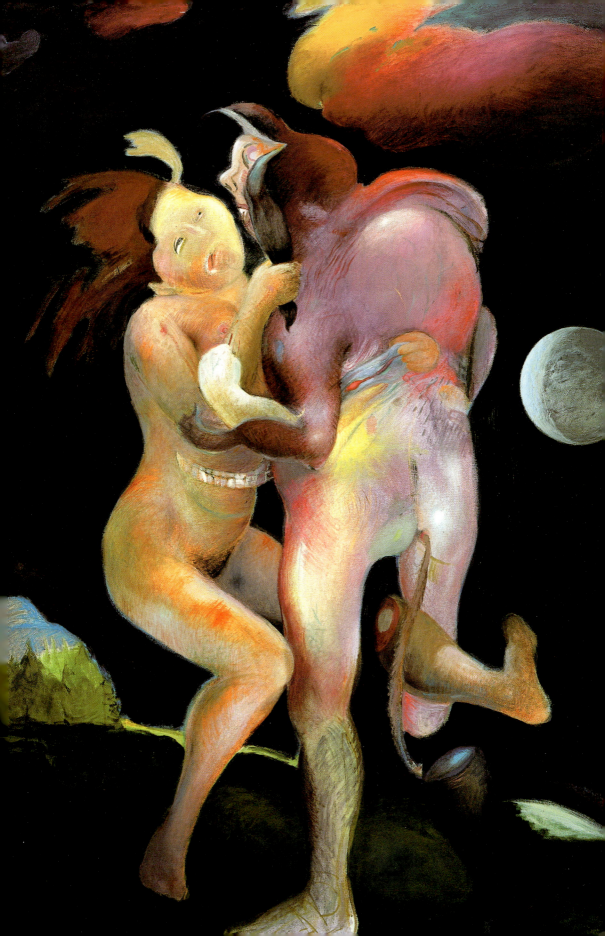

figures, one female and one male, wrestle on the surface of the curved earth, with a full moon hanging in the dark sky in the background. The female figure, whose face resembles Joyce's, is standing on her right leg with her left in an upward swing between the legs of the male figure. Her belly has a large scar and her eyes, half open, are rolled up into her head. She is grabbing the nearly translucent skin of the humped male figure, tearing it off. His tail reveals the demon-like figure is a beast.

This painting has been called the most personal of Joyce's works, "both

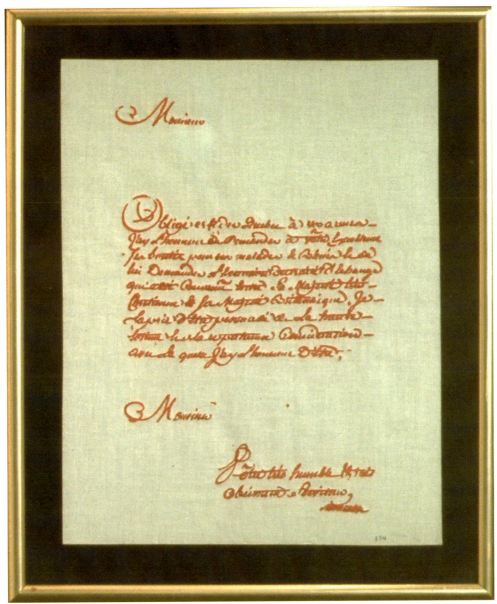

Montcalm's Last Letter/Wolfe's Last Letter, 1971.

allegory and catharsis."[99] In fact, it has to do with the phantom she created as a replacement for her father after he died, as well as the consequences of that loss within herself and in her relationships with men. "If one doesn't have a father, one has him live on in fantasy."[100]

Artist on Fire is another oil painting dense with personal meaning. It reveals how Joyce chose pieces of history and integrated them into her personal life as a way of constructing herself and building images. Here, the artist is in flames, reminiscent of Joyce's sister's dramatization of the Joan of Arc story when she was a child. The artist stands to one side of her easel holding a painting of yet another winged male figure in profile, this one with an erect penis and a laurel wreath on his head.

On the right side of the artist's head is a hint of a horn growing. Her right eye is blue, appearing small and vulnerable; her left eye dark brown. Perhaps she was emulating a Rembrandt self-portrait she liked in which, she said, he painted one of "his eyes like that of a baby, soft and hurt, while the other was the eye of a man."[101] In the artist's right hand is a brush with flaming bristles. Instead of her left hand, Joyce has given herself an animal's black hoof.

In the background, the outdoor setting includes a curious-looking building standing on a lake. The grass, which one would expect to be green, is a golden-rod yellow, perhaps a reflection of the artist's fire.

Joyce wrote at least three accounts of making this painting.[102] In each one she said she painted herself as Madame de Pompadour, who was the consort — the Lady of Honour at Court — of France's King Louis XV for nearly twenty years. The hairstyle of the female figure is Pompadour's, and the building is the *Trianon, Pavillon Français*, which "stands in the French Gardens between the Grand Trianon and the Petit Trianon."[103]

Madame de Pompadour, born Jeanne-Antoinette Poisson in 1721, virtually ruled France during the time she spent in the court of Louis XV. Louis XV would have interested Joyce because of the impact of his regime on Canadian history; his general, Louis-Joseph de Montcalm, lost to the English general James Wolfe, in trying to defend Quebec in the Battle on the Plains of Abraham in 1759, a subject explored in one of her embroidery-on-cloth works, *Montcalm's Last Letter/Wolfe's Last Letter* (1971).

A gardener and botanist, Madame de Pompadour, had qualities that Joyce admired, in particular her ability to understand artists, and her support of France's arts and culture. Not only was she a friend of such writers as Voltaire, but books were a great love of her life. By the time she died she had more than 3,500 volumes in several languages. She also loved theatre, and soon after she arrived in Versailles, she founded a theatre company called the *Théâtre des Petits Cabinets*.

Pompadour also loved houses and bought one after the other, redecorated them, and collected beautiful things to fill them — silver, china and flowers. Some months she ordered china every other day from the French factories, as well as from India, Japan, Korea and China.[104]

Toward the end of her life — only a year before she died — the king took another mistress, who bore him a son. Madame de Pompadour disguised herself and went to the house the king had given the young woman, where, undetected, she observed the mother and child nursing. Given Joyce's experience, she would not have missed noticing this incident in the life story of Madame de Pompadour, which she read, for she left among her papers photocopied chapters from Marcelle Tinayre's Pompadour biography.

In one set of notes on the painting, Joyce gave her reason for portraying herself as Madame de Pompadour. She did it to ennoble herself, she said. "I've flattered and imbued myself with a period of history which I've romanticized and put above me. Now in this painting [I] dared to take some of these attributes of it for myself. It was like stealing. I dared to take these attributes even though I wasn't good enough for them. The problem is most of this was unconscious to me until later."[105]

In these same notes, Joyce said that in this painting she is showing the difference between herself and "the Bellevedere" [sic], the male figure on her canvas. Joyce used this term rather loosely. The Belvedere is a statue court and garden in the Vatican, where the *Torso Belvedere*, a powerful, extremely muscular male figure, and the *Apollo Belvedere*, a striding male, are exhibited. The latter is a Roman copy of a Greek bronze at the Apollon Patroos temple in Athens.[106] Many artists have created their own interpretation of this ancient statue; Joyce painted hers in *Artist on Fire*, and she thought he looked like Napoleon. She portrayed herself as a match for him, both in aligning herself with a powerful woman in history, and in her personal passion as represented by fire.

"Something in me wants to enjoy this new found image," she wrote. "It wasn't enough that I express the fiery feeling of the engagement with myself on the canvas ... I have to show the difference between me and the Bellevedere [sic] — This is the only way I can show how good or bad I am."[107] Surely her need to show that she could measure up to the Belvedere is related to her feeling over the years that Michael was better than she was, that the art world saw the couple that way.

The painting brings together many threads that ran through Joyce's life and work over the years: seeing herself as a pioneer in demolishing the stereotype of the female as passive; the Trudeau-Napoleon twinning; her love of French culture, which encompassed the French-Canadian culture and Michael's family; eroticism and male-female relations; feminism — women as autonomous agents in society. All these she claimed in this image of herself on fire, the person she felt herself becoming.

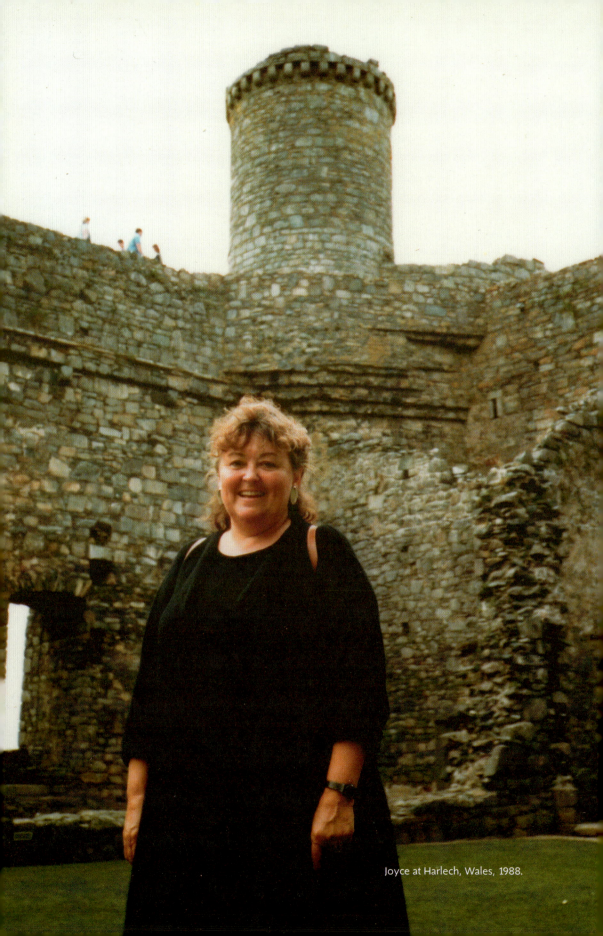

Joyce at Harlech, Wales, 1988.

9

Artist on fire

In our culture it is no easy task to accept the validity of experiences that are called "visionary." The modern personality is much more respectful of the rational aspects of the psyche. — Suzi Gablik[1]

IMAGINE JOYCE WIELAND, a vibrant, dark-haired woman about five-foot-three, facing the front of a castle surrounded by a high wall. She climbs up the wall and once inside opens the locked castle gates. Outside, a crowd of women is also waiting to enter. With a shout, Joyce throws open the gates, and one by one the women walk through. Joyce saw the art establishment and art institutions this way — castles whose walls she wanted to scale, or better yet, to batter down. She thought the Art Gallery of Ontario needed to "have its mind blown," and she wanted to be the one to do it, to loosen up the place.[2]

As the story goes, one day when Joyce felt fire in her belly, she walked into the office of William Withrow, then the director of the Art Gallery of Ontario, and asked for a retrospective. She had complained to her psychiatrist that the establishment was passing her by, and he finally told her, "Joyce, you *are* the establishment," and with that she looked surprised.

He suggested that she call the AGO and propose a show, which she did.[3] It was high time, she thought.

Withrow remembers the origin of Joyce's retrospective somewhat differently: he had a long list of artists that included the "Isaacs all-stars" whom he wanted to show, and Joyce was on that list. "She claimed — and it gave her a great deal of satisfaction to do so months after — that she had talked me into having a show out of the blue which wasn't the case at all. But I wasn't going to argue since she got so much pleasure out of telling that story. So be it."[4]

It's interesting that a page of "Director's Remarks" for a press preview of Joyce's show states "Clarify that this exhibition was a mutual decision by both Joyce and the AGO."[5] Was the administration of the AGO somewhat uneasy with what might have been seen as reluctance, or at least a tardiness, in offering Joyce a retrospective? No art institution is comfortable with being seen as slighting women, but the truth is that even as late as 1996, in a show called "The Group of Seven: Art for a Nation," of 179 works listed in the exhibition catalogue, only twenty-one were by women. The women working during the period covered by the exhibition were simply not included in Canadian art history, as *Toronto Star* art critic Christopher Hume pointed out, even though research reveals a large number of women artists at the time.[6]

Joyce knew all about the place of women in art history from personal experience, which is why she took the initiative in getting her retrospective. Withrow, who was director at the AGO for thirty-one years, reminisced about his "dear enemy" relationship with Joyce. He liked Joyce, but he had confronted her and her compatriots in the early seventies, when she was a ringleader in protests at the gallery, events that he found annoying because he believed that a curating job in the area of "Old Masters" could be carried out by an American without disadvantage to Canadian art and artists. "These sorts of things were a bit of a trial. Because I always thought that artists had a rough time, I bent a little."[7]

He met with Joyce in the Members' Lounge at the AGO on Friday, January 21, 1983. Withrow assigned Joyce's retrospective to the late Marie Fleming, who was then Associate Curator of Contemporary Art. A year after her first meeting with Withrow, in January 1984, Joyce received from Fleming a letter confirming her show for 1987.[8]

In the meantime, much else claimed Joyce's attention. For one thing, she was working on a proposal for a flower sculpture for an eastern slope of the Don Valley Parkway in Toronto. It was to be a goddess of love made up of 6,000 flowers, titled "Toronto's Venus of Flowers." But Joyce could not get the financial backing she needed, and in March, Metro Council turned down her idea. The grassy bank remained an unremarkable grassy bank.

That spring, Joyce was happy to be among ten Canadian artists invited to go on a tour of Israel, sponsored by the Canada-Israel Cultural Foundation. The purpose of the trip was to develop an exchange with Israeli artists, curators and critics. The group visited museums, galleries, art schools, and a print workshop, as well as a kibbutz.

Just as Joyce had noticed the light when she visited the Arctic, so in Jerusalem she experienced another kind of light, an intense whiteness bathing the city. For Joyce, the trip was a deeply spiritual experience. She had an appreciation for this part of the world as the origin of the religions of the Jews, Muslims and Christians. When she visited the Wailing Wall she responded to the acoustical effect of the wailing of prayers. "The sound was in waves," she said, "buzzing in the ceiling ... Celestial, religious music made from praying. The whole thing is so spiritual it's like nothing else."[9]

While she was in Israel, she discovered what to do with the film footage of birds she had made in the early mornings on Summerhill Avenue, the year after she returned from New York to live in Toronto. She had felt secure and happy in her "little cottage" back in 1972. In contrast to her feeling of comfort, she saw the birds in the cold; yet they seemed triumphant in surviving, giving her joy in their chirping, offering "life and hope for spring."[10] In Israel, she thought of the Jews surviving, like the birds, with the same spirit of hope and joy. She saw the signs of their hope everywhere, even on the site of a bomb shelter where carefully watered flowers grew.

Joyce absorbed the resonance of the Hebrew language and decided she wanted the sound of a Hebrew cantor in her film about the birds. That is how *Birds at Sunrise* came to have Psalm 23 in Hebrew at the beginning, laying out the "spiritual ground" of a film that was layered with the symbolism of survival.

Joyce was not the only artist for whom the trip was a spiritual experience. Montreal artist Irene F. Whittome felt the same way. Before 1984, she and Joyce knew each other's work, but they had not met until they arrived at Montreal's Mirabel Airport for their flight. As it turned out, she and Joyce and Sylvain Cousineau, another Montrealer, had the same quarters in an artists' residence in Jerusalem. That is when Joyce and Irene discovered they were soul mates. The tour of Israel was a mystical experience for both of them, so much so that they each decided they wanted to be baptized in the Sea of Galilee. Sylvain Cousineau was born a Catholic, so he acted as the "priest" who baptized them. And they each brought back to Canada a small bottle of water from the Sea of Galilee.[11]

Irene and Joyce spent most of that two-week tour in Israel together and discovered the common bond of two artists on a mythical journey, talking about the mystical aspects of life. However, some days Joyce's behaviour was puzzling, even disturbing. She went through enormous swings of emotion, extreme highs — almost ecstatic — and then for no obvious reason became depressed, or she drifted off, one didn't know where. Several times Joyce panicked and said, "I can't move." She asked Irene to go on, saying she would catch up later. Fortunately, Irene stayed with Joyce when panic struck, but she wondered about these incidents.[12]

They formed an enduring friendship, and after they each returned home, Irene and Joyce spoke to each other frequently on the telephone. Irene had come to know the two sides of Joyce: the woman with an inner light, who was bubbling and laughed easily; and the woman with the "heavy cast of something," very sad. Irene would later learn from Joyce about her grief at not having been able to conceive a child, and the loss she sustained in her separation from Michael; she would often talk to Irene about those two sadnesses.

Around this time Michael initiated efforts at working out a legal divorce, something he continued for a number of years until the legal settlement in 1989. Several of their properties were points of disagreement and contention, especially the beloved Newfoundland property, which Joyce was determined to keep. She felt it was hers, and she cringed at the idea of Michael in the cabin with another woman.[13]

The files in the archives at York University contain numerous scraps of paper with notes in Joyce's handwriting to herself and to lawyers, listing what she thought Michael owed her and what she wanted from the settlement. The Newfoundland property figures prominently in these jottings. In the course of working on the divorce, her lawyer, Erica James, told Joyce she should execute a will and suggested that she ask Douglas McPherson to be her executor. James was also McPherson's lawyer.

McPherson had met Joyce in the early seventies, and in the mid-seventies he and Penelope Glasser happened to live in the neighbourhood where Joyce and Michael lived. They occasionally saw each other at parties, and in the early eighties Joyce sometimes went to their cottage on Manitoulin Island, which is where she adopted her cat Thomas. When James phoned McPherson to ask whether he would be the executor of Joyce's will, he knew Joyce well enough to make a decision. He agreed, but heard nothing more about it from James.[14]

Joyce changed lawyers several times during the course of the divorce negotiations. One lawyer, who became exasperated with how the negotiations between Joyce and Michael were going, dropped the case in frustration. The negotiations came to a stand-still for a while. It is not surprising that Michael wanted this business finished. An undated Christmas card to Joyce reads, "Merry Christmas ... and Happy New Year, but PLEASE!

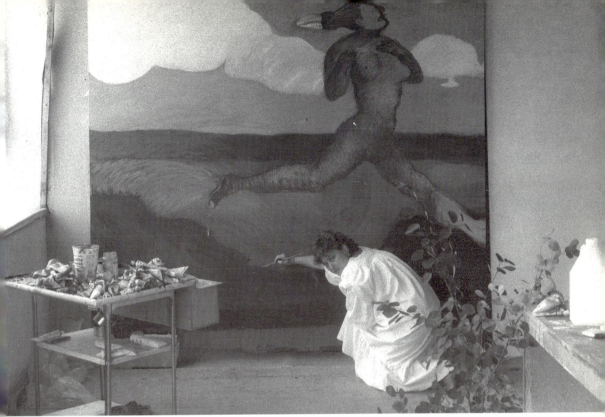

Joyce painting in her King Street studio in the mid-eighties.

CLOSE THE COMPANY and DO The Divorce in Jan! Michael."[15] It seemed Joyce deliberately avoided working on the divorce, most likely because she did not like making the end of her marriage official. She preferred to work on her art.

For one thing, she wanted to complete her unfinished films, a decision for which Kay Armatage had been the catalyst. During the winter of 1983, Armatage, a filmmaker and now chair of Women's Studies at the University of Toronto, phoned Joyce one day after teaching a class about Joyce's films. She felt impelled to tell her how impressive her films were — a spontaneous gesture. It had a big impact on Joyce; as a result of that phone call, Armatage and Joyce met weekly during the winter and went through her old film footage, which she had not seen for a long time. With this encouragement, Joyce began work on completing her films from the old footage. Armatage also helped Joyce get funding for the films by writing the grant applications; Joyce then signed them and mailed them.[16] As a result, Joyce made *Birds at Sunrise* and *Peggy's Blue Skylight*, and got a new print made of *Larry's Recent Behaviour* (1963).

Joyce had black-and-white footage for a film she and her close friend Hollis Frampton had shot in the summer of 1967, chasing each other with their cameras, beginning at Wendy Michener's home in the Casa Loma area of

Toronto and ending at Ward's Island. They didn't complete it before Frampton died of lung cancer in the spring of 1984 at the age of forty-eight, just when the Albright-Knox Gallery in Buffalo, New York, was mounting a major travelling retrospective of his work. Considering the importance of this film, the Albright-Knox wanted to see *A and B in Ontario* completed.

Su Rynard — who to Joyce would always remain her niece even though she was Michael's niece — worked with Joyce in editing the footage she and Frampton had shot. It was completed that year. Su also helped Joyce edit *Birds at Sunrise* and *Peggy's Blue Skylight*, both of which were completed the following year.

Joyce wanted to develop her stored material for a film she and her dear friend Wendy Michener had begun. Wendy, at age thirty-five, had died of an embolism on New Year's Day in 1969. The disparate film footage and photographs required total concentration — something that Joyce did not seem to have, and she made no progress. She was also unable to get the funding she needed. "Wendy and Joyce" was never completed.

About three months after Joyce received the letter confirming her retrospective at the Art Gallery of Ontario, another letter came from Janis Crystal Lipzin of the San Francisco Art Institute, offering her the post of visiting instructor at the school in 1985. Her responsibilities during the fifteen-week semester in the first half of that year would include teaching both graduate and undergraduate seminars. For the semester from January 1 to May 15, 1985, she would be paid $4,713.[17] Joyce accepted. While she was away, Su Rynard lived in her house, and Stella Kyriakakis continued to look after her business.

Lipzin arranged for Joyce to stay at Steve Anker's place. Anker, the Director of the San Francisco Cinémathèque, had moved into a new apartment and had an extra room. He remembers that Joyce spent a lot of time by herself, setting up her easel in her room and working on her Mozart paintings. She was obsessed with Mozart during this period, fantasizing that she could travel back in time to when he was alive. In fact, she felt she drew spiritual strength from Mozart, and that his spirit helped her make the transition to San Francisco — she had discovered him two months before she left Toronto and read everything she could find about him. Because she imagined that he went from great heights of spirituality into the depths of despair, she felt some kinship with him. In jottings in her notebook, she said she wondered if her friends thought she was crazy for feeling she could know Mozart in this way, but she felt she did not have "the strength to make the transition alone."[18]

Though Joyce spent a lot of time in her room, she was open, enthusiastic and joyful at times, and entered into conversations with Anker. The politics

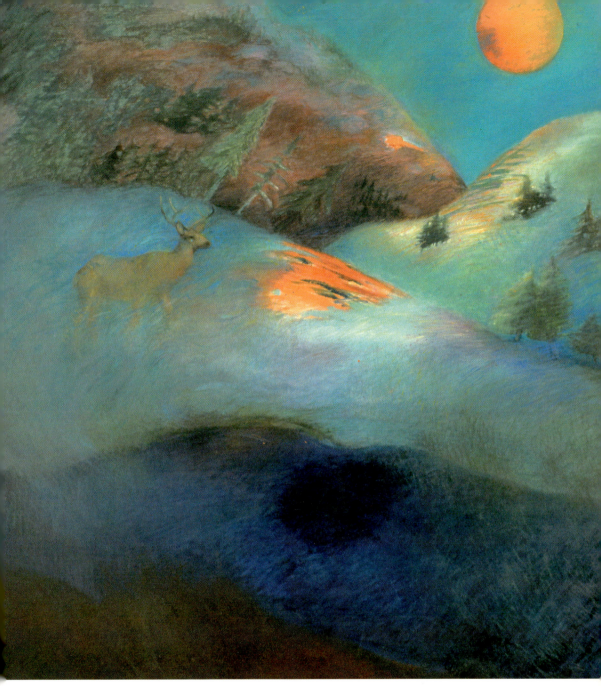

Mozart and Wieland, 1985.

of the Ronald Reagan era was one of their topics of conversation. With Reagan in power in the United States, Margaret Thatcher in England, and Brian Mulroney's Parliament in Canada a year old, talking about politics in 1985 upset Joyce. For her, the Western world was moving in the wrong direction. A number of years later she would call Canada "tired and confused. You never know what the fuck Mulroney's going to do. He makes everybody

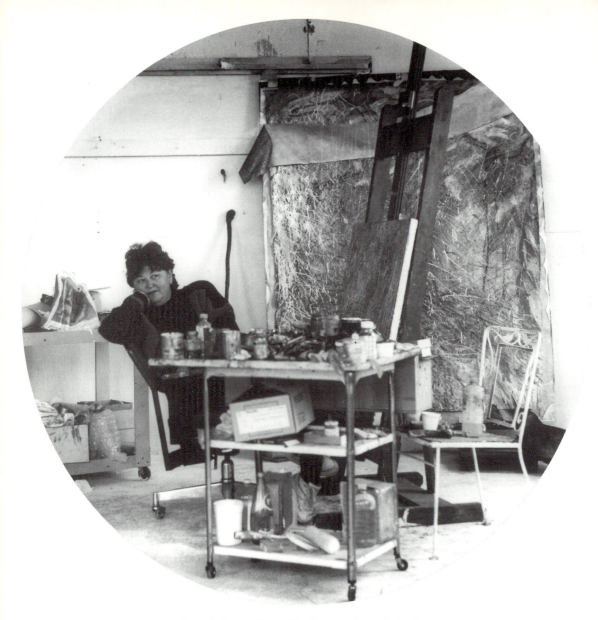

Joyce in her studio on King Street in the mid-eighties.

drunk, in a way, or powerless." By the late eighties she would say that Canada was being dismantled, to be left in the same kind of numbness she sensed in the United States.[19] She had seen it coming nearly twenty years earlier, but she likely had not imagined the extent of the change.

Talking about angels rather than politics was much more inspiring. Of course, Joyce and Anker also discussed films and the Cinémathèque, and Joyce did not hold back on her opinions. "I keep people at arm's length because of business," Anker said, "and she'd cut through that and sometimes she'd be cross with me. She was incapable of NOT speaking her mind."[20]

Joyce loved teaching, and her approach was completely her own. Anker thought she made a course plan, but in notes she wrote after she had returned to Toronto, she said she did not have a course outline, but just acted as though she did.[21]

She used an intuitive approach in her teaching, and did exercises that required students to work with their dreams, an approach that was not typical in a film class. According to Anker, Joyce "resolutely tried to do the surprising and unconventional thing. She thought of ways of provoking dialogue." She was nurturing and encouraging, but at the same time, she was "totally sharp ... precise and very critical. She was plain speaking ... critical and harsh if she felt something was 'bullshitty.'"[22]

Anker felt Joyce changed during the time she was in San Francisco. When she arrived, he sensed that she was somewhat depressed, and he assumed her depression resulted from the difficult times she had experienced in recent years. He attributed the change partly to the drugs she took — she participated in group sessions in which Ecstacy, then legal, was administered as a way of opening people to each other and to psychic healing.[23] These sessions made her feel she was being reborn. She later wrote about having felt like a baby, and realizing she had to take care of that baby. She also felt the experience had put her in touch with the little girl inside of her who had been unloved and forgotten, and that she began being able to allow people to love her.[24]

Joyce also consulted a psychic in San Francisco. The psychic told her she had just passed through a traumatic period — this was not news to Joyce. Following the psychic's suggestions, Joyce began using affirmations in an attempt to reprogram herself. Among her papers are many loose sheets with the same statements written over and over, more than a hundred times, often in red ink: "Thy will not mine O Lord" and "Divine love is doing its perfect work in this situation now and all is well" and "I will do my best without limitation."[25] She also used a "scientific healing affirmation" about little cells in her body, saying that "This affirmation has stimulated many ink drawings, and now, today, I think could be translated into a painting."[26]

By the time Joyce's contract at the Art Institute had ended, she did not want to go home. According to Anker, she was desperate to stay permanently in San Francisco and continue teaching there. After the several new approaches she had tried in an attempt to resolve her inner turmoil and confusion, apparently she saw this as a place where she could break out of her shell. It was also characteristic of Joyce, particularly from the mid-eighties on, that when she liked a place and the people there, that's where she wanted to live. She sometimes said she wanted to move to Montreal to be closer to Phyllis Lambert; she talked about moving to Cabbagetown, where artist Jane Martin lived because that area was a friendly community; she also looked at a house in Brantford on Kathy Dain's street. These other places offered something she wanted, that she seemed to feel she was missing at home. However, with her love of learning and exploring all kinds of approaches to personal growth, San Francisco had special appeal.

While Joyce was in San Francisco, Sandra Paikowsky had mounted a show of her work at Concordia University in Montreal. Called "A Decade of Painting," the exhibition consisted of forty-five of her paintings from 1956 to 1966. The show traced how Joyce had moved from the subject matter of domestic situations to more abstract work, such as her *Time Machine* series, the rough collages and the plane-crash paintings in the early to mid-sixties, revealing the strength of the early part of her career.

When she returned to Canada, Joyce was shocked to find out that Jean Sutherland Boggs had been fired from her position as director of the Crown corporation responsible for new buildings for the Museum of Man and the National Gallery of Canada. She suspected this was a case of bureaucratic disregard for women.

Boggs had become the first female director of the National Gallery in 1966. She had brought to the job a broad experience of teaching art history as well as curating. With her education at Harvard in the museum training program, she had the necessary qualifications, and she also became an authority on Degas. While she was at the National Gallery, a number of institutions awarded her honorary degrees, something she attributed to the times and the need to begin recognizing women, which she saw as a kind of tokenism, so she was not flattered.[27]

Two years after her appointment as Director of the National Gallery, the National Museums of Canada Corporation had been formed, a reorganization that meant the museums were in competition for funds, and Boggs no longer had the support of trustees whose primary interest was the National Gallery. Though she enjoyed the job, after ten years she left and took a teaching position at Harvard. From there she went on to become director of the Philadelphia Museum of Art. By then the Government of Canada had decided to construct new buildings for both the National Gallery and the Museum of Man. A Crown corporation was formed for this purpose, and Boggs was asked to return and be the director.

Boggs was sixty years old in 1985, and liked the idea of spending the last five years of her career at this job. It did not work out that way — she was fired and she never found out the real reason. She was "called in by the clerk of the Privy Council and told that at two o'clock that afternoon a bill would be passed in the House of Commons cancelling my Order in Council appointment. That would be my last day."[28] She was told that the Privy Council decided the Department of Public Works should be the administrator of the project instead. However, in hindsight Boggs speculates that she was fired because she was not interested in power games and politicking; she just wanted to get the job done.[29] Michael Pantazzi remembers helping Boggs pack her things on that Friday afternoon and having lunch with her and Joyce the next day.[30]

It is not hard to imagine the indignation with which Joyce would have responded to Boggs's situation because she understood what it was like to come up against power games. Nor had she forgotten Boggs's total support for the *True Patriot Love* show in 1971. The action of the National Museums of Canada Corporation was just the thing to set in motion an avalanche of ideas in Joyce's head to do something dramatic and lavish to honour Boggs. Joyce found two women to help her, Phyllis Lambert and a former National Gallery curator, Mimi Cazort. They threw a party to overshadow all parties.

To begin with, Joyce created the invitation, a composite of scenes on a large, folded card, printed in red ink. All over the card, small figures, drawn in dots and lines, dance and play music. A man holds up a banner with the words "TRUTH" and "JOY" written on it. In the spirit of two countries in one, another sign says "VÉRITÉ à Joie." The words "Thank you Jean" rise up from a swirl of mist — or is it a river? In a large pillared pavilion on the left, a costumed man carrying a sword comes running.[31]

The drawing on the invitation set the celebratory tone for the evening, as did the request for "festive dress." One hundred guests were invited to the party on September 7, 1985, in Phyllis Lambert's home in Old Montreal. Boggs remembers that the whole house was filled with people talking — "an extraordinary number of people," and it was both "gala and informal" at the same time, "with wonderful food all over the place."[32]

Boggs was not prepared for the scale of the party, which included performing mimes and musicians, and women wearing wreaths in their hair. A bower had been built especially for her, and guests strewed flowers in her path when she arrived. It was Joyce's idea to have a performance that would tell Boggs's story, but in fact, the performance was a mixture of true Boggs and true Wieland: the bureaucracy Boggs faced and Wieland's innocence and humour expressed in her dream of changing that bureaucracy. Joyce orchestrated the event, including directing the performers.

A mime carried in a model of a Greek temple, which was a stand-in for the new National Gallery. A big scroll of paper represented the plans, which the bureaucrats wrenched away. Of course, they also carried giant scissors and a six-foot-long dollar bill, which they had the power to cut as they pleased. And in the spirit of Wieland-romanticism, silver dust filtered through the air. The female mime representing Boggs carried the gallery in her hands, and the men — bureaucrats — carried Boggs. The message was that she would

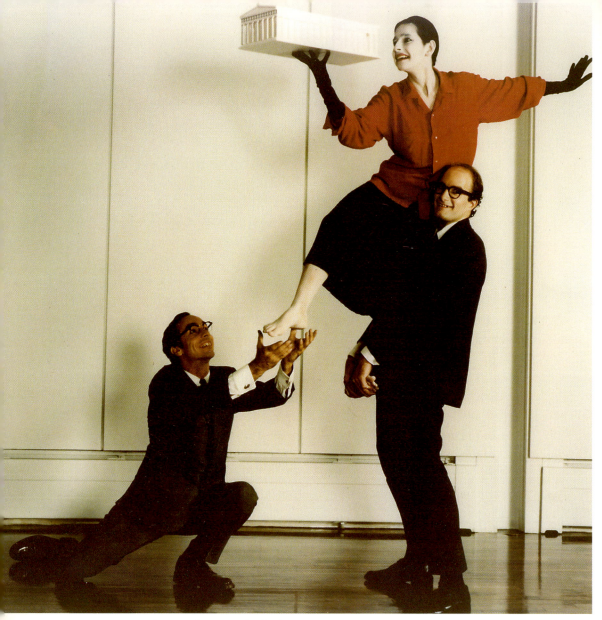

Mimes at the party for Jean Sutherland Boggs.

inspire them to change their minds. Pierre Elliott Trudeau, who had dressed in a cowboy outfit for the evening, afterward quipped, "So you think bureaucrats can change their minds like that?" Joyce took it all in her stride. Trudeau's comment simply added to her pleasurable memory of the party — she was in "seventh heaven about it all," and summed up the extent of her pleasure with the evening when she said, "You'd think you were at the Petit Théâtre at Versailles."[33] Joyce was still Madame de Pompadour!

The party marked the contribution of Jean Boggs, but it also marked Joyce's love of celebration and her great sense of the dramatic — qualities threading back through her 1971 show, the demonstrations she staged at the

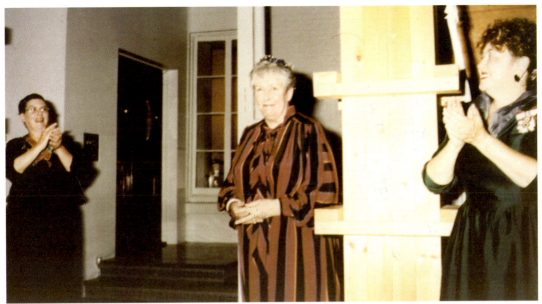

Phyllis Lambert, Jean Sutherland Boggs, and Joyce at the party for Boggs.

Canadian embassy in New York, her performances in George Luscombe's theatre group in 1962, and further back even to her childhood, when she and her friends built a theatre in a garage and created stage plays in her working-class neighbourhood in Toronto.

Immersed in these projects — her teaching in San Francisco and the party for Boggs — Joyce did not really begin focusing on her retrospective until about a year and a half before it was scheduled. And even then she was working on other projects that ended up consuming her time and attention. After Joyce's return from San Francisco, Stella Kyriakakis gave notice that she was moving on to a new job, but first she helped with the search for her replacement. Joyce wanted to hire an applicant who was an orphan, even though she was not really suitable. Stella insisted that Frances Patella would be the best person for the job, and in the end Joyce hired her. But Joyce was angry that Stella was leaving — Joyce felt abandoned, while, from Stella's perspective, "I just thought I was switching jobs. I thought we could still stay friends and have tea, but she saw it as I'm leaving her."[34]

Stella, as would the assistants after her, had learned to set certain boundaries. If they were having a meeting to discuss the day's work, Joyce had difficulty keeping her attention on her business. She might suddenly get up and start "dancing around by herself, sort of Isadora Duncan [style]."[35] Like Stella, Frances, who worked as Joyce's administrative assistant from 1985 until the spring of 1987, remembered that in the middle of a business meeting Joyce would suddenly jump up and say something like, "Oh, I have to go measure the curtains." Frances would ask Joyce to please do it later so

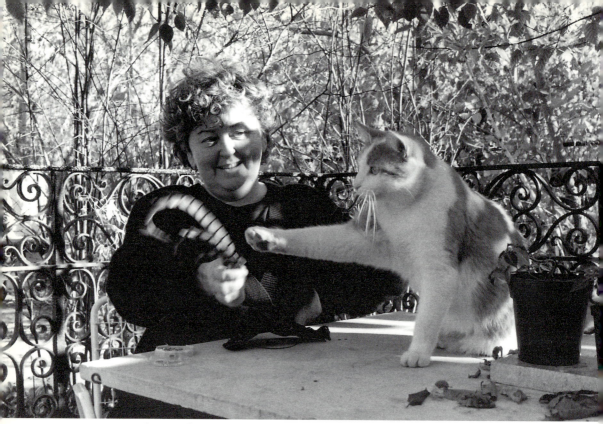

Joyce making a Halloween mask on her back patio with Thomas, fall 1986.

they could focus on the work at hand. Not only that, but sometimes Joyce would completely forget what had happened that morning or the day before. Before she went home at the end of the day, Frances had to put up notes for Joyce so she would remember what she was doing that evening.

One evening Joyce had an important meeting scheduled, and Betty Ferguson stopped in and asked if she'd like to go out for dinner. Joyce agreed to go, but Frances, on her way out the door, reminded Joyce of her appointment. Just then the phone rang, and another friend asked her to dinner, and again Joyce said she would love to go. "Betty and I are just like — Joyce, you can't go! I left and said to Betty, make sure she gets to this meeting. In a matter of minutes she'd forget these things, but she could remember things that happened way back when."[36] Because Joyce seemed so scattered and forgetful — she also came across to people as being needy — Frances and the other employees became protective of Joyce, as well as somewhat suspicious of others, because they were afraid people would take advantage of her. However, to the extent that her assistants maintained a calm control of Joyce's business, she became more relaxed and focused.[37]

Regardless of her commitments, she also had other priorities, and if a sick cat showed up, taking care of it was added to the list of tasks for the day. In Frances's daily log recording phone calls and tasks completed, she noted that she phoned the humane society about how to catch Ian. This was a cat Joyce had named, a mangy, ragged alley cat that she claimed her own cat Thomas had brought home, so she intended to adopt him and take care of him. She managed somehow to get him into the house, and he went berserk and raced madly about inside till she finally let him out. Obviously, he was an outdoor cat and did not want confinement. She set food — to which she added vitamins — on the ground outside her back door and in winter put out a little house heated with a light bulb. With her care, Ian revived and grew back his fur. Though he continued his wanderings, Ian used her back patio as his home, which gave Joyce a measure of satisfaction.

"Little" things, like looking after cats, aside, Joyce was working on many ideas. She wanted to start a gallery for young artists who did not have a place to show their work. Also, since the beginning of 1984, she had been developing ideas for several paintings she called the "Laidlaw Group," because Nicholas Laidlaw had agreed to fund the project with $25,000, and she suggested he could dedicate them to a member of his family. Joyce worked on one painting off and on for several years. It was to be a landscape, an homage to the Group of Seven, and would include Lawren Harris along with her psychiatrist, Dr. Mary McEwen, Joyce's god-daughter Allison Ferguson with her baby, and her foster child in Kenya. She also intended to put Nick Laidlaw into it with a grandchild, and "somehow Trudeau arrived [in the painting]. I wasn't trying to paint him, [but] there he was."[38] It's not too surprising that Trudeau showed up, since he still had a prominent place in her mind. She decided she would write to him and invite him to be her escort for her opening at her retrospective.[39]

Joyce wanted to donate these paintings to the United Nations because their subject was to be world peace, an expression of her awareness of conflict in other parts of the world. She also felt that a concrete way of making a difference in developing countries was to sponsor a foster child, and for a number of years she wrote letters to the boy she "adopted," as well as including him in one of the paintings. She only ever completed the one painting, now owned by the Laidlaw Foundation. It is a large painting of a big lake, with a tree on the left, one that she obviously intended to reflect Tom Thomson's tree in The West Wind. In the lower right-hand corner, the group of people she felt belonged in this painting are sitting around an open camp fire. She had difficulty finding time to work on the painting, which is one reason it was frequently on her mind during the eighties, judging by letters in her archival material.[40] Even now, some of the figures seem incomplete.[41]

Joyce also investigated teaching and showing her work in China, until finally in January 1986 she decided to put it "on the back burner" when she discovered the difficult bureaucratic aspects of the venture.[42] She was a member of several boards and committees of arts organizations. One of the committees was the Wendy Michener Memorial committee that met from time to time to initiate events and lectures in memory of Wendy Michener.

Another, which Joyce enjoyed, was the Committee for '94. This group of professional women who, at the impetus of Judy Steed had first met at her house in 1984, were interested in politics. One of the women, Maude Barlow, now Volunteer Chair of Council of Canadians, was thinking of making a run at becoming a Member of Parliament. The discussions moved from Barlow's prospects to talk of how few women were elected representatives and what could be done about it. Joyce was the only artist in the group, and she did not attend meetings regularly. Writer Christina McCall, the group's first president, thinks that some of the women in the group had never met anyone like Joyce, who was "famous as a rebellious person." She did not talk a lot, but when she did, she said things that were meaningful. "She always wanted to have a march," and of course, she would be able to visualize how the march could be staged, the lighting at nightfall and the impression it would make. McCall remembers that Joyce contributed her own essence in the group, her radical spirit. Joyce was someone who wanted "to turn society on its head. That's the voice she brought [to the group]."[43]

The goal of this bi-partisan group was to have Canadians elect a Parliament that was at least fifty per cent female. Later, they expanded their aims to include the election of a female prime minister by 1994. They held conferences and lobbied in twos and threes at Queen's Park and Parliament Hill in Ottawa. Joyce was not among the lobbyists. However, the name of the group was her idea. She wanted to put a time-frame into the scheme and gave it ten years. According to McCall, the name later became a source of embarrassment because, obviously, the goal was not achieved and, unfortunately, Parliament Hill is still populated by a large proportion of men. And, when a female prime minister, Kim Campbell, finally assumed office in 1993, she was in power for a very short time.

Joyce designed a bright pink button with the profile of a woman on it for a Committee fund-raiser in '94. Frances Patella remembers that working on this button took Joyce much longer than she had anticipated and added to the general panic in Joyce's day-to-day life.

Besides all these activities, there were grant proposals to write. She applied to the Canada Council and the Ontario Arts Council. She had to determine the condition of all her films and have prints made of them, both for her retrospective at the Art Gallery of Ontario and for a retrospective of her films being planned for Canada House in London. From time to time Michael came to Joyce's house to talk about settling the divorce. They would begin their meetings in a friendly way, but ended up in disagreements and a stalemate by the time he left.

Joyce also put a lot of time and energy into personal therapy during the year leading up to her retrospective. For six months she had four different therapists, "a bioenergetist, a shrink psychiatrist and a gestalt, and another one, and I quit that one. For six months I did just that, and I was being thrown from pillar to post — it was wild, but I wanted to break through this stuff." With the help of personal therapy, she felt she was rebuilding herself "from the ground up."[44] Joyce had been her father's favourite child, but the level of their interaction had cast her as a plaything. She described herself as "being brought out of the box, being on display and when the show's over being put back in the box, put on the shelf until you're called out again."[45]

She desperately had wanted her father's attention and recognition, and became a playful, entertaining little girl. However, performing for her father did not get her the love and acceptance she longed for. She had always felt there was something wrong with her, a feeling that might have originated because her conception had been a "mistake."[46] She craved an acceptance that would eradicate that mistake and take her beyond the working class into which she was born.

As an adult, even when she was given recognition, she felt it was not enough, or it was not the right kind of recognition she as a major artist deserved. She convinced many people she was right. The feeling that she did not get her due sometimes puzzled other artists. "It's very hard to explain because Joyce seemed so successful," Jane Martin said. "... There was always this feeling of injustice, that somehow Joyce was treated like a bit of a bimbo or an airhead. There was a complete inability of the professional curator, critic, analyzer and ranker of male artists to understand a brain that was so different as Joyce's was, so non-linear, so right-lobe, so original, so enthusiastic."[47]

Martin touched on a major area in which Joyce, justifiably, felt she did not get what she deserved. A survey of the many articles and reviews written about her over the years, and after her retrospective, for example, reveals that they mostly dwell on her personal life. "Very few people were able to understand the real importance of her work," said writer Joyce Zemans.[48] Consequently, serious critical thinking about and understanding of her work was frequently missing.

Joyce's feeling of being unaccepted, though based in her childhood and in the lack of understanding of her work, can also be attributed to a broader reason. The kind of person she was, and what she symbolized for other women who also wanted to be successful, meant that she carried the rejection women had experienced for many generations, when "artists" meant men, for whom the attention was their birthright, and artists who happened to be female had to carry with them the extra designation of "woman artist." We have not yet shed this part of our culture. In a book about the American artists Eva Hesse, Lee Krasner and Georgia O'Keefe, Anne Middleton Wagner states that "being a woman ... has been *the* condition of artistic identity, bracketing and modifying it in ways that were and continue to be inescapable. ..." Wagner goes on to say that the qualification of "woman artist" has been used "as a limit to, rather than a guarantee of, suitability for the artist's role ..."[49] For Joyce, being imprinted as Canada's "foremost woman artist" and becoming a part of the art establishment implied a disloyalty to other women. To maintain her solidarity with them, she simply denied the recognition she was given. This was Joyce's reality, and her inner turmoil extended into the hectic pace of her day-to-day life, as she tried to focus on preparing for her retrospective.

By the fall of 1986, Kay Armatage was working on a documentary film about Joyce. Armatage had begun thinking about a film on Joyce's work during the winter she had screened old film footage with her. Joyce readily agreed when Armatage proposed the film. She seemed somewhat nervous during the filming and was always very, very conscious of her appearance, but otherwise Joyce was cooperative — she understood the filmmaking process. Armatage had asked her whether there was any painting she would like used as a motif. Joyce loved the work of the Italian painter Giambattista Tiepolo for his use of light and colour, an artist whose work, like that of Jean Chardin, art historians have described as "feminine."[50] She suggested Tiepolo's self-portrait, *Apelles painting Compaspe*, a painting that includes a page boy and a man wearing a wreath and draped in a red mantle.[51] The elaborate elements of the painting appealed to Joyce — she wanted to pose in a similar scene in the place of Tiepolo in the film.

Recreating a semblance of the Tiepolo painting was complicated. On the day the shoot was scheduled, Joyce didn't show up. Armatage phoned her house, but she wasn't there, and no one, not even her assistants, knew where she was. Finally, after five hours of waiting, Joyce arrived and Armatage asked her where she had been. Joyce said, simply, she had been swimming. "I thought that's the way it is to deal with someone who's always had that kind of freedom in her life ..." Armatage said. "I just thought ... the normal everyday things of the world don't concern her and isn't she clever to have organized her life in such a way that she doesn't have to be concerned with it, that she has these assistants."[52]

From time to time Joyce had employed as many as four or five people to work on different projects, including the bibliography for the retrospective catalogue. The documentation Joyce had was disorganized and incomplete. Someone had to spend days in the library tracking down missing articles.

Joyce tried to find a place in her house where she could safely keep all the accumulated boxes of documentation. She was relieved that the York University Archives and Special Collections asked her to donate her papers in exchange for a tax receipt.

Frances described Joyce's place before the retrospective as "a zoo," but she thinks Joyce loved the chaos and "almost purposely went out of her way to bring in more stuff and more people. How to keep track of this?"[53] Joyce's ideas continued flowing and she wanted to carry through on all of them. To her, it didn't seem that preparing for a retrospective should restrict whatever else she wanted to do.

However, in August of 1986, when I interviewed Joyce extensively — adding to her already full weeks — she said the details of the retrospective preparations were taking their toll on her creative work, particularly the painting she wanted to do. She often ended up painting in the evenings. But she acted as though there was nothing in the world she would rather be doing than talking with me at that moment.

Perhaps because of all these other interests, as well as Joyce's inclination to be somewhat scattered, Philip Monk, who curated the show, concluded that he could not count on Joyce for many aspects of organizing the retrospective. Monk, who began working as Curator of Contemporary Canadian Art at the Art Gallery of Ontario in 1984, took over the work on Joyce's show when Marie Fleming, the assigned curator, became ill. Mounting the exhibition became what Monk described as "pretty well the curator's exhibition." He remembers thinking that Joyce seemed ill.[54] His memory of the process agrees with the way Joyce described it in August of 1986, saying that he chose the pieces he wanted to include and then checked with Joyce.[55]

Kathy Dain, who had been one of Joyce's students at Artsake and by then was a close friend, remembers that Joyce asked her to go along to a meeting with Monk. Joyce also brought Frances to one of the meetings to operate a tape recorder and tape the meeting. Although Monk has no memory of it, Kathy recalls that Monk seemed taken aback by the tape recorder. Joyce was uneasy at first about working with Monk. She thought of him as an "analyzer of things," and she was afraid her show would not be mounted the way she wanted. Kathy tried to reassure Joyce. When Kathy pointed out that Monk was young, and relatively new in his job at the AGO, Joyce's attitude changed somewhat, and she became almost maternal.[56]

Several months before the show opened, a newspaper article entitled "Wieland faces another historical first" stated that this would be the first time the AGO had presented a retrospective exhibition of a living female artist.[57] Randall Speller, a librarian at the AGO for nearly twenty years, remembers that when AGO director William Withrow discovered the article he came to the library, and "we were running around" to find out if that was true. They discovered that the article was right, and Withrow expressed surprise.[58] In fact, in the archives of the AGO is a photocopy of the article, with the statement underlined and notes showing that someone had checked the claim — jottings in pencil in the margins mention Paraskeva Clark's exhibition in 1982, Emily Carr's small exhibition of paintings in 1943, and "very few retros of living male artists."[59]

A large retrospective of Emily Carr's work had been held at what was then the Art Gallery of Toronto in October and November 1945, seven months after Carr's death.[60] Though the number of shows of women's work did increase at the AGO in the eighties, more than thirty years after Carr's retrospective, Joyce's show was something of a landmark.

Knowing where she belonged in Canadian art history gave her satisfaction, but other circumstances impinged on what Joyce felt was an opportunity for recognition. Just over two weeks after her retrospective opened, an exhibition of Montreal artist Betty Goodwin's work from 1971 to 1987 also opened at the AGO. This bothered Joyce. Here she was, finally having a retrospective at the major gallery in her province, and she had to share the attention with another senior female artist.[61]

In the back of her mind were memories of the unique aspects of her 1971 show in Ottawa, and she wanted to do something dramatic again. She wanted to bring huge trees into the gallery, and set up trellises with plants. However, she had to make compromises. The gallery did budget $500 for a variety of bulbs, flowers and pussy willows to create an atmosphere that Joyce liked. Monk remembers that at the last minute she wanted to rebuild one of her original studios from the fifties as the entrance to the exhibition, but it was too late in the process and the fire marshall would likely not have approved it.

On a cool, cloudy Wednesday evening at six-thirty — April 15, 1987 — the AGO held the opening ceremony for Joyce's retrospective. Margo Bindhardt, who was president of the AGO at the time, gave the first words of welcome. Philip Monk also spoke briefly, followed by Pierre Théberge, who declared the exhibition open. Then it was Joyce's turn, and she simply thanked all the guests for coming "to my harvest. It's upstairs. I made it with my love and I give it to you with love." With a performance of Gustave Charpentier's "Depuis les Jours" by the soprano Rosemarie Landry, who offered to sing when she heard about Joyce's show, the ceremonies came to an end and Joyce's thirty-year career was put on the public stage. More than four thousand people visited the show on the opening day.

Joyce was pleased with the way the show was hung.[62] Beginning with a 1955 collage, the retrospective covered her work, which moved freely

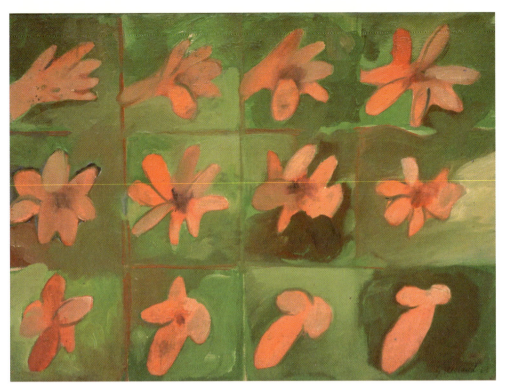

Nature Mixes, 1963.

between drawing and painting, constructions and collage, quilts and films, printmaking, and even her 1971 Sweet Beaver Perfume. It is ironic that Joyce, who had protested American curators at the AGO, wanted American critics — Lucy Lippard and Lauren Rabinovitz — to write essays in her catalogue, and she liked what they said. Particularly, Joyce felt vindicated by Lippard's essay. Lippard acknowledged that Joyce was criticized for making art that was awkward, sentimental, and as if that were not enough, also naive. However, she pointed out that "... without these elements it [the art] would not have been able to stretch and flex to accommodate so many different ideas and subjects."[63]

The "many different ideas and subjects" became apparent as one walked through the Zacks wing of the AGO, or viewed her films. The show was arranged chronologically and hung according to periods in her prolific art-making history: her work of the fifties and sixties, which included most of the New York years; the quilts and other pieces embedded in nationalism through the 1970s; and the later pieces from the first half of the 1980s.

In the first room, Joyce included photographs of herself at different ages and other small pieces in a glass case: the button she designed for the Committee for '94, along with her sketches, her Sweet Beaver Perfume and two small self-portraits.

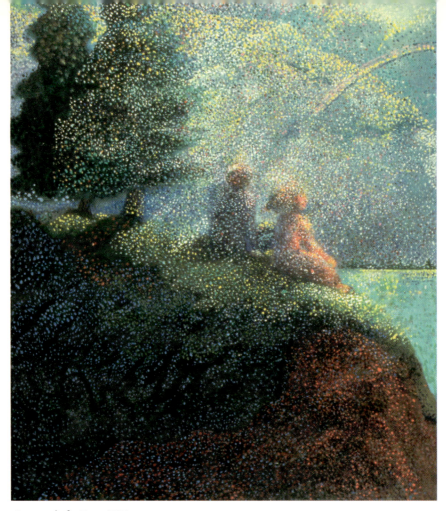

Crepuscule for Two, 1985.

Among the early works was *Penis Wallpaper* (1962), a small oil painting of penises like rockets zooming across the sky. "I'd go for a whole wall of that," was one woman's response.[64] Susan Crean speculated that Joyce's humour is one of the things that saved her from the morality squad when she was painting penises back in the sixties. The cover of *This Magazine*, in which Crean's article appeared, sports a very funny Wieland drawing of a large, erect penis with a smiling face on its head against a background of a blue sky where two Canadian flags blow in the wind.[65]

More than a dozen of the stuffed plastic hangings Joyce called "home totems" were included in the show. Certainly these can be seen as the forerunners of the quilts, which she began around the same time — Joyce used a sewing machine to stitch the pockets of the clear plastic, into which she stuffed photographs, small objects and folded newspaper clippings. Some of these plastic hangings were obviously political, but the political content of others was less apparent because the messages were invisible inside the pockets. In the spirit of sixties pop art, these pieces reveal the workings of

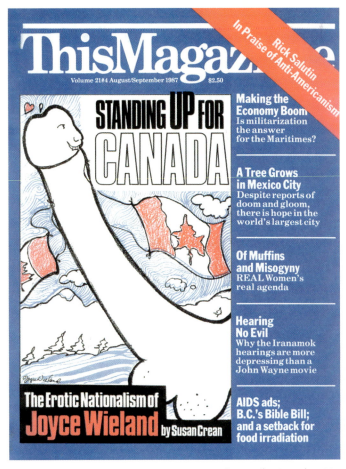

ThisMagazine

Volume 21#4 August/September 1987 $2.50

In Praise of Anti-Americanism   Rick Salutin

STANDING UP FOR CANADA

The Erotic Nationalism of Joyce Wieland by Susan Crean

Making the Economy Boom
Is militarization the answer for the Maritimes?

A Tree Grows in Mexico City
Despite reports of doom and gloom, there is hope in the world's largest city

Of Muffins and Misogyny
REAL Women's real agenda

Hearing No Evil
Why the Iranamok hearings are more depressing than a John Wayne movie

AIDS ads; B.C.'s Bible Bill; and a setback for food irradiation

Standing up for Canada, 1987.

this artist's mind and emotions to create visual images that encompassed serious issues, but with a light touch.

More than a dozen embroidered cloth works and quilts were included in the exhibition, for which Joyce had hired other women. These innovative, collaborative works are part of the reason Joyce is often seen as a pioneer. In the retrospective catalogue, Lucy Lippard noted that Joyce Wieland preceded Judy Chicago.[66] In fact, the summer that Joyce's quilts were exhibited in a museum for the first time — in 1971 at the National Gallery — Chicago first discovered china painting, which led to *The Dinner Party*.[67]

A number of the coloured-pencil drawings from "A Bloom of Matter," shown in 1981 at the Isaacs Gallery, appeared in the retrospective. These were images of healing and celebration, to which Joyce felt she had a right because she had emerged from her personal wilderness experience. These drawings were part of her quest for spiritual rejuvenation and healing. The writer Carol Becker articulated what artists such as Joyce attempted: "how to chart the development of the soul; how to give physical shape to the metaphysical; and

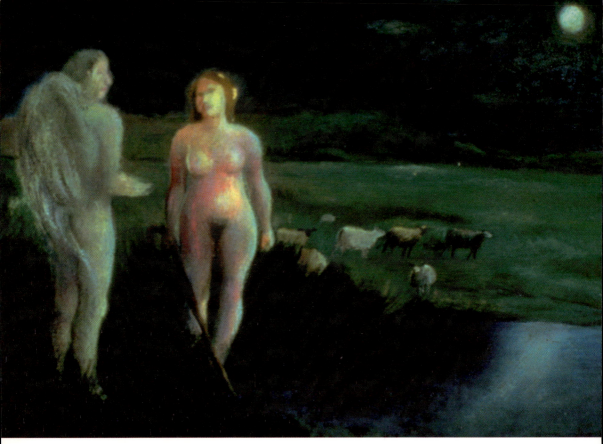

She will remain in the phenomenal world filled with ignorance
with her sheep, and not go with him, 1983.

how to develop a personal symbolic system through which to explain, examine, and represent the process through which individuals come to understand their lives in relationship to a cosmic order."[68]

From the pencil drawings Joyce had returned to oil paintings.[69] The title of one, *She will remain in the phenomenal world filled with ignorance with her sheep, and not go with him* (1983), reveals her focused drive to stay on the course she had begun, her pursuit of the extraordinary in life, even though others might perceive this path as "filled with ignorance" and naive. Joyce was nothing if not consistent, for this title is in the spirit of her journal jottings from her mid-twenties. This is how she carved out a place for herself, channelling her personal passions into her art, even if it meant revealing her disturbances and struggles, which a number of the oil paintings from the eighties certainly do.

Early One Morning (1986), which appears on the cover of the exhibition catalogue, at first glance appears to be a bucolic landscape. But what are the blue and brown forms in the middle of the painting — a river, a mudslide? At the foot of these in the lower right-hand corner is a barn toppled on its side and a tiny figure beside it waving her arms. Something about the red sky with its lumpy clouds adds to the ominous feeling. One is left wondering

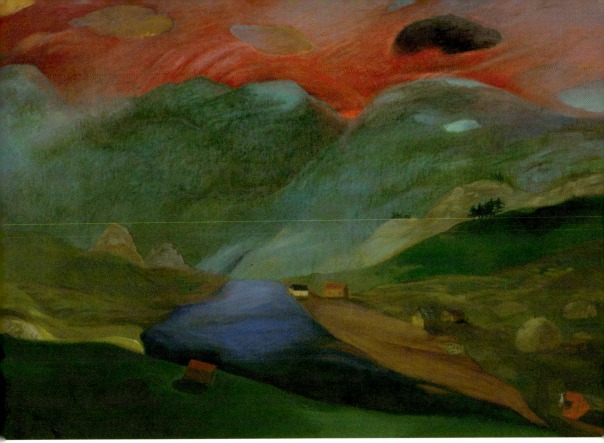

Early One Morning, 1986.

what the unsettling story is behind this painting.

The Wieland retrospective provided an overall picture of Joyce's vision. She exposed her vulnerabilities, her struggles, her lifelong passion for ecology, her country, and her female aesthetic, along with her sense of humour and capacity for celebration — these all vibrated through the Zacks gallery. And it revealed the workings of her mind, "a mind where the emotive and the idea were so conjoint that I think that was the miracle of Joyce," as her friend Phyllis Lambert once said.[70]

What were the catalysts for this artist who created such a body of work? What made her do it? What drove her on? We can never definitively answer these questions, but perhaps Dr. Kay Redfield Jamison's studies of artists and writers provide some clues. Jamison says that "learning through intense, extreme, and often painful experiences, and using what has been learned to add meaning and depth to creative work, is probably the most widely accepted and written-about aspect of the relationship between melancholy, madness and the artistic experience." She then goes on to quote John Berryman's famous statement that "the artist is extremely lucky who is presented with the worst possible ordeal which will not actually kill him."[71] Berryman's assertion, whether or not we think Joyce was lucky, does describe her.

She had an erratic emotional life, with intense highs and lows, something she herself recognized from the time she was in her early twenties. Jamison maintains that the ability to reconcile opposite states "is a critical part of any creative act," what Virginia Woolf called "... two edges, one of laughter, one of anguish, cutting the heart asunder."[72] It's as though Joyce herself was a boulder with a crevasse, and coming up between the two edges like a geyser was her urge to create.

Jamison states that if "a highly imaginative person's thinking processes are hastened and loosened by mild manic states, it is likely that a distinctive quality will be added to the creative process. The grandiosity of spirit and vision so characteristic of mania, coupled with manic drive and intensity, can add an expansiveness and boldness as well."[73] Again, this description fits Joyce. She was not manic-depressive, but she did experience what could be described as mild manic states with "restlessness, ebullience, expansiveness, irritability, grandiosity, quickened and more finely tuned senses, intensity of emotional experiences ..."[74] She entered a state of mind in which she floated and danced in a kind of ethereal excitement.

Joyce believed her art was healing. The healing power of art is an ancient belief, according to Jamison. "To the extent that an artist survives, describes, and then transforms psychological pain into an experience with more universal meaning, his or her own journey becomes one that others can, thus better protected, take."[75] Joyce's faith in this healing power gave her the courage she needed, and with its healing properties art also became a bridge to the outside world. Her retrospective gave her yet another link.

She entered into the events connected with her retrospective with characteristic exuberance and enthusiasm. On a Sunday in May she led a tour of two hundred people through her show and talked about the work. She visited the show frequently and observed people's responses. Comments in her guest book showed that no one was indifferent to Joyce and her work and ranged from antagonism to adoration: "Rubbish" and "Trivial and meaningless" on the one hand, and "Wonderful, inspirational, amusing and thought-provoking" on the other. One man expressed appreciation for the "diversity of subjects and media" in the exhibition and "the inspired production ... and the probable complications (and exhaustion) involved in being a woman Canadian painter contemporary feminist artist."[76]

The retrospective travelled to Charlottetown that fall, and in the winter to Fredericton and Regina. The AGO offered the show to galleries in many other cities, national and international: Vancouver, San Francisco, New York and the Pompidou in Paris, but none of these proposals materialized.

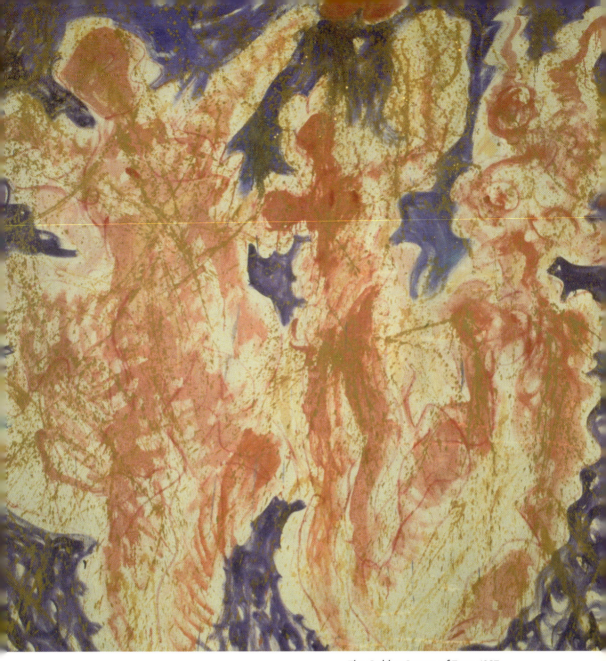

The Golden Semen of Zeus, 1987.

In 1987 articles about Joyce proliferated in many Canadian publications. *Globe and Mail* critic John Bentley Mays wrote a somewhat dismissive article that such art historians as Rozsika Parker and Griselda Pollock would describe as gender-biased.[77] Among other things, he criticized Joyce for being a dabbler, using one medium and then dropping it and moving on to something else, a criticism that Mays would not likely level at Michael Snow, or other male artists who work in a variety of media. He interpreted the "lots of talk" about the first "career-long exhibit of a living Canadian woman" at the AGO as an "occasion to shower bouquets on Wieland as phenomenon — a woman of great personal charm and beauty, an exemplary Canadian patriot, feminist, defender of the earth, survivor of many neglects and troubles ..." rather than to honour Wieland the visual artist.[78] It's interesting that Mays would write just as dismissively of Emily Carr three years later, saying that interest in her work was inspired more by "her usefulness as an example than by her accomplishment as a visual artist."[79]

Writer Jay Scott felt that critics' difficulty with Joyce was not about the forms she used, but about what she said "in a remarkably consistent and integrated way in each medium she adopted. She was asking Canadians to love themselves and she was exhorting women to love themselves." Joyce's work was the antithesis of the rational, the linear, "that paragon of reason over passion, the powerful North American man — she is female and Canadian, and her art is a fascinating public record of her quest to affirm that in the case of Canada, thinking patriotism is a positive and life-enhancing act ... and that in the case of her own person, self-embracing affection is a positive and life-enriching attitude."[80]

To be faced with more than a hundred of Joyce's works did give viewers a concentrated dose of Wieland, and perhaps that was too much for some people. During many years of her productive life, "cool was the thing, and she wasn't cool ... [She was] passionately involved in the world and it may have been one of the reasons why she wasn't appreciated. People were a little bit embarrassed by the fire in her," Pierre Théberge once said.[81]

People were also embarrassed by her sense of humour and her sharp satirical comments about politicians or institutions. "Humour is the hardest things for Canadians to accept," Joyce stated. "I had a tough enough time myself when I found out it was half of my personality ... There is humour everywhere you go in Canada ... I guess where humour might appear, like on CBC, it is hopeless. Their displays of humour aren't even of an institutional quality. In the first place they wouldn't even show a conversation between two men at the Cheticamp post office even if it was funnier than the *Goon Show*. By the time they ran it through their system, through their glass asshole, it would come out looking like Howard Johnson's."[82]

When the Mays article in Saturday morning's *Globe and Mail* hit the news stands on April 18, 1987, the telephone lines between the homes of certain artists began humming. A group of women, ranging in age from their early twenties to mid-forties, had been meeting regularly for a number of months in bars and in one anothers' studios to talk about the difficulties of trying to build a career in the kingdom of art. This diverse group of women met sometime after Mays's article appeared, and they all agreed on two things: Joyce was important because of what she had accomplished, and the Mays

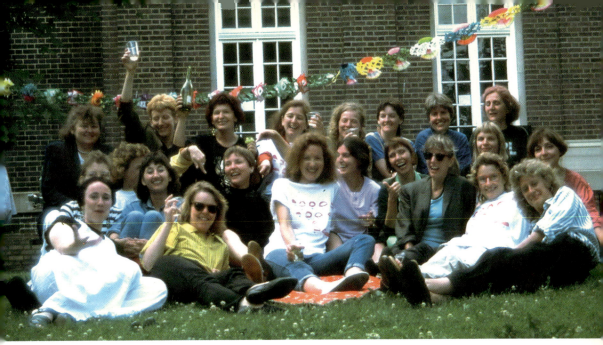

The picnic in Grange Park. Joyce is in the back row on the far left.

article called for a response. "We were so upset at that review, the condescension of that review, that we decided to advertise for a decent critic," Jane Martin said.[83] This is the ad they wrote, taking their name from the Mays description of Joyce:

Canada's leading national newspaper desperately needs responsible visual arts critic, not interested in "mastery" and not threatened by "the other", to provide informed responses to contemporary work by women artists.

Search committee: The League of Women of Great Personal Charm and Beauty, Exemplary Canadian Patriots, Feminists, Defenders of the Earth, Survivors of Many Neglects and Troubles.

Apply: Box 5663, *The Globe and Mail*[84]

The Women of Great Personal Charm and Beauty shared the cost of running the ad in *The Globe and Mail.* They did not receive any applications. I remember clipping that ad when it was published, and I knew enough about Joyce's sense of humour that I wondered whether she placed it. However, she knew nothing about it until later.

Joyce's pioneering spirit in pushing the boundaries of the art system for women had special meaning for these artists, who were all younger than she was. As Martin explained it, "There was Emily Carr and then there was Joyce and then — gap — all the rest of us."[85] To express their support, The Women of Great Personal Charm and Beauty decided to have a potluck picnic for

Joyce in Grange Park, directly south of the AGO, on the last day of her exhibition, June 28, at four o'clock, with artists Elizabeth MacKenzie, Jane Martin and Arlene Stamp organizing the event. It turned out to be a beautiful sunny day, despite the thunderstorms in the forecast.[86] Some of the women wore Joyce's lip-imprinted T-shirt produced for the show. Joyce responded with delight, and when she was asked to speak, she told with a flourish her story of meeting William Withrow and demanding her retrospective.

Why did so many women love Joyce Wieland? "We loved her because she was full of contradictions. She was human and didn't hide her contradictions," said Kass Banning, a critic who wrote on Joyce's retrospective.[87] The picnic was an expression of this love for her, but it also reflected Joyce's own generosity, and let her know that other artists would follow her inside the institutions' walls and keep the doors open for women.

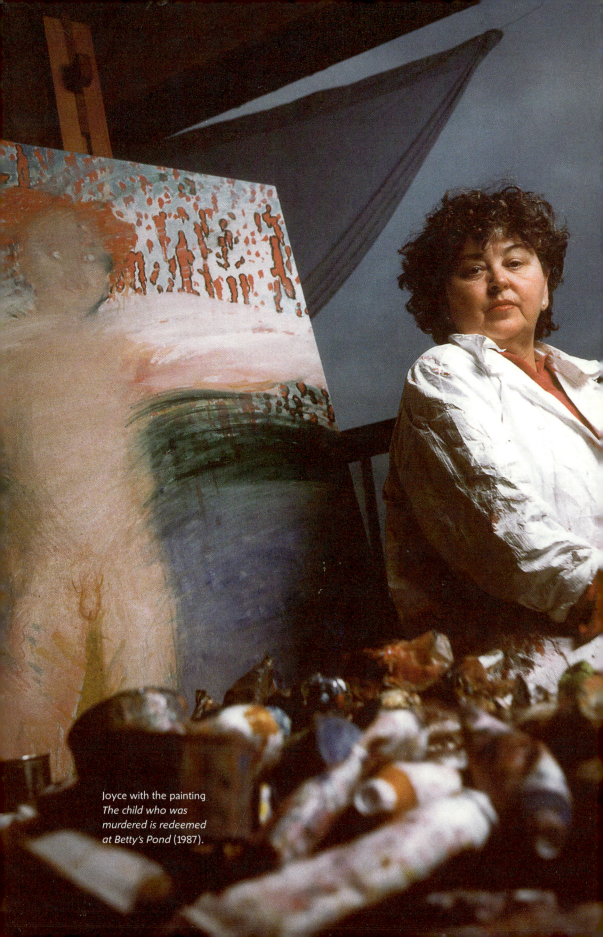

Joyce with the painting *The child who was murdered is redeemed at Betty's Pond* (1987).

10

"Planetary dream sight" lost

It may well be that nothing solid actually exists, but what might exist is energy, is space. And I have not discovered a more energetic space than art. —Jeanette Winterson[1]

Awards, honours, tributes — Joyce craved recognition and felt bereft if she didn't get it. Of course, she already had her Order of Canada, but what about recognition from her home town? To be given two of Toronto's highest honours the same year she had her retrospective gave her great pleasure. She took home an Aggie in the spring of 1987, and that fall received the Toronto Arts Award.

The Women of Distinction award was founded by Agnes Blizzard, for whom the Aggie was named, as a way to honour women who do outstanding work in their chosen field. Joyce used the awards night as an opportunity to credit the women who were important in her life. In notes she made for the organizers of the event, she mentioned her sister, Joan, as the woman who influenced her most in childhood. She also credited her teacher, Doris McCarthy.[2] As a pioneer for women in the art world, Joyce took her place in

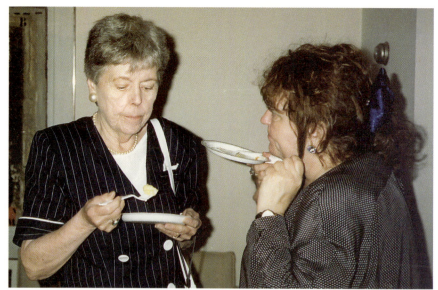

Joan and Joyce in the late eighties.

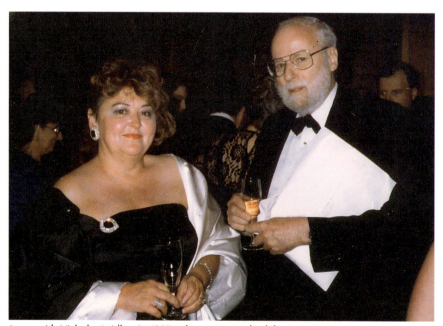

Joyce with Nicholas Laidlaw in 1987 at her arts award celebration.

the company of generations of women in a variety of fields who broke new ground. This is what the Aggie was about.

The Toronto Arts Award ceremony was a different kind of event. Joyce asked her friend and patron Nicholas Laidlaw to present the award, a somewhat dubious choice, as it turned out, for he made disparaging remarks about the portrait of him she had done, and then covered over the

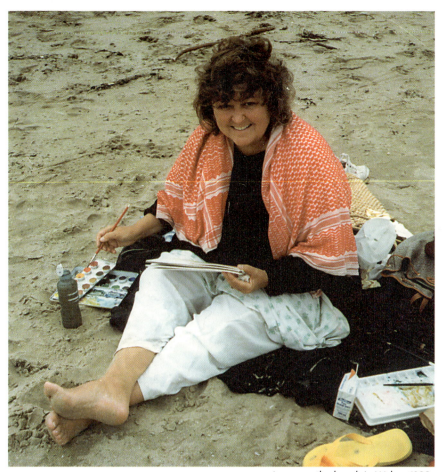

Joyce on the beach in Wales, 1988.

comments by calling her a "dear friend." To feel critical of the work was certainly his right, but an occasion to honour Joyce was not the time to tell the world that his children did not much like the portrait. There was a pause after he made his short speech — Joyce did not appear instantly, and he asked, "Is she coming?" Then Joyce appeared, looking magnificent in a long, black silk dress, off the left shoulder, designed by her friend Linda Gaylard, whom Joyce had hired as a fashion consultant by then.

Linda remembers a hesitancy when Joyce accepted the award, as though "a lot of wind had been taken out of her sails by Nick."[3] Joyce's short speech was not typical of her; she had an ability to be both articulate and funny. Joyce simply told her guests that she was born on Claremont Street, gave her thanks to Toronto, and spoke of her love for the city's trees, which make Torontonians feel they live in a forest. She must have felt hurt and stunned by Laidlaw's comments. Once the formal part of the ceremony was over, Joyce responded with enthusiasm to the reception that followed. But Linda stayed close by Joyce that evening because she perceived Joyce needed the security her presence provided.[4]

During the two months following her retrospective, she took a holiday, another cruise with Phyllis Lambert, this time to Greece.[5] She also travelled to London — she was still determined to find out more about her ancestors, so much so that she phoned every Wieland in the phone book. On several London trips, Joyce stayed with her friend Enid Irving. The two went to Wales, and in one small village, to Irving's astonishment, "as soon as she was out of my sight," Joyce somehow ended up as a judge of a flower show being held there: "Madame — from Toronto — just arrived from the intricacies of horticulture in Canada!"[6]

Back in Toronto, Joyce received a commission to paint a large mural for the Pantages Theatre on Yonge Street in the fall of 1987. She called it *Celebration* — a very large, lively, colourful scene bursting with an energy that seems to emanate from the sun. She also had started some new, large oil paintings and wanted to continue working on these after her retrospective. The new oils included *Journey to Omega (at Betty's Pond)* and *The child who murdered is redeemed at Betty's Pond*. This latter painting was based on the rage Joyce experienced at the death of her parents, as well as a schoolgirl memory. When she was sixteen she had picked a fight with a boy in the school yard and frightened him. The look of fear in his eyes stayed with Joyce to such an extent that she was never violent again with anyone.[7]

In another new oil painting, *The Murder of Marat by Charlotte Corday*, a flaming-red Charlotte Corday stands defiantly over Marat's dead body, a knife with blood on the blade in her right hand. Jean Paul Marat (1743-93) was a French revolutionist whose writings were instrumental in overthrowing the monarchy. Because of a severe skin disease, he spent much of his time in the bath, which is where Corday stabbed him. She was guillotined for this deed. These paintings reveal a side of Joyce that she rarely showed, feelings she attributed to her "twelve-year-old [self] that would like to shoot people through the car window" — feelings she said she no longer had.[8]

Another painting in a very different spirit, also completed that year, is entitled *Veriditas* (small truths), a large, green and pink abstract canvas, which was a spontaneous response to the extraordinary twelfth-century musician, poet, scientist and artist, Hildegard of Bingen (1098-1179). For a number of years Joyce drew strength from reading Hildegard's works, and introduced her to her friends. "She's my greatest inspiration," Joyce said. "She was so filled with love and so filled with the idea of the greening of the world and the raising up of women in the church, making the church realize that women have been left out."[9] Joyce drew great satisfaction from narrative painting that included historical figures even though she also continued using personal subject matter in her work.

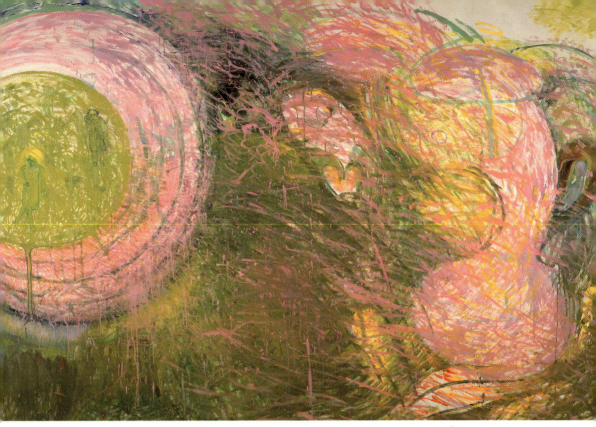

Veriditas, 1987.

The months following her retrospective in 1987 turned out to be productive, partly because she had received a Canada Council grant of more than $20,000, which meant she did not have to worry about expenses, giving her clear mind-space to focus on her work. Certainly the fee she was paid for the retrospective did not take her very far. It was organized as a national touring exhibition and the Canadian Artists' Representation (CAR) rate for this category was $3,744. When Joyce received a cheque from the AGO for $2,600 several weeks into the exhibition, she contacted Philip Monk. As it turned out, she was confused about the fee and had expected $1,750 from each of the other galleries to which her show travelled. Artists' fees were based on whether a show toured nationally or not. Since the Vancouver Art Gallery did not book the show as the AGO had hoped, it had designated the show as inter-regional rather than national; hence the lesser amount. Joyce appealed to the Toronto office of CAR, and with their intervention, she was paid $3,744.[10]

With the AGO's attempts to tour the show internationally, Joyce had high hopes for exposure abroad and was disappointed when that did not happen. However, in January and February of 1988, Canada House in London hosted a film retrospective and in the summer and early fall, an exhibition of her quilts, paintings and works on paper.

She went to England and Scotland that summer, and for several weeks travelled around Scotland with filmmaker Leila Sujir and her mother Ruth Sujir. Joyce asked Gerald Robinson and Linda Gaylard to oversee some renovations on her house while she was gone, according to a list she gave them. She wanted her attic fixed up to create a pleasant space to be used as a guest room — with a sky light — along with a storage area for some of her work. Besides renovating the attic, Joyce's bedroom was redecorated. The changes included a new frieze of green vines and flowers, which Cynthia Lorenz helped to handpaint; and a new carpet was installed in the bedroom and down the stairs.

Partly as a result of her retrospective, Joyce received and accepted more invitations to give slide lectures about her work, often on the topic of creativity. Her fees varied widely, depending on what her hosts could pay, ranging from $50 (Hart House on February 13, 1987) to $400 (University of Regina, April 7, 1988).[11] Even though she frequently gave the impression that she was short of funds, she had a steady income from investment interest, sales, film royalties, grants, lecture fees and commissions, and could live comfortably on what she earned.

For years Joyce had thought about starting a gallery to provide a place where younger artists could show their work. The idea would not go away. She believed that established artists had a responsibility to their younger colleagues. When Artsake had folded, and her students wanted to continue working with her, she had rented a large warehouse space on King Street, a short walk from her home, and that had become her studio for large works. She also taught there and painted alongside her students. She felt she benefitted from working with students and discovered she preferred painting with other artists rather than working alone. However, they could not find galleries to show their work, and Joyce knew there were many more artists like them.

Joyce occasionally looked for a suitable space for a gallery in buildings in her part of the city and nothing she found seemed right. She had been renting a small second-floor space on Markham Street in Toronto's Mirvish Village, with large front windows overlooking the street. Although she never used it for a studio herself, she had been reluctant to give it up because the space had good light and was cheap, about $150 a month.[12] She sometimes sublet it to younger artists. Finally, she decided she would use that space for a gallery, and for three years Alma Gallery would show artists' work, until its closing in the spring of 1991. Joyce chose the name because she said it means soul, and "fostering the protege."[13]

On March 4, 1988, Alma Gallery held a press preview and the next day opened its first show, an exhibition of Kate Brown's works on wood. Word of

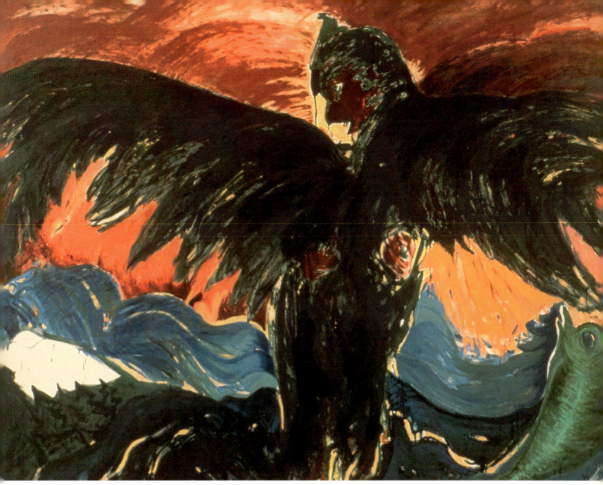

Alma, 1988.

the gallery had spread fast, and upon opening, it was already scheduled till the end of the year. By then Fran Hill, who had an art history degree from York University, was working as Joyce's administrative assistant, and she handed over to Hill the responsibility of running the gallery.

When the artist who was scheduled for the second show at Alma cancelled, Joyce decided to hang a show of her small drawings, which included "delicate line drawings, softly coloured portraits of Mozart, tiny ink studies, vibrant abstract watercolours and rough sketches on steno-pad paper."[14] She filled the gallery with white lilies.

Av Isaacs, Joyce's dealer, was not pleased that she made sales from her show without giving him a commission. This was not the only irritation he felt. That spring she entered into negotiations with the Vancouver Art Gallery to sell one of her large paintings, titled *Alma* (1988), and in June the VAG sent Joyce a cheque for $25,000 for the painting.[15] Records show that as early as February of that year Joyce had also sold through Moore Gallery, then in Hamilton, Ontario.[16] According to Ron Moore, he had been interested in her painting and that of other Toronto artists for many years. He had mounted a major show of Gordon Rayner's work, who had showed with Isaacs, and Moore wanted to show Joyce in Hamilton as well. Joyce agreed to a studio visit, and subsequently allowed him to show her work.[17] However, Isaacs wanted a commission on everything that had been sold. When Joyce refused, she found herself in a full-scale legal dispute with Isaacs, who had shown her work for nearly thirty years.

In Joyce's 1989 appointment book, on the January 14 page, she wrote notes about how she felt. "Av Isaacs takes me to a downward spiral — as I wish to spiral upwards and give hope, I suffer from being unable to get up again ..." She wrote about her attempts to leave his gallery, that when she talked to him about it he made comments about her having difficulty with menopause. Months later she was still fretting; in the September 11 space of her calendar she jotted questions for which she needed guidance from a counsellor with whom she had an appointment that day: "How to deal with a man who has all my work."[18]

According to Isaacs, he had an agreement with his artists that he had exclusive rights and would receive a commission on all works sold. However, Joyce had no agreement in writing. When he found out in 1987 that Joyce had sold paintings directly from the studio without going through him, and he had not received a commission, he "wouldn't put up with that nonsense, so I called her into the gallery. She admitted to it and I asked her to leave the gallery and then I went to the lawyer." Isaacs also said he was hurt because he felt he was not consulted about her retrospective at the AGO.[19] And yet, according to Philip Monk's memory, Isaacs had been consulted.[20]

For Joyce's part, she felt her dealer was not giving her the publicity she wanted, and during the eighties she had found a publicist and paid him out of her own pocket. She claimed she was the one who did the work to find commissions, got her shows in London and Dublin, and called up people to ask them if they wanted to buy art. She was also unhappy because immediately following her retrospective hardly any works had been sold. In notes she wrote in preparation for a meeting with her lawyer, she said "If ever there was a time to make money it was 1987 ... from that time forward I decided to do my own work in terms of sales."[21] She claimed there was not one sale with Isaacs in 1988. This made no sense to her — she had expected that the retrospective would help to increase sales, particularly because she had had a show at the Isaacs Gallery the same year, and she was extremely disappointed and angry.

In her anger, she began thinking about other things that had happened over the years that she did not like. Because of *The Far Shore*, she had had no shows at the Isaacs Gallery between 1974 and 1981. When she was ready for a show of her drawings in 1981, she felt Isaacs had not given her enough publicity. Also, she wanted to charge higher prices than her dealer did. She hired two young women to publicize the show, and when she sold many of the drawings in "The Bloom of Matter," she felt vindicated.[22]

However, from Isaacs's point of view, he felt he had put up with a lot. When she was making films during the New York years and wasn't painting, he claimed, "I would put shows together every two years just to keep her name before the public."[23] He went on. "I don't know if there's any appreciation. The artist-dealer relationship is a rough one, 'cause no one makes any money and ... if you have an exhibition of an artist and it doesn't sell, you're a lousy dealer. If it does sell, she's a great artist so that [you're] kind of caught." Isaacs said he did not know what Joyce's attitude had been toward him over time, especially since she was the only woman in his gallery for most of those years. "I don't think there was warmth between Joyce and myself, nor was there any antagonism."[24] Whatever the feelings were in the past, by the late eighties there was hurt and antagonism on both sides, despite several discussions. Fran Hill, Joyce's assistant, remembers frustrated phone calls from Isaacs, and feels he tried to discuss things with Joyce. But Joyce felt so betrayed she simply turned against him. Hill said Isaacs "couldn't understand why she was being impossible to deal with," and looking back she thinks it was because Joyce was becoming ill.[25]

At one point Joyce made notes for a letter to Isaacs, saying that her psychiatrist suggested she discuss the breakdown in their relationship, and that she would like to do this, and she gave him the option of answering the letter or not.[26] Despite the contrite notes of her letter to Isaacs, the matter was settled in the courts in Isaacs's favour. "She backed off and I got all my demands," Isaacs recalled.[27] Those "demands" translated into $28,000 that he claimed in lost commissions, which he wanted in a cash settlement of $20,000 or the equivalent of $28,000 worth of paintings. Joyce settled for the latter, and with the return of more than $500,000 worth of works and archival material, the matter was closed.[28]

An undated note in Joyce's handwriting reads, "Joyce Wieland is no longer with the Isaacs Gallery ... Thank heaven I'm free at last J Wieland"[29] Joyce also had a letter printed in *Now* magazine in April 1989, saying she was no longer associated with the Isaacs Gallery.[30] The *Toronto Star* also carried a brief story noting that Joyce had left Isaacs and that he chose not to comment. In that story, Joyce again talked about becoming free: "'I'm leaving to be free,' she said. 'To run my own life. I think I'll do my own dealing from now on. I'd never have an exclusive arrangement with a dealer again.'"[31]

However, Joyce did have another dealer, and she had been receiving payments from Moore Gallery for work sold a year before the story was published.[32] Obviously, Joyce's feelings about dealers were not entirely

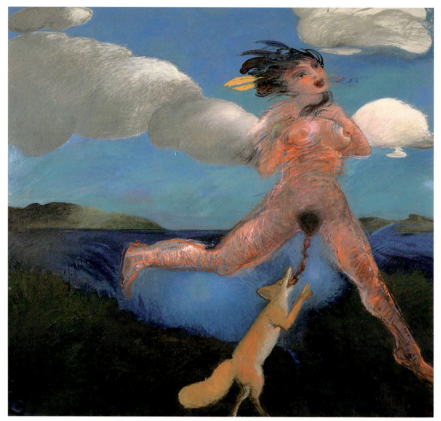

Untitled (Woman and Fox), 1986-88.

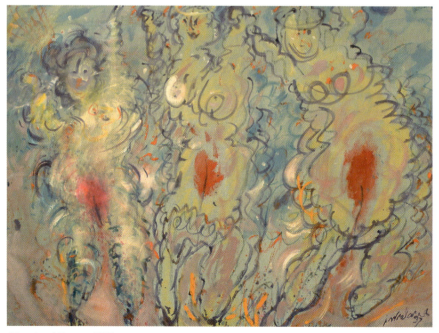

Menstrual Dance, 1987.

consistent from one time to the next. She sometimes made declarative statements about freedom, or about having resolved certain conflicts in her life, and like most of us, would later discover that things were not quite as simple as they had first seemed. This was one of those times.

As in two previous periods of her life — after finishing her feature film and in the early eighties — Joyce again consulted a nutritionist and also went to see a homeopathic doctor. Her weight was up again, this time to almost 180 pounds.[33] With so much stress over the Isaacs dispute and the divorce, controlling her weight was extremely difficult.

Joyce also consulted a number of different types of professional healers. Several paintings from that period include images having to do with bleeding, among them *Menstrual Dance* (1987), a painting she worked on for several years. In this piece she deliberately put the subject of menstruation before the public. But it embodies two separate issues: the impact on her personally of her mother's death from bowel cancer and the subject of female experience, which was a part of her work from the beginning. "Something that has never left me is this whole idea about blood," she said, "... and it's really hard to put this into the world ... This is me and my mother and it's sort of like, what do you feed the world with if you don't have milk?"[34]

Menstrual Dance could be considered one of those paintings described by art historian Marsha Meskimmon that by "representing menstruation subverts the codes which define female sexuality as image rather than physical body."[35] At the beginning of her career, Joyce's erotic drawings, subversive in the fifties and sixties, showed that the female experience included sexual pleasure. Near the end of her career, her painting about menstruation was subversive in a different way, reminding viewers that bodily functions are also part of who a woman is.

For Joyce, that female body in her paintings and drawings was also the site of pain, which she carried all her life in the images of her mother's suffering and death — she openly acknowledged that this childhood trauma was a part of her and her work. Is it surprising, then, that she carried a fear of her body? According to her psychiatrist, she had a terror of haemorrhaging to death.[36]

By the time Joyce had finished *Menstrual Dance*, and during the next several years, she was aware that something disturbing was happening to her. According to Allison Ferguson, who had moved to British Columbia in 1986, Joyce phoned her to talk about how worried she was about her mind. She was upset because she did not feel she could tell her friends about it as they did not take the problem seriously.[37] But at least one of her friends, Judy Steed, had known Joyce's behaviour in the past had sometimes been erratic to the point of being almost intolerable. Occasionally they planned to meet for a visit, and when they talked on the phone, Joyce became rude, swore at Judy and yelled at her. Other times she called and "freaked out" over the phone. Judy would go to Joyce's house to calm her down — not the only friend who had tried to help Joyce when she was in a state of distress. Judy finally had enough, and asked Joyce to call her back when she felt she could have a sane conversation. Judy assumed Joyce would call back and apologize, and they'd maintain their friendship. Joyce never called. "She just dropped me out of her life ... and I realized I was totally dispensable."[38] Though Joyce never treated Betty Ferguson this way, Betty knew Joyce was having difficulty settling the business with Isaacs as well as handling the divorce, two issues that would have upset anyone.

Joyce was holding back from the legal settlement of the divorce because she still did not want to give up the Newfoundland place. She often called Betty, who spent hours on the phone with her — Joyce knew Betty had successfully gone through her own divorce case. "I'd go over it, and go over it with her and she had changed lawyers — it was a mess."[39] When it all seemed too much, particularly after talking with Michael on the phone, Joyce would simply collapse on her couch and cry and cry. Other times she might pull out her "murder Michael" picture, a painting she had made of a woman strangling a man, which she kept hidden behind her upstairs studio door. As an antidote to her crying, she would pull it out and look at it and laugh. The setting of the painting was the green grass fields below their cabin in Newfoundland.[40]

For Joyce, as for many of us, her sense of place was invested with deep emotion. Virginia Woolf's *A Room of One's Own* evoked in women a feeling about their personal space, a sentiment to which women still relate nearly three-quarters of a century later. Joyce, wherever she lived, transformed the space into her own. Her sense of place meant a total environment, a feeling larger than the trendy idea of "nesting." It was an extension of her inner space into the spaces closest to her skin — her bedroom, her kitchen, her living room, her studio — and from these intimate spaces outward to wherever she was. A few years after she had moved into her Queen Street house, Joyce talked about wanting to live in a house with rooms like those Chardin painted. "I haven't quite achieved it," she had said in 1981, "but I want to live in another period. I'd take it even further back, if I could."[41] Living in this kind of environment was inspiring to her because it was like living within a still life.

Like Pompadour, Joyce loved beautiful objects and loved buying them, filling her house with ornate collections of things she loved, as though making up for the poverty of her early life. She lived within her own still life:

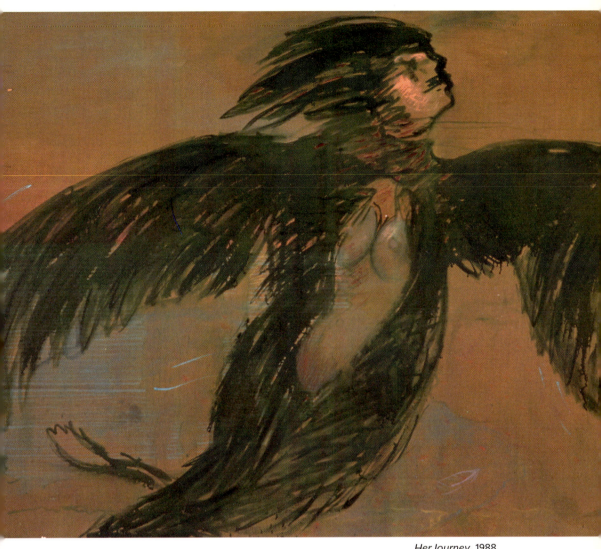

Her Journey, 1988.

in her living room were a stuffed beaver and on her fireplace mantle a jumble of photos, feathers, a small orange glass vase, figurines, Inuit carvings, a clock and a large mirror with an ornate wooden frame; shelves filled with her art books; West Coast native masks and drawings on the walls, as well as a deer's head; her dining room table with its long, richly patterned rug covered with papers, books, ceramic pots, a box of chocolates, coloured glass, a big bouquet of lilies; and on her walls her paintings and an engraving of her great aunt Zaeo, called "Zaeo Triumphant," drawn by Enoch Ward, which appeared in a supplement to the *Music Hall and Theatre Review* more than a hundred years ago; geraniums in her kitchen inside the sliding glass doors that let in the sunshine and illuminated her Welsh cupboard, with delicate china cups hanging on hooks and a silver tea service on the shelf. Upstairs in her studio, a stuffed goose hung from the ceiling above a table of tubes of oil paints. Her pride in her bedroom was her bed covered in pink, with its canopied headboard in salmon and pink hues.

Joyce nourished her feelings about her space through her bond with, in particular, the writers Colette and Katherine Mansfield, and with her friends — to name only two, Betty Ferguson and Phyllis Lambert. At Betty's place, Joyce felt her connection to the earth and enjoyed the out-of-doors, the pond, the deer, the trees, the wild strawberries and the patterns of clouds in the sky, whereas her friendship with Phyllis nourished the cosmopolitan and the urbane. Joyce needed both.

In a way, she took with her these two elements wherever she went. Not only did she need both among her friends, but she also needed her own spaces that included both her city home and her country home. If either one of these was threatened, she could not avoid feeling distressed.

She had her city home, and the cabin on a Newfoundland cape had been the earth-place where Joyce had invested her heart and soul. She had dreamed of growing fruits and vegetables there. One summer she and Michael had a few chickens and they had more fresh eggs than they could eat. They had intended to eat the chickens, too, but when it came down to the final act, they couldn't do it and gave the hens to someone in the village.[42] Joyce dreamed of cultivating nut trees and growing berries. She wanted to nourish the earth and believe the earth would, in turn, nourish her and her beloved. On an emotional level, it was clear to her friends that Joyce had woven a fantasy around herself and Michael and the Newfoundland place, like a web in which she nestled. It is easy to understand why in such a beautiful spot.

All around the cabin, which is like a tiny dot in the expanse of a wild summer landscape, stretches a meadow of purple irises and other wild flowers in an intoxicating mix of colour. Walking down a grassy slope towards the sea, Joyce often sat above the cliff, a drop of four hundred feet to the water's edge, and looked across the curve of the land to other black cliffs in the distance, dark and ominous against the blue of the water. She watched the constant change on this cape, with veils of fog and mist giving way to bright sunshine and blue sky, and then more fog. The light played on the wild grasses, the cliffs and the ocean every hour, transforming the entire landscape within the scope of a few minutes. In the evening, the intensity of the sunsets, the dark, billowing clouds, the black sky and the orange and yellow bands of colour were like no sunsets she had ever seen. This was a landscape of the emotions, and it became her own, for it spoke to her passionate, joyful nature, her romanticism and her sense of tragedy, and she took it in, this visceral quality that became part of her soul.[43]

By 1988 she knew she would lose her piece of land, and with it a piece of her mind. For eight years she had rummaged about in her mind over the dilemma of the Newfoundland place, and though Joyce and Michael met periodically to discuss their disagreements, that summer their lawyers made attempts to bring the process to a conclusion. According to Joyce's many jottings on scraps of paper in her archives, she had thought a lot about what she wanted to do with the Newfoundland place. These notes reveal that she had wanted Michael to build her another house there; they could either divide the land or hold joint ownership of their cabin, which did not interest Michael. But the intensity of Joyce's feeling about wanting the place is expressed in one of her notes: "With my last penny I will buy you out." She also wrote, "Just remember you said in separation you would provide my (sic) with land and cabin of equal value. ... The land is my investment for old age how will I live?"[44] Clearly, she not only wanted the place, but the thought of losing it evoked worries about being alone with no money as she aged, even though in reality this piece of land would not determine her future financial security.

The divorce proceedings finally ended in the summer of 1989, with the Newfoundland property in Michael's hands and Joyce receiving a small financial payment. That fall, Joyce wrote her farewell elegy to this place she loved.

In Newfoundland
up high in Mountains
over the sea where (else)?
have lost it but continue
to want to sea it (all) now in
the Hands of Mike & Peggy
the joy to sea its face again
yet now on seeing it, everyone
owns it, I am no longer its keeper
it is no longer mine — my beloved
home has been taken from me
the place of all possibilities —
the planetary dream sight —
filled with my prayers desire for
the eternal love always present.
Cruel and divine. the flowers the
field I wanted to work with — the
field that helped me grow the first
tomatoes in that side of Newf
please let me have it *too* [underlined][45]

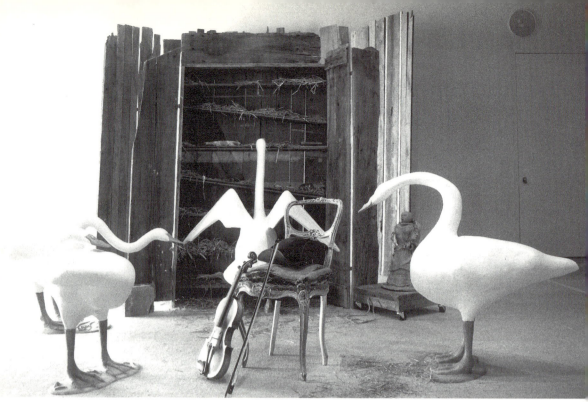

Swan's Cupboard, 1990.

Joyce also poured out her love for the place in a series of fifteen tiny ink drawings on the backs of New Democratic Party candidate Lynn McDonald's business cards. On one of these cards, Joyce drew the vast sky, the hill and the tiny cabin, and wrote "vegetables and trees grow." In another similar drawing she wrote along the hillside, "my love is the sea my house my country thee."[46] Her loss was almost unbearable.

For some time Joyce had been turning over in her mind an idea about creating something really different, something cathartic, to symbolize her efforts at letting go of her grief during this period of loss. It seems she wanted to give a visual form to her spiritual life and its significance in her desire for peace of mind, images arising from this stage of her life — an installation about transformation. She worked on the idea while she was artist in residence at the University of Toronto School of Architecture during the 1988–89 school year and considered the possibility of hiring a sculptor to create certain elements of the project. She found the right person when she saw the work of Nicola Wojewoda at one of the Alma Gallery shows.

As was characteristic of Joyce, she chatted with the young artist while she admired one of her sculptures, a piece that on one side was like a fish-woman and on the other side, a man dancing with a fish. As Wojewoda looked at Joyce's face, she realized that the round face in her own sculpture resembled Joyce's. Then, as Joyce had the same thought simultaneously, she said the face in the sculpture looked like her own face.

Joyce asked Wojewoda if she would be interested in a commission and described what she had in mind. "She had this vision, and it was a broken-down cupboard such as you'd find in a barn, broken and slanted, covered with chicken poop and objects that were gestures of a life lived. And she saw it surrounded by swans." Wojewoda still remembers clearly what Joyce said the significance of this piece was for her — "profound transformation, beyond the transformation of going from one life stage to another, but the swans represented the kind of transformation from life to death." She spoke of it as "a profound shift of perspective."[47]

The swan as an archetypal symbol in art and literature is extremely complex. The long, phallic neck is masculine, and yet the round, silky body is feminine. For this reason, according to *A Dictionary of Symbols* by J.E. Cirlot, "the swan always points to the complete satisfaction of a desire, the swan-song being a particular allusion to desire which brings about its own death." The swan, together with the harp, are symbols of the mystic journey we make to the other world. It is also seen as a representation of the "mystic Centre and the union of opposites."[48] This latter meaning has particular significance for Joyce, who throughout her life, lived and worked out of the tension of two polarities she experienced, her joy and her pain.

In the completed installation, which Joyce called *Swan's Cupboard*, four large, white swans, each in a different position, stand in front of a rough wooden cupboard. A violin and a bow lean against an old, ornate chair, as though the musician who sat there had just gone elsewhere, leaving behind the instrument and the accoutrements of life in the dilapidated cupboard: a paintbrush, embroidery hoops, feathers, a glass egg, a small stone, and a canvas banner with "Veriditas" written on it. Against one side of the cupboard stands a small, terracotta female figure, a goddess, Joyce called her, wearing a long billowing dress. She stands on a trolley. As in *Artist on Fire*, one of her eyes is larger than the other.

The evolution of *Swan's Cupboard* is an instance of synchronicity that characterized many of Joyce's encounters with others. Wojewoda, almost thirty then, was experiencing a shift in her own life. She had just quit her job, left the gallery where she had shown her work, and without knowing what was next, she decided to go in a totally different direction. At that cusp in Wojewoda's life, Joyce commissioned her to make the swans, sculptures into which Wojewoda poured her own feelings about experiencing a kind of transformation.

Wojewoda made ten maquettes, and Joyce chose four. They agreed on a fee, and Joyce arranged for the sculptor to work in an unused classroom where she was in residence at the University of Toronto. Wojewoda built the

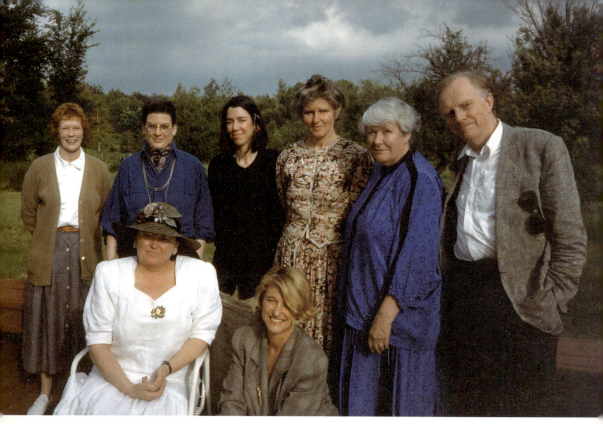

Joyce's sixtieth birthday celebration in Sharon, Ontario. Standing left to right: Donna Montague, Phyllis Lambert, Linda Gaylard, Frieda Hjartarson, Jean Sutherland Boggs, Gerald Robinson. Seated: Joyce, Irene F. Whittome.

swans with armatures and plaster, with beaks and feet cast in bronze. Wojewoda recalled that when she delivered the swans she thought Joyce seemed fragile. She mentioned only in passing that she was having trouble with her memory, and talked about trying to let go of her grief and pain.

Wojewoda never saw Joyce again, and did not know what happened to the swans until five years later, when she was married, had a family and was living in Hamilton, Ontario. She thought no one knew she had made the swans, until I phoned her. One day she went into the Art Gallery of Hamilton, picked up a sculpture catalogue called *Shape Shifters*, and as she flipped through it to her surprise she saw a photograph of *Swan's Cupboard*. She visited the installation when it was exhibited there in the summer of 1999.

When Joyce's friends wanted to do something special for her sixtieth birthday, they planned an elegant summer picnic. Their location of choice was just north of Toronto in Sharon, once an Upper Canada village called Hope, now hedged in by recent housing developments. In this town stands Sharon Temple, significant for its unusual architecture, on a green lawn shaded by giant old trees. The temple was conceived by David Willson, a

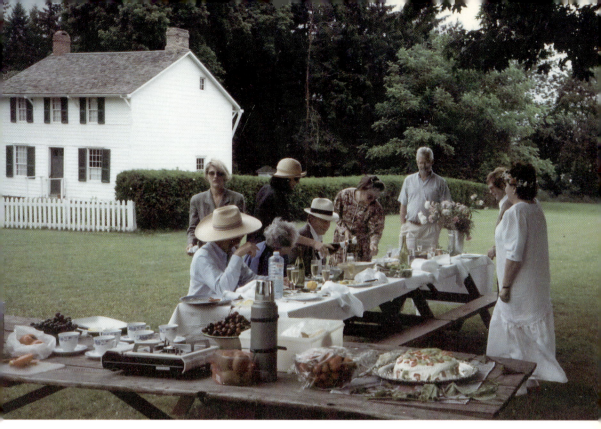

The sixtieth-birthday picnic.

religious leader who came to the Sharon farming community from New York State in 1801 to settle on two hundred acres of Upper Canada's Crown Land. Sharon Temple was built in 1825-1831 as a meeting place for special celebrations of The Children of Peace. This was a group — also called Davidites — led by Willson when he broke with the Quakers because they did not use music in their meetings, something he believed belonged in a worship service. Willson, whose group included many new immigrants to the farming community as well as nearly a quarter of the local Quakers, established a band and a choir.

Joyce had an appreciation for this unique building, with its structure based on mathematical and Biblical symbolism. "The three stories represent the Trinity. Twelve pillars supporting the upper storeys bear the names of the apostles. The foursquare plan permits equal access on all sides to all who come. In the centre of the Temple, surrounded by four columns standing for the virtues of Faith, Hope, Love and Charity, stands the Ark, a masterpiece of cabinetmaking which hid a collection of Willson's papers from 1832 undiscovered until 1990."[49] A golden globe representing peace on earth is suspended on top of the building between the four spires. Other buildings on the site include builder Ebenezer Doan's house, his workshop, a log house and a 1967 museum building.

Sharon Temple, now owned by the Sharon Temple Museum Society, carries on the original tradition of holding musical performances by small groups. Gerald Robinson and Linda Gaylard had once taken Joyce there to a concert, and knew Joyce would enjoy a picnic on the lawns.

The picnic was a small, intimate event, with the friends Joyce chose: Montrealers Irene F. Whittome and Phyllis Lambert, Frieda Hjartarson, who came from Ottawa, Jean Sutherland Boggs, as well as Linda and Gerald and Donna and George Montague.

Photographs from that day depict a beautiful table, laid with white tablecloths and napkins, wine glasses, blue-and-white china, silver cutlery; bouquets of lilies, carnations and baby's breath; lush salads and bowls of cherries, grapes, strawberries — the kind of elegance Joyce loved. Joyce wore a new white dress Linda designed for the occasion, and Phyllis Lambert brought a wreath for her hair. Everyone brought her presents.

Saturday, the 30th of June, 1990, had started out with sun and cloud, and a comfortable temperature for an afternoon picnic. Later in the day the sky became ominously dark, and a violent rain storm drove Joyce and her friends to take shelter in the temple, where Harry Somers and his musicians were rehearsing. The drama of the weather and the music added to the magic of the day, the kind of magic that, according to her friends, Joyce brought with her time after time.

It was a beautiful celebration marking this woman's extraordinary sixty years. As several of her friends said, they paid money just to be present at a celebration for Joyce — people would do almost anything to come to a special event for her. But that day her friends knew that Joyce's remarkable presence and agility of spirit showed signs of cracking. This awareness was like an unspoken question that had its own presence among them, but it did not dampen the outpouring of love and the spirit of celebration.

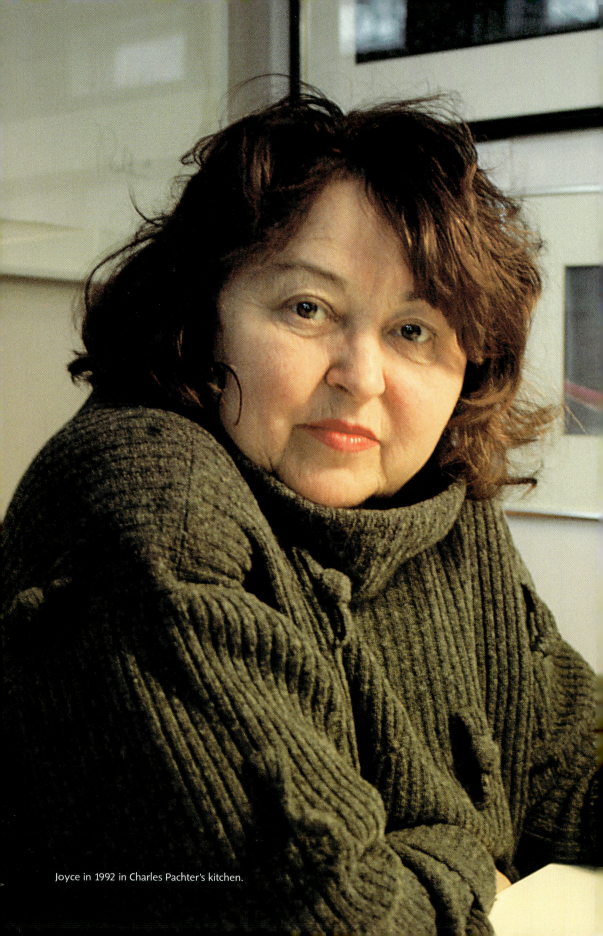

Joyce in 1992 in Charles Pachter's kitchen.

11

An enveloping fog

They say I have Alzheimer's — I even hate the sound of
the word. —Joyce Wieland to Betty Ferguson

"IT'S IN the brain" appears written in Joyce's handwriting in one of her
address books, under Dr. Rennie's name and phone number; and again, "Its
all in the Brain" on the "Y" page under "Yoga classes."[1] She was right, though
she likely did not fully understand what was happening. The outer, wrinkled
layer of her brain, the cortex, was deteriorating, the part that enabled her "to
plan, calculate, imagine and create."[2]

The function of the cortex seems almost miraculous because it
"... produces an individual pattern of emotions, aspiration and experience
that defines the character and personality."[3] In other words, the cortex is the
physical aspect of ourselves that makes us unique individuals — the cortex
makes us human.

Different parts of the cortex are responsible for different functions: insight
and planning take place in the frontal lobe, while the temporal lobes give us

memory and the ability to process sounds and understand speech. The ability to use numbers and to absorb what we experience through our senses is also a part of the function of the cortex. In the centre of our brains, neurons located where the spinal cord begins, regulate such basic functions as hunger and thirst, and sexual drive. At the back, the cerebellum is "responsible for the complicated processes of movement."

Knowing something about the functions of the cortex, we can understand why, if that part of the brain is damaged, a person begins to disappear. The changes in Joyce were typical in that the first sign of the illness was her memory loss. And there was the vacancy in her presence that would come and go. Some of her friends were convinced the illness began as long ago as twenty years before Joyce's death. This is possible, for at least one study suggests that Alzheimer's disease could be "like hardening of the arteries, resulting from a lifelong biological deterioration that becomes apparent only when people are older ..."[4] However, other friends say Joyce was always scattered, and that she did not become ill until 1989 or 1990. Still others question whether the diagnosis of Alzheimer's disease was correct, citing her exposure to harmful chemicals in paints and her use of drugs. Despite the differing opinions, Joyce's symptoms throughout her illness do point to Alzheimer's disease.

As people reviewed their memories of Joyce, many incidents came to the surface that in hindsight could be attributed to the disease. Betty Ferguson recalls that in 1984 Joyce phoned her one day in tears because she had forgotten how to run her camera. Although she never was adept at mechanical things, she certainly knew how to use her camera — in New York she used to take cameras apart and put them back together again because she wanted to "really get inside cameras."[5] The truth is that Joyce had great difficulty managing her life during the years leading up to her 1987 retrospective, a fact to which her assistants can attest in some detail.

In the late eighties, incidents occurred that strained Joyce's professional relationships. For example, she borrowed a painting for a show and forgot to return it to the owner. When she was in Vancouver for a visit, she talked to several people about trying to get a job at the Emily Carr Institute of Art and Design, and then told her friends she was promised a job there, which was not true. And Fran Hill, who was Joyce's assistant in 1988, remembered the work on Joyce's show at Canada House that year; as plans were finalized, Joyce repeatedly phoned London in the middle of the night to change things in a way that did not make sense. Each time, the following day Fran helped Joyce put the original plans in place again.[6]

When she gave slide lectures on her work, she increasingly became scattered and disorganized. In May 1989 at an Experimental Film Congress at the Art Gallery of Ontario, Joyce was scheduled for an hour-long presentation on her films. When she loaded her slide carousel into the projector, the slides were not the ones she wanted. She was about to leave when filmmaker Barbara Sternberg, the one who had asked Joyce to speak, suggested she show the slides anyway and talk about them, so she did that in about five minutes. Sternberg suggested she go through the slides again more slowly, which she did. At the end of all this, Sternberg and the others were, understandably, perplexed.[7]

Occasionally other kinds of difficulties had surfaced, and no one could understand Joyce's behaviour. Several times Phyllis Lambert took Joyce with her to Kripalu, a yoga centre in New England. The last time they went, Joyce continually became lost and frequently ended up in Phyllis's room, thinking it was her own.[8] On another occasion, Joyce stayed with Irene F. Whittome in Montreal, and Irene gave her a key so she could come and go. Irene came home to discover her door wide open, and Joyce was oblivious to what she had done.

Kay Wilson, who shared Joyce's studio, always left her paintings out when she finished working, and once when she returned she discovered that Joyce had painted on them. That was when Kay knew something was wrong.[9] In 1987 Joyce was working on *Celebration*, the large mural commissioned by Toronto's Pantages Theatre for its lobby. When Joyce ran out of paint, Diane Pugen went with her to an art supply store to help her set up an account so she could buy what she needed. She could not manage to do that herself.[10]

Cynthia Lorenz, who began working as Joyce's assistant early in 1988, remembered that when she accompanied Joyce on a trip to Ottawa that spring, Joyce carried her money around in a plastic grocery bag, and several times nearly left it in a taxi. During Joyce's stint as artist in residence at the University of Toronto in the 1988-89 school year, she frequently talked to Cynthia about being terribly forgetful; sometimes she couldn't get her keys to work and often lost them. Cynthia and Joyce laughed off these recurrences. However, one day the room that had been set aside for Joyce to use as a studio was to be prepared for use by someone else for the day. Joyce had not told Cynthia about it and then became very angry because Cynthia had not prepared the space.[11] Increasingly, people were puzzled by her behaviour, thinking that her zaniness had become exaggerated.

Since about 1984 Joyce had been attending Reiki sessions from time to time. She consulted with a Buddhist teacher, went to Al-anon sessions and tried a variety of approaches to therapy. She continued her sessions with her psychiatrist, Dr. John Rennie, sometimes more frequently than others. One of the things she talked about with Dr. Rennie was that she had never had any children, an issue that was still painful for her. He suggested finding opportunities to nurture children and young people, and as a result, she had another, shorter stint as artist in residence at the University of Toronto, this time at University College. In the spring of 1990, she concluded her residency with "Tears in the Rainbow," a show of forty-four of her drawings and watercolours from 1960 to 1988.[12]

She also contacted the school board in Toronto and arranged to do art projects with children. One day she had arranged to go to St. George's Junior School in Etobicoke. She had been there before and thought she knew the way. However, on a brisk, sunny November day, when she was scheduled to paint with the children, she became lost and disoriented en route. After driving around for a while, she parked her car and cried. Somehow she managed to find her way home, but she never got to the school. She left a short note — probably for one of her assistants, Norine Weiss — about the incident on November 23, 1989: "N. went insane in my car and couldn't find my way home was lost to the world."[13] It didn't help that around the same time her car was stolen, and she had to cope with sorting out details with the insurance company, from whom she received payment for the value of the car.[14]

The next time Joyce went to see her psychiatrist, she recounted to him the fiasco of trying to find the school. Though she had always seemed childlike, Dr. Rennie had seen a definite change in her during the 1980s, and he recognized her disorientation — linked with an inability to cope — as a classic symptom of Alzheimer's disease, and told her it was possible she had this disorder. She became subdued, and sobered, and it seemed to make sense to her because she had known for some time that something was wrong. They spent a few sessions after that talking about it.[15]

In December of 1989 she consulted her general practitioner, Dr. Gina Shochat, and told her she had had a three-month period of memory loss and disorientation. The doctor referred her to specialists, but Joyce did not keep the appointments.[16] Yet she was definitely considering consulting neurologists, for around the same time she consulted Dr. Shochat, I met with Joyce to propose writing this book, and she told me she had to "get her head examined." In January, she noted in her appointment book that she began taking tranquilizers.[17]

Even with all this, it seems Joyce's imagination had not slowed down. She applied for a Canada Council grant to work on a project called "Marika's Nine Visions of the Imagination," based on the life of Serbian-American inventor Nikola Tesla (1856-1943). Tesla, who designed the power system of Niagara Falls and whose discoveries made possible missile science, captured Joyce's imagination for his love of experimentation and his intuition. He had his own laboratory, where he conducted experiments with electricity and at one point claimed he had received signals from outer space.

Notes for her grant, which was turned down, described her project as nine paintings culminating in a sacred tent where viewers could explore their own imagination. She wanted the tent to be an extension of her fabric work, with images painted on the tent surface. This multi-layered project would have allowed her to explore a number of areas: Tesla's relationship with his mother; how extrasensory perception influenced his imagination; the relationship between genius and madness — the genius of space technology and the madness of weapons.[18] This project was never realized.

The jottings in Joyce's 1989 appointment book, which she used somewhat like a journal to make short notes about what was on her mind, reveal a deep neediness and depression. Undated notes on loose sheets of paper show she was trying to sort out her thoughts about the connection between the brain and spirit. "The Brain is a high organ which receives the spirit through thinking — of spiritual. The spirit enters when Brain is pressed to think of Spirit."[19] Other undated jottings reveal how she tried to deal with her fears: "Tell Joyce to be careful not to go where there are no angels."[20]

It was around this time that the Ontario College of Art had announced a policy of hiring only women to rectify the imbalance of male/female instructors, a decision that created a "ruckus," according to the OCA president of the time, Tim Porteous.[21] In March 1990, Joyce had an appointment with Colette Whiten at OCA to discuss taking on the job of chairperson of fine art. That the opportunity came so late in her life must have saddened Joyce. She wrote in her March 13 calendar page: "I don't want this job I'm going to be 60 in June I understand they need me and my name — but I can't run the Fine Arts Chair when there is so little time."[22] Her comment that she had "so little time" must have meant that she had some understanding of the disease. Even if she decided she could not take the job, she was delighted with all the controversy at OCA.[23]

In the spring of 1990, Joyce went to Fredericton, New Brunswick, to give a speech and to conduct a drawing workshop. Just before her slide lecture, she discovered she had brought an empty slide tray. An article described the evening as having had "special magic," instead of becoming the disaster it could have been. Joyce was her passionate self, still able to cover her difficulty by "speaking in flashes of disconnected ideas, unfinished sentences and phrases, descriptive images and passionate beliefs ..."[24] She talked about light, the spirit and soul of colours and their healing power. Her art was still her way of making connections with others. Of course, some lectures did not turn out so well.

She went to Dublin, Ireland, for the first week of April when she had an exhibition at the National Centre for Culture and the Arts in a seventeenth-century building, the Royal Hospital Kilmainham. The Canadian Embassy officials looked after arrangements for her stay there, and it seems she managed adequately. The next month, when she travelled to give a lecture at Carleton University, she had to get detailed instructions about how to get to Ottawa, what to do when she got there and where to go.

On a Saturday in July she received an invitation to the twenty-fifth wedding anniversary celebration for Sheila Curnoe and the late Greg Curnoe in London, Ontario. When Joyce arrived, Greg and Sheila welcomed her and introduced her to other people. The party was videotaped, and later when Sheila looked at it, she saw that after the introductions and initial chatting, Joyce had stood there looking confused, but she and Greg had not noticed at the time. Without their knowing, Joyce stayed for the night. There she was the next morning, saying, "Oh, I came in and saw this lovely comfortable bed and I thought I'd just lie down and have a nap."[25]

Pierre Théberge was at that celebration and the next day after breakfast drove from London to Toronto, giving Joyce a ride. "It was a beautiful day, one of those impressionist days ... We listened to French songs, Piaf and others, and it was a wonderful moment, but she was starting to forget things. I remember she kept saying, 'Oh, what's wrong with me, I'm forgetting things' ... But I would say this was the last time I saw her as a whole personality. She was buoyant, funny as ever, and original, the originality of her thoughts — she was really special."[26] That was the last conversation Théberge had with her.

Joyce experienced intense frustration and distress with her memory loss, and as the number of troubling incidents escalated, she still did not tell her friends that her psychiatrist had mentioned Alzheimer's months earlier, though by the end of 1990 many of them knew something was wrong. They were aware that she often lost her purse, forgot where she put things, suspected that people were stealing from her, and missed appointments.

In her September 13, 1990, page in her appointment book, Joyce wrote that she had missed her appointment with Dr. Rennie, "But will go to Toronto General Hospital for check up to see if something can be done for chronic memory loss."[27] Almost a whole year had passed since Dr. Rennie had first told her she might have Alzheimer's and had made referrals, and she still had not undergone neurological examinations. Finally, according to her appointment book, on October 11 she went to "Toronto General Hospital to see doctor," but more extensive tests and scans were not scheduled until December.

The same year that all this was happening, she painted a large, stark, untitled self-portrait, in which she stands in profile on the left side of the painting, her eyes wide open, holding a large palette and a paintbrush. The

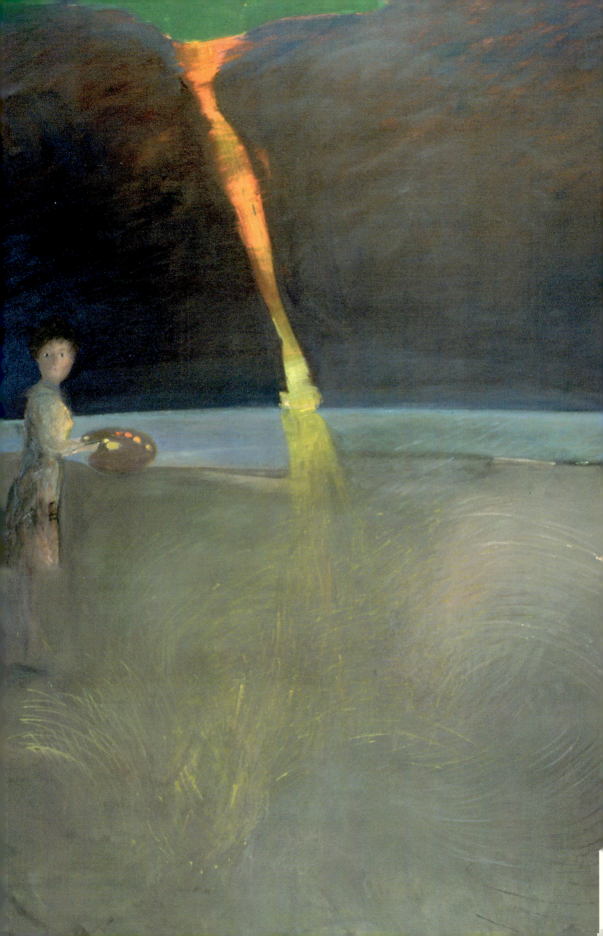

painting seems all the more enormous because this tiny figure stands to the side of an ominous landscape composed of a great, dark sky, topped by a green cloud, from which pours an orange streak that turns a golden colour as it approaches the earth. The dark sky and the earth are divided horizontally by a thin strip of blue water. Munro Ferguson, who owns the painting, thought Joyce had called it "Bolt." Joyce would have been working on this painting while trying to come to terms with the illness, when she had not yet told many people about it.

For many years at Christmas, Joyce had gone to the home of her neighbour, Georgia Nayyar, to bake Christmas cookies, which they arranged in baskets to give to friends. One day when they had baked the cookies, Joyce went back to her house to get baskets. She stayed at home for a while, then returned and asked what she was supposed to get. She did the same thing again, and Georgia told her to repeat to herself, "baskets, baskets, baskets." When she forgot the baskets the third time, Georgia wondered what was going on. She asked Joyce, "Are you all right?" and Joyce said she was doing a lot of meditation and healing, but she did not mention Alzheimer's. When Joyce went home the fourth time for the baskets, she remembered to bring them. Soon after, she began bringing things from her house to the Nayyars — once a tray and another time a chair — asking Georgia to hide them because there were people coming to steal them.[28]

Sara Bowser recalled one Saturday morning when she went shopping at the St. Lawrence market and was loaded with heavy bags of food, she stopped to rest on a park bench. She saw Joyce "barrelling down the street" in her convertible Volkswagen. When she saw Sara she jammed on the breaks, pulled to the curb and jumped out of the car. As she came within about three feet of Sara, Joyce said, "Oh, I thought you were Sara," and turned around and ran back to the car and started the engine. "I'm standing there with my jaw hanging — this is after thirty years — and I'm yelling, 'Joyce, Joyce, it is me, it is Sara' and she came back and we both laughed our heads off. But it was so shocking."[29]

One day after a doctor's appointment, when the reality of her health gripped her, Joyce broke down. She tried to call Betty Ferguson but couldn't reach her. Somehow she managed to dial the Montagues' number, which is when Donna and George received a call from her in complete distress. The Montagues and Joyce had not seen much of each other for many years because she had been disappointed and offended that they had chosen not to invest in *The Far Shore*. Joyce was sobbing on the phone and told Donna the doctors said she must get her affairs in order because she has Alzheimer's. Donna said she would come right over, but Joyce was not at home and was too confused to tell her where she was. Donna drove around looking for her, guessed she might be at the McGill Club, and sure enough there she found a completely disconsolate Joyce standing on the steps.[30]

Donna took Joyce home with her, gave her something to eat and suggested she sleep for a while. In the evening, Donna made dinner for Joyce and then drove her home. After that day, every now and then Joyce phoned Donna in a state of panic because she had either lost her purse or forgotten where she had parked her car. Donna and George frequently took Joyce to their farm in the Caledon Hills north of Toronto when they went there on the weekends. One weekend she told the Montagues there were always people wanting her money, asking her to sign cheques. Donna tried to find out what Joyce was talking about. Joyce finally asked Donna to help her out with her financial business, and when Joyce was advised to get a power of attorney, she signed it over to the Montagues. Joyce did not tell Betty Ferguson about her diagnosis until after the legal business was settled, and never talked about it again to Betty.[31]

By then Linda Abrahams, now the editor of *Matriart*, was working for Joyce as an administrative assistant, and she looked after day-to-day office matters. When Abrahams began the job in 1990, Joyce was still working.[32] She completed a commission for Via Rail that year, a mural she called *The Ocean of Love*. In November and December, she had simultaneous shows in Hamilton, Ontario, at the Moore Gallery and at the McMaster University Art Gallery, where she was Visiting Hooker Professor, which meant she was available to students, including those in the Women's Studies program. Mary Keczan-Ebos, who had arranged to interview Joyce, described her as having been so vulnerable and nervous that she put away her pen and paper and they just talked.[33]

Joyce must have summoned up a great reservoir of courage to carry on with these exhibitions, for she already knew she was ill, and it was exactly during this block of time that she was undergoing extensive neurological testing. Of course, people she encountered sometimes wondered what was happening to her, but few knew what it was because she was able to carry on conversations. Like many Alzheimer's patients in the early stages, she was very clever at compensating when she could not remember certain words or if she forgot the identity of someone she had known for years.

Joyce went to Ottawa to stay with her friend Frieda Hjartarson when her husband, the late Bishwarup Bhattacharya, a psychiatrist, became very ill and was admitted to a chronic care hospital. Joyce visited Bhattacharya in the hospital. It must have been a sobering experience for her because he showed her around the hospital and explained later to Frieda that "he was getting her accustomed to what was going to happen."[34]

Despite her increasing confusions, Joyce continued with a surprising

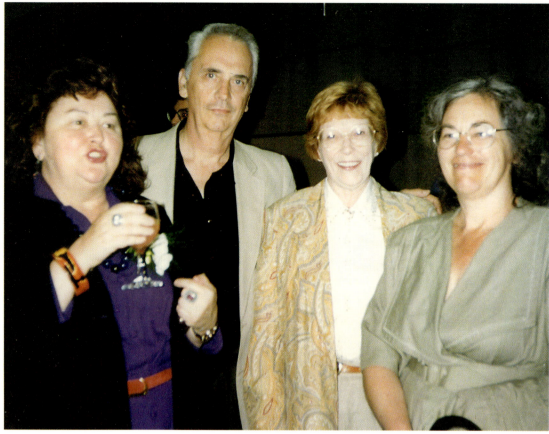

Joyce, Bryan Barney, Donna Montague and Betty Ferguson at the ceremony when Ontario College of Art and Design awarded Joyce an Honourary Fellowship in 1992.

number of lectures, including a panel discussion at the Vancouver Art Gallery in February 1991. Joyce did not say much at that event, but when she did talk she seemed confused, and she deferred to Greg Curnoe, who was also on the panel.[35] In March, by invitation from the Department of Art and Film Studies, she was Visiting Woman Scholar at Queen's University in Kingston, Ontario. In April she went to Sudbury for a slide lecture at Laurentian University. Donna Montague and Linda Abrahams helped her assemble her slides and prepare her notes, and Donna took Joyce to the airport, got her through security and put her on the plane, with instructions about what to do when she arrived. Someone was going to meet her at the other end. However, Joyce took a cab when she got there, and went to the university, but no one was around since it was a Saturday. The trip was a disaster. When she returned home, Joyce "talked about walking through fields of mud and snow, that she got to her hotel, and eventually the Sudbury people found her."[36]

Perhaps it was this Sudbury experience that prompted Joyce to begin cancelling professional commitments she had made earlier — for example, a

CARFAC Saskatchewan panel that spring — and turning down new engagements. Considering how much she had loved San Francisco in 1985, declining the Art Institute invitation to become part of a faculty pool in filmmaking, painting, and photography for the 1991-92 academic year must have been a great disappointment. A note in Joyce's handwriting says that her schedule prevents her participation.[37]

The British literary critic John Bayley, who looked after his late wife, the novelist Iris Murdoch, when she had Alzheimer's disease, described the illness as an "insidious fog, barely noticeable until everything around has disappeared. After that, it is no longer possible to believe that a world outside fog exists."[38] As the fog enveloped Joyce more and more, her confusions and panicked phone calls in the middle of the night signalled that she needed more help, and Donna began spending more time with her and asked other friends to help out. Diane Rotstein looked after Joyce, often several days a week — sometime after she herself had undergone brain surgery. Joyce and Diane had many laughs about their memory. "We used to make a joke out of the fact that I had half a memory and she had half a memory, but together we were 100 percent." Diane described how she often forgot details of one part of an event, and Joyce another part, but together they had the whole thing. The same thing with songs. Diane remembered the tune and Joyce the words. And Diane knew that Joyce would not remember whatever she said. She was in the process of separating from her husband at the time, and the two of them had "marvellous discussions."[39] Since no one would ever know, and neither of them would remember, they were free to say whatever they liked about men.

The Montagues began sorting out Joyce's financial affairs, with the help of Linda Abrahams. Whenever Joyce had doctors' appointments, Donna accompanied her and tried to keep abreast of Joyce's needs as the illness progressed. When it no longer seemed safe for Joyce to drive her car, Donna discussed with Dr. Shochat what to do since she knew Joyce would not want to give it up. Donna arranged for Joyce to be sent a notice requiring that she take a new driving test, and then explained to her what she would have to do on an examination.[40] Joyce decided she did not want to go through all that and sold her car, a Honda she had bought after her Volkswagen had been stolen two years earlier, to Kathy Dain. Kathy had a history with Joyce and driving. When she was teaching at Artsake in 1981, Joyce had confided in Kathy that she had failed her driver examination, and she didn't know what to do. In fact, the evaluation stated that Joyce had failed to obey signals, blocked crosswalks at intersections and straddled lanes. Joyce had needed practice, so Kathy offered to go with her. Joyce's second try at her test had been better, and by the third try she had passed.[41]

Joyce was sad about giving up her Honda, but as a replacement, Donna set up an account with a taxi company. Eventually, Joyce had difficulty even dialling the number for a cab.

As Joyce's condition deteriorated, several incidents occurred that frightened the neighbours. Helene St. Jacques, a businesswoman, had bought the house adjoining Joyce's on the west in November 1984, to be used as her office and residence. Joyce immediately tried to talk her into selling it to her, offering an exorbitant amount as a point of persuasion. St. Jacques refused to sell, after which Joyce became rude to her, and the two were off to a rocky start as neighbours. But one day a subdued Joyce showed up at her door, not apologizing for her behaviour, but simply asking St. Jacques to help her with her radio, which she did. After that, Joyce was friendly.

In the early nineties, St. Jacques and Georgia Nayyar became alarmed when they saw a fire truck parked in front of Joyce's house. She had started a fire in the fireplace, had failed to open the damper, and police had happened to notice smoke pouring from the house and had called the fire department. The two women were distressed enough to send a letter to the Montagues, then in Vancouver, suggesting that Joyce needed round-the-clock care.

In another bizarre situation, Joyce rang St. Jacques's doorbell late one Saturday night and said a woman was sitting in her living room and wouldn't leave. She wanted help to get the woman out. It was true; a white-haired woman wearing a nice dress and socks and sandals sat in Joyce's living room. Joyce relaxed as soon as St. Jacques returned with her and began talking about what she had done that day. She had been to Hamilton to see a friend's exhibition — likely Dorothy Cameron's show.

The woman then said she came from Hamilton, and St. Jacques wondered if Joyce had brought a friend home and had forgotten who she was. After asking the woman a few questions, St. Jacques learned that the woman had been out walking and became tired, so she had knocked at Joyce's door because a light was on. St. Jacques also learned that the two had never met before, and she tried to find out where the woman lived. Finally, she asked whether the woman was lost, and she said she was. She also learned that these two women had tried to call someone and couldn't figure out how. It became clear to St. Jacques that this woman also had memory loss. She called the police at Toronto's Fifty-one Division and learned that, yes, a woman who had Alzheimer's was missing from a seniors' residence farther east on Queen Street.

"Isn't this wild," St. Jacques said as she concluded her story, "the serendipitous nature of it all, the blind leading the blind. And here the two of them had sat for a couple of hours, I gathered, trying to puzzle out what to do next."[42] Though the incident had a humorous side, the possible danger was not lost on the neighbours — that another kind of person ringing Joyce's

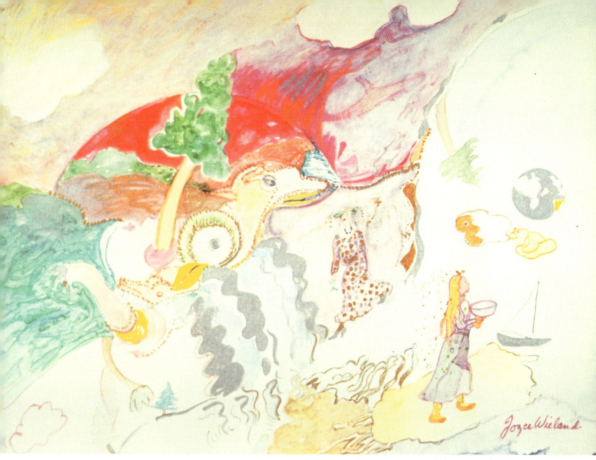

Her Love is so Strange, n.d. (circa 1992).

doorbell at two o'clock in the morning could have meant a completely different ending to the story.

Eventually, Joyce's needs prompted an assessment by Joan York from Community Occupational Therapists and Associates, and from then on she checked in on her several times a week. A home-care worker also began visiting as Joyce's need for care increased. When Donna took Joyce to medical appointments, doctors warned her that she would burn out, that the needs of Alzheimer's patients were too great for one person to shoulder, but Donna felt she could manage with a group of people helping. Donna asked Joyce's friends to take her to their homes for dinner several nights a week and take her home and see that she got to bed. Then Donna drove to Joyce's house first thing in the morning. Other friends spent weekends with Joyce, and George and Donna often took her with them to their farm for the weekend. Eventually, they had the gas turned off on her stove so she would not burn herself or start a fire. The next step Donna took was to hire someone to stay with Joyce several nights a week, but it was difficult to find people Joyce liked.

In the summer of 1993, Joyce's friends organized a birthday party for her. Donna had just learned of Joan's death and asked several friends to stay after

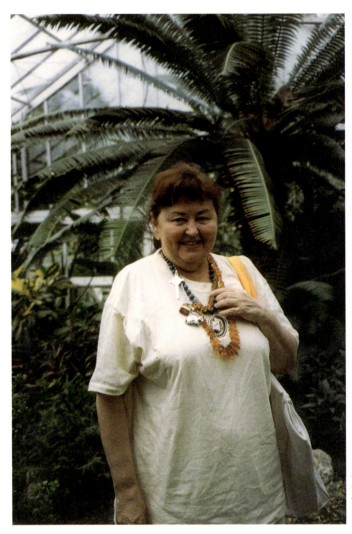

Joyce in Allen
Gardens in
Toronto,
probably 1993.

the party while she gave Joyce the sad news. When Donna told Joyce she had
something sad to tell her, Joyce responded with something like, "Oh dear,
she died."[43] And then she began crying. Joan's death was the final family loss
Joyce would experience.

By January 1994, it was abundantly clear that Joyce needed someone with
her twenty-four hours a day. Donna called a meeting of friends who had been
helping her look after Joyce to discuss what the alternatives were. A place was
available in a retirement home, but some people felt it should still be
possible for Joyce to live in her own home with round-the-clock care.

After that meeting, Betty Ferguson relieved Donna, who was worn out.
Also, Joyce's lawyer contacted Doug McPherson, Joyce's executor, to take on
the power of attorney, and her long-time friend, Colette Perron Sharp, was
also named. She would be responsible for supervising Joyce's day-to-day

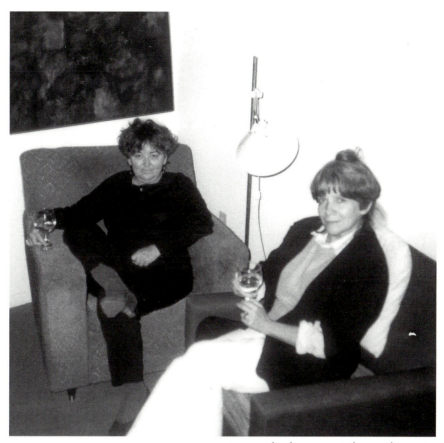

Joyce and Colette Perron Sharp in the 1980s.

care.[44] Both of the new powers of attorney had as their goal to keep Joyce in her own home for at least another year, if possible, by hiring the necessary caregivers. As it would turn out, she was able to live at home for two more years. Meanwhile, McPherson took responsibility for the financial and administrative part of Joyce's care, sorting out her tax returns and setting up a proper payroll for those who would be looking after her. Colette took responsibility for interviewing and hiring staff.

For security in case of emergency, Colette wanted two people around the house with Joyce. Because someone was with her all the time and went with her if she wanted to go outside, they did not keep the door locked. When Joyce realized she was not locked in, she stopped trying to get out. She also stopped hiding things — at first, she would open the door and throw things on the street or into the crawl space behind her kitchen. But she stopped doing all those things.[45]

Another reason Colette hired two people was to create something like a family environment, a lively, chatty atmosphere, because Joyce herself did not talk much any more. Cynthia Lorenz had earlier worked as Joyce's administrative assistant, and Joyce liked her, so Colette hired her to be there every day and take Joyce to galleries or doctors' appointments, and to generally look after her. Flora Ramos, an experienced caregiver, was responsible for the cooking and other household tasks. There was also someone for the night shift, and on weekends Colette arranged for a friend to look after Joyce on Saturdays, while she herself stayed with Joyce on Sunday nights.

In the beginning, Cynthia and Joyce spent time drawing listening to music, and painting. Cynthia mixed whatever colours Joyce asked for and encouraged her to paint and talk about painting. Sometimes Joyce talked about projects she thought she was working on, "something important and big."[46] Joyce also loved looking at her art books. Sometimes Cynthia took her to free noon-hour concerts, to the Art Gallery of Ontario or the Museum for Textiles. If she was not feeling well — sometimes she was too frightened to go outside — they stayed at home and listened to music.

Joyce's caregivers had a gentle approach in relating to her, and went along with her perceptions and sense of humour. But she could not differentiate between fantasy and reality, which is why they did not watch television because Joyce could easily become frightened. Whatever was on the TV screen would be just as real for her as the person beside her. Colette remembers that once when she took Joyce to Harbourfront they saw a large, life-size cut-out of the opera singer Luciano Pavarotti. Someone took her photo beside the cut-out, and later with great excitement she told her friend Vincent Sharp that she had met Pavarotti, and he was such a nice man.[47] Joyce also enjoyed looking at old photos, and Colette kept several boxes available for Joyce to look through whenever she wanted. She could not remember names; Bryan Barney, with whom she had lived when she was in her twenties, was simply "my lover," and that is also what she called Michael Snow.

Joyce loved Flora, and after she had been there for a few months, she began calling her "Mom." As Alzheimer's disease progresses, and the deterioration of the cortex advances, the afflicted person also regresses in age, loses her adulthood, and is propelled further and further back into childhood. In the years after her marriage dissolved, Joyce had feared that when she became old she would be alone and uncared for, perhaps a valid fear. The cruel irony is that her illness "created a situation where she was well taken care of. She got to be a child again, she got to have someone with her all the time."[48] In other words, through Alzheimer's disease she regained her mother, and this time around, instead of Rosetta, her name was Flora.

Joyce was cared for in her home until practical matters made it nearly impossible. The disease affected her bodily functions; she became incontinent and her interest in eating diminished. She had to be fed her Christmas dinner in 1995 because she wouldn't eat on her own, except for the dessert, which she ate without help. That was the last time she fed herself. She began pacing the floor for six hours at a time, and someone had to follow her around. Also, around that time she had several seizures. Her safety was at risk, particularly because of the stairs. It became obvious that she required a level of professional care that could not be provided at her house, and her friends realized they had to give up the hope of keeping Joyce in her own home for the rest of her life.[49]

On Monday, January 22, 1996, Joyce was taken to Chester Village, just east of Toronto's Don Valley, to a long-term care home with an Alzheimer's wing. To make the transition, the plan was that Cynthia and Flora would stay with Joyce in the daytime until she was familiar with the place and the staff. During the next six months, Joyce's health deteriorated rapidly, and she lost a lot of weight. She became hunched over and held her head down so that her chin was on her chest. Flora, whom Joyce loved, stayed with her in the mornings, but no one Joyce knew was with her the rest of the day.

Colette decided to hire someone for the afternoons. Christine Oksanen, a slim, down-to-earth woman with a calming, mellow voice, became the afternoon person. She began in August 1996 and at first spent most of each afternoon trying to get Joyce to take medication to control seizures, along with an antidepressant. "She wouldn't even open [her mouth] to take liquid, so I had to crouch underneath her to get a tiny spoonful of liquid into her."[50] With someone she knew with her all day, Joyce began responding. After about a month, Christine could "slip pieces of cantaloupe or watermelon into her. She would start drinking a bit and taking the medication, but it would still take the whole time."

Christine had no training to work with Alzheimer's patients, and had never worked in a nursing home. In many ways, she did not relate to Joyce as someone who had Alzheimer's. As Colette explained, "What was so good about her, she did not see her as a sick person. We had been doing everything for her. She tells Joyce, my hands are full, can you open the door?"[51] And Joyce opened the door. Somehow, Christine also got Joyce to drink, and the nurses were astonished. "After I'd been at Chester Village for a few months and she was able to drink, one day she just took the glass out of my hand."[52]

That fall, on Saturdays Colette began taking Joyce home to visit her Queen Street house, and Linda Abrahams and Kay Wilson took her out for a few hours on Sundays. She responded remarkably well to these excursions. In fact, sometimes when Colette arrived, Joyce would say, "Go home," which indicated she knew what was going on at least some of the time. At her house, Joyce would sit on a chair in the kitchen while Flora and Colette cooked and chatted, with Joyce sometimes giggling or just sitting, seemingly enjoying the activity and the cooking smells. Sometimes the neighbours dropped in to say hello, or chatted on the street when Joyce and Colette were out walking.

Ever since Joyce had gone to Chester Village, the neighbours kept an eye on the house, and cleaned up any garbage that accumulated. They felt Joyce's absence, according to Ingrid Gadsden, who lived a few doors to the east. Whereas Joyce used to put paintings in her front window, now there was a black curtain. "Nobody had to be told that she's sick, but we all sort of knew that she had gone."[53] That she received the care she needed was a testament to what Joyce had given to all who knew her. As Sara Bowser said, there's a poetic irony that Joyce, who "sought family all her life," ended up with care from friends who did a better job than most families.[54]

One weekend, when Joyce had been at Chester Village for about a year and was no longer able to walk up and down stairs, Flora and Colette took Joyce to her house for the day. Joyce went to the stairs and put her foot on the bottom step. It was obvious she wanted to go upstairs. Flora went with her, and Joyce walked upstairs and into her studio and sat down. She sat there with the sun pouring in her window, with tears in her eyes. What was happening in her mind during those two hours she sat in the studio? Flora helped Joyce down the stairs, and, with tears still in her eyes, Joyce gave Colette a big hug.[55]

Ignoring opinions that Joyce could no longer understand language, Christine talked to her anyway about all kinds of things. Joyce herself rarely spoke. Knowing how fond she was of Robbie Burns, when Robbie Burns Day arrived in the winter of 1997, Christine told Joyce what day it was. "Aye Lassie," Joyce said, and then, to Christine's surprise and amusement, Joyce tried to dance a jig. "I remember how the doctor tried not to look at me when I told him that Joyce spoke," Christine said, because by this stage of the illness, doctors, as well as others, did not think Joyce had any capacity to comprehend or to respond.[56]

When Joyce did say a few words, she usually did not speak about people she knew. However, she mentioned her sister a few times, though not by name, and occasionally she said Betty's name. One day after she had been napping, she sat up on the edge of her bed and said, "I had a dream about Betty." No one could explain these flashes of understanding in the mind of someone so engulfed in Alzheimer's disease.

That fall, Joyce was given Toronto's Lifetime Achievement Award, too late for her to understand what was going on. After the awards ceremony, which she could not attend, during the last six weeks of 1997, Joyce became extremely wakeful and agitated. Christine remembered spending most of the time following her around the hallway of Chester Village, staying close enough to catch her if she fell. As they walked along the hall, once Joyce said, looking at the floor, "I really like the way this is done here. This is really good, isn't it?" as though she were looking at a painting. Christine agreed, and on they went. After those six weeks, Joyce had a major seizure.[57] She became weaker and weaker throughout the first six months of 1998.

As spring turned into summer and the days of June went by, the illness closed down the person who was Joyce Wieland.

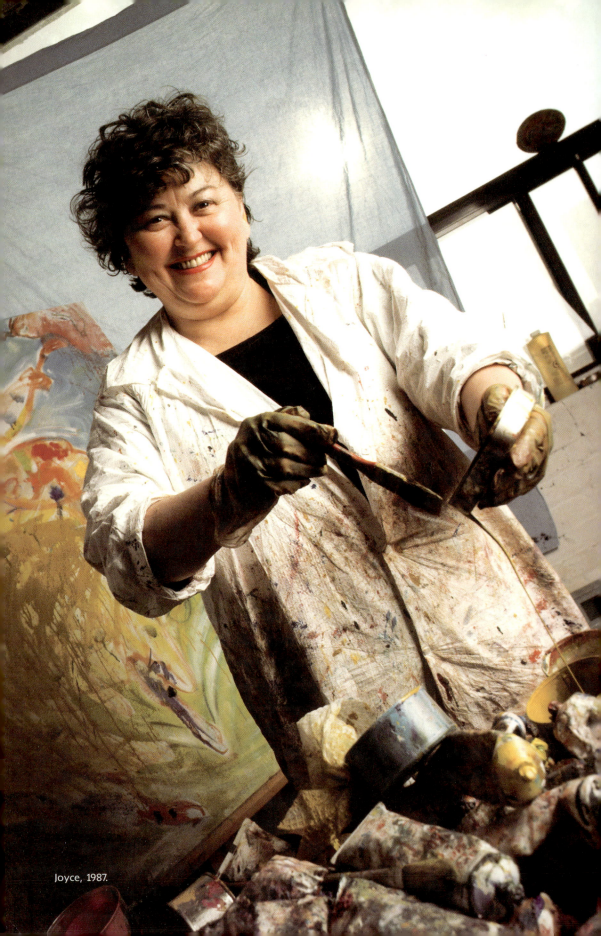

Joyce, 1987.

Foremost and fearless

It's been my experience that if you open up new territory
you're viewed as an enemy. If you investigate or bring
new things to light first, then you're the one to get a kick
in the butt for it. Then Later you become an institution.
—Joyce Wieland, 1980[1]

How can we know the reverberations of the life of Joyce Wieland? We can only trace a few examples of the women who influenced her, and how her energy altered the lives of others and left behind her legacy.

From the beginning, Joyce was someone who did not fit into the female gender conventions of her time. As we know from her diaries, her perception of who she was gave rise to inner turmoil because she had absorbed the current gender constraints, in spite of her understanding about herself. Between these two parts of herself, she discovered her special gift, her Wieland-vision. What came with her vision was a desire and determination to be seen — a need for recognition. It is a matter of good fortune for succeeding generations that Joyce was born at her particular time and place, that she wove together the strands of her life in such a way as to leave behind a legacy that continues far beyond what she could have imagined, even beyond her sometime dream of becoming famous. She is at the forefront of a long line of women who now offer to the world their gifts in their own ways.

Joyce outreached her mother's attempts at breaking the gender stereotype. As a teenager, Rosetta Amelia Watson ventured on her own to the city, changing her name from Rosetta to Billy, gestures that reveal a spirited young woman. But she was caught in the conventions of the times, and according to Joyce's accounts, lived these conventions to the hilt because she saw herself as less important than her husband. Still, Billy passed on something of her own spirited nature to Joyce. But the circumstances of poverty, intensified by the death of Sidney, on whom she was dependent, placed real limitations on Rosetta's life, limitations her daughter surmounted.

Two photographs of round-faced Joyce with dark curly hair, probably taken when she was about eight years old — within a year after her father's death — reveal two sides of the little girl, the same two sides that were also part of the adult woman. In one photo, she stands in the backyard of her family's house, on her face an expression of pain, her left hand held tense, the same hand that forty-five years later she portrayed as a hoof in *Artist on Fire*. In the other photo, a headband in her hair, the little girl stands with her legs crossed, holding an umbrella. She is smiling, self-assured, and looks into the camera, conscious that she is posing.

In another family photo, this one of Joan and Sidney, taken when the children were sent to Canada on the ship to meet their parents, the brother and sister stand rigidly beside a chair, posed as in the old traditional studio photos of men and women, he with his hand around her shoulders, she holding roses in her left hand. Joan's round, plump face wears a faint smile; her eyes, elusive, look off to the left, away from the camera. There is something stoical about these two little children, who seem almost like miniature adults.

These photographs suggest the way the two sisters each responded to the loss they experienced. Joyce used the tension between the two parts of herself revealed in the photos as a catalyst for the body of work she gave us — the visual images of her own inner world. Joan, on the other hand, enclosed her bitterness within, enduring in a kind of stoicism, and defended herself with a rigid stance early in her life. Though she did her best to come to terms with her grief and pain, she carried a resentment toward her father all her life, not only because he abandoned her when he left England, but also because he was to blame for her mother's disappearance when Joan was so young. And she never could forgive him for his favouritism toward Joyce. Another great regret and sadness she carried all her life was that she never had a chance to learn to play the piano; nor did she become the writer she

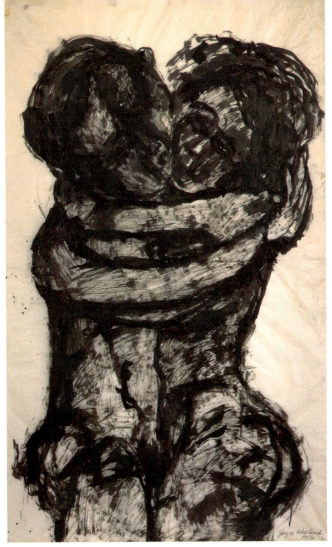

Untitled (two children holding each other), 1956.

dreamed of. In a sense she also blamed her father for these regrets because his illness prevented her from continuing her education.

Though the two sisters' experiences and feelings differed, they shared their deep losses. In the roles they each assumed as orphans they became opposites: Joan became the loving parent, caring for young Joyce with admirable devotion and understanding; Joyce remained the little girl. Joan in her role became an adult far too soon. At the same time, they clung to each other for comfort while having to fend for themselves, and in that sense Joyce also mothered Joan. These strands of experience became part of their emotional lives in the way they were entwined. When Joyce reached the age of independence, and it became evident that she could make her own way, she felt overwhelmed by her sister's continued need for her, and felt guilty for establishing her own life. And as a mature adult, when Joyce eventually tried to break what she saw as the unhealthy part of the tie with her sister,

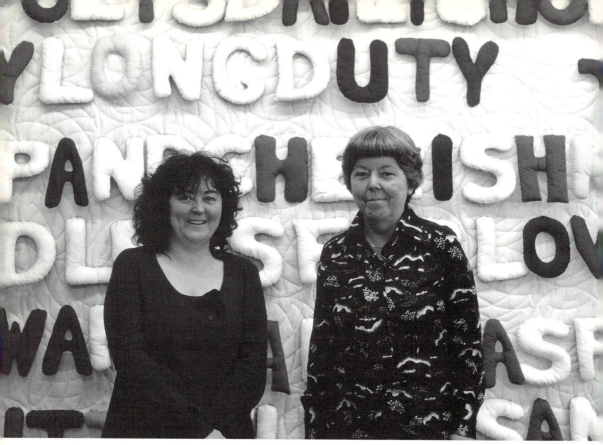

Joyce and Joan with *Lens* (1978-79) in the background.

and went her own way, Joan felt hurt. This was Joyce's perception.[2]

Joyce was grateful that Joan had introduced her to music and art but was disappointed that her sister did not develop her own gifts. She saw Joan as intelligent, talented and having a great mind. She tried to encourage her by hiring her to work on her quilts. By making quilts with her sister, Joyce was once again using her art to connect with someone who had meant so much to her in her early life. Each brought to a quilt project a different, necessary component of the process: Joyce had the vision, and Joan the skills to give that vision its physical presence.

The observation Berthe Morisot's biographer made about women in the nineteenth century, which sometimes is still true, applies to Joyce. "Behind every great woman there is another woman. Perhaps the only common denominator among nineteenth-century women of outstanding public achievements is their private bond to a female relative, almost always a sister, very often a sister with considerable talents of her own."[3] At the end of her life, Joan knew that Joyce could not have accomplished what she had with her quilts if it had not been for her own work. She did not appreciate the comment Joyce made while they were working on *Barren Ground Caribou* (1978): "You're the only one I know who is fool enough to do anything like this." Joan wanted more than just the money she got for her work.[4]

Joan's hurt was exacerbated when a newspaper article quoted Joyce as saying her friends were her family. To Joan, this was a slap in the face. "Am I a piece of chopped liver, or what? This is what happens when you live totally different lives, separate lives." Their separateness was partly because of the difference between her family and Michael's; he seldom went to Joyce's family gatherings. And yet, despite Joan's resentment, she quickly added, "I'm glad she's got friends. Thank god she's got friends! I don't know what she'd do without them."[5] Around the time Joyce became ill, because she did not live in Toronto, Joan felt she could not get enough information about what was happening to Joyce. She had someone drive her from her home near Owen Sound to Toronto to find out, wanting to have some say in the power of attorney, but by the time she got to the city, Joyce had already signed it over.

Joan felt she did not have a big enough place in Joyce's life, as her letters to her sister show. Like Joyce, she also felt she did not get the recognition she deserved. A few days before she died in 1993, when Joan was in the hospital and Joyce came to visit, Joan said afterwards, "'She's still a pain in the ass,' or something along that line."[6]

As Joyce entered her teenage years, she began separating herself from Joan, seeking out others, both her age and older, and from that time on she always had close friends her age. Even when she was in her twenties, and the thing for young women to do was to be seen mostly with men, Joyce went around with her women friends. Marjorie Harris, who worked at Dorothy Cameron's Here and Now Gallery in the late fifties and is now a well-known writer on gardening, recalls that Joyce "was one of the first people I knew who had a very specific group of women friends, which was not usual in those days."[7] Harris, then in her early twenties, was impressed that a woman would seek out other women as friends.

Also, when Joyce was in her twenties, she adopted Michael's mother, whose "idiosyncratic, expressionistic aesthetic" was different from hers, but which she liked in Antoinette from the beginning. Su Rynard observed that her grandmother's aesthetic was tamer than Joyce's, but in some ways the two were similar. Antoinette had a "collector's aesthetic where nothing is exactly the same, one of these and four of these and two of these."[8] Antoinette had a huge bed, high off the floor, and in Joyce's Queen Street house, she, too had a high bed with piano legs on the four corners.[9] Daughter- and mother-in-law shared in their pleasure in cooking up a bouillabaisse, or just the two of them chatting.

Joyce loved the company of women. Over the years she developed a number of distinct circles of friends, and this pattern becomes most clear

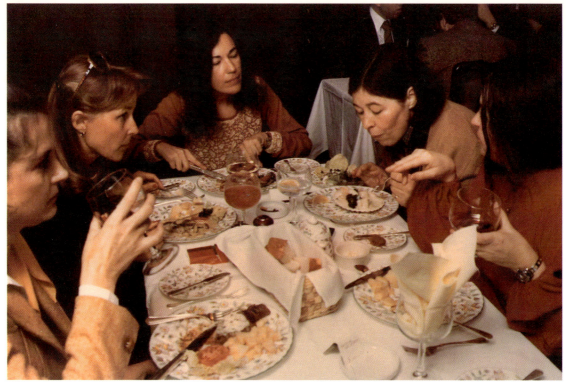

Some of the "dinner bunch" in the 1970s. Left to right: Sylvia Tyson, Christine Wookie, Betty Ferguson, Sara Bowser, Joyce.

when one looks at her friendships after *The Far Shore* years: younger women who were her students at Artsake and then in her studio; a group of professional women who met regularly in the early eighties; "the dinner bunch," who met for lunch or dinner once a week for thirty years. This last group, which had remarkable staying power even though it was made up of women of diverse political points of view, had started when Diane Rotstein and Ellen Godfrey each had small children at home and asked their husbands to babysit one day a week so the mothers could have some time out. Joyce had joined in with this group when she returned to Toronto from New York. Very quickly the women discovered Joyce's sharp wit and sense of humour.

Many years later, when the group was having dinner in a restaurant, Joyce vividly described a sexual encounter. Her story was hilarious. The women were almost thrown out of the restaurant because they were howling with laughter so loudly they disturbed the other diners.

"It's hard to explain," Betty Ferguson said. "Joyce could always talk about everything in a way that wasn't distasteful ... It was never dirty," regardless of the topic, likely because to her sex and bodily functions were just part of life, and there was no reason to be hush-hush about anything.[10]

Two of the women in the dinner group, who were perhaps the most constant in Joyce's life, were Sara Bowser and Betty Ferguson. In the

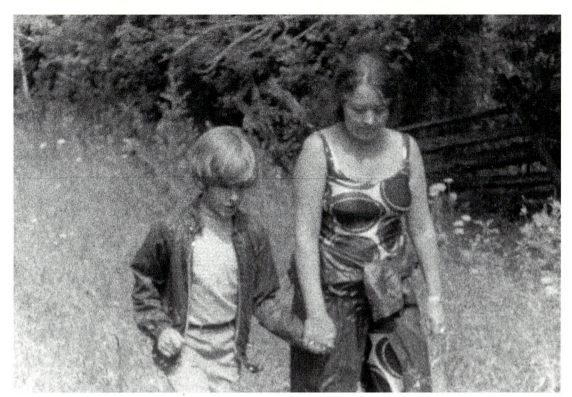
Munro Ferguson and Joyce, probably 1971.

beginning, Joyce and Sara's friendship had a rocky start, with them yelling at each other one night at a party, and according to Sara's memory, they fought a lot from time to time.[11] But they developed a fondness for each other and for many years lived in the same part of the city, often meeting at the St. Lawrence Market on Saturday mornings.

Betty Ferguson, also a filmmaker, became a friend Joyce could always count on. While Joyce was still living in New York, Betty and Graeme had rented a house in Toronto's Rosedale while they built the first Imax projector at McMaster University in Hamilton, Ontario. Betty then decided she wanted to live in the country, and do the "back to the earth sort of thing."[12] She and Graeme bought a one-hundred-acre farm in the southern end of Wellington County in Puslinch Township. The land included a hardwood bush and a pond surrounded with trees and wildlife. The house, part of it an old stone post office, was little more than a shell, with no wiring or plumbing. The Fergusons lived with plastic on the windows at first, and they had most of their meals outside. Betty began having the house rebuilt, using wood from trees on the farm.[13]

By 1972 Betty and Graeme had separated, and they divorced in 1974. Joyce was living in Toronto by the time the Fergusons separated, and she spent a lot of time at Betty's farm. She was extremely supportive of Betty during

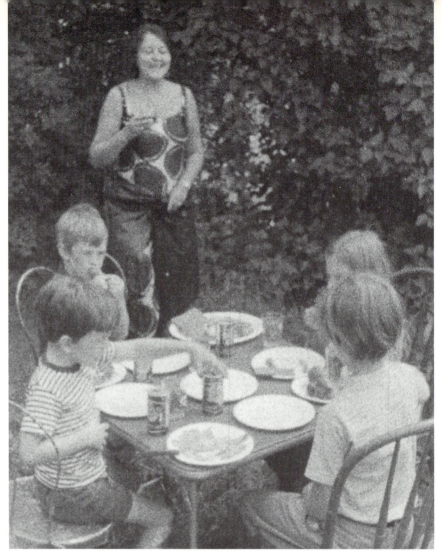

Joyce at Betty Ferguson's farm, probably 1971. The two Ferguson children are to the right.

those difficult years. Betty, Allison and Munro became like an adopted family;
Joyce included the children in invitations to special events, "adult" parties
that children usually did not attend. She did not make a distinction between
adults and children at social events.[14]

Betty had been squeezed out of Imax as a minority shareholder. In a four-
year court battle with Imax, she won a landmark ruling that gave her a
handsome settlement, including court costs. She had spent much time and
effort studying the implications of the case, and during those four years her
friends, including Joyce, rallied around her.

Betty's farm, and "Betty's pond," as Joyce called it, became one of her
favourite places, and she loved to swim there. "It was like her Walden pond,
very quiet, very private, she just loved it," Betty said. Deer and many different
kinds of birds, including great blue herons, lived around the pond, and Joyce

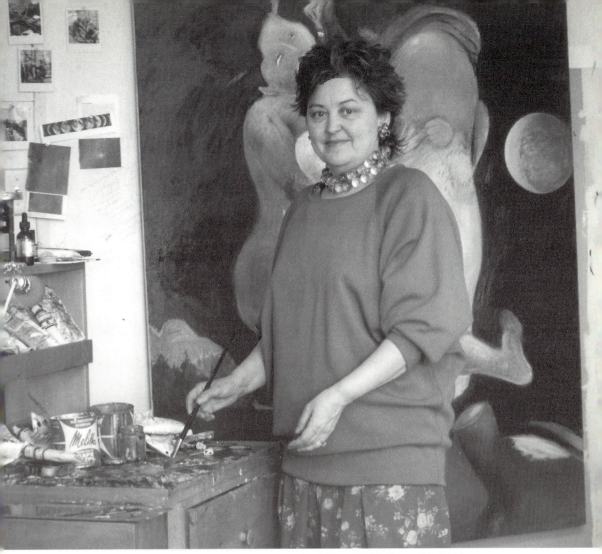

Joyce in 1983 or 1984 in front of *Paint Phantom*.

spent hours there, absorbed in the landscape.[15] She came on weekends and entered into family life with Betty and the children, going for long walks with Munro and Allison, and cooking and talking with Betty.

When asked whether she became a mother figure for Joyce, Betty replied, "She turned everybody into a mother figure, I think. She wanted a mother. She was somebody you tried to look after. She didn't really need looking after. She was good at looking after herself." Betty articulated what many people felt about Joyce — here was this very intelligent, creative woman; yet you sensed a winsome, childlike attitude that made you want to take care of her. It was as though a big part of this woman had never grown up, but it was also her childlike view of the world that made her so delightful. The friendship between Joyce and Betty was a mutual pleasure, remarkable for its strength and consistency over thirty-six years.

Joyce was among those artists — Nancy Spero, Louise Bourgeois, Frida Kahlo and many others — who created images from her inner being. In the fearlessness of her choice to work this way, she left her mark on many artists, both women and men, but particularly on women, who felt they did not have a voice, and who did not have a recorded history on which to build. She had a gift for teaching. What she absorbed from women all her life and fused with who she was gave rise to her uniqueness and an inclination towards nurturing. She elicited from other artists a desire to emulate her — she always insisted that her friends do what they really wanted to do. Once, Joyce and painter Helen Lucas went together to an art supply store in Scarborough, and on their way Helen confessed that secretly she wanted to paint large, five-foot-square canvases. "Go for it!" Joyce said, and Helen launched into her large, colourful flower paintings.[16]

Meeting Joyce and working with her made a big impact on Judy Steed's adult life because of what Joyce taught her. When they began making films together, Judy was surprised to find out how much hard work was a part of the creative process. Joyce, "an unbelievably hard worker," taught Judy how to work, how to do research. "She did what very few women of her generation managed to do," Judy said, "which is to focus in on her own creativity and experience, and it was radical, revolutionary and it was exciting and she reached a lot of people." Perhaps the most exciting part for Judy was that Joyce was the first woman she encountered who spoke in her own voice. "We were all conditioned into supporting male voices, listening to male voices, never speaking in our own voices. We didn't know how to do that." From Joyce, Judy learned that she, too, could speak in her own voice.[17] As would happen with many of the women whom Joyce taught, Judy's friendship, and her own unique qualities and skills.

For Joyce, doing creative work with others did not seem much different from teaching a class. She firmly believed it was a matter of encouraging creativity and helping students overcome their own inhibitions or timidity. Her students at Artsake — Kay Wilson, Kathy Dain, Ettie Shuken, among others — became Joyce's friends, and the student-teacher relationship was one of sharing common interests. When Joyce offered a course in her studio in 1984, she called her "school" École des Beaux-Arts de Toronto. Her course outline consisted of six pages of photocopied reproductions of paintings — among them Tiepolo's self-portrait — with humorous captions. The concluding statement was, "For the development and affirmation of each student's individual creativity."

For Kay Wilson, who at age fourteen had first seen one of Joyce's paintings, the course at Artsake changed her life. "It was as though for thirty-two years I'd been blind and all of a sudden I was beginning to see." Joyce had a gentle approach to teaching, asking students to paint from inside themselves, to give image to their own vision. She commented on students' work, and she sometimes said things that made little sense, but if you "wrote it down, followed it, you found you started to ... notice things you didn't before." Drawing and painting became an obsession for Kay. When Joyce was no longer teaching, Kay rented space in Joyce's studio and the two of them painted together for seven years.[18]

The two artists also spent hours talking about art. "I asked her one time why do you paint and she said because I love it." Joyce spoke about art as "being given from a divine source of love," and that art is love. But the love of art included hard work. She told her students to go to museums to learn, and to learn from nature. If they were painting animals, she would tell them to go to the zoo and also to rent films about animals; and to go to the reference library and look at pictures, not to draw there, but to absorb, absorb.[19]

Kay's memories included hours of fun with Joyce, who had a great capacity for laughter. One day when Joyce's house was cold — besides being a mess — the two of them sat as though trying to keep warm in front of the fireplace, which had no fire in it, and laughed themselves silly. They shared the same sense of the ridiculous. They both loved to shop and eat, and often stuffed themselves in restaurants.[20] One of Joyce's favourite paintings at the AGO was about food — Jean-Baptiste Chardin's painting *Bocal d'abricots* (*Jar of Apricots*), a beautiful still life of a round of cheese, a jar of apricots, bread, tea cups and wine goblets. Joyce and Kay loved standing in front of that painting and feasting their eyes.

That this woman, so intelligent, witty, and creative, who had such a huge impact on Kay's life, should be crushed by Alzheimer's disease seemed utterly cruel. "I would have accepted cancer or heart disease," Kay said, "but someone with a mind like Joyce had —"[21]

It was that sharp mind that gave Joyce her attentiveness, her notice of those who were working in their own creative spirit. Michaele Jordana Berman, a lithe, dark-haired, passionate painter and performer, remembers that in 1976 she had made a series of drawings printed as a little booklet. "Before I knew it, she had picked up about sixty of these and bought them, these booklets I had done. We were out there to stop the James Bay project. It was the level of support, the vengeance with which she was behind me, that I'll never, ever forget," Michaele said.[22] This was around the same time that Michaele, in her late twenties, had an exhibition at Isaacs Gallery called "Oceans of Blood," large, airbrush whale paintings with titles like "I cry tears of blood for the power man wields over the hierarchy of being." When she told Joyce she had a vision of "the whales in their death," that she wasn't sure if she should paint them that way, Joyce responded, "Yes, you should."

Michaele had always wanted her work to speak to people about injustices, and Joyce's support gave her permission.

Michaele loved Joyce, not just for her encouragement, but also for her sense of aesthetics. "We'd go over there and she'd have pink depression glass, and in the middle of the winter she'd cut strawberries, cut them up nice and thin and put it right in front of you as you were just awed by this scent of the strawberries. She'd want to feed you." Joyce did not serve "ordinary food, but it was always something spectacular, whether it was funny or really beautiful."[23] She understood how food nourishes us, physically, aesthetically, and in good company, spiritually.

Joyce mixed together her strong belief in a better world with a sense of fun. "She was crazy and a dare-devil and wanted me to be a dare-devil, and often — I dare you to do this — and I would do it because she was behind it." One evening when Michaele and her husband, Douglas Pringle, who wrote the music for *The Far Shore*, were at Joyce and Michael's house on Summerhill. In one of those situations where the men were in their place and the women in theirs, she and Joyce and Judy Steed were in the kitchen, while the men — Doug and Michael — were playing music. As Michaele remembered it, the three women did not want to be in the kitchen. "I certainly didn't," she recalled. "They dared me to go in there, so I ran in and did something crazy on the piano and ran out and Mike looked at me like, what are you doing? Joyce and Judy were using me, and I didn't mind being used." And later she added, "Did you ever notice that Joyce was so lady-like in her appearance, and what a mouth, though!"[24]

Sometimes Joyce used her daring spirit to help her friends. Though she was afraid to drive her car at night, she instigated an escapade in the middle of the night to help a friend get her car back from her former husband. In 1984 singer Selma Lenchener-Frankel had left her marriage — something Joyce, of course, identified with — and since she and her husband had two cars, she wanted one of them. Joyce insisted that the two of them go together and get the car. She had Selma phone her at two o'clock in the morning, and Joyce picked her up. They drove to her former husband's place and found the car. The gas tank was empty, but Joyce knew of a twenty-four-hour gas station at Bathurst Street and St. Clair Avenue, so she drove behind Selma in case she ran out of gas. They made it, got the gas and returned to where Selma was staying, and Joyce told her to lock the car into the garage, and that was that.[25]

Towards the end of her life, Joyce liked being called "foremost," because she knew she had been a pioneer. Many have added another description — "fearless." The second term applies to the daring range of emotions in her work: her rage, her pain, her darkness, and also her joyful celebrations, emotions that in the past were outside of women's prerogative. This was the route she took to becoming our cultural heroine, the feminist artist, all the while exposing her personal contradictions. Becoming a symbol for us came with a price — she had to live up to being Canada's foremost feminist artist and carry the weight of its meaning, but she was willing.

That Joyce continuously dared to range to the edge of experience in her art encouraged other artists to explore their own passions. The circle of artists she touched extends far beyond those with whom she formed friendships, and includes many whose work seems completely unrelated to hers. Some artists who were part of the generation after Joyce saw art as an intellectual activity, whereas, even though Joyce was highly intelligent, her work was emotive, not based on theoretical processes. Joyce was of the generation that worked from what was meaningful to their personal lives, and they insisted, as Jessica Bradley observed, "that it was okay to make things that were personal — the personal is political ... and in fact we saw that the whole landscape of the art scene shifted considerably as more women came into it and were working in a very different way." During conceptualism and minimalism in the sixties and seventies it was women who began doing work "that was more materially present, that had narrativity in it, that was diaristic, all of those things that we tend to rightly attribute to the work of women at that time."[26]

Perhaps what some women artists have objected to in Joyce's work is what Bradley described as "pink and sweet and all those things we're supposed to be and that kind of irks us," and the fact that some of her work "flies in the face of what we wanted Joyce Wieland to be for us."[27] Perhaps we wanted a certain kind of heroine, or an icon, but the truth is that Joyce was more spirited — and whole — than an icon can ever be. Artists of each generation are a part of their own culture, and each generation moves into its own visual expression, building on earlier artists' work, as well as forging new directions that, because of previous societal restrictions, were not possible before.

Liz Magor, a sculptor who teaches at Emily Carr Institute of Art and Design in Vancouver, from the time she was a young artist in the early seventies, was aware of Joyce and her work. Knowing how difficult being an artist is, Magor admired Joyce's courage, but saw her art as "declarative" and dealing with issues of Joyce's generation — celebrating female sexuality. In Magor's work, issues of gender difference are more integrated. "There's no place where gender difference isn't involved. That first blatant difference of women didn't seem to be my experience. I didn't have a 'pink' life. ... I would express gender difference in much different terms."[28] Although Magor did not reject Joyce's ideology, it was not her own personal experience.

Another Vancouver artist, Elizabeth MacKenzie, had a similar response.

She felt that many of the women of the next generation owe a great debt to Joyce. "But these artists don't necessarily engage with ideas of 'the feminine' in the way that Joyce did. Joyce's work is based on certain assumptions about being women that my generation may reject or ignore. This is reflected in a general way in feminism and any other social movement," MacKenzie observed. "The leaders focus on different issues ... than the generations that follow."[29] In other words, artists of each generation make art based on ideas current to their particular time.

Carol Laing, an artist, writer and critic who teaches at the Ontario College of Art and Design in Toronto and is of the same generation as Magor and MacKenzie, was an education officer at the National Gallery in 1971, when Joyce had her exhibition there. She immediately liked Joyce's work for its relationship with popular culture. And she also loved the idea that Joyce "could actually make a film by getting on a train," a reference to Joyce filming from a train window for *Reason over Passion*.[30]

Laing felt that Joyce did much for women in art, despite what she saw as an unevenness in her work. "Considerable differences emerged with the next generation of feminist artists," Laing said, "especially around the issues of theory. But she was very important to me ... and her *True Patriot Love* and experimental films remain among my all-time favourites of women's work."[31] Despite the respect that these artists had for Joyce, the interest some of that generation had in art couched in theory rubbed Joyce the wrong way — she thought making art had little to do with theory.

The truth is, Joyce had little tolerance for those who disagreed with her on any issue that she considered very important, not just her art — the environment, for instance. Singer Sylvia Tyson remembers that when the "dinner bunch" met, "If you did not agree with her, then there was no hope for you." Sometimes "it would go head on and she would get really angry and she would not just agree to disagree."[32] She did not seem worried about being abrasive if a disagreement had to do with something important to her.

The other side of her fierce defense of her opinions was a great generosity, which became obvious in her visits to classes at the Ontario College of Art & Design. Students responded to her sense of humour and her down-to-earth way of presenting herself, but sometimes they could not relate to her work. Part of the reason was that students "increasingly see themselves as part of multicultural and global culture," whereas much of her work "turned on certain feelings of nationalism."[33] Another difference was that Joyce's "art of feeling" did not fit in with many students' technologically saturated approach to making art. But often they appreciated that she was not elitist and saw her as working-class, which she was.

One student who did connect with Joyce on a deep level was Madonna

Andress, who grew up in Masey, Ontario, a small town of eleven hundred people near Elliot Lake. For a project in a class called "Women and Art" in 1996, Andress created *The Body Quilt*. This "quilt" is made of thirty-five, eight-inch-square handmade sheets of flax noil paper in their natural colour. Andress tied the sheets together using black eyelets and string of a colour similar to the paper. A black-and-white photo of different parts of Andress's body were imprinted on twenty-four of the sheets, some of which were covered with a paper flap that could be lifted to see the body part underneath.

Andress chose flax paper for this piece because "it reminded me of dried, stretched skin ... Despite its thin, translucent and delicate appearance, it is an extremely strong paper. I began to realize that women have often been perceived in much the same way."[34] Andress acknowledged the impact not only of Joyce's work, but also her courage and strength.

Another artist whose work echoes Joyce's art is Mireille Perron. Perron, who grew up in Montreal, began teaching at the Alberta College of Art and Design in Calgary, Alberta, in 1990 and is now the Academic Head of Liberal Studies there. As a student, she discovered Joyce in reproduction and in exhibitions and was impressed by her "energy and interdisciplinarity." In *inversions*, an annual journal on women's art published in Winnipeg, Alberta, Perron described her personal encounters with Joyce. Close to thirty years younger, Perron had her first solo exhibition outside Montreal at the Isaacs Gallery in 1985. At Perron's opening, she met Joyce for the first time. Joyce had come to the gallery with Perron's aunt, Colette Perron Sharp. Perron, who was in awe of Joyce, very much wanted to converse with her, but was too shy and unsure about speaking English, even though Joyce was encouraging.

Ten years later, in Kingston, Ontario, Perron showed her *Dear Gertrude* (1993), a mixed-media installation on Gertrude Stein, in a group show at the Agnes Etherington Gallery, where a show of Joyce's drawings was hanging at the same time. Though by now Perron felt able to speak with Joyce, she, because of her illness, was not able to have a conversation with Perron. The two missed encounters of inverse circumstances led to "fictive conversations" within Perron's mind many times. These gave birth to her *Index of Intents ou elle à le vague à l'âme*, with the imaginary setting of a laboratory designated as a world centre for feminist pataphysics and an extension of the "Alberta College of Art, Design and Pataphysics," an institution "which attempts to link art and life in a more socially responsible matter."[35] *Index of Intents*, exhibited at Calgary's Banff Centre off-site location in 1996, consisted of multimedia installations that included a playful dialogue between, among others, the artist, Joyce and beavers.[36] The characters, who "narrate because it

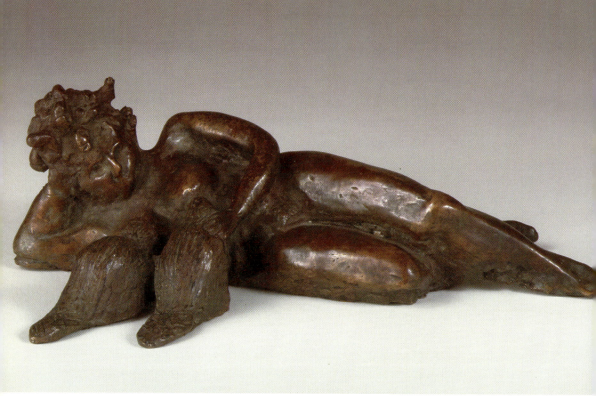

The Spirit of Canada Suckles the French and English Beavers, 1971.

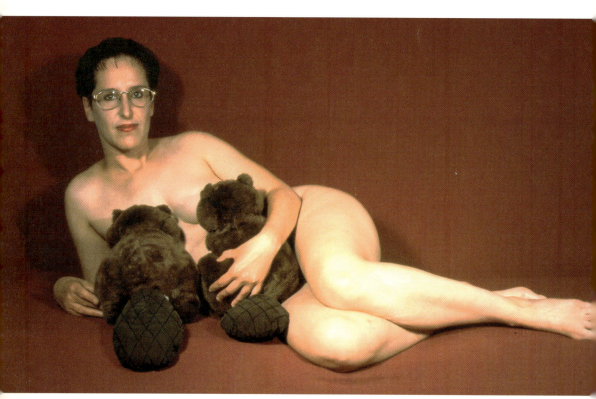

Mireille Perron, *Homage to Joyce Wieland #1*, 1996.

feels good," embodied aspects of the visual part of the show. *Joyce et moi* included two small, ceramic nude female figures lying on their stomachs, facing each other, how Perron imagined herself and Joyce having a conversation together. Other parts of *Index of Intents* made references to the two lovers in *The Far Shore* and the scene in which they mouth poetry to each other through a magnifying glass.

Homage to Joyce Wieland #1 was striking for transforming Joyce's small bronze, *The Spirit of Canada Suckles the French and English Beavers* (1970-71), into a real-life rendition. A large photo of the nude Perron herself personified the "Spirit of Canada," and the French and English beavers were two Hudson's Bay stuffed toy beavers, made for the three hundred and fiftieth anniversary of the Bay, another irony inlaid into Perron's piece. Perron would have one more final missed encounter with Joyce, her "grand-mère spirituelle."[37]

Ellen Rosenfeld, a jazz musician living in the state of New Jersey, was one of the girls in Joyce's art class of the sixties, when she was working on sinking sailboats and crashing planes. In the late seventies, Rosenfeld met Joyce for the last time to discover that after more than twenty years, Joyce had kept one of the paintings Rosenfeld had done when she was a little girl, a series of frames in which a creature becomes smaller in each frame, with "The Man, he dies." written on it. When the two met at Rosenfeld's father's funeral in 1979, Joyce gave Rosenfeld the painting she had saved for her, now one of her most precious treasures.

From Joyce, Rosenfeld gained "a hands on first concept of aesthetics … I am passionately in pursuit of playing jazz now with the same continuation of patterns I developed as a child in Joyce's art class … The concepts of juxtaposition of different objects into patterns put together by collage is not only my aesthetic point of view, but also symbolic of life."[38] The sentiment in Rosenfeld's words speak for many of us, just as the many stories of Joyce that thread in and around our lives become like a long procession of hundreds of women, with Joyce humming and singing, in the lead.

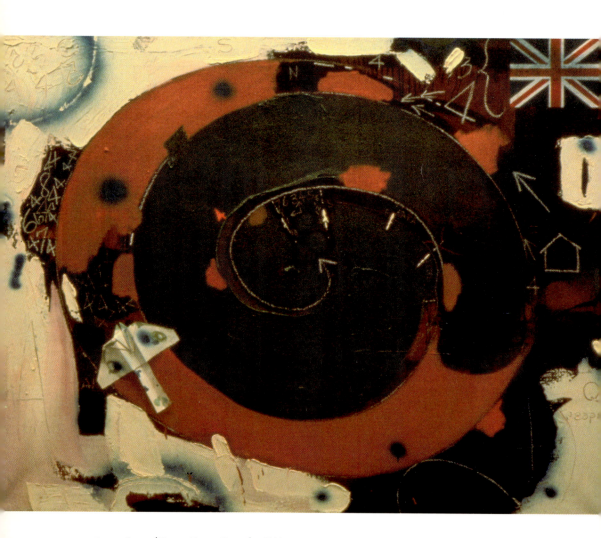

Laura Secord Saves Upper Canada, 1961.

Epilogue

**Although we're in life, what's interesting is creating eternals.
What we leave behind us when we die are all these wonderful
forms and sounds for people to remember us by. The poet Blake
reached into the lowest part of heaven to receive a fragment of
the divine. So all the work I've done has really become an entity
that's beside me and with me. —Joyce Wieland, 1980[1]**

AT THE TIME of the death of a person as loved as Joyce was, we want to
believe that she was courageous to the end and that she died in peace. We
also know the reality that Alzheimer's disease is a horrible way for this life to
end — in a struggle for each breath — especially for a woman of such
boundless energy, creativity and intelligence.

Just before dawn on a beautiful, clear, blue-sky day — June 27, 1998 —
Colette Perron Sharp received a phone call at four-thirty from a nurse at
Chester Village urging her to come immediately because Joyce had had a very
bad night. Colette took a cab to the nursing home, and for the last time,
spent a few hours with her long-time friend. Colette called the other power
of attorney, Douglas McPherson, who also came for a while that morning.

Around noon, the head nurse suggested that arrangements be made
because Joyce's vital signs pointed to an imminent death. By then, Linda

Abrahams had arrived, and Colette went home to make phone calls. While Colette was at her house calling a funeral home, Joyce died, surrounded by Linda, Kay Wilson, Kate Brown and Flora Ramos, Joyce's beloved "mom" at the end of her life. For Kay Wilson, the light she saw emanating from Joyce at the end was a gift — Kay's experience of seeing light around a dying person is more common than most people think.

For Colette, an apt conclusion to that day unfolded in the person of the woman from the funeral home, who came to pick up Joyce's body. A tall, beautiful, "dashing young woman" wearing high heels, who reminded Colette of Superwoman, carried Joyce's body out with no help. "It was a beautiful thing for Joyce," Colette said. "It was just like in a movie ... It was surrealistic, I couldn't believe it. Joyce would have loved it, to go like this."[2]

Because Colette's power of attorney ended with Joyce's death — she was responsible only for her care — she phoned others to help with planning a memorial. Gerald Robinson and Linda Gaylard planned the liturgy. A group of friends, the director of the Art Gallery of Ontario and several curators developed a plan for a reception at the gallery after the ceremony at the church.

July 8, 1998, was a hot, sultry day in Toronto. At the Church of St. George the Martyr, with its chapel closer than any other to the Art Gallery of Ontario, Joyce's friends met to mourn her death and to celebrate her life. People arrived dressed every which way, from a man in a bright red shirt and black shorts to a woman wearing a filigreed black hat with a brim six inches wide. Gradually the church, with its yellow brick interior and arched stained glass windows, filled as people seated themselves on the red velvet cushions in the cream-coloured pews.

On a table at the front lay a pink, lace-covered pillow on which sat a plain box containing Joyce's ashes; a yellow lily lay in front of the box.

Before the service began, old friends greeted each other, introducing people who had not met before; others chatted, telling stories about Joyce Wieland. Two women stood in the aisle unwrapping something folded into a raincoat. It was a small painting, and in a touching gesture, Colette Perron Sharp placed one of Joyce's small self-portraits at the front of the chapel as the pianist played the prelude. Kathy Dain, who had gathered and arranged more than two thousand stems of flowers and herbs — picked in the light of dawn that morning in her Brantford garden and by her niece from roadsides between Stayner and Toronto, along with a few purchased on Queen Street — adjusted one of the luxuriant bouquets to her satisfaction. A mixture of formality and informality, this ceremony.

Rev. David Brinton, a former priest at St. Matthias on Bellwoods Avenue — the same little Anglican church where Joyce was baptized when she was six months old and to which she returned to have her cat Thomas blessed — was among those leading the service and offering prayers. Rev. Canon Elizabeth Kilbourn read from the book of Revelation in the Bible, verses that included these lines: "And there appeared a great wonder in heaven; a woman clothed with the sun, and the moon under her feet, and upon her head a crown of twelve stars …" (12: 1). This was a Christian service, Anglican, with Bible readings, prayers and tributes to this quintessential Canadian artist whose irrepressible life force was mentioned in the same breath as that of Jesus Christ! Would Joyce have preferred a reference to Mary Magdalene?

After the service, during the recessional anthem, the guests, picking up flowers that had been placed on a table, filed into the courtyard garden for the final ceremony, the interment of Joyce's ashes in a grey brick garden wall standing in a perennial flower bed at the Church of St. George the Martyr. Earlier, a niche had been made at eye-level in the wall, just above a round-leafed perennial called *Ligularia Desdemona*, an appropriate spot.[3] Flora Ramos, Joyce's final "mom," placed the box of ashes in the garden wall. With a hammer, a man dressed in blue work clothes tapped the plaque into place; it says only "Joyce Wieland 1931–1998." Later, it would be neatly cemented in.

During these solemn moments of the final ritual with the ashes, a beautiful black-and-white cat sat in the grass washing itself, and then sprawled out in the sunshine, accompanied by a short-haired grey one. It was almost as though Joyce's spirit, and her love of cats, had brought these two to the ceremony.

At the end, pipes led a procession through Grange Park and into Walker Court at the AGO for the reception, which, after the speeches and tributes, was something like a tea party. Interestingly enough, this part of her memorial was very close to what Joyce had contemplated for herself. Though she had left behind no formal plans for a funeral, she had thought about it, for she had made notes on loose pieces of paper: "a high tea to be served in a cosy atmosphere that I love — a large table laden with a ham, little salmon sandwiches with butter evident." She also wanted "to spend whatever is necessary" to hire "the very best" musicians to play Mozart's flute and harp Concerto in C Major, K.299 "in a suitable place where refreshments can be served." And the place of her funeral would have to have "a beautiful piano."[4] In her wildest dreams, Joyce could have imagined the Walker Court as the place for this farewell tea party, the place where *Bill's Hat* had taken place thirty-one years earlier, within the institution where she had caused such consternation in the early seventies. Perhaps she would have seen it as a swing from the position of renegade to sainthood in the institution, an ironic, just conclusion. And perhaps she still would have insisted that she had been ignored by the art establishment!

The gallery's director, Matthew Teitelbaum, was the Master of Ceremonies. Dennis Reid, the Chief Curator at the AGO, who held Joyce in high regard, spoke of her contradictions, the range of her work — the treasure she left behind — and her vision. "Her visions might on the surface seem simple, but when they get hold of you they drive you crazy, joyfully mad, with their sophisticated layerings of often seemingly contradictory emotions, confronting relationships, searing truths."

Jean Sutherland Boggs, former Director of the National Gallery of Canada and now retired, told of her memories of this artist, who made for her a special gift. It was an exquisite cover for the book Boggs wrote for the National Gallery, in delicate spring colours — greens, mauves, yellows — with the words art and heart embroidered on it. Boggs forecast that in future years, the complexity of Joyce's work would be more and more appreciated.

The art and heart of which Boggs spoke dotted the other tributes to Joyce that afternoon. And then the third missed encounter occurred for artist Mireille Perron. In a meeting with those organizing the event, Dennis Reid's assistant, Anna Hudson, had suggested that Perron speak to represent the artists who follow in Joyce's footsteps. In the press of finalizing plans, somehow her name was omitted from the printed program, and somehow no one remembered to call on her. Since in her life and work Joyce integrated the French- and English-Canadian cultures — in her marriage and in *The Far Shore* — she would have been pleased by Perron's contribution at the time of her death.

One of the last tributes, a song written by Canadian songwriter Les Smith, who lost a family member to Alzheimer's, "Piece by Piece," sung with feeling by Sylvia Tyson, moved many of Joyce's friends to tears. Those who were close to her knew from experience the meaning of "Piece by piece and day by day I'm losing you." And the line, "Piece by piece your ship is sinking," had particular meaning, as though written specifically for Joyce. The formal part of the memorial concluded with Alexander Kats at the beautiful piano Joyce wanted, in a rendition of Chopin's *Berceuse* in D-flat Major, op. 57, and the Étude No. 1 in C Major, op. 10.

Afternoon tea consisted of tables filled with sweets, scones, jam, cream, tea and coffee. In a thoughtful gesture on the part of the AGO, guests had been given tickets that admitted them into the gallery to see a special exhibition of Joyce's work, a most appropriate expression of love and respect for Joyce.

On the wall with the exhibition appeared a brief biography and two photos, along with one of Joyce's November 1990 statements: "More and more I do what I want, and more and more I become what I'm supposed to be." The bitter irony is that when she said those words, she already knew she was ill, and just when she felt she was becoming more and more Joyce Wieland, the disease had already begun dismantling her, "piece by piece."

One of the most arresting works in this show was a 1955 pencil drawing with a prophetic title, *Lady Examining Her Magic and Protective Circle*. This title can be read in several different ways — the magic is in the person of the female figure in the drawing, or in the protective circle; or the magic applies to the protective circle. Perhaps it is both, for within the walls of the AGO that day, as we shared our grief and our joy in her life, even in her death her magic touched us all.

Endnotes

Sources cited only as a number refer to file numbers at the York University Archives and Special Collections in Toronto, where Joyce Wieland's personal archives are housed.

Acknowledgements

[1] Virginia Woolf, *A Room of One's Own* (London: HarperCollins, 1977), p. 47.

Introduction

[1] Author's interview with Joyce Wieland, August 14, 1986.

[2] Kathleen Barry, "Toward a Theory of Women's Biography: From the Life of Susan B. Anthony," in Teresa Isles, ed., *All Sides of the Subject* (New York: Teachers College Press, Columbia University, 1992), p. 33.

[3] See Anne Middleton Wagner, *Three Artists (Three Women)* (Berkeley/Los Angeles: University of California Press, 1996), p. 2 for a discussion of (women) artists' identity as "bracketed."

[4] Jeanette Winterson, *Art Objects: Essays on Ecstasy and Effrontery* (New York: Vintage Books, 1995), p. 138.

Chapter 1

[1] Virginia Woolf, *Women and Writing* (New York and London: Harcourt Brace Jovanovich, 1980).

[2] Edward Banes, *History, Directory and Gazetteer of the County Palatine of Lancaster*, Volume 2 (Devon: David and Charles Publishers, reprint of 1825 edition), p. 603.

[3] Ibid.

[4] Author's interview with Paula Letki, February 26, 1998.

[5] 1993-009/008-113.

[6] Joan's account is the more accurate one since the dates fit with the rest of the story.

[7] Black notebook in 1992-018/009-134.

[8] Author's interview with Joan Prowd, May 21, 1993.

[9] Dennis Wheeler, ed., *Form and Structure in Recent Film*, Vancouver Art Gallery, from October 29-November 5, 1972 (Vancouver: Vancouver Art Gallery, 1972), p. 84.

[10] Author's interview with Joan Prowd, May 21, 1993. Sidney fudged his age all his life, but since he said he was thirteen years older than Billy, he must have been born in 1877.

[11] Author's interview with Joan Prowd, May 21, 1993.

[12] Author's interview with Joan Prowd, September 23, 1992.

[13] Letter from Martha Hart, in Joan Prowd's collection of family memorabilia.

[14] Ibid.

[15] Joan Prowd, "The Early Days," p. 3, unpublished manuscript.

[16] Author's interview with Joan Prowd, May 14, 1993.

[17] Author's interview with Joan Prowd, September 23, 1992.

Chapter 2

[1] In conversation with the author, August 27, 1986.

[2] Previous writings on Joyce Wieland give her birth year as 1931. However, according to her early diaries, her baptismal and medical records and her driver's licence, she was born in 1930. Also, Joan, Joyce's sister, verified that Joyce was born on June 30, 1930. That this error occurred and was repeated early in Joyce's career resulted in some discrepancies in documentation.

[3] *The Canadian Encyclopedia*, Volume II (Edmonton: Hurtig Publishers, 1985), p. 771.

[4] Statistics Canada, *Toronto 150: Portrait of a Changing City* (Ottawa: Statistics Canada Catalogue No. 11-X-523E, 1984) p. 15; and G.P. det. Glazebrook, *The Story of Toronto* (Toronto: University of Toronto Press), 1971.

[5] Ibid.

[6] H. Blair Neatby, *The Politics of Chaos* (Toronto: Gage Publishing Limited, 1972), p. 25.

[7] Alison Prentice, et al., *Canadian Women: A History* (Toronto: Harcourt Brace Jovanovich Canada, 1988), p. 216.

[8] Ibid.

[9] See Atwood's "Afterword" in *The Journals of Susanna Moodie* (Toronto: Oxford University Press, 1970), p. 62.

[10] Author's interview with Joan Prowd, September 23, 1992.

[11] 1992-018/003-117.

[12] Joan Prowd, "The Early Days," an unpublished manuscript, pp. 8, 9.

[13] Joyce once described this dream to Munro Ferguson, musing on whether this might have been an out-of-body experience. Author's interview with Ferguson, July 26, 1997.

[14] 1992-018/003-117.

[15] Joan Prowd, "The Early Days," unpublished manuscript, p. 18.

[16] Author's interview with Joyce Wieland, August 27, 1986.

[17] Author's interview with Joan Prowd, September 23, 1992.

[18] Unpublished document, "Kindergarten Course of Study: Toronto Public Schools" September 3, 1935, Toronto Board of Education Archives.

[19] Ibid.

[20] Author's interview with Joyce Wieland, August 27, 1986.

[21] Author's interview with Dr. John Rennie, December 7, 1999.

[22] James King, *The Life of Margaret Laurence* (Toronto: Alfred A. Knopf Canada, 1997), p. 17.

[23] Adele Freedman, "Roughing It with a Brush," in *Toronto*, April 1987, p. 78.

[24] Might's Directories, 1941, Toronto City Archives.

[25] Might's Directories, 1942, Toronto City Archives.

[26] Author's interview with Joyce Wieland, August 27, 1986.

[27] A 1926 edition of the Ontario Public School History of Canada includes a C.W. Jefferys drawing of a frightened Laura Secord about to cross a stream on a log before she enters a dense forest on the other side.

[28] Might's Directories, 1942-1946, Toronto City Archives. After the 1942 entry recording her Shirley Street address, Joan's name disappears entirely from the directory, though several of the Kerr women continue to be listed at the Sylvan Avenue address until 1946.

[29] 1990-014/002-20.

[30] 1990-014/002-20.

[31] Ibid.

[32] This painting was identified in a November 4, 1998, note to the author from Charles Hill, Curator of Canadian Art at the National Gallery of Canada.

[33] Honora M. Cochrane, ed., *Centennial Story* (Toronto: Thomas Nelson & Sons (Canada) Limited, 1950), p. 217.

[34] 1993-009/007-78.

[35] Author's interview with Doris McCarthy, November 29, 1993.

[36] By that time, guidance was part of the grade-nine curriculum in the Toronto school system.

[37] Author's telephone interview with David Etherington, March 3, 2000.

[38] Author's interview with Barbara King Graham, March 7, 2000.

[39] 1993-009/009-104.

[40] David Etherington pointed out that Joyce would likely have needed an address within the City of Toronto to attend Central Tech. Because Sammon Avenue was in East York, she would have used Joan's address on Jones Avenue, which was where Etherington thought she lived. However, Barbara King Graham feels sure that Joyce lived with her brother's family during the three years they knew each other in high school.

[41] Author's interview with Barbara King Graham, August 11, 1997.

[42] Ellen Bot, "Artist has evolved from a 'bohemian bargain hunter,'" *The Toronto Star*, September 28, 1989.

[43] Author's interview with Barbara King Graham, March 7, 2000.

[44] Author's interview with Joyce Wieland, August 26, 1986.

[45] Author's interview with Melita Stewart Waterman and Victor Waterman, June 10, 1996.

[46] Author's interview with Joyce Wieland, September 10, 1986.

[47] Kay Armatage, *Artist on Fire*, film, 1987.

[48] Author's interview with Doris McCarthy, November 29, 1993.

Chapter 3

[1] Quoted in Elizabeth Bronfen, "The knotted subject: hysteria, Irma and Cindy Sherman" in Griselda Pollock, ed., *Generations and Geographies in the Visual Arts* (London and New York: Routledge, 1996), p. 43.

2 Alison Prentice, et al., *Canadian Women: A History* (Toronto: Harcourt Brace Jovanovich, 1998), pp. 304, 305.

[3] Beth Light and Ruth Roach Pierson, eds., *No Easy Road: Women in Canada 1920s to 1960s* (Toronto: New Hogtown Press, 1990), p. 65.

[4] Ibid, p. 69.

[5] Doug Owram, *Born at the Right Time: A History of the Baby Boom Generation* (Toronto: University of Toronto Press, 1997), p. 12.

[6] Ellen Stafford, *Always & After — A Memoir* (Toronto: Penguin Books, 1999).

[7] 1990-014/004-53.

[8] Ibid.

[9] *Women, Art, and Society* (London: Thames and Hudson, 1996), p. 230.

[10] Anne Higonnet, *Berthe Morisot* (Berkeley: University of California Press, 1995), p. 51.

[11] 1990-014/004-53.

[12] Author's interview with Anna Karch, May 30, 1996.

[13] 1990-014/004-53.

[14] Ibid.

[15] 1990-014/004-53.

[16] Ibid.

[17] Author's interview with Joyce Wieland, August 26, 1986.

[18] Doris Anderson, *Rebel Daughter* (Toronto: Key Porter Books, 1996), p. 95.

[19] Author's telephone interview with Les Parkes, January 8, 1999.

[20] 1990-014/004-53.

[21] Ibid.

[22] Ibid.

[23] 1993-037/002-04. Phyllis was not traceable since the Karches did not remember her last name, and none of Joyce's friends from that time knew Phyllis. Joyce found her studio through her friend Mel, with whom she had shared a room at the Stewarts. Mel married Victor Waterman, who had a studio at 700 Bathurst Street.

[24] Author's interview with Sheila McCusker, July 26, 1995.

[25] Author's interview with Sara Bowser, June 5, 1995.

[26] Author's interview with Sheila McCusker, July 26, 1995.

[27] Author's interview with Chris Yaneff, April 25, 1996.

[28] Author's interview with Anne Dydich Robbins, May 2, 1996.

[29] Ibid.

[30] Author's interview with Barbara King Graham, August 11, 1997.

[31] 1990-014/004-530.

[32] Author's interview with Sheila McCusker, July 26, 1995.

[33] 1993-009/004-028.

[34] 1990-014/004-53.

[35] 1993-009/004-028, letter from Joyce to Bryan Barney, February 12, 1952.

[36] 1990-014/004-53.

[37] Ibid.

[38] Ibid.

[39] Ibid.

[40] Ibid.

[41] Harold Town, *Albert Franck: His Life, Times and Work* (Toronto: McClelland & Stewart Limited, 1974), p. 18.

[42] Author's interview with Bryan Barney and Sara Bowser, February 21, 1996.

[43] Author's interview with Dr. John Rennie, December 7, 1999.

[44] Author's interview with Bryan Barney, February 21, 1996.

[45] Jill Ker Conway, *When Memory Speaks* (New York: Alfred A. Knopf, 1998), p. 176.

[46] 1993-009/004-028, letter from Joyce to Bryan Barney, dated September 3, 1953.

[47] Ibid. Undated letter.

[48] Ibid.

[49] 1988-003/001-003.

[50] Ibid.

[51] 1990-014/004-53.

[52] 1994-004/001-05.

[53] 1993-009/004-028, letter to Bryan Barney marked "date unknown." In a letter to Joan, Joyce also mentions seeing *Die Fledermaus* and *The Magic Flute*.

[54] 1988-003/001-003.

[55] Ibid.

[56] Author's interview with Jim MacKay, February 24, 1999.

[57] 1990-014/004-53.

[58] Author's interview with Bryan Barney, February 21, 1996.

[59] 1990-014/004-53.

[60] Lauren Rabinovitz, "An Interview with Joyce Wieland" in *Afterimage* (Volume 8, No. 10, May 1981), p. 1.

[61] Ben Viccari, "Belfast on the Don," *Performing Arts* (Vol. 32, No. 1, October 1998), p. 38.

[62] 1990-014/004-53.

[63] Ibid.

[64] Author's interview with Donna Montague, October 18, 1995.

[65] Author's interview with Bryan Barney, February 21, 1996.

[66] Author's interview with Sara Bowser, February 21, 1996.

[67] Author's interview with Bryan Barney, February 21, 1996.

[68] 1988-003/001-03.

[69] Colette, *The Vagabond* (London: Secker and Warburg, 1954), p. 13.

[70] Michele Sarde, *Colette* (London: Michael Joseph, 1978), p. 405.

Chapter 4

[1] In *The Anatomy of Freedom* (Garden City, New York: Doubleday, 1984), p. 275.

[2] 1990-014/004-53.

[3] The street directories in Toronto's Archives for 1955 list Hattin Funeral Service at 525 Sherbourne in 1955. However, an envelope postmarked May 29, 1955, in the Joyce Wieland Fonds (1988-003/001-003) is addressed to her at 525 Sherbourne, which means she was living there by then.

[4] Author's interview with Donna Montague, May 31, 1995.

[5] Author's telephone interview with Graham Coughtry, May ll, 1997.

[6] Author's interview with Michael Snow, June 5, 1995.

[7] This book was published in Europe in 1956. According to Marie Fleming in *Joyce Wieland* (Toronto: Key Porter/Art Gallery of Ontario, 1987, p. 182, fn.7), Joyce bought her own copy in 1959. As it turned out, these drawings had a major impact on Joyce's work at that time.

[8] Ibid. and Art Gallery of Ontario Archives, Michael Snow Fonds, Box 2, File 4.

[9] Author's interview with Sara Bowser, June 5, 1995.

[10] Author's interview with Donna Montague, July 5, 1995.

[11] Author's interview with Michael Snow, April 16, 1997.

[12] Author's interview with Vivienne Muhling, March 9, 1999.

[13] 1993-009/009-104.

[14] 1990-014/004-53.

[15] Ibid.

[16] Author's interview with Jo Haines, November 3, 1997.

[17] 1990-014/004-53.

[18] Ibid.

[19] Author's telephone interview with Graham Coughtry, May 11, 1997.

[20] 1990-014/004-53.

[21] Ibid.

[22] Anne Higonnet, *Berthe Morisot* (Berkeley: University of California Press, 1995), p. 204.

[23] Gillian E. Hanscombe, *The Art of Life: Dorothy Richardson and the Development of Feminist Consciousness* (Athens, Ohio: Ohio University Press, 1982), fn. 25, p. 38.

[24] Author's interview with Anne Robbins, May 2, 1996.

[25] Author's interview with Barbara King Graham, August 11, 1997.

[26] 1992-018/003-117.

[27] 1993-009/008-114.

[28] 1993-009/008-114. Joyce's journal from her 1956 trip to France does not give Lydie's last name.

[29] Ibid.

[30] 1993-009/008-114.

[31] Ibid.

[32] Letter dated June 3, 1955, in 1988-003/001-005.

[33] Ibid.

[34] Author's interview with Joyce Wieland, August 27, 1986.

[35] Author's interview with Sara Bowser, May 18, 1995.

[36] Author's interview with Sara Bowser, June 5, 1995.

[37] Dennis Burton, letter to the author, June 7, 1997.

[38] Author's interview with Robert Hedrick, April 6, 1999.

[39] Author's interview with Michael Snow, June 5, 1995.

[40] Art Gallery of Ontario Archives, Michael Snow Fonds, Box 13, File #1.

[41] Author's interview with Michael Snow, June 5, 1995.

[42] 1994-004/001-012.

[43] Art Gallery of Ontario Archives, Michael Snow Fonds Box 13, File #6.

[44] Author's interview with Gordon Rayner, April 21, 1997.

[45] Author's telephone interview with Sylvia Fogarty, January 23, 1998.

[46] Jim MacKay still has Joyce's invoices for art work for Minute Maid and Campbell Soup ads. Joyce's casual nature is evident in these invoices, written on scraps of paper in pencil. One was written on the back of a card printed by the "Independent Order of Foresters."

[47] Author's interview with Jim MacKay, February 24, 1999.

[48] Author's interview with Michael Snow, April 13, 1999.

[49] Dennis Reid, "Remembering Walking Woman," in *Visual Art, The Michael Snow Project* (Toronto: The Art Gallery of Ontario/The Power Plant, 1994) p. 23.

[50] Author's telephone interview with Sylvia Fogarty, January 23, 1998.

[51] Letter from Sylvia Fogarty to the author, March 12, 1998.

[52] Letter to the author from Sylvia Fogarty, March 12, 1998; author's telephone interview with Sylvia Fogarty, January 23 and 27, 1999.

[53] Author's interview with Warren Collins, July 26, 1995.

[54] Author's telephone interview with Sylvia Fogarty, January 27, 1999.

[55] Author's telephone interview with Sylvia Fogarty, January 23, 1999. Dorothy Cameron (author's interview, June 26, 1995), who had her own gallery from 1959 to 1965, and Elizabeth Kilbourn, who knew Joyce well during that time, also described Joyce as being like Giulietta Masina. Kilbourn said, "It was that kind of feminine style — I don't know how to explain it — if you know Colette and Giulietta Masina." (Author's interview, September 12, 1995).

[56] Robert Fulford, "Turning Point," *Canadian Art* (Vol. 10, No. 3), Fall 1993.

[57] Barrie Hale and Dennis Reid, *Toronto Painting: 1953-1965*, (Ottawa: National Gallery of Canada, 1972), exhibition catalogue, p. 5.

[58] Author's interview with Michael Snow, June 5, 1995.

[59] Harold Town, *Albert Franck: His Life and Times and Work* (Toronto: McClelland & Stewart Limited, 1974), p. 19.

[60] Author's interview with Av Isaacs, June 29, 1995.

[61] "Painters Laugh It Up," *Toronto Daily Star*, February 23, 1959.

[62] Author's interview with Elizabeth Kilbourn, September 12, 1995.

[63] 1990-014/004-20.

[64] Jan Allen, Joyce Wieland Twilit Record of Romantic Love, (Kingston, Ontario: Agnes Etherington Art Centre, Queen's University, 1995), exhibition catalogue, p. 7.

[65] Joyce gave this drawing to Betty Ferguson years later, and it is now in Ferguson's collection.

[66] Author's interview with Joyce Wieland, August 20, 1986. The tower visible through the window in the upper left corner of the painting is the square bell tower of St. Paul's church on Queen Street at Power Street, just east of Parliament. Joyce was working at a printing place on Sherbourne at the time and could see the tower from there. In later years, she could see the other side of the tower from her house on Queen Street.

[67] Gillian E. Hanscombe, *The Art of Life: Dorothy Richardson and the Development of Feminist Consciousness* (Athens, Ohio: Ohio University Press, 1982), p. 19.

[68] Author's telephone interview with Sylvia Fogarty, January 23, 1999. Jacqueline Park

expressed the same point of view in the author's interview with her on July 20, 1998. The term "Mike's shadow" was used by Ray Jessel (written communication, April 27, 1999) and Marjorie Harris (interview with the author, September 13, 1999).

[69] Author's interview with Robert Fulford, January 20, 2000.

[70] Apparently this concept of Michael Snow continued, given the media hype over his 1994 Toronto exhibition in a number of venues in the city, called "The Michael Snow Project."

[71] See Christine Battersby, *Gender and Genius: Towards a Feminist Aesthetics* (Bloomington/Indianapolis: Indiana University Press, 1989) for a discussion of the concept of genius in our culture, a term that comes from the Latin, meaning being handed down to the male child. Thus a woman cannot be a genius.

[72] *Three Artists (Three Women)* (Berkeley and Los Angeles: University of California Press, 1996), p. 285.

[73] Author's interview with Robert Fulford, January 20, 2000.

[74] Author's interview with Marjorie Harris, September 13, 1999.

[75] Author's telephone interview with Ross Mendes, January 26, 1999.

[76] According to the author's conversation with Irene F. Whittome (November 25, 1997), Joyce talked about this issue from time to time.

[77] Anne Middleton Wagner, *Three Artists (Three Women)*, (Berkeley, California: University of California Press, 1998), p. 11, 12. For comments on the complexity of marriage between artists, see also Elaine Showalter's "Towards a Feminist Poetics" in *Women Writing and Writing about Women* (London: Croom Helm, 1979), p. 30.

[78] Elizabeth Kilbourn, "Pianist — painter Showing Works at Westdale," *Hamilton Spectator*, November 28, 1959.

[79] Author's interview with Donna Montague, October 18, 1995.

[80] 1993-009/004-28. Perhaps an example of Joyce's "amateur journalism" was a sarcastic letter in *Canadian Art* (May-June 1961): "Dear Sir, I did not like the January issue of Canadian Art. There is too much in it about artists. Give us more issues on cars and typography. Yours truly, Joyce Wieland" (1992-018/003-113).

[81] Author's interview with Dorothy Cameron, June 26, 1995.

[82] Ibid. Cameron regretted that she sold this piece when Joyce left her gallery. She had limited funds and had a policy of buying for herself works of the artists she showed, so at the time she felt this one by Joyce had to go, and later regretted it.

[83] Author's interview with Av Isaacs, June 29, 1995.

[84] Marie Fleming, "Joyce Wieland: A Perspective," in *Joyce Wieland* (Toronto: Art Gallery of Ontario and Key Porter Books, 1987), p. 42.

[85] Emil Ludwig, *Napoleon* (Garden City, New York: Garden City Publishing Co., 1926), p. 485.

[86] *evidence*, Toronto, n.d.

[87] Lauren Rabinovitz, "An Interview with Joyce Wieland," *Afterimage* (Vol. 8, No. 10) May 1981, p. 2.

[88] The Dada show ran from December 21, 1961, until January 20, 1962.

[89] The invitation addressed the public: Dear Gallery Goer, Because of the unusual content of our next exhibition we have been unable to think of a suitable title for it. So you may order the title of your choice after seeing our show by printing it on a slip of paper and mailing it to us in the inclosed [sic] envelope. You may order in any of the following sizes large, med, small. (Thanks to Av Isaacs for a copy of the invitation.)

[90] Michel Sanouillet, "The Sign of Dada," *Canadian Art* (19:2 1962), p. 111.

[91] January 31-February 20, 1962, at the Isaacs Gallery.

[92] Author's interview with Joyce Wieland, August 27, 1986.

[93] Author's interview with Av Isaacs, August 19, 1986.

[94] Doug Richardson, "Snow in the Gallery," *The Varsity*, October 19, 1962.

Chapter 5

[1] In *The Canadian Forum*, May/June, 1974.

[2] Bruce Jenkins and Susan Krane, *Hollis Frampton Recollections: Recreations* (Cambridge, Massachusetts: MIT Press, 1984) pp. 107 ff.

[3] Audio tape #78, 1971, a recorded conversation between Joyce Wieland and Hollis Frampton, Cinémathèque Québécois archives in Boucherville, Quebec. The archive in Boucherville houses many of Joyce's film fragments and a number of audio tapes made in the sixties and seventies, mostly conversations, but a few appear to be Joyce practising speeches, or recording her ideas on various topics on tape.

[4] Author's telephone interview with Jamie Erfurdt, January 11, 2000.

[5] Kay Armatage, "The Feminine Body: Joyce Wieland's Water Sark," in Pierre Veronneau, Michael Dorland and Seth Feldman, eds., *Dialogue: Canadian and Quebec Cinema* (Montreal: Media Texte Publications Inc., 1987), p. 293.

[6] Jeanette Winterson, *Art Objects: Essays on Ecstasy and Effrontery* (New York: Random House, 1995), p. 142.

[7] The cut-out letters also give the sound credits: Carla Bley, Ray Jessel, Mike Mantler.

[8] Audio Tape #78, 1971, Joyce Wieland Holdings, Cinémathèque Québécois, Boucherville, Quebec.

[9] Lauren Rabinovitz, Points of Resistance (Chicago: Chicago University Press, 1991), p. 151.

[10] Author's interview with Michael Snow, June 5, 1995.

[11] It must have been around this time that Joyce wrote a letter to Duchamp, whether or not she mailed it. "Dear Mister Duchamp Enclosed you will find a picture of myself as I really am. Thank you for the lively pictures of you. We find they are exactly what we need for our delightful bourgeois avant garde little magazine. If you ever make a little magazine ever again please feel free to use my picture." She went on to say that the English Canadian painters are good. "It may be the nordic clime which invigorates and tortures them." 1993-009/008-120.

[12] Author's conversation with Betty Ferguson, September 3, 1986.

[13] Author's telephone conversation with Betty Ferguson, June 6, 2000. The results of the tubal insufflation are not included with Joyce's medical papers in 1990-084/004-57 in the archives at York University.

[14] Author's interviews with Michael Snow, February 21, 1996, and April 13, 1999.

[15] Author's interview with Jo Haines and Paul Haines, November 3, 1997.

[16] Author's interview with Munro Ferguson, July 26, 1997.

[17] 1993-009/009-104, Joyce's typed notes.

[18] Author's interview with Jacqueline Park, July 20, 1998.

[19] Letter to the author from Jo Haines, August 16, 1997.

[20] Author's interview with Rose Richardson, March 22, 1999.

[21] Author's interview with Michael Snow, April 13, 1999.

[22] Letter to the author from Jo Haines, August 16, 1997.

[23] Author's interview with Donna Montague, May 31, 1995.

[24] 1990-014/002-24.

[25] Author's interview with Jo Haines and Paul Haines, November 3, 1997.

[26] Author's telephone conversation with Jo Haines, June 14, 2000.

[27] Author's telephone conversation with Betty Ferguson, June 14, 2000.

[28] Author's interview with Michael Snow, April 13, 1999.

[29] Joyce Wieland A Decade of Painting, exhibition catalogue, Concordia Art Gallery, Montreal, 1985, p. 5.

[30] Author's interview with Les Lawrence, October 7, 1998.

[31] Art Gallery of Ontario Archives, Michael Snow Fonds, Box 2, File 4; and author's interview with Michael Snow, February 21, 1996.

[32] Helen Parmelee, "Joyce is a Zen Cook", *Toronto Telegram*, November 23, 1963.

[33] Norma Broude and Mary D. Garrard, eds., *The Power of Feminist Art: The American Movement of the 1970s, History and Impact* (New York: Harry N. Abrams, Inc., Publishers, 1994), p. 16.

[34] Author's interview with Jacqueline Park, July 20, 1998.

[35] Around the time that Joyce made *Water Sark*, women in the anti-Vietnam War circles and in the civil rights movement became discontent with being shunted aside. In November 1967 the first Women's Liberation meeting was held in New York. See Susan Brownmiller's *In Our Time: Memoir of a Revolution* (New York: The Dial Press, 1999) for a record of the women's movement at that time.

[36] *Old Mistresses: Women, Art and Ideology* (London: Pandora Press, 1989), p. 78.

[37] Norma Broude and Mary D. Garrard, *The Power of Feminist Art: The American Movement of the 1970s, History and Impact* (New York: Harry N. Abrams, Inc, Publishers, 1994), p. 237.

[38] Rozsika Parker, *The Subversive Stitch: Embroidery and the making of the feminine* (New York: Routledge, 1989), p. 215.

[39] Author's interview with Joyce Wieland, August 14, 1986.

[40] Author's interview with Allison McComb, Nadine Schwartz and Lois Taylor, August 18, 1994.

[41] Lauren Rabinovitz, "An Interview with Joyce Wieland," *Afterimage* (Vol. 8, No. 10, May 1981) p. 5.

[42] 1993-009/009-104, Joyce's typed notes.

[43] Lee Hall, *Elaine and Bill: Portrait of a Marriage* (New York: HarperCollins, 1993), p. 93.

[44] Author's interview with Eugene Lion, June 11, 1998.

[45] Kathleen Walker, "The artist as patriot," *The Citizen*, Ottawa, October 23, 1976, p. 30.

[46] Author's interview with Michael Snow, February 21, 1996.

[47] Author's interview with Michael Snow, April 13, 1999.

[48] Written communication from Ellen Rosenfeld to the author, May 1999.

[49] Letter to the author from Sara Jane Arnold, April 20, 1999.

[50] Author's telephone interview with Florence and Ken Jacobs, April 1, 1999.

[51] Ibid. and 1999-044/003-002.

[52] Ibid.

[53] Ibid.

[54] Author's interview with Michael Snow, February 21, 1996.

[55] Author's interview with Eugene Lion, June 11, 1998.

[56] Joyce Wieland fonds 1990-014/004, File 53.

[57] Ray Jessel, "Joyce Wieland Remembered," unpublished memoir of Joyce Wieland written for the author, April 1999.

[58] 1993-009/010-116.

[59] Author's interview with Michael Snow, April 13, 1999.

[60] The seven children are, in order of age: David, Michael, Lonnie, Cindy, Glenn, Steven, Paul.

[61] Author's interview with David Wieland, June 26, 1996.

[62] Author's interview with Glenn Wieland, May 20, 1996.

[63] Ibid.

[64] Author's interview with Joyce Wieland, August 1986.

[65] Jonas Mekas, "Movie Journal," in *the village VOICE*, April 3, 1969.

[66] "Debbie Magidson and Judy Wright Interview Joyce Wieland," in *The Canadian Forum*, May-June, 1974.

Chapter 6

[1] In *By a Lady* (Toronto: Penguin, 1992), p. 151.

[2] Marilyn Beker, "Expanded Cinema Rocks Gallery," *The Globe and Mail*, July 8, 1967.

[3] This commission came about at the urging of prominent women, including Laura Sabia, Judy LaMarsh, the only female cabinet minister, and Doris Anderson of *Chatelaine* magazine. A remarkable number of women — 11,000 — replied to a three -hour questionnaire *Chatelaine* published. The summarized results were presented in a brief to the Royal Commission. See Doris Anderson's *Rebel Daughter: An Autobiography* (Toronto: Key Porter Books, 1996), p. 158.

[4] Author's telephone conversation with Diane Rotstein, May 17, 1999.

[5] Harry Malcolmson, *The Telegram*, March 25, 1967, p. 16.

[6] The new Canadian flag, featuring our maple leaf, was chosen in Parliament on December 15, 1964, after a six-month debate. The government invoked closure to get the business settled.

[7] The information here about *Bill's Hat* comes from the undated audio tape #70, Wendy Michener interviewing Joyce Wieland, housed at the Cinémathèque Québécois archives in Boucherville, Quebec.

[8] Marilyn Beker, "Expanded Cinema Rocks Gallery," *The Globe and Mail*, July 8, 1967.

[9] Stephen Clarkson and Christina McCall, *Trudeau and Our Times*, Volume 1 (Toronto: McClelland & Stewart, 1990), p. 107.

[10] Joyce Wieland in *A Film about Joyce Wieland* by Judy Steed, 1972.

[11] In the 1987 retrospective at the Art Gallery of Ontario, the title of this piece was given as *The Life and Death of the American City*.

[12] Audio Tape #78, Hollis Frampton and Joyce Wieland conversation, Archives of Cinémathèque Québécois, Boucherville Quebec.

[13] Ibid.

[14] Steven Clarkson and Christina McCall, *Trudeau and Our Times*, Volume 1, *The Magnificent Obsession* (Toronto: McClelland & Stewart, 1990), p. 196.

[15] Press release May 10, 1968, Canadians Abroad for Trudeau, and author's interview with Betty Ferguson, October 11, 1994.

[16] Author's telephone interview with Ray Jessel, May 14, 1999. Used by permission.

[17] Author's interview with Rose Richardson, March 22, 1999.

[18] Joyce also wanted to commission a hooked piece that was to be called "True Patriot Love," but she had no way of financing this work (1993-009/009-104).

[19] The source for quotes and other material in this section about *Reason over Passion* is a taped conversation of Joyce Wieland and Hollis Frampton.

[20] Notes about work on Joyce's films in 1993-009/009-104. *Reason over Passion* premiered in Canada in 1969 at the National Arts Centre in Ottawa, was shown at Jonas Mekas's Christmas Festival in 1969, and later at the Museum of Modern Art in New York.

[21] Ibid.

[22] In 1934, Riefenstahl made the film *Triumph of the Will* about that year's session of the Nazi Party Congress and the mass rallies of thousands of people. Riefenstahl was not a Nazi and the Nazi propagandists resented that Hitler appointed her to make this film.

[23] Audio tape #78, 1971, Cinémathèque Québécois archives, Boucherville, Quebec.

[24] Kay Armatage, "Joyce Wieland, Feminist Documentary, and the Body of the Work," in *Canadian Journal of Political and Social Theory* (Vol. XIII, no. 1-2, 1989), p. 93.

[25] Ibid.

[26] Author's interview with Eugene Lion, June ll, 1998.

[27] Author's telephone interview with Jonas Mekas, May 29, 1999.

[28] Susan Crean, "Notes from the Language of Emotion: A conversation with Joyce Wieland," in *Canadian Art* (Spring 1987), p. 65; and Robert Everett-Green, "Bold Strokes" in *Saturday Night* (May 1987), p. 59.

[29] Geoffrey James, "The Protean Vision of Joyce Wieland" in *Maclean's* (April 27, 1987), p. 53.

[30] Barry Hale, "Canadian artists in N.Y. bravely waving our flag," in *Toronto Daily Star*, March 7, 1970.

[31] Author's interview with Betty Ferguson, October 11, 1994.

[32] Barrie Hale, "Canadian artists in N.Y. bravely waving our flag," *Toronto Daily Star*, March 7, 1970.

[33] Author's interview with Joyce Wieland, August 14, 1986.

[34] Robert Everett-Green, "Bold Strokes," in *Saturday Night* (May 1987), p. 59.

[35] Author's interview with Pierre Théberge, November 26, 1997.

[36] Joyce Zemans at the WARC/WCA International Conference, February 25, 1998.

[37] Author's interview with Pierre Théberge, November 26, 1997.

[38] Author's interview with Joyce Wieland, August 14, 1986. Very few of these catalogues are still available.

[39] Kay Kritzwiser, "A woman's work in the National Gallery," *The Globe and Mail*, February 19, 1971.

[40] Ibid.

[41] Audio Tape #78, Cinémathèque Québécois in Boucherville, Quebec, Hollis Frampton in conversation with Joyce Wieland.

[42] Author's interview with Joyce Wieland, August 14, 1986.

[43] Letter from D.W. Pettit, National Capital Commission to Pierre Théberge, April 6, 1971,

in National Gallery of Canada Archives.

[44] Another translation, the one Joyce gives in Audio Tape #37 at the Cinémathèque Québécois, which seems to be her rehearsal of a speech she might have been asked to give in connection with her exhibition, is somewhat different: "The great sea has set me adrift/It moves me as a weed in the great river/The earth and the great weather have moved me/Have carried me away/Have moved my inward parts with joy."

[45] Roszika Parker, *The Subversive Stitch: Embroidery and the Making of the Feminine* (New York: Routledge, 1989), pp. 191, 215.

[46] Author's interview with Michael Pantazzi, March 24, 1999.

[47] Three videos of preparatory work for *True Patriot Love* are housed in the National Gallery of Canada Archives, labelled "Installation — Ducks/Arctic Day," "Studio 1" and "Studio 2."

[48] Printed interview folded inside the back cover of Joyce Wieland, *True Patriot Love* (Ottawa: National Gallery of Canada, 1971).

[49] Ibid.

[50] Anne Wordsworth, "An Interview with Joyce Wieland," *Descant Magazine* (Spring/Summer 1974), p. 110.

[51] "Afterword" in *The Journals of Susanna Moodie* (Toronto: Oxford University Press, 1970), p. 62.

[52] Author's interview with Michael Snow, September 11, 1997.

[53] Author's interview with Eugene Lion, June 11, 1998.

[54] George Kuchar and Mike Kuchar, *Reflections from a Cinematic Cesspool* (Berkeley, California: Zanja Press, 1997), p. 60.

[55] "Movie Journal," June 27, 1968.

[56] Lauren Rabinovitz, "The Films of Joyce Wieland," in *Joyce Wieland* (Toronto: Art Gallery of Ontario and Key Porter Books, 1987), fn. 15, p. 189.

[57] Author's telephone interview with Jonas Mekas, May 29, 1999.

[58] Joyce Wieland in *Form and Structure in Recent Film*, Dennis Wheeler, ed. (Vancouver: Vancouver Art Gallery,), p. 91.

[59] The selection committee was James Broughton, Ken Kelman, Peter Kubelka, Jonas Mekas, P. Adams Sitney.

[60] "Debbie Magidson and Judy Wright Interview Joyce Wieland," *The Canadian Forum*, May-June, 1974, p. 61.

[61] Ibid.

[62] Ibid.

[63] Kay Armatage, *Artist on Fire*, film, 1987.

[64] Author's interview with Michael Snow, April 13, 1999.

Chapter 7

[1] Quoted in *The Sunday Star*, April 27, 1980.

[2] Marion Fowler, *The Embroidered Tent*, (Toronto: Anansi Press, 1982), p. 169.

[3] Interview in *Criteria* (Vol. 2, #1, February 1976), p. 17. Around this time, New York artist Robert Frank and painter June Leaf, whom Joyce admired, also bought land near Mabou, Nova Scotia. Joyce and Michael bought 200 acres of wild Cape Breton land in November 1970 for $3,500. They would sell it for $20,000 five years later, when they held a $10,000 mortgage for the new owners, so for some time they made nearly $200 a month on a property, in addition to its increase in value. (Art Gallery of Ontario Archives, Michael Snow Fonds, Box 2, File 2 and Box 2, File 5).

[4] Author's interview with Michael Snow, April 16, 1997.

[5] Jean MacDonald et. al., *Toronto Women Changing Faces 1900-2000* (Toronto: eastend books, 1997), p. 105.

[6] *Rebel Daughter* (Toronto: Key Porter Books, 1996), p. 175.

[7] Author's interview with Marjorie Harris, September 13, 1999.

[8] Susan Crean, "Two Decades of Cultural Nationalism and the Arts in Canada," in *Fuse Magazine* (Vol. 19, No. 3, Spring 1996), p. 14.

[9] The name was a take-off on the 1948 Refus Global of the Quebec artists.

[10] Susan M. Crean, "Notes from the Language of Emotion: A conversation with Joyce Wieland," in *Canadian Art*, Spring 1987, p. 65.

[11] Susan M. Crean, "The Heart of the Matter: The Cultural Legacy of CAR," in *The Power of Association: Twenty Years of Canadian Artists' Representation* (Toronto & Ottawa: CARO & CARFAC, 1989), p. 10.

[12] "Protesters at Art Gallery put themselves in chains," *The Toronto Star*, July 5, 1972. Legend has it that Joyce also chained herself to office furniture at the AGO, but that is not the case.

[13] Author's interview with Michael Pantazzi, March 24, 1999.

[14] Author's interview with Joan Murray, September 23, 1999.

[15] Author's interview with Judy Steed, April 21, 1998.

[16] Pierre Vallières, *White Niggers of America* [English translation] (Toronto: McClelland & Stewart, 1971), p. 204.

[17] Ibid., p. 205.

[18] Unpublished statement by Joyce Wieland, "Pierre Vallières Notes from the Filmmmaker," Filmmakers Distribution Centre archives.

[19] 1994-004/003-02.

[20] Lauren Rabinovitz, "An Interview with Joyce Wieland," in *Afterimage* (Volume 8, Number 10, May 1931), p. 8.

[21] Author's interview with Joyce Wieland, August 14, 1986. The date of 1975, given in the section on commissions in Joyce Wieland, her Art Gallery of Ontario retrospective catalogue, is incorrect.

[22] The account of Gorky's childhood, *The Childhood of Maxim Gorky*, directed by Mark Donskoi, is the most famous of the three films. Gorky lived with his grandparents after his parents' death. His grandfather was a cruel man, so Gorky left home at age twelve and went from job to job.

[23] Interview with Joyce Wieland, by Brian Charent, Peter Harcourt and Margo Blackell in *Motion* (Volume 5, No. 2, 1976), p. 32.

[24] Charent, Harcourt and Blackell, p. 32.

[25] Joyce recounted this early history of Michael Snow's parents in a taped interview (copyright by Janis Crystal Lipzin) in March 1978 with Janis Crystal Lipzin and Lisa Lewis at Antioch College, Yellow Springs, Ohio. My thanks to Lipzin for sending me this tape.

[26] Telephone conversation with Denyse Rynard, February 10, 2000.

[27] (Don Mills, Ont.: General Publishing) p. 65.

[28] According to Crean, the Quebec wing of the NFB fostered a new generation of filmmakers and French Canada led the way with producing feature films. The effect of CFDC support is revealed in that by 1974, the sales of Canadian films at France's Cannes Film Festival were eight times higher than they had been in 1973.

[29] Author's interview with Sara Bowser, August 14, 1996.

[30] Judy's brother, Ian Ewing, was hired, but left in August. Deanne Judson was hired in August and left in November.

[31] Doug Fetherling, "Joyce Wieland in Movieland," in *Canadian Weekly*, January 24, 1976, p. 12. The sequence of events in this section on making *The Far Shore* is drawn from this article.

[32] According to Kay Armatage ("Joyce Wieland, Feminist Documentary, and the Body of the Work," in *Canadian Journal of Political and Social Theory*, Volume XIII, no. 1-2 1989) the other two were Nell Shipman (*Back to God's Country*, 1919) and Sylvia Spring (*Madeleine Is ...*, 1969).

[33] Letter from Bernard H. Solomon & Associates to Cemp Investments, and letter from Joyce Wieland to Phyllis Lambert, March 20, 1975, in Phyllis Lambert personal archives, Canadian Centre for Architecture, File # C6/14.1.

[34] Ibid.

[35] Robert Martin, *The Globe and Mail*, August 7, 1976.

[36] Author's telephone interview with Boris Zerafa, April 11, 1999.

[37] Author's interview with Robert Fulford, January 20, 2000.

[38] Author's interview with Céline Lomez, June 10, 1998.

[39] Author's interview with Frank Moore, April 13, 1999.

[40] Author's interview with Céline Lomez, July 29, 1998.

[41] Despite repeated efforts, I was unable to contact Lawrence Benedict and Sean McCann.

[42] Author's telephone interview with Richard Leiterman, May 1, 1999.

[43] According to a letter dated May 23, 1974, Joyce paid Pringle $3000 for composing the music (1999-044/001-36).

[44] Author's interview with Frank Moore, April 13, 1999.

[45] Author's telephone interview with Richard Leiterman, May 1, 1999.

[46] Robert Martin, "Canada's mini-epic film costing 6 years, $450,000," in *The Globe and Mail*, August 7, 1976.

[47] *The Globe and Mail*, July 6, 1974.

[48] Author's interview with André Théberge, June 11, 1998.

[49] Ibid.

[50] Author's telephone interview with Keith Lock, November 3, 1999.

[51] Debbie Magidson, "Joyce Wieland's Vision," in *The Canadian Forum*, September 1975, p. 71.

[52] Author's interview with Frank Moore, April 13, 1999.

[53] Ibid.

[54] Ibid.

[55] Author's interview with Judy Steed, April 21, 1998.

[56] Author's interview with André Théberge, June 11, 1998.

[57] Author's telephone interview with Richard Leiterman, May 1, 1999.

[58] Author's interview with Céline Lomez, June 10, 1998.

[59] Author's interview with André Théberge, June 11, 1998.

[60] Ibid.

[61] Author's interview with Anne Pritchard, November 25, 1997.

[62] Author's interview with Larisa Pavlychenko, May 4, 2000.

[63] Fetherling, Doug, "Joyce Wieland in Movieland," in *Canadian Weekly*, January 24, 1976, p. 12.

[64] Author's interview with Michael Snow, April 13, 1999.

[65] See Judith Findlayson, *Trailblazers — Women Talk about Changing Canada* (Toronto: Doubleday Canada, 1999) for excellent personal stories that document the struggles of women to enter fields of their choice.

[66] Audio tape labelled June 6, 1974, 1993-002/012-137.

[67] Audio tape labelled October 4, 1974, 1993-009/012-137.

[68] Audio tape labelled June 6, 1974, 1993-009/012-137.

[69] Audio tape 1993-009/012-137.

[70] Audio tape 1993-009/012-138.

[71] Author's telephone interview with Louise Ranger, May 19, 1999.

[72] Fetherling, p. 12.

[73] In *Some Canadian Women Artists* (Ottawa: The National Gallery of Canada, 1975), p. 13. This show included Gathie Falk, Sherry Grauer, Mary Pratt, Leslie Reid, Colette Whiten, An Whitlock and Shirley Wiitasalo.

[74] Author's interview with Michael Snow, April 13, 1999.

[75] Kathleen Walker, "The artist as patriot," *The Citizen*, Ottawa, October 23, 1976.

[76] Author's telephone conversation with Jo Haines, June 14, 2000.

[77] They paid $13,000 on the house, which meant the mortgage was $16,500. (1994-004/002-05).

[78] Author's interview with Michael Snow, April 13, 1999.

[79] Author's interview with Betty Ferguson, May 23, 1998.

[80] Author's interview with Judy Steed, March 16, 1998.

[81] Author's interview with Michaele Jordana Berman and Douglas Pringle, May 3, 1999.

[82] Author's interview with Frank Moore, April 13, 1999.

[83] Michele Landsberg, "Joyce Wieland: Artist in Movieland," in *Chatelaine*, October 1976, p. 59.

[84] Author's telephone interview with Louise Ranger, May 19, 1999.

[85] Doug Fetherling, "Joyce Wieland in Movieland," in *Canadian Weekly*, January 24, 1976.

[86] Frank Rasky, "Painter and film-maker directs a classical romance," in *The Toronto Star*, September 16, 1976.

[87] Wayne Sumner, "Far Shore More Ripple than Wave," *The Toronto Clarion*, October 15, 1976.

[88] Marshall Delaney "Wielandism: a personal style in full bloom," *Saturday Night*, May 1976.

[89] Author's interview with Robert Fulford, January 20, 2000.

[90] "The Far Shore: Feminist Family Melodrama" in *The Films of Joyce Wieland*, Kathryn Elder, ed., (Toronto: Toronto International Film Festival Group, 1999), p. 119.

[91] Author's interview with Susan Crean, October 7, 1998.

[92] Rabinovitz, Ibid., p. 126.

[93] Brian Baxter, London, November 30, 1976.

[94] Lauren Rabinovitz, *Points of Resistance* (Chicago: University of Illinois Press, 1991), p. 211.

[95] Valerie Ross, "A thing of beauty is a Joy forever, and/or a tax write-off," in *Maclean's* (March 22, 1976, Volume 89 No. 5).

[96] Alison Reid, *"The Film" in Joyce Wieland: Drawings for "The Far Shore"* (Ottawa: The National Gallery of Canada/National Museums of Canada, 1978), p. 3.

Chapter 8

[1] Quoted in *The Sunday Star*, April 27, 1980.

[2] Lauren Rabinovitz, "An Interview with Joyce Wieland," in *Afterimage* (Volume 8, Number 10, May 1981), p. 8.

[3] Author's interview with Charles Pachter, January 27, 1998.

[4] Ibid.

[5] Author's interview with Judy Steed, April 21, 1998.

[6] Thanks to Charles Pachter for making records in his personal archives available, January 27, 1998.

[7] Marsha Meskimmon, *The Art of Reflection* (New York: Columbia University Press, 1996), p. 28.

[8] Author's interview with Helen Lucas, July 20, 1999. Her sister, Mary Geatros, who was also close to Joyce, chose not to be interviewed.

[9] 1988-003/002-18.

[10] Author's interview with Joyce Wieland, August 26, 1986.

[11] Author's interview with Joan Prowd, May 14, 1993.

[12] Author's interview with Joyce Wieland, August 26, 1986.

[13] Joyce paid Jasmine Jones $3.00 an hour to stay with the quilt (1993-004/001-02). Other women who also worked on the quilt were Esmi Hedrick, Laurisa Leighton, Eo Sharp, Sara Barney, Betty Ferguson and Hanni Sager, who was commissioned to do the finishing work.

[14] I have found sources that give three different dates for Joyce's trip to Cape Dorset: a Canada Council grant application for funds to return later to the Arctic states she went there in 1977; Marie Fleming in *Joyce Wieland*, the AGO 1987 retrospective catalogue, gives the date as November 1978 (page 92); in an interview with Lauren Rabinovitz (*Afterimage*, May 1981) Joyce said she went to Cape Dorset early in 1979. The date on the print of *Soroseelutu* is 1979, which leads me to believe this is the correct date because she made the lithograph while she was in Cape Dorset.

[15] An Interview with Penelope Glasser, "Problems and Visions: Joyce Wieland Now," *Spirals* #2 (Winter, 1981-82), p. 7.

[16] Joyce Wieland to Phyllis Lambert, Phyllis Lambert personal archives, File #C6/14.1, Canadian Centre for Architecture.

[17] Gerald Hannon, "Provocateur," *Toronto Life* (April 1994), p. 58.

[18] Author's interview with Michael Snow, April 13, 1999.

[19] Author's interview with Michael Snow, April 13, 1999.

[20] Author's interview with Judy Steed, March 16, 1998.

[21] Gerald Hannon, "Provocateur," *Toronto Life* (April 1994), p. 53.

22. 1994-004/003-05. In the May 8 block of her 1979 calendar, she had written "Mike to call." On the June 12 calendar space, Leah Koman's name appears. Joyce had contacted Koman, who by then was separated from her former husband, George Gingras, when she wanted to pick up her friendship with him again. These clues lead one to believe that by May Joyce was living on Queen Street, though she and Michael did not draw up a legal separation

agreement until 1981 (1993-037/001-04).

[23] Author's interview with Denyse Rynard and Su Rynard, July 29, 1998.

[24] Author's interview with Betty Ferguson, May 23, 1997.

[25] Author's interview with Michaele Jordana Berman and Douglas Pringle, May 3, 1999.

[26] Author's interview with Joyce Wieland, August 27, 1986.

[27] 1993-037/001-04.

[28] Author's interview with Su Rynard, June 3, 1998.

[29] Letter from Pierre Théberge, then Curator of Contemporary Canadian Art at the National Gallery (1994-004/002-07). The National Gallery had mounted a touring exhibition of these drawings in 1978.

[30] 1988-003/001-13.

[31] James King, *The Life of Margaret Laurence* (Toronto: Knopf Canada, 1997), p. 273.

[32] Joan Mackie, *A Culinary Palette: Kitchen Masterpieces from Sixty-Five Great Artists* (Toronto/Vancouver: Merritt Publishing Co., 1981), p. 190. I acknowledge the insights of Kate Brown (interview, August 24, 1999) regarding this stage of Joyce's life.

[33] *The Legacy of Mary McEwan*, National Film Board of Canada, 1988.

[34] April 1999 issue.

[35] Francine Barry, "Fee Place: A Bit of Corktown History" in *Corktown News*, April 1999.

[36] Author's interview with Ingrid Gadsden, April 6, 1999.

[37] Author's interview with Georgia and Vijay Nayyar, September 22, 1997.

[38] Author's interview with Munro Ferguson, July 26, 1997.

[39] Sandra Naiman, "Joyce Wieland is really living!" in *The Sunday Sun*, March 1, 1981.

[40] Letter to the author from George Gingras, February 10, 1999.

[41] Author's interview with George Gingras, March 23, 1999.

[42] 1993-009/004-028.

[43] Author's interview with George Gingras, March 23, 1999.

[44] 1980 letter to George Gingras. My thanks to Gingras for making a copy available.

[45] Letter, dated July 14, 1980, copied to the author, courtesy of George Gingras.

[46] 1993-009/004-028.

[47] Jo Haines, in the author's interview with Jo Haines and Paul Haines, November 3, 1997.

[48] Author's interview with Linda Gaylard, October 7, 1998.

[49] Author's interview with George Gingras, March 23, 1999.

[50] Olivia Ward, "Artist Joyce Wieland: Blossoming at 50," in *The Toronto Star*, February 8, 1981.

[51] Author's interview with Kathy Dane, September 16, 1999.

[52] Author's interview with Jessica Bradley, October 18, 1999.

[53] Undated Joyce Wieland Canada Council grant application, Joan Murray's Artists Files, Robert McLaughlin Gallery, Oshawa.

[54] Penelope Glasser, "Problems and Visions: Joyce Wieland Now — An Interview," in *Spirals* #2, Winter, 1981-1982.

[55] Pierre Teilhard de Chardin, *The Phenomenon of Man* (New York: Harper & Row, 1959), p. 264.

[56] Pierre Teilhard de Chardin, *Hymn of the Universe* (New York: Harper & Row, 1965), pp. 41-46.

[57] Marie Fleming, "Joyce Wieland," in *Joyce Wieland* (Toronto: Art Gallery of Ontario/Key Porter Books, 1987), p. 93.

[58] "Ted Hughes: My Life with Sylvia Plath," in *The National Post*, November 3, 1998.

[59] Author's interview with Joyce Wieland, August 14, 1986.

[60] This description of the opening is from the author's telephone conversation with Betty Ferguson, October 14, 1994.

[61] Author's interview with Jessica Bradley, October 18, 1999.

[62] From Jessica Bradley's unpublished presentation of Joyce Wieland's work at Queen's University, January 30, 1995, upon the occasion of a show of Wieland drawings, Twilit Record of Romantic Love at the Agnes Etherington Art Gallery, December 18, 1994, to March 25, 1995.

[63] Marie Fleming, "Joyce Wieland: A Perspective," in *Joyce Wieland* (Toronto: Art Gallery of Ontario/Key Porter Books, 1987), p. 98.

[64] Author's interview with Marie Lynn Hammond, September 13, 1999.

[65] Author's interview with Joyce Wieland, August 27, 1986.

[66] Author's interview with Joyce Wieland, August 26, 1986.

[67] 1991/014/004-59.

[68] Phyllis Lambert archives, C6/14.1 Correspondence — Personal 71-89.

[69] My thanks to Gerald Robinson for telling me about the origin of this inscription in an interview, May 30, 1996.

[70] J. Middleton Murray, editor, *Journal of Katherine Mansfield* (New York: Ecco Press, 1983), p. 132.

[71] Val Ross, "Phyllis of Montreal," *The Globe and Mail*, February 27, 1999.

[72] Author's interview with Phyllis Lambert, November 26, 1997.

[73] Ibid.

[74] Phyllis Lambert archives, C6/14.1 Correspondence — Personal 71-89.

[75] 1993-009/008-115.

[76] Phyllis Lambert Archives, C6/14.1 Correspondence — Personal 71-89.

[77] Author's interview with Phyllis Lambert, November 26, 1997.

[78] Author's interview with Marie Lynn Hammond, September 13, 1999.

[79] Ibid. I question the accuracy of the date given on the painting because she received the Laidlaw commission in 1981, and the portrait was unveiled in February 1983. It seems Joyce would have made the phone call to Hammond before she received the commission, or she would have known how to reach Laidlaw.

[80] Adele Freedman, "Portraits from a daring artist," *The Globe and Mail*, January 4, 1983.

[81] Author's interview with George Gingras, March 23, 1999.

[82] Joyce ran this ad in *The Globe and Mail*: "Midsummer Nights Dream — Strong sensitive established woman in her 50s who is creative passionate, sensitive. Loves books, music, nature. Seeks caring confident successful man 45-65 with warm heart who is comfortable in 'Black Tie' evening dress or overalls; to root around with (Till the end of time.)" 1990-014/005-71.

[83] Author's interview with Helen Lucas, July 20, 1998.

[84] 1990-014/005-71.

[85] Ibid.

[86] Author's interview with Kathy Dain, September 16, 1999.

[87] 1999-044/001-23.

[88] Author's interview with Stella Kyriakakis, August 5, 1998.

[89] 1999-044/001-003.

[90] Art Gallery of Ontario Archives, Michael Snow Fonds, Box 2, File 4.

[91] Author's interview with Stella Kyriakakis, August 5, 1998.

[92] Ibid.

[93] 1988-003/002-018.

[94] Author's telephone conversation with Michael Snow, February 1, 2000.

[95] Author's interview with Sara Bowser, May 18, 1995.

[96] 1990-014/02-22 and 1993-009/008-114.

[97] Author's interview with Allison McComb, Nadine Schwartz and Lois Taylor, August 18, 1994.

[98] 1993-009/008-116.

[99] Marie Fleming, "Joyce Wieland," in *Joyce Wieland* (Toronto: Key Porter/Art Gallery of Ontario, 1987), p. 106.

[100] Author's interview with Joyce Wieland, August 14, 1986.

[101] 1988-003/001-008.

[102] 1988-003/002-29 and 1990-014/03-30. Also, a letter to Joan Murray dated September 17, 1986 (1988-003/01-08).

[103] James Borcoman, *Eugene Atget* (Ottawa: National Gallery of Canada, 1984), p. 132. My thanks to Michael Pantazzi of the National Gallery of Canada for telling me of this source on the Trianon. Borcoman's photograph of the Trianon shows the roof ornamentation that is included in Joyce's painting.

[104] Nancy Mitford, *Madame de Pompadour* (New York: Bantam Books, 1956), p. 170.

[105] 1988-003/002-029.

[106] Hans Henrik Brummer, *The Statue Court in the Vatican Belvedere*, (Stockholm: Kungl. Boktryckeriet P A Norstedt & Soner, 1970), p. 58.

[107] 1988-003/002-029.

Chapter 9

[1] In *The Reenchantment of Art* (New York: Thames and Hudson, 1991), p. 43.

[2] Author's interview with Joyce Wieland, August 20, 1986.

[3] Author's interview with Dr. John Rennie, December 7, 1999.

[4] Author's interview with William Withrow, October 28, 1999. My research in the Art Gallery of Ontario exhibition records, with the help of Randall Speller and other researchers, did not yield a copy of a list.

[5] Art Gallery of Ontario Archives, Exhibition Records Box A2-1-4, File 2.

[6] "Emergence of women subtext of AGO show," April 27, 1996.

[7] Author's interview with William Withrow, October 28, 1999.

[8] Ibid.

[9] "Canadian Artists on 'The Far Shore,'" in *The Art Post* (Volume 2, No. 2, Sept/Oct, 1984), p. 19.

[10] "In Search of the Far Shore, the Films of Joyce Wieland," program notes for the January-February 1988 show of Joyce Wieland films at Canada House, London, England.

[11] Author's interview with Irene F. Whittome, November 25, 1997.

[12] Ibid.

[13] Ibid.

[14] Author's interview with Douglas McPherson, August 30, 1999.

[15] 1990-014/03-34.

[16] Author's interview with Kay Armatage, January 25, 2000.

[17] 1988-003/002-26.

[18] 1990-014/005-69.

[19] Elizabeth Hay, *Captivity Tales — Canadians in New York* (Vancouver: New Star Books, 1993), page 145.

[20] Author's telephone interview with Steve Anker, August 17, 1999.

[21] 1990-014/005-69.

[22] Author's telephone interview with Steve Anker, August 17, 1999.

[23] Telephone interviews with Jamie Erfurdt, November 21, 1999, and January 11, 2000.

[24] 1990-014/005-69.

[25] 1990-014/006-92, 1990-014/005-71, 1988-003/2-20.

[26] Undated note, 1990-014/002-24.

[27] Jean Sutherland Boggs in Judith Findlayson, *Trailblazers: Women Talk about Changing Canada* (Toronto: Doubleday Canada, 1999), p. 44.

[28] Ibid, p. 46.

[29] Author's interview with Jean Sutherland Boggs, June 10, 1998.

[30] Author's interview with Michael Pantazzi, March 24, 1999.

[31] My thanks to Phyllis Lambert for providing me with an original invitation.

[32] Author's interview with Jean Sutherland Boggs, June 10, 1998.

[33] Adele Freedman, "Roughing it with a Brush," *Toronto* (The Globe and Mail, April 1987), p. 79.

[34] Author's interview with Stella Kyriakakis, August 5, 1998.

[35] Ibid.

[36] Author's interview with Frances Patella May 26, 1998.

[37] Ibid.

[38] Author's interview with Joyce Wieland, August 20, 1986.

[39] Notes from the daily log of Norine Weiss, given to the author August 5, 1999.

[40] 1991-014/003-043.

[41] My thanks to Nathan Gilbert of the Laidlaw Foundation for making this painting available to me for viewing.

[42] Frances Patella Daily Log, January 1986, Frances Patella personal papers.

[43] Author's telephone interview with Christina McCall, November 2, 1999.

[44] Author's interview with Joyce Wieland, August 20, 1986.

[45] Author's interview with Richard Todhunter, October 28, 1999.

[46] Author's interview with Joyce Wieland, August 27, 1986.

[47] Author's interview with Jane Martin, April 6, 1999.

⁴⁸ Author's telephone interview with Joyce Zemans, February 11, 2000.

⁴⁹ *Three Artists (Three Women)* (Berkeley: University of California Press, 1996), p. 2.

⁵⁰ Alice Mansell, "Contemporary Art and Critical Theory in Canada" in Christine Mason Sutherland and Beverly Matson Rasporich, *Woman as Artist* (Calgary: University of Calgary Press, 1993), p. 151.

⁵¹ This painting, according to *Giambattista Tiepolo; His Life and Art* (New Haven and London: Yale University Press, 1986) by Michael Levy, is owned by the Montreal Museum of Fine Arts.

⁵² Author's interview with Kay Armatage, January 25, 2000.

⁵³ Author's telephone interview with Frances Patella, October 26, 1999.

⁵⁴ Author's interview with Philip Monk, October 18, 1999.

⁵⁵ Author's interview with Joyce Wieland, August 14, 1986.

⁵⁶ Author's interview with Kathy Dain, September 16, 1999.

⁵⁷ Marilyn Linton, *The Sunday Sun*, February 22, 1987.

⁵⁸ Author's conversation with Randall Speller, November 5, 1999.

⁵⁹ Personal conversation with Randall Speller, November 5, 1999. Marilyn Linton, "Wieland faces another historical first," *The Sunday Sun*, February 22, 1987, in the Art Gallery of Ontario archives, Exhibition Records, Box A2-1-4, File 2.

⁶⁰ *Emily Carr: Her Paintings and Sketches*, Ottawa: National Gallery of Canada, 1945.

⁶¹ Author's interview with Irene Whittome, November 25, 1997.

⁶² Ibid.

⁶³ In *Joyce Wieland* (Toronto: Art Gallery of Ontario/Key Porter Books, 1987), p. 1.

⁶⁴ Susan Crean, "Forbidden Fruit: The Erotic Nationalism of Joyce Wieland," *This Magazine* (Volume 21, No. 4, August/September 1987), p. 12.

⁶⁵ Ibid.

⁶⁶ In Joyce Wieland (Toronto: Art Gallery of Ontario/Key Porter Books, 1987), p. 11.

⁶⁷ Lauren Rabinovitz, "Issues of Feminist Aesthetics: Judy Chicago and Joyce Wieland," in *Woman's Art Journal* (Vol. 1, No. 2, Fall 1980/Winter 1981).

⁶⁸ Carol Becker, *Zones of Contention: Essays on Art, Institutions, Gender and Anxiety* (Albany, New York: State University of New York Press, 1996), p. 147.

⁶⁹ Joyce loved working with tapered Filbert paint brushes in hogs hair — she liked the feel and sound of them brushing across the canvas — according to Kay Wilson who painted with her during much of the eighties (Author's telephone conversation, November 26, 1999).

⁷⁰ Author's interview with Phyllis Lambert, November 26, 1997.

⁷¹ Kay Redfield Jamison, *Touched with Fire* (New York: The Free Press, 1994), pp. 114, 115. My thanks to Dr. John Rennie for suggesting this book as a source.

⁷² Quoted in Jamison, p. 128.

⁷³ Ibid., p. 109.

⁷⁴ Ibid., p. 105.

⁷⁵ Ibid., p. 121.

⁷⁶ 1993-009/010-112.

⁷⁷ In *This Woman in Particular: Contexts for the Biographical Image of Emily Carr*, Stephanie Kirkwood Walker (Waterloo, Ontario: Wilfrid Laurier University Press, 1996, p. 128) says the same thing about Mays's article on Emily Carr.

⁷⁸ "AGO enshrines the myth surrounding Wieland," *The Globe and Mail*, April 18, 1987.

⁷⁹ In *The Globe and Mail*, July 7, 1990.

⁸⁰ Jay Scott, "Full Circle," in *Canadian Art* (Volume 4, No. 1, March 1987), p. 59.

⁸¹ Author's interview with Pierre Théberge, November 26, 1997.

⁸² In "Interviews with Canadian Artists," Debbie Magidson and Judy Wright, *The Canadian Forum* (May-June, 1974), p. 63.

⁸³ Author's interview with Jane Martin, April 6, 1999.

⁸⁴ Jane Martin, "She Brought the Sun: Glimpses of Joyce Wieland," in *CARO Dispatch* (Volume 4, #3, September 1998), p. 3. This is a tribute heard on *This Morning*, a CBC program. It was broadcast on July 5, 1998, after her death.

⁸⁵ Author's interview with Jane Martin, April 6, 1999.

⁸⁶ E-mail from Jane Martin, November 12, 1999. Among the other women who attended

were Sheila Ayerst, Joan Borsa, Wendy Coe, Anna Gronau, Janice Gurney, Lynn Hughes, Toby MacLennan, Jeanne Randolph, Judith Schwartz, Cynthia Short, Barbara Sternberg, Elke Town, Colette Whiten, and Irene F. Whittome.

[87] Author's telephone interview with Kass Banning, November 26, 1999.

Chapter 10

[1] In *Art Objects: Essays on Ecstacy and Effrontery* (New York: Vintage Books, 1995), p. 169.

[2] 1988-003/002-29 and 1992-018/010-151, which is a video, Brian Bobbie Productions, May 20, 1987.

[3] Author's interview with Linda Gaylard, October 7, 1998.

[4] Ibid.

[5] 1992-018/003-130.

[6] Letter to the author from Enid Irving, October 28, 1997.

[7] 1991-014/002-24.

[8] Author's interview with Joyce Wieland, August 20, 1986.

[9] Author's interview with Joyce Wieland, August 14, 1986.

[10] Letters in 1998-003/002-33.

[11] 1992-018/002-69.

[12] 1992-018/003-130.

[13] Notes for a press release, 1989-014/007-81.

[14] Deirdre Hanna, *Now*, April 7-13, 1988, p. 17.

[15] 1992-018/002-54c.

[16] 1992-018/002-69.

[17] Author's telephone interview with Ron Moore, November 17, 1999.

[18] 1993-009/006-100.

[19] Author's interview with Av Isaacs, June 29, 1995.

[20] Author's interview with Philip Monk, October 18, 1999.

[21] 1990-014/007-86.

[22] Ibid.

[23] During the years when Joyce lived in New York and when she was making *The Far Shore*, she had shows at the Isaacs gallery in 1962, 1963, 1967, 1972, and 1974. *Joyce Wieland* (Toronto: Art Gallery of Ontario/Key Porter Books, 1987), p. 205.

[24] Author's interview with Av Isaacs, June 29, 1995.

[25] Author's interview with Fan Hill, July 20, 1998.

[26] 1991-014/004-62.

[27] Author's interview with Av Isaacs, June 29, 1995.

[28] 1992-018/002-58a.

[29] 1991-014/004-62.

[30] *Now*, April 6-12, 1989.

[31] *Toronto Star*, March 27, 1989.

[32] 1992-018/002-69.

[33] 1990-014/006-76.

[34] Author's interview with Joyce Wieland, August 26, 1986.

[35] Marsha Meskimmon, *The Art of Reflection* (New York: Columbia University Press, 1996), p. 172.

[36] Author's interview with Dr. John Rennie, December 7, 1999.

[37] Author's interview with Allison Ferguson, November 27, 1994.

[38] Author's conversation with Judy Steed and Betty Ferguson, May 23, 1998.

[39] Ibid.

[40] Author's interview with Fran Hill, July 20, 1998.

[41] Penelope Glasser interview: "Problems and Visions: Joyce Wieland Now," in *Spirals #2* Winter, 1981-82.

[42] Author's telephone conversation with Michael Snow, November 3, 1999.

[43] My thanks to Su Rynard for sharing with me her photographs, June 3, 1998.

[44] 1988-003/002-20.

[45] 1990-014/002-23.

[46] 1994-004/001-01.

[47] Author's telephone interview with Nicola Wojewoda, December 14, 1999.

[48] (London: Routledge & Kegan Paul, 1984) p. 322.

[49] From a brochure on the Sharon Temple, produced by the Sharon Temple Museum Society. My thanks to Anne Corkett for her time, who by coincidence dropped in at the Temple when I happened to stop in to see the place in off-season on November 24, 1999.

Chapter 11

[1] 1993-009/009-131.

[2] Dr. William Malloy and Dr. Paul Caldwell, *Alzheimer's Disease* (Toronto: Key Porter Books, 1998), pp. 17, 18. This excellent book is the source for the information on the illness in this chapter.

[3] Ibid.

[4] *The Toronto Star*, February 21, 1996.

[5] Lauren Rabinovitz, "An Interview with Joyce Wieland," in *Afterimage* (Vol. 8, No. 10, May 1981), p. 3.

[6] Author's interview with Fan Hill, July 20, 1998.

[7] Author's interview with Barbara Sternberg, April 26, 1999.

[8] Author's interview with Phyllis Lambert, November 26, 1997.

[9] Author's interview with Kay Wilson, June 5, 1995.

[10] Author's interview with Diane Pugen, June 26, 1997.

[11] Author's interview with Cynthia Lorenz, July 29, 1998.

[12] 1993-009/005-33.

[13] 1990-014/003-33.

[14] 1993-009/009-126.

[15] Author's interview with Dr. John Rennie, December 7, 1999, and a telephone conversation December 17, 1999.

[16] Author's interview with Dr. Gina Schochat, December 16, 1999.

[17] 1993-009/008-102.

[18] 1990-044/001-20.

[19] 1988-003/002-20.

[20] Ibid.

[21] Lynda Hurst, *The Toronto Star*, January 21, 1990.

[22] 1993-009/006-100.

[23] Lynda Hurst, *The Toronto Star*, January 21, 1990.

[24] Christina Sabat in *Fredericton Gleaner*, March 24, 1990.

[25] Author's interview with Sheila Curnoe, April 10, 1997.

[26] Author's interview with Pierre Théberge, November 26, 1997.

[27] 1993-009/008-102.

[28] Author's interview with Georgia and Vijay Nayyar, September 22, 1997.

[29] Author's interview with Sara Bowser, May 18, 1995.

[30] Author's interview with Donna Montague, June 29, 1995. This interview is also the source for the following paragraph.

[31] Author's interview with Betty Ferguson, October 16, 1997.

[32] According to Joyce's appointment book for 1990 (1993-009/008-102), Joyce hired Linda Abrahams in July.

[33] In "Joyce Wieland Re-inventing the Artist," *Site*, January/February, 1991, p. 7.

[34] Author's telephone interview with Frieda Hjartarson, November 23, 1999.

[35] Author's interview with Sheila Curnoe, April 10, 1997.

[36] Author's interview with Donna Montague, October 18, 1995.

[37] 1992-018/002-56.

[38] John Bayley, *Elegy for Iris* (New York: St. Martin's Press, 1999), p. 218.

[39] Author's interview with Diane Rotstein, June 26, 1995.

[40] Author's interviews with the late Donna Montague, June 29 and July 5, 1995.

[41] 1990-014/004-54.

[42] Author's interview with Helene St. Jacques, September 11, 1997.

[43] Author's interview with Donna Montague, June 29, 1995.

[44] Author's interview with Doug McPherson, August 30, 1999.

[45] Author's interview with Colette Perron Sharp, November 30, 1999.

[46] Author's interview with Cynthia Lorenz, July 29, 1998.

[47] Author's interview with Colette Perron Sharp, November 30, 1999.

[48] Author's interview with Dr. John Rennie, December 7, 1999.

[49] Author's interview with Colette Perron Sharp, November 30, 1999.

[50] Author's interview with Christine Oksanen, January 12, 2000.

[51] Author's interview with Colette Perron Sharp, November 30, 1999.

[52] Ibid., Christine Oksanen.

[53] Author's interview with Ingrid Gadsden, April 6, 1999.

[54] Author's interview with Sara Bowser, June 5, 1995.

[55] Ibid., Colette Perron Sharp.

[56] Ibid., Christine Oksanen.

[57] Ibid.

Chapter 12

[1] In *The Sunday Star*, April 27, 1980.

[2] Author's interview with Joyce Wieland, August 26, 1986.

[3] Higonnet, Anne, *Berthe Morisot* (Berkeley/Los Angeles: University of California Press, 1990), p. 10.

[4] Author's interview with Joan Prowd, May 14, 1993.

[5] Author's interview with Joan Prowd, May 21, 1993.

[6] Author's interview with Joan's daughters, Nadine Schwartz, Lois Stewart and Allison McComb, August 18, 1994.

[7] Author's interview with Marjorie Harris, September 13, 1999.

[8] Author's interview with Su Rynard, June 3, 1998.

[9] Ibid.

[10] Author's interview with Betty Ferguson, October 16, 1997, and telephone conversation June 19, 2000.

[11] Author's interview with Sara Bowser, May 18, 1995.

[12] Author's interview with Betty Ferguson, February 23, 1999.

[13] Author's interview with Betty Ferguson, May 23, 1997.

[14] Author's interviews with Betty Ferguson, October 16, 1997, and January 23, 1999.

[15] Ibid.

[16] Author's interview with Helen Lucas, July 20, 1998.

[17] Author's interview with Judy Steed, March 16, 1998.

[18] Author's interviews with Kay Wilson, August 19, 1986, and June 5, 1995.

[19] Ibid.

[20] For a number of years Joyce loved to cook and could prepare an elegant dinner. Her menu for a dinner on February 10, 1984, was as follows: Roast pork with ginger and garlic, stuffed tomatoes, basmati rice with sweet rice and nuts, black beans (hot), orange salad with olives, marzipan with raspberry, watermelon, fruit ice, coffee — and red wine. (1988-003/001-001).

[21] Author's telephone conversation with Kay Wilson, November 26, 1999.

[22] Author's interview with Michaele Jordana Berman and Douglas Pringle, May 3, 1999.

[23] Ibid.

[24] Ibid.

[25] Author's interview with Selma Lenchener-Frankel, September 21, 1999.

[26] Author's interview with Jessica Bradley, October 18, 1999.

[27] Ibid.

[28] Author's telephone interview with Liz Magor, February 1, 2000.

[29] Author's telephone interview with Elizabeth MacKenzie, January 15, 2000, and e-mail March 29, 2000.

[30] Author's interview with Carol Laing, November 8, 1999.

[31] Author's interview with Carol Laing, November 8, 1999, and telephone interview, April 3, 2000.

[32] Author's interview with Sylvia Tyson, August 4, 1999.

[33] Author's interview with Carol Laing, November 8, 1999.

[34] Unpublished "Artist's Statement 'The Body Quilt'", by Madonna Andress.

[35] inversions, (Winnipeg: MAWA, 1998), p. 48.

[36] The "textual transcreation" of the show was written in collaboration with Amy Gogarty, a Calgary artist.

[37] Author's telephone interview with Mireille Perron, December 17, 1999; Perron's letter to the author, December 17, 1999; inversions (Winnipeg: Mentoring Artists for Women's Art, 1998), pp. 44-53.

[38] Ellen Rosenfeld letter to the author, May 1999.

Epilogue

[1] Quoted in *The Sunday Star*, April 27, 1980.

[2] Author's interview with Colette Perron Sharp, November 30, 1999.

[3] My thanks to Christine Oksanen for pointing out the name of this flower.

[4] 1988-003/002-20 and 1990-014/005-69, 70.

Permissions

Art, photographs or other material without a credit or courtesy line belong to the Estate of Joyce Wieland. This material is © the Estate of Joyce Wieland and is reproduced by permission of the Estate.

Frontispiece

Collection Robert McLaughlin Gallery, Oshawa, Courtesy of the Isaacs Gallery

Introduction

Page 13: Arnold Matthews; Page 14: Arnold Matthews; Page 13: Courtesy of the Isaacs Gallery; Page 15: Credit George Whiteside; Page 16: Credit Larisa Pavlychenko.

Chapter 2

Page 48: Courtesy of York University Archives and Special Collections; Page 50: Courtesy of Nadine Schwartz.

Chapter 3

Page 58: Courtesy of York University Archives and Special Collections; Page 62 bottom: Art Gallery of Ontario, gift from the McLean Foundation, 1966; Page 61: Private Collection, Credit Vince Pietropaolo; Page 66: Courtesy of Leslie A. Parkes; Page 70: Courtesy of Arthur Grinstead; Page 82: Credit Warren Collins; Page 85: Credit Warren Collins; Page 90: Credit Warren Collins.

Chapter 4

Page 92: Courtesy of Sara Bowser; Page 93: Credit Warren Collins; Page 95: Credit Warren Collins; Page 96: Credit Warren Collins Page 97: Collection Art Gallery of Hamilton, Gift of Irving Zucker, 1992, Credit Robert McNair; Page 100: Courtesy of Robert Hackborn; Page 103: Credit Warren Collins; Page 106: Credit Warren Collins; Page 107: Private Collection Courtesy of the Isaacs Gallery; Page 111: Private Collection; Page 112: Credit Warren Collins; Page 114 top: Collection Art Gallery of Ontario, Gift of Betty Ramsaur Ferguson, 1998; Page 114 bottom: Private Collection Courtesy of the Isaacs Gallery; Page 115: Collection Art Gallery of Ontario, Gift of Betty Ramsaur Ferguson, 1998; Page 116 top: Collection Art Gallery of Ontario, Gift of Betty Ramsaur Ferguson, 1998; Page 116 bottom: Private Collection; Page 118: Art Gallery of Ontario, Gift of Betty Ramsaur Ferguson, 1998; Page 120–121: Courtesy of the Isaacs Gallery; Page 122 top: Courtesy of Sara Bowser; Page 122 bottom left: Courtesy of Sara Bowser; Page 122 bottom right: Courtesy of York University Archives and Special Collections; Page 126: Credit Warren Collins; Page 127: Courtesy of the Isaacs Gallery; Page 128: Courtesy of the Isaacs Gallery.

Chapter 5

Page 130: Credit John Reeves; Page 132: Private Collection Courtesy of the Isaacs Gallery; Page 134: Courtesy of Canadian Filmmakers Distribution Centre; Page 137: Private Collection; Page 138: Private Collection Courtesy of the Isaacs Gallery; Page 142: Credit Warren Collins; Page 143: Courtesy of the Isaacs Gallery; Page 144 top: Courtesy of the Isaacs Gallery; Page 144 bottom: Private Collection; Page 146: Collection National Gallery of Canada; Page 148: Collection Vancouver Art Gallery, Murrin Estate Funds; Page 150: Credit John Reeves; Page 153 top and bottom: Photos Courtesy of Betty Ramsaur Ferguson; Page 159: Courtesy of Canadian Filmmakers Distribution Centre.

Chapter 6

Page 162: Photo Courtesy of Sara Bowser; Page 164 top: Collection National Gallery of Canada; Photo 164 bottom: Collection Art Gallery of Hamilton, Gift of Irving Zucker, 1992; Page 172 top and bottom: Credit Harold Barkley, courtesy of the Toronto Reference Library; Page 176: Collection National Gallery of Canada; Page 179: Credit Arnold Matthews; Page 180 top: Credit Arnold Matthews; Page 180 bottom: Credit Arnold Matthews; Page 181 top: Collection York University; Page 181 bottom: Credit Arnold Matthews; Page 182: Collection Mackenzie Art Gallery, Regina; Page 183: Collection Mackenzie Art Gallery, Regina; Page 185: Credit Arnold Matthews; Page 186: Collection Art Gallery of Ontario, Purchase, 1977 with Assistance of Wintario; Page 187 top and bottom: Collection Art Gallery of Ontario, Purchase, 1977 with Assistance of Wintario; Page 188: Credit Arnold Matthews; Page 189: Collection Art Gallery of Ontario, Courtesy of the Isaacs Gallery; Page 191 top and bottom: Credit Arnold Matthews; Page 192: Credit Arnold Matthews; Page 196: Credit Rose Richardson.

Chapter 7

Page 198: Credit Larisa Pavlychenko; Page 200 bottom: Private Collection, Courtesy of Joan Murray, Joan Murray's Artists Files, Robert McLaughlin Gallery, Oshawa; Page 202: Courtesy of the Isaacs Gallery; Page 203: Private Collection, Courtesy of the Isaacs Gallery; Page 206: Courtesy of the Canadian Filmmakers Distribution Centre; Page 208: Courtesy of the Canadian Filmmakers Distribution Centre; Page 211: Courtesy of the Canadian Filmmakers Distribution Centre, Credit Vince Pietropaolo; Page 212: Credit Larisa Pavlychenko; Page 213: Credit Larisa Pavlychenko; Page 216: Credit Larisa Pavlychenko; Page 221: Credit Larisa Pavlychenko; Page 222: Credit Larisa Pavlychenko; Page 223: Credit Larisa Pavlychenko; Page 227: Credit Larisa Pavlychenko; Page 229 top and bottom: Credit Larisa Pavlychenko.

Chapter 8

Page 237: Collection Toronto Transit Corporation, Toronto; Page 242: Courtesy of Denyse Rynard; Page 243: Courtesy of Denyse Rynard; Page 244:

Courtesy of Denyse Rynard; Page 246: Credit Vincent Sharp; Page 247: Credit Vincent Sharp; Page 251: Credit The Toronto Star; Page 252 top and bottom: Courtesy of the Isaacs Gallery; Page 254: Private Collection; Page 255: Credit Vincent Sharp; Page 264: National Gallery of Canada; Page 265 National Gallery of Canada; Page 266: Courtesy of the Isaacs Gallery; Page 267: Courtesy of the Isaacs Gallery.

Chapter 9

Page 270: Courtesy of Enid Irving; Page 275: Credit: Vincent Sharp; Page 277: Private Collection, Courtesy of the Isaacs Gallery; Page 282: Courtesy of York University Archives and Special Collections; Page 283: Courtesy of York University Archives and Special Collections; Page 284: Credit Frances Patella; Page 291: Private Collection Courtesy of the Isaacs Gallery; Page 292: Cover for This Magazine; Page 293: Private Collection; Page 294 bottom: Private Collection Courtesy of the Isaacs Gallery; Page 297: Courtesy of the Isaacs Gallery; Page 299: Credit Elizabeth MacKenzie.

Chapter 10

Page 302: Credit Jim Allen; Page 305: Courtesy of Enid Irving; Page 307: Credit Gregory Dru; Page 309: Collection Vancouver Art Gallery Acquisition Fund; Page 312 top: Credit Gregory Dru; Page 312 bottom: Courtesy of the Isaacs Gallery; Page 315: Credit Gregory Dru; Page 318: Collection Art Gallery of Hamilton; Gift of Irving Zucker, 1992; Page 320: Courtesy of Irene F. Whittome; Page 321: Courtesy of Irene F. Whittome.

Chapter 11

Page 324: Credit Charles Pachter; Page 331: Private Collection, Credit Munro Ferguson; Page 334: Courtesy of Sara Bowser; Page 337: Collection Art Gallery of Ontario, Gift of Betty Ramsaur Ferguson, 1998, Courtesy of Betty Ramsaur Ferguson; Page 338: Courtesy of Sara Bowser.

Chapter 12

Page 344: Credit George Whiteside; Page 347: Private Collection, Credit Vince Pietropaolo; Page 348: Credit Charles Pachter; Page 350: Courtesy of Sara Bowser; Page 351: Courtesy of Betty Ramsaur Ferguson; Page 352: Courtesy of Betty Ramsaur Ferguson; Page 353: Credit Dr. Paul Chapnick; Page 360 top: Collection Art Gallery of Hamilton, Gift of Irving Zucker, 1992, Credit Robert McNair; Page 360 bottom: Courtesy of Mireille Perron.

Index